PRENTICE HALL'S

# DICTIONARY
# OF AMERICAN CRIMINAL
# JUSTICE, CRIMINOLOGY,
# AND CRIMINAL LAW

### Second Edition

## DAVID N. FALCONE, PH.D.

**Prentice Hall**
Upper Saddle River, New Jersey 07458
Columbus, Ohio

**Library of Congress Cataloging-in-Publication Data**

Falcone, David N.
  Prentice Hall's dictionary of American criminal justice, criminology, and
criminal law / David N. Falcone.—2nd ed.
    p.  cm.
  ISBN-13: 978-0-13-515402-1 (alk. paper)
  ISBN-10: 0-13-515402-2 (alk. paper)
    1. Criminal justice, Administration of—United States—Dictionaries.   2. Criminal law—
United States—Dictionaries.   3. Criminology—United States—Dictionaries.   I. Title.
II. Title: Dictionary of American criminal justice, criminology, and criminal law.
KF9223.A68F35 2010
345.73'003—dc22

2008035586

**Vice President and Executive Publisher:**
  Vernon Anthony
**Senior Acquisitions Editor:** Tim Peyton
**Editorial Assistant:** Alicia Kelly
**Media Project Manager:** Karen Bretz
**Director of Marketing:** David Gesell
**Marketing Manager:** Adam Kloza
**Marketing Coordinator:** Alicia Dysert

**Production Manager:** Kathy Sleys
**Creative Director:** Jayne Conte
**Cover Design:** Margaret Kenselaar
**Full-Service Project Management/**
  **Composition:** Sadagoban Balaji/
  Integra Software Services
**Printer/Binder:** Bind-Rite, Robbinsville/
  Command Web

Pearson Education Ltd., London
Pearson Education Singapore, Pte. Ltd
Pearson Education, Canada, Inc.
Pearson Education–Japan
Pearson Education Australia PTY, Limited

Pearson Education North Asia, Ltd., Hong Kong
Pearson Educación de Mexico, S.A. de C.V.
Pearson Education Malaysia, Pte. Ltd.
Pearson Education Upper Saddle River,
  New Jersey

**Prentice Hall**
is an imprint of

www.pearsonhighered.com

10 9 8 7 6 5 4 3 2 1
ISBN-13:  978-0-13-515402-1
ISBN-10:      0-13-515402-2

This work is dedicated to my patient wife Joan,
for her encouragement and support.

# Preface

This dictionary was written expressly for the convenience of students in criminal justice and criminology, although it will clearly be of use to practitioners and laypersons alike. The author has made available, in one comprehensive volume, a ready reference for the interdisciplinary study of criminal justice, criminology, and criminal law. A list of the major criminal appellate cases is included for reference purposes, along with a brief biographical sketch of U.S. Supreme Court justices. Every effort was made to include virtually all words, phrases, and terms used interchangeably across the various social sciences and the law, which comprise the study of criminal justice.

# About the Author

David N. Falcone received his B.A. in sociology from Elmhurst College, his M.S. in criminal justice sciences from Illinois State University, and his Ph.D. in American studies from Saint Louis University. He has been a member of the faculty at Illinois State University since 1988 and is currently Professor and Interim Chairman of the Department of Criminal Justice Sciences at Illinois State University, with a speciality in American policing and law enforcement. He has served on the editorial boards of well-known criminal justice journals and was a member of the U.S. Army Military Police Corps and of a number of county- and municipal-level police agencies in Illinois. He has coauthored a number of research monographs resulting from grants from the National Institute of Justice and the AAA Foundation for Traffic Safety. He is recognized as a national expert on police vehicle pursuits and has testified as an expert witness in numerous related cases. He is the coauthor of a number of books in criminal justice and has authored or coauthored dozens of articles appearing in leading scholarly and professional journals spanning criminal justice, policing, crime and delinquency, history, and transportation. His current research involves an analysis of the assumed relationship between community variables and police service styles and the identification and conceptualization of the various models that constitute the American policing mosaic.

# A

AA, atomic absorption
AAPL, Afro-American Police League
AAPLE, American Academy for Professional Law Enforcement
ABA, American Bar Association
ABF, American Bar Foundation
ABFO, American Board of Forensic Odontology
ACIA, Advisory Commission on Intergovernmental Affairs
ACJS, Academy of Criminal Justice Sciences
ACLU, American Civil Liberties Union
ACIR, Advisory Commission on Intergovernmental Affairs
ADIT, Alien Documentation, Identification, and Telecommunications
ADPRIN, Automatic Data-Processing Intelligence Network
AELE, Americans for Effective Law Enforcement
AFIS, Automated Fingerprint Identification Systems
AFP, American Federation of Police, Inc.
AG, Attorney General
AJS, American Judicature Society
ALEOA, American Law Enforcement Officers' Association
ALI, American Law Institute
ALJ, Administrative Law Judge
ALR, American Law Reports
AMA, American Municipal Association
ANACDUTRA, Annual Active Duty Training
APCO, Association of Public Safety Communications Officials
    International, Inc.
ASC, American Society of Criminology
ASIS, American Society for Industrial Security
ATF, United States Bureau of Alcohol, Tobacco, and Firearms
ATLA, Association of Trial Lawyers of America

**abandoned property.** Property over which ownership has been voluntarily relinquished, surrendered, deserted, or abandoned.

**abortion, criminal.** The purposeful and unlawful destruction of an unborn human fetus via any means including drugs, instruments, or physical extraction.

**abrogate.** *v.* To abolish, annul; repeal; cancel.

**absolute liability offense.** In criminal law, an offense category where liability for the violation of a criminal or quasi-criminal offense can be established irrespective of whether intent (*mens rea*) can be established. See *strict liability*.

**abuse of authority.** Actions by criminal justice officials, under "color of law," tending to violate citizens' civil liberties or rights, and which injure, insult, or demean human dignity.

**Academy of Criminal Justice Sciences (ACJS).** A scholarly and professional society for criminal justice educators, researchers, and criminal justice administrative practitioners. Formally organized in 1963 as the International Association of Police Professors, the ACJS holds its annual meeting in March of each year and publishes the journal *Justice Quarterly.*

**accelerant.** *n.* A substance, chemical, or compound that speeds the combustion process; e.g., gasoline is commonly used as an accelerant at arson scenes.

**accessory.** *n.* One who assists in a subordinate capacity in the commission of an offense; one who aids and abets.

**accessory after the fact.** One who obstructs justice by knowingly assisting a criminal offender in the avoidance of capture or process.

**accessory before the fact.** One who plans, counsels, encourages, or orders another to engage in a criminal act, but who himself or herself is not present during the commission of the offense.

**accomplice.** *n.* A partner in a given crime. One who knowingly and voluntarily assists another in the commission of an unlawful act. See *Model Penal Code,* § 2.06(3).

**accountability.** *n.* The state of being culpable, answerable, liable, or responsible.

**acculturation.** *n.* The adaptation to a new culture. The process of conditioning a person to new cultural values, attitudes, and patterns of behavior.

**accusatorial system.** A system for administering justice based on the premise that the most advantageous way of achieving just results in disputes is to place the opposing parties in a contest. For example, in the United States, the defendant (the accused) is pitted against the prosecution (the state).

**accusatory stage.** That portion of the criminal justice process where a suspect has been identified and an accusation is made, e.g., a complaint, information, charging document, or indictment.

**acid phosphatase test.** A mapping technique—using an enzyme (phosphoric acid monoesterase) found in the secretions of the male prostate gland—used by forensic scientists in searching for semen stains found on objects at sexual-assault scenes.

**acquittal.** *n.* A setting-free, absolving, release, or discharge of a defendant from a formal accusation.

**Act of God.** An occurrence for which no human being is accountable or legally liable. Any natural event not attributable to the carelessness or negligence of another.

**Act of providence.** See *Act of God.*

**actus reus.** *(Lat.)* The overt criminal act, action, or omission that caused harm.

**ad alium diem.** *(Lat.)* At another day.

**addendum.** *n.* Something added at the end of a document; e.g., an appendix or other supplement.

**addict.** *n.* One who habitually uses any drug, thereby endangering public morals, health, safety, and/or welfare.

**adduce.** *v.* To bring forward; to offer as a reason for proof.

*ad hoc. (Lat.)* For this only; for this specific purpose exclusively.

*ad hominem.* "To the person." An attack on the person as opposed to the argument, subject, or issue in controversy.

**adjective law.** The entire corpus of the rules of procedure and court practice.

**adjourn.** *v.* To terminate, defer, suspend, recess, or postpone.

**adjudge.** *v.* To decide or settle judicially; to pass sentence; a judicial determination. See *judgment.*

**adjudicate.** *v.* To settle an issue in dispute through the formal process of a hearing or litigation.

**adjudication.** *n.* The judicial processing of a case and the rendering of a final judgment.

**adjudicatory hearing.** A fact-finding hearing before a juvenile court judge, held for the purpose of determining whether sufficient evidence exists to sustain the allegations set forth in the petition.

*ad litem. (Lat.)* Something for the purpose of a suit or litigation. See, e.g., guardian *ad litem*; one appointed to litigate a suit on the behalf of a juvenile.

**administrative courts.** Courts with jurisdiction over administrative rules and regulations, presided over by an administrative law judge (ALJ). Courts that adjudicate violations of administrative regulations enforced by regulatory agencies, e.g., the EPA.

**administrative law.** A body of law generated by an administrative agency or agencies. The authority to create such law is delegated by the legislature of a sovereign government. Administrative laws are also known as rules, regulations, orders, and decisions. Despite the fact that they may provide for a criminal-like sanction, they are technically not cited as criminal laws.

**administrative law judge (ALJ).** A judge who presides over a court that adjudicates alleged violations of the administrative codes generated by the various administrative or regulatory agencies, e.g., the EPA, having the authority to administer oaths, to rule on questions of admissibility, and to make determinations of fact. Formerly known as a "hearing officer or examiner." See *Administrative Procedure Act,* § 556.

**administrative search.** A search conducted under the authority of administrative law for the purpose of protecting public safety. Importantly, the level of force allowable in executing an administrative search under the authority of a warrant is lower than for a criminal search warrant, where all reasonable force may be used.

**admiralty.** *n.* That body of law pertaining to navigable waters and navigation thereon. See *admiralty law.*

**admiralty law.** That particular branch of law dealing with marine commerce and navigation, especially on the high seas. In the main, it is considered an area of law falling within federal jurisdiction.

**admissibility of evidence.** The ruling by the trial judge as to whether evidence is admissible at trial. The rules of evidence in most state courts are founded on appellate case law, which guides the judge's decision. In federal and some state courts, however, the admissibility of evidence is found in a codified Rules of Evidence, supplemented by case law.

**admission.** *n.* A voluntary acknowledgment made by a suspect to the existence of a fact or facts at issue in an investigation. An admission falls short of a confession, as it is not a full acceptance of criminal culpability.

**adversarial proceeding.** A legal proceeding consisting of opposing parties as contrasted against an *ex parte* (a one-sided) hearing.

**adversarial system.** Characterized as a contest between a plaintiff in civil proceedings or the prosecutor in criminal cases (the initiating parties) and a body of inter-related laws, rules, and procedures, wherein parties seek to find a ruling favorable to their interests. The judge functions as a disinterested independent magistrate rather than as a prosecutor, as in an inquisitorial system (found in many European nations), where he or she is called an investigative magistrate.

**Advisory Commission on Intergovernmental Affairs (ACIA).** As an organization that addresses areas of friction between the federal and state governments in inter-state and inter-local relations, the ACIA has been supported by Congress since its beginnings in 1959. It publishes the quarterly journal *Intergovernmental Perspective.*

**advocacy.** *n.* The act of speaking or writing in support of something or someone; in law the act of actively pleading in one's behalf.

**affiant.** *n.* One who swears to and signs an affidavit.

**affidavit.** *n.* A written statement of facts voluntarily made under oath.

**affirmance.** *n.* A confirming or reassertion of an existing law or former judgment. The confirmation of an appellate court on a lower court's ruling, order, or decree.

**affirmation.** *n.* A formal declaration (in place of an oath) that an affidavit is accurate and true and that the witness will tell the whole truth.

**affirmative action.** Programs instituted by the federal government (by statutes and regulations) to affirmatively assist minority persons in remedying discriminatory hiring and promotional practices by employers. The National Labor Relations Board is mandated to effectuate affirmative action provisions under the National Labor Relations Act.

**affray.** *n.* A public brawl or riot constituting a breach of the peace.

**Afro-American Police League (AAPL).** Established in 1968 and headquartered in Chicago, the organization represents black police employees and publishes two quarterly periodicals: the *Bulletin on Special Events* and the *Grapevine.*

**aftercare.** *n.* A program whereby an adjudicated juvenile who has been committed to a treatment facility as part of his or her treatment or sanction is conditionally released and placed in a supervised treatment program outside a juvenile treatment facility.

**agent.** *n.* One empowered to act for another; in law enforcement, e.g., an FBI agent.

**agent provocateur.** An undercover agent who incites others to perform overt acts for the purpose of compromising them or placing them under criminal arrest.

**age of accountability.** The minimal age at which one is legally considered to have the mental capacity to be held accountable for his or her actions or inactions in a criminal context. The specific age varies between jurisdictions, usually from twelve to fourteen. Traditionally, however, most Anglo-American jurisdictions have set the age at seven.

**age of consent.** The minimal age at which a female may legally consent to sexual intercourse without placing her sexual partner in criminal jeopardy for charges of statutory rape or some like offense.

**age of maximum criminality.** The chronological age range at which, statistically, most people will likely offend against the criminal law. That age is somewhere between sixteen and twenty for serious property offenses and somewhat higher for offenses against the person. As a general rule, criminal activity noticeably declines after the age of twenty-one and very rapidly drops off after forty.

**agglutination.** *n.* The phenomenon of particles in a fluid, especially red blood cells, clumping as a result of the action of an antibody.

**aggravated assault.** An assault where the assailant flourishes a deadly weapon, or attempts to cause serious bodily injury to another intentionally, knowingly, purposely, or recklessly, while demonstrating extreme indifference for human life. See *Model Penal Code, § 211.1(2).*

**aggravation.** *n.* Actions or circumstances that increase the gravity of a crime and its legal consequences.

**aggregate, social.** The bringing together of various components into an identifiable but unorganized whole.

**aggression.** *n.* In international law, the forcible attempt by a state to intrude on another state's sovereignty, without legal or moral justification.

**Agnew's general theory of strain.** The General Strain Theory (GST) developed by sociologist Robert Agnew, identifying microlevel (individual) influences of strain, as opposed to Robert Merton's social-class differences in criminality or delinquency. Agnew's theory attempts a more general explanation of criminality across all strata of society rather than delimiting the theory to only lower-class offenders.

**agnomen.** *n.* A secondary name or nickname.

**aiding and abetting.** The affirmative assistance or facilitation in the commission of a crime through various forms of encouragement or support. It involves any form of assistance, e.g., words, acts, or encouragement.

**albastone.** *n.* A substitute for plaster of Paris, used in casting various indentations for comparison purposes.

**Alcohol, Tobacco, and Firearms (ATF).** The United States Bureau of Alcohol, Tobacco, and Firearms, originally a division of the Department of the Treasury, has been transferred under the authority of the Department of Homeland Security bill to the U.S. Department of Justice. The agency's name was also altered to the United States Bureau of Alcohol, Tobacco, Firearms, and Explosives (see that title). It investigates crimes involving explosive devices and illegal firearms. The agency also formerly served a regulatory and licensing function in the sale, distribution, and licensing of alcohol, tobacco, and firearm products.

**aleatory element.** The element of the inexplicable and unpredictable; largely dependent upon chance.

**Alford plea.** A plea allowed in some criminal courts in the United States, wherein the defendant neither admits to the alleged criminal act(s) nor claims his or her innocence, although the defendant does recognize that there exists sufficient evidence for a reasonable jury to convict. In some jurisdictions, the judge may immediately sentence the defendant, while in others, the judge may continue the case, pending further inquiry. That inquiry may lead to a dismissal of the charges—the ultimate hope of the defense counsel in making the plea. The plea is similar to a plea of *nolo contendere*; although in a *nolo contendere* plea, the defendant clearly is not making any admission regarding criminal culpability. The subtle difference between the two pleas is that in the Alford plea the court may use the plea against the defendant's interests in a subsequent civil or criminal trial. And, in jurisdictions where a "three-strikes" rule is used, the Alford plea counts as one of the three strikes. A *nolo contendere* plea, on the other hand, may not be used against the interests of the defendant in a subsequent adjudication. See *North Carolina v. Alford* 400 U.S. 25 (1970).

**alias dictus.** *(Lat.)* The popular form of this term is "alias" (otherwise known as "a.k.a.").

**alibi.** *n.* An excuse or explanation that the accused was elsewhere or otherwise could not have committed the alleged offense; a defense of impossibility.

**alien.** *n.* A foreign-born resident of a given nation who does not hold citizenship in that nation.

**Alien Conspiracy Theory.** The perspective holding that organized crime was imported into the United States from foreign nations. This perspective also holds that organized crime syndicates limit membership to those of their ethnic origins.

**Alien Documentation, Identification, and Telecommunications (ADIT).** A computerized data base operated by the Immigration and Naturalization Service for purposes of tracking aliens.

**alienation.** *n.* A state of separation or estrangement from a person, organization, culture, or other thing.

**allocution.** *n.* A formal warning from the court that unless the prisoner shows cause otherwise, the court will pass judgment on him or her upon conviction.

**altercation.** *n.* A heated dispute, often ending in an assault or a battery.

**ambulance chaser.** A slang phrase for an attorney or one who on the behalf of an attorney solicits legal business contrary to the standards of professional ethics; a metaphor for any person who fails to observe professional behavioral standards.

**American Academy for Professional Law Enforcement (AAPLE).** The academy, established in 1973, stresses education and the development of programs in the areas of professional and ethical standards for police officers.

**American Bar Association (ABA).** Headquartered in Chicago, the ABA is the national professional association for lawyers. Its fundamental purpose is to maintain and improve the standards of legal service and the overall administration of justice in the United States. Any licensed attorney in any of the various states who is in good standing may be accepted as a member.

**American Bar Foundation (ABF).** Established in 1952 as the research arm of the American Bar Association, the ABF is located in Chicago. It serves as an organization that sponsors and funds projects in legal research and education.

**American Board of Forensic Odontology (ABFO).** Organized in 1976, under the aegis of the National Institute of Justice, the ABFO serves the forensic needs of the nation's police and law enforcement agencies by providing expert witnesses during litigation. The Board's primary mission is to maintain qualification standards for those practicing odontology (forensic dentistry) in North America. (An odontologist is one holding a DDS or DMD degree or a graduate degree in dentistry with a specialty or graduate degree in odontology). Odontologists are often used as expert witnesses in cases where bite marks are involved.

**American Civil Liberties Union (ACLU).** As a privately funded organization whose primary purpose is the defense of the individual's civil rights and liberties as enumerated in the U.S. Constitution, the ACLU has been socially, politically, and legally active since its inception in 1920. Headquartered in New York City, the ACLU has nearly 2,000 lawyers representing the agency without remuneration.

**American Federation of Police, Inc. (AFP).** The Federation, established in 1966, is comprised of federal, state, county, local, and private security officers; it publishes the monthly periodical *Police Times.*

**American Judicature Society (AJS).** Headquartered in Chicago, the AJS is dedicated to the promotion of the effective administration of justice in the United States. It publishes the monthly *Judicature* and a bimonthly newsletter, the *AJS Update.*

**American Jurisprudence.** A legal encyclopedia that replaced *Ruling Case Law.* In its revised form (*American Jurisprudence Second Edition—Am. Jur.* 2d), it is cross-referenced with an annotated case series, *American Law Reports* (ALR).

**American Law Enforcement Officers' Association (ALEOA).** Located in Washington, DC, the ALEOA was established in 1976 and is comprised of both full- and part-time employees in the criminal justice system. Private security personnel may also hold active membership. The organization's primary intent is to foster cooperation between police, law enforcement, and security personnel.

**American Law Institute (ALI).** A national association of legal scholars who, with the assistance of the National Conference of Commissioners on Uniform State Laws, draft many of the Uniform State Laws (model state codes), e.g., the *Model Penal Code,* with the intent of bringing uniformity to state laws.

**American Law Reports (ALR).** A compilation of cases with annotations for researching specific cases on specific points of law; it is composed of three volumes.

**American Municipal Association (AMA).** Headquartered in both Chicago and Washington, DC, the AMA is comprised of the state leagues from numerous municipalities. The association's primary purpose is to provide consulting services concerning problems confronting municipal governments in the United States.

**American Society of Criminology (ASC).** Located in Columbus, Ohio, the society is an interdisciplinary scholarly and professional organization dedicated to the spreading of social scientific, legal, historical, and applied knowledge for the study of criminology. Affiliated with the American Association for the Advancement of Science, the organization assimilated the Association of College Police Training Officials in 1947. The ASC publishes the quarterly *Criminology: An Interdisciplinary Journal.*

**American Society for Industrial Security (ASIS).** Headquartered in Washington, DC, the ASIS is the national organization for private security officers and administrators in the United States.

**Americans for Effective Law Enforcement (AELE).** The AELE, established in 1966 and located in Evanston, Illinois, provides research services in the area of civil liability for police and law enforcement administrators.

*amicus curiae. (Lat.)* "Friend of the Court." Frequently referred to as "amicus briefs," interested individuals and organizations who are not a party to the litigation are permitted by the court to file a brief in appellate cases in order to provide a rationale for a ruling consistent with their views on the issue at hand. These briefs are frequently filed in appeals having compelling public interests.

**amido black.** A protein-based dye solution used to amplify various bloody impressions, e.g., bloody footprints left at crime scenes, to obtain clearer crime-scene photographs.

**amphetamine.** *n.* A drug commonly used as a nasal inhalant. Technically it is benzedrine sulfate, a synthetic drug that is a stimulant to the central nervous system.

**ANACDUTRA.** An acronym used by the U.S. armed forces for Annual Active Duty Training; it applies to reservists and national guard personnel who have been activated for the customary annual two-week training period, often held during the summer months. During ANACDUTRA, reservists and guard personnel are subject to the Uniform Code of Military Justice (UCMJ). As a result, crimes committed during this period may be prosecuted under military law.

**analgesic.** *n.* A drug or chemical substance for reducing or eliminating pain.

**anarchism.** *n.* A political ideology holding that the absence of a permanent centralized government best serves the relationships between individuals. The absence of centralized state authority.

**anarchist.** *n.* One who holds to the principles of anarchism; that is, the absence of government and its coercive control over individuals.

**ancient document rule.** Under the *Federal Rules of Evidence* (Fed. Evid. R. 901 b, 8) documents having been in the custody of an official source and that are twenty to thirty years old are presumed genuine without proof to the contrary.

*animus. (Lat.)* Mind; intention; design; something done with intention and design.

**annotated statutes.** Statutes of a sovereign state that have been annotated with explanatory notes.

**annulment.** *n.* The invalidation or cancellation of something; to make void or abrogate. The annulment of a judgment is the stripping of all legal force and authority.

**anomaly.** *n.* An abnormality, deviation, or departure from the general pattern. In criminology, anomalies have been associated with Cesare Lombroso's physical anomalies, whereby certain physical characteristics of the head were correlated with criminal behaviors. This discredited theory has been revisited in recent years by a minority of conservatively oriented physical anthropologists.

*anomie. (Fr.)* Originally from the Greek *anomos*, meaning without law or norms. It is commonly referred to as a state of normlessness; however, that definition is somewhat wanting. It is more accurately a state during which the traditional social and cultural ways, rules, regulations, and laws have broken down as a result of some major social upheaval and are no longer applicable or functional, leading to a generalized social and cultural malaise. It is a state or condition associated with social disorganization, often accompanied by demoralization and its numerous dysfunctional behaviors.

**Anomie Theory.** Early theoretical development is traced to Emile Durkheim's concept of anomie, taken from the Greek word *anomos* (without law or norms). Durkheim posits that an anomic society has experienced a breakdown of behavioral rules or norms as a result of rapid social change or a social crisis such as war. Durkheim's theory was applied to modern criminology by Robert K. Merton in a somewhat modified version.

**antabuse therapy.** The treatment consists of the introduction of a negative experience with certain forms of behavior, of which the use of the chemical disulfiram is key. Disulfiram is a chemical compound that has been commonly applied in the treatment of alcoholism. Once introduced into the system, disulfiram causes a number of symptoms, when alcohol is ingested, causing increased blood pressure, skin flushing, and an accelerated heart rate. If further alcohol usage continues, dizziness, nausea, a rapid decrease in blood pressure, and eventually unconsciousness results. See *aversion therapy.*

**antecedent.** *adj.* Prior; preceding; before; any thing or event occurring before another.

**anthropology, criminal.** The measurement and categorization of bodily characteristics in an attempt to predict a predisposition toward criminality.

**anthropology, cultural.** In its most restrictive meaning, cultural anthropology deals with the social life of primitive peoples. In its more fully developed sense, it is likened to sociology, the scientific study of the social behavior of people.

**anthropology, physical.** See *anthropology, somatic.*

**anthropology, somatic.** That branch of anthropology commonly known as physical anthropology, concerned with the study of the human organism, its evolutionary iterations, life cycles, and the variations existing among diverse racial categories.

**anthropometry.** *n.* The measurement of notable features of the human body and the classification of those features into an organized system.

**anthropophagy.** *n.* Cannibalism; the act of devouring another human being.

**anticipatory search warrant.** Also known as a "prospective" search warrant, it is a search warrant issued for a particular place, vehicle, container, person, and item(s) not yet at the place where the search is to be conducted. See, e.g., *People v. Glen,* 30 NY2d 252, 331 NYS2d 656, 282 NE2d 614 (1972).

**Anti-Racketeering Act.** The federal act that prohibits robbery, extortion, and numerous other illegal acts interfering with interstate commerce. See the *Hobbs Act* and *RICO statutes.*

**antitrust acts.** Public laws at both the federal and state levels protecting trade and commerce against unlawful restraints, price fixing, and monopolies. The primary antitrust acts include the Sherman Act (1890); the Clayton Act (1914); and the Federal Trade Commission Act (1914).

**Apalachin meeting.** The 1957 meeting of highly placed Cosa Nostra officials at Apalachin, New York, where police and law enforcement officers interrupted the meeting, detaining and questioning those in attendance. The meeting erased any doubt regarding a nationally syndicated criminal organization and forced the

FBI to actively address organized crime in the United States, something Hoover (the then head of FBI) earlier had avoided.

**apparent danger.** A critical element of self-defense in homicide cases, requiring an overt act or conduct on the part of the assailant that is designed to take a life or subject the intended victim to serious bodily harm, without which the claim of self-defense is not viable, as there is no apparent or necessary action to secure self-preservation.

**appeal.** *n.* A review of the decision by a lower court by a higher court. Generally, in both the federal and state court systems, an appeal involves the review of a decision by a court of general jurisdiction (trial court) to an appellate court, usually an intermediate court of appeals. From the intermediate appellate court, the case may be appealed to the highest court of appeals, usually the supreme court of the state and then occasionally to the U.S. Supreme Court. In states employing a nonunified court system, where a system of inferior courts exists, a case may be heard *de novo* in the state trial court, after adjudication in an inferior court. Technically, this is not an appeal, but, rather, an entirely new case, as no transcript is available from the inferior court for the appellate court to review.

**appeal bond.** A bond posted when pursuing an appeal, under which the appellant is bound to incur all costs if he or she fails to go forward reasonably with the appeal.

**appearance.** *n.* The submission of a defendant to the court's authority and jurisdiction by voluntarily attending a hearing either in person or through his or her attorney.

**appearance bond.** Bail bond used to ensure the presence of the defendant at trial. See *bail.*

**appellant.** *n.* The person who initiates and carries forward an appeal from a lower court to a higher court.

**appellate.** *adj.* The distinction between courts of original jurisdiction and appellate jurisdiction.

**appellate court.** This class of court includes (in most jurisdictions) both intermediate courts of appeals and the highest court of appeals (in most jurisdictions and the federal judiciary, the Supreme Court). A court of review and generally not a court of first instance, except in cases like treason, where the High Court sits as the court of original and exclusive jurisdiction and from which the defendant has no right to appeal.

**appellate judge.** A judge appointed or elected (depending on the jurisdiction) to the appellate bench. Formally known as a "justice" of the appellate court, he or she sits with a number of other justices.

**appellate jurisdiction.** The legal right vested in an appellate court to review the record and judgment of an inferior court.

**appellee.** *n.* The party against whom an appeal is submitted, sometimes called the respondent.

**apprehension.** *n.* The physical seizure, taking, or arresting of a person for violation of a law. In a military context, e.g., for military police, apprehension is the technical term used as a substitute for the civilian criminal justice procedure known as arrest, as arrest in a military context has an entirely different meaning, i.e., the confinement of a person to a particular place.

**Aquinas, St. Thomas (circa 1225–1274).** A Dominican philosopher and theologian and the author of the *Summa Theologica.* Drawing a sharp distinction between reason and faith, he stressed the role of free will in human acts and reasoning. He was an adherent of a well-ordered society and efficacious rule that would ward off tyranny.

**arbitrator.** *n.* A neutral person chosen to settle disputes, outside of the formal justice system.

**archetype.** *n.* An original prototype or pattern upon which others are modeled.

**argot.** *n.* Jargon or slang used by criminals and those who are incarcerated.

**argument.** *n.* A discussion in which there is disagreement on an issue, where logic is used to bring forth support or refutation of or for a position, an effort to gain belief through reason. In law there are a number of types and reasons for offering an argument, e.g., argument by counsel, used during an opening statement to the jury, or argument in mitigation before sentencing.

**argument in aggravation.** An argument offered by the prosecution, during the sentencing phase of the criminal trial, presenting facts regarding the defendant that increase the probability the judge will render a more severe sentence in the interest of justice.

**armorer.** *n.* In a military or police context, an armorer is the person placed in charge of the armory, responsible for the repair and the safekeeping of firearms; he or she is also responsible for the storage and dispensing of ammunition.

**armor-piercing bullet.** A bullet having a projectile made of lead, covered with a hard metal jacket, often hardened brass that is cone shaped. This configuration allows the armor-piercing projectile to penetrate armor (metal) plating.

**armory.** *n.* (1) A building or secure room within a building intended for the storage and dispensing of firearms and ammunition. (2) A building having a drill hall and command offices of a militia, military reserve, or national guard unit.

**arms-reach doctrine.** A court generated doctrine allowing officers to search not only the person who is being placed under arrest but also any places under his or her immediate physical control, that is, ". . . any area into which the arrested subject might reach in order to grab a weapon or evidentiary items . . . ." See the ruling case law in *Chimel v. California,* 395 U.S. 752, 762–763, 89 S.Ct. 2034, 2040, 23 L.Ed.2d 685, 694.

**arousal theory.** A criminological perspective (theory) holding that people who have high levels of arousal actively seek strong stimuli, in order to sustain a high level of arousal, e.g., violence and aggression leading to criminality. Some criminologists suggest that sociopaths are likely to seek this type of stimulation at the expense of their victims.

**arraignment.** *n.* A hearing before a court of competent jurisdiction wherein the defendant pleas to the alleged charge(s). The plea must be one of the following: guilty, not guilty, or *nolo contendere* (if the jurisdiction allows). The charge(s) is/are read in open court directly from the information, complaint, or indictment before the defendant makes his or her plea.

**array.** *n.* (1) The entire body of potential jurors who have been summoned for jury duty. (2) The formal arrangement of the selected jurors, once assembled and impaneled.

**arrest.** *n.* The deprivation of one's liberty through legal authority, usually for the purpose of formally charging him or her with a crime or quasi-criminal offense. (It should be noted that both persons and property are sometimes subjected to civil arrest). An arrest involves two essential elements: (1) the assertion of legal authority to restrain, and (2) a physical act in the furtherance of the arrest by an officer or (in the case of civilian arrest) by a citizen to detain or place another in custody for the purpose of officially charging and processing him or her.

**arrest of judgment.** An act by the judge either before or after conviction that stays the execution of the judgment or impending judgment, as a result of an issue that would render it either erroneous or reversible, e.g., if the case were tried before a court not having jurisdiction.

**arrest rate.** The ratio of persons arrested per thousand or one hundred thousand in a given population, community, or jurisdiction.

**arrest record.** (1) The official record of an arrest created by a policing or law enforcement agency, including the disposition of the charge(s). (2) The official record kept on file at the state or national level.

**arrest register.** In some jurisdictions the register is known as the "police blotter," and was traditionally a written document kept by the desk sergeant. Today, it is usually a record containing a complete chronological accounting of all criminal arrests made by police or law enforcement agencies in digital format. The record is readily retrievable by official agencies and contains at a minimum the name and date of birth of the arrested person and the offense(s), date, and time of occurrence.

**arrest warrant.** See *bench warrant.*

**arson.** *n.* (1) The intentional and malicious burning or explosion of another's building, vehicle, or property or the burning or explosion of one's own for the purpose of insurance fraud. See the *Model Penal Code,* § 220.1(1). Some jurisdictions divide arson into three degrees. (2) To unlawfully and intentionally damage, or attempt to damage, any real or personal property by fire or incendiary device (FBI Uniform Crime Definition).

**arsonist.** *n.* One who intentionally sets fires or causes explosions for the purpose of injuring or destroying property or life. These acts may be done for financial gain, even against one's own property for the purpose of fraud.

**article 15 hearing.** A nonjudicial punishment hearing conducted by the commanding officer of a military or naval unit, for relatively minor criminal and/or quasi-criminal offenses or infractions of military discipline or protocol. It is known by different terms among the various armed services, i.e., in the Army and Air Force an "article 15," while in the Navy a "captain's mast," and the Marine Corps "office hours." While the sanction never involves any confinement, its consequences can be potentially career ending for the offender. See Art. 15 (UCMJ) and Part V, para. 1e of the *Manual for Courts Martial* (1998 ed).

**article 32 hearing.** (1) In the armed forces it is a probable-cause hearing (for what in the civilian criminal justice system would be a misdemeanor violation) to determine whether the alleged offender should go forward to a "special" court martial for trial. (2) For what would constitute an alleged felony violation in the civilian criminal justice system, the article 32 hearing amounts to a grand jury or preliminary hearing or investigation to determine whether the alleged offender should stand trial at a "general" court martial. Although the Constitution requires a grand jury hearing before a federal felony trial may begin, this provision is not applicable in the military justice system. The grand jury provision is supplanted by an article 32 hearing (inquiry) by a military officer, under article 32 of the Uniform Code of Military Justice, § 832 Title 10, USC. This section mandates an impartial investigation of the charge(s) and a recommendation to go forward with or to decline a prosecution.

**Articles of Confederation.** The original organic law of the (these) United States, which granted most of the power to the states, as it denied the newly formed federal government the power to levy taxes, raise troops, and regulate commerce, all of which constitute the basic elements of sovereignty. The document proved a severely delimited and unworkable document for the federal government and was later replaced by the U.S. Constitution. The Articles of Confederation became the document that the southern secessionist states wanted to go back to during the Civil War and the reason why the South was known as the Confederacy.

**artifact.** *n.* (1) In forensic science, any characteristic or feature altered by the deteriorating forces of nature or another agency, and not an original feature or characteristic. (2) In the social sciences, including history, any characteristic, feature, tradition, item, practice, or pattern of behavior associated with a given time period or social, racial, or ethnic group, i.e., something produced reflecting a socially shared world view, philosophy, or ideological persuasion. (3) An object produced through human effort.

**Aryan Brotherhood.** A Caucasian gang originating in the prison at San Quentin, California.

**Ashurst-Sumners Act (1935).** The federal law (18 USC §§ 1761–1762) making it a federal offense to transport prison-made goods between states, regardless of existing state laws providing for such transportation and sale.

**asportation.** *n.* The taking and transporting of goods from one place to another. A requisite for the charge of larceny.

**assassination.** *n.* Murder of a public figure for personal, social, religious, or political motives. Until the assassination of President John F. Kennedy (1963), the assassination of the president or vice president was entirely a state offense. Today it is a federal crime under 18 USCA § 2385.

**assault.** *n.* A willful and unlawful attempt to deliver a battery or a gesture that places another in the position to reasonably expect to receive a battery. An unlawful touching, with the intent to do harm (a battery), is not an element in the offense of assault; it is, however, a necessary element in the offense of battery. When carried out with the intent to cause great bodily harm or death or with a deadly weapon, the charge is elevated to aggravated assault.

**asset forfeiture proceeding.** An *in rem* procedure instituted against the property, as opposed to the person, that was either an instrumentality of a crime or the fruits of a crime (in whole or in part); or it may constitute the civil arrest and seizure of property to be forfeited, independent of a criminal arrest and/or conviction of the person responsible for the commission of a crime. Thus, an asset forfeiture is not part of the sanction of a criminal arrest for a crime and is not to be confused with the civil seizure, which takes place only after a conviction for a criminal offense.

**assignation house.**  A house of prostitution; house of ill fame; a bawdy house.

**assigned counsel.**  An attorney appointed by the court to represent an indigent defendant, usually in a criminal case.

**Assimilative Crimes Act.**  The federal act assimilating state criminal and quasi-criminal law into federal law, violations of which are to be tried in federal court. The act does not apply where Congress has previously enacted a penal code. That is, the act incorporates state law only in instances where no federal law addresses certain acts. The act stipulates: "Whoever within or upon any of the places now existing or hereafter reserved or acquired as provided in Section 7 of this Title, is guilty of any act or omission which, although not made punishable by any enactment of Congress, would be punishable if committed or omitted within the jurisdiction of the state, territory, possession or district in which such place is situated, by the laws thereof in force at the time of such act or omission, shall be guilty of a like offense and subject to like punishment." See 18 USCA § 13; and 21 *Am. Jur. 2d*, Criminal Law, § 395. The constitutionality of the Assimilative Crimes Act was upheld by the U.S. Supreme Court in *United States v. Sharpnack,* 355 U.S. 286, 78 S.Ct. 291 (1958).

**Assistant United States Attorney.**  An attorney employed in a U.S. Attorney's Office in one of the U.S. District Courts. Assistant U.S. attorneys act in the place of the U.S. attorney and have all the authority and powers inherent in the Office of the U.S. Attorney. Their duties include the prosecution of violations of the U.S. Code, the prosecution or defense of the U.S. government, or its agents, the defense of the government against civil suits or proceedings in which the United States is a party, the recovery of all fines and seizure and forfeiture assets, and the collection of revenue in cases arising out of the revenue law of the United States. See 28 USCA § 547.

**assize.** *(Fr.)*  Also spelled *assise,* it is a sitting court, or one that is in session. In earlier times, a court comprised of knights and other men of high social standing in a given venue.

**Association of Public Safety Communications Officials International, Inc. (APCO).**  The world's largest communications association, founded in 1935 with nearly 15,000 members worldwide, providing communications training, products, and services. The APCO produces the standard police brevity code for use in the United States, known as the APCO 10 signals.

**Association of Trial Lawyers of America (ATLA).**  Headquartered in Washington, DC, the Association was originally founded in 1946 as the National Association of Claimants' Compensation Attorneys (NACCA); it was renamed ATLA in 1977 and includes in its membership attorneys from the United States and Canada. ATLA publishes *Trial* magazine.

**assumed facts.**  Relevant facts for which no evidence has been introduced during the course of litigation. A set of hypothetical facts employed to illuminate a point of law.

**asylum.** *n.*  A venue that offers sanctuary from prosecution for criminal offenders. The right of asylum is vested in the asylum state and cannot be claimed by the alleged offender without the granting of asylum status by the state. The privilege of asylum has been greatly diminished in recent years by international treaties on extradition of fugitive criminals that limit the kinds of offenses that can be considered and the conditions under which asylum may be granted.

**asylum state.** The state, its protectorates, vassal states, and legations where a criminal fugitive may be secreted and granted immunity from prosecution.

**atavism.** *n.* A throwback to a more primitive type. A resemblance of a person to an ancestor in some characteristic not noticeable in more recent relatives; a genetic throwback.

**atavistic anomalies.** A fundamental element in Lombrosian criminology, holding that "born criminals" have genetic and overtly noticeable physical traits that are throwbacks to more primitive human forms. Lombroso believed, e.g., that most criminals had notable physical features like protruding jaws.

**at large.** (1) Something not limited to a specific place, venue, person, issue, or question. (2) An elected official who has been chosen by the collective voters of a political entity as a whole, as opposed to one selected from a specific district within a political entity.

**atomic absorption.** A method of analysis employed by forensic scientists to detect trace elements of antimony and/or barium, used in the production of firearm ammunition primers.

**attaché.** *n.* One attached to a foreign legation, embassy, or office of an ambassador; one otherwise connected to a public office or officer.

**attachment.** *n.* The physical act of seizing and taking into custody a person, persons, or property through a judicial writ for the purpose of securing a judgment in a civil, administrative, or criminal matter.

**attainder.** *n.* The formal extinguishment of all civil liberties, rights, and privileges under early English law, following a legislative condemnation for any felony. The attained person not only had all property seized, he or she lost the legal right to inherit from or bequeath property to his or her heirs. He or she also lost the right to have standing in court. In the United States, bills of attainder are forbidden by the Constitution, Article I § 10, 1. See also *corruption of blood.*

**attempt.** *v.* A purposeful effort taken to accomplish a crime, entailing more than simple planning, which if not frustrated would have led to the accomplishment of the criminal act. The necessary elements of a charge of criminal attempt include (1) intent, (2) an overt act carried out in the furtherance of the crime, (3) the failure to accomplish the criminal act, and (4) the possibility of the criminal act being successfully carried out.

**attenuation doctrine.** One of several doctrines under which the Supreme Court has recognized exceptions to the otherwise nonadmission of tainted evidence at suppression and/or trial. The High Court's holding in *Nardone v. United States,* 308 U.S. 338 (1939) argues that despite the fact that evidence was gathered as a result of an illegal search and seizure, at some juncture the nexus between the illegal conduct and the eventual discovery of the evidence " . . . may have become so attenuated as to dissipate the taint." The Court in *Brown v. Illinois,*

422 U.S. 590 (1975), however, declined to establish a "bright-line" rule for the application of the attenuation doctrine. Rather, the High Court cited a number of factors that might establish sufficient attenuation for non-Mirandized statements; they include "[the] temporal proximity of the arrest and the confession, the presence of intervening circumstances, and, particularly, the purpose and flagrancy of the official misconduct." See also *United States v. Ceccolini,* 435 U.S. 268 (1978).

**attestation.** *n.* The act of swearing or affirming to something, as the signature of a witness to the drafting of a document.

**Attica Prison riot (1971).** Nearly, 1,200 prisoners rioted for four days at the state prison at Attica, New York, where thirty-eight guards were held as hostages. On the last day of the revolt, a massive assault was made by the combined efforts of the New York National Guard's Military Police, New York State Police, and other police agencies. Nine hostages and twenty-eight prisoners were killed in the withering gunfire laid down by the assault teams.

**attorney.** *n.* An agent or proxy authorized to act in another's place. Unless otherwise stipulated, the term denotes an attorney-at-law.

**attorney-at-law.** A professional person or corporation licensed to practice law in a given jurisdiction with all of the rights and privileges appertaining thereto.

**attorney–client privilege.** According to the laws of evidence (whether codified or case-law generated), a client's privilege to disallow disclosure of any confidential communications between himself or herself and the attorney of record. This privilege belongs to the client alone and may be waived with his or her consent only, independent of the attorney.

**attorney general, state.** The state attorney general is the chief legal officer of the state. This officer gives legal advice to the executive branch, represents the state and any of its departments or agencies against litigation, and renders legal opinions regarding unsettled issues of law to the executive branch or any state agency or department, upon request.

**attorney general, United States.** The U.S. attorney general is the legal head of the U.S. Department of Justice and the chief legal officer of the federal government. This officer gives legal advice to the executive branch and represents the government in cases of extreme importance; otherwise cases are handled by a U.S. attorney or one of his or her assistant U.S. attorneys. The attorney general also has administrative authority over all U.S. attorneys throughout the network of federal judicial districts and circuits.

**attorney general's bill.** An indictment prepared by the attorney general's office, expressly for presentation to a grand jury (usually a statewide grand jury) without first presenting a complaint before a judge.

**attorney general's opinion.** An opinion offered by an attorney general on an issue in controversy (often the interpretation of a statute, public law, or constitutional provision) that has not been the subject of appellate review to either the executive department or a governmental agency upon request. It does not carry the same weight in litigation as an appellate decision.

**attorneys general.** Plural form of attorney general.

**Auburn system.** A penal philosophy initiated at the Auburn State Prison in New York in 1816, requiring complete silence for inmates. Prisoners were placed in separate cells during nighttime hours and were made to perform physical labor in complete silence during waking hours.

*audita querela. (Lat.)* A writ seeking to set aside the execution of a judicial judgment because of an alleged injustice committed by the party who sought the ruling; it is assumed that this pleading could not have been made during the course of the trial. See *arrest of judgment.*

**Augustus, John (1784–1859).** Credited as unofficially establishing the first effort at probation in the United States, this Boston shoe cobbler acted between 1841 and 1859 as the supervisor for nearly 2,000 offenders. He argued that the purpose of the law was not to maliciously punish, but rather to reform offenders and to deter.

**authenticating witness.** One who testifies that a written document is what it purports and that it was generated by the party to whom it is attributed.

**authoritarianism.** *n.* The practice of unquestioned obedience to authority figures.

**authority.** *n.* In law, the legal right to direct and command; the legal right to exercise power in the enforcement of laws; to exact obedience; to command; and to make judgments.

**autoerotic death.** An accidental death resulting from an attempt to reach sexual gratification while approaching death, usually by hanging.

**Automated Fingerprint Identification Systems (AFIS).** As a relatively recent computer-based fingerprint recording and classification technology, many AFIS computers have the ability to live-scan prints, thereby supplanting the traditional paper and ink method of fingerprint taking.

**Automatic Data Processing Intelligence Network (ADPIN).** A computerized network for the collection and dissemination of intelligence data for the purpose of combating smuggling, usually of illicit drugs. The system is almost exclusively used by the U.S. Bureau of Customs, now the Bureau of Immigration and Customs Enforcement (ICE), under the newly formed Department of Homeland Security (DHS).

**automatic reversal rule.** A rule promulgated by the U.S. Supreme Court, holding that certain constitutional errors are of such fundamental importance in the American scheme of justice as to require an automatic reversal of a lower court conviction. In *Tumey v. Ohio*, 273 U.S. 510 (1927), e.g., the High Court held that the Fourteenth Amendment's due process provision demanded a fair trial before a neutral judge and reversed the decision of the lower court.

**automatic weapon.** (1) A firearm that continues to fire once continuous pressure is placed on the trigger; that is, unlike a semi-automatic, where the trigger must be actuated separately for each round; the true "automatic" fires continuously until finger pressure on the trigger is released. (2) In common usage, any handgun that is not a revolver or "wheel gun" and which reloads automatically by the recoil or expanded gases of the fired round, often called simply an "automatic." Technically, this type of handgun is a "semi-automatic" firearm, as it will continue to fire only when the trigger is manually depressed for each round.

**autopsy.** *n.* The physical examination and surgical dissection of a body in order to determine the cause of death. Often conducted by a coroner or his designate or a medical examiner, autopsies are performed when no physician was present at the time of death or the cause of death suggests foul play; it is often known as a postmortem.

**autrefois.** *(Fr.)* Formerly; heretofore; before; predating.

**aver.** *v.* To make a declarative statement or assertion; to posit or allege.

**aversion therapy.** A behavior modification treatment based on the association of a negative experience with certain behaviors. The therapy can also consist of positive reinforcements for desired behaviors. See *antabuse therapy.*

**axiom.** *n.* A maxim; a statement universally considered to be true; a statement requiring no proof because of its obvious truth; a widely accepted principle of law, science, or art.

# B

BAL, blood alcohol level
BATF, see *BATFE*
BATFE, Bureau of Alcohol, Tobacco, Firearms, and Explosives
BCCI, Bank of Commerce and Credit International
BFOQ, bona fide occupational qualification
BIA, Bureau of Indian Affairs
BJA, Bureau of Justice Assistance
BJS, Bureau of Justice Statistics
BLM, Bureau of Land Management

**bail.** *n.* The surety or sureties, deposited with the court, procuring the release of a person under pretrial custody, for the purpose of ensuring the defendant's appearance at trial. See *Illinois plan.* Bail is categorized into two separate types: (1) nonfinancial release, including (a) release on recognizance, and (b) conditional release; and (2) financial release, including (a) unsecured bail, (b) privately secured bail, (c) property bail, (d) deposit bail, (e) surety bail, and (f) cash bail.

**bail bondsman.** One who may be either licensed or bonded or both who posts the bail for persons who are in custody for alleged offenses. Some jurisdictions disallow bail bondsmen to operate within their jurisdiction.

**Bailey, F. Lee (1933– ).** A well-known criminal defense lawyer, who early in his career organized a private detective agency and who became an authority on the use of the polygraph. Best known for his successful 1966 appeal and retrial of Dr. Samuel Sheppard of Cleveland, Ohio, who had been convicted in 1954 for the murder of his wife.

**bailiff.** *n.* An officer of the court established as early as 1285 under the Statute of Winchester, responsible for the custody of prisoners while in court, the security of the court, as well as the protection of its personnel, property, and processes. Usually the bailiff is a member of the county sheriff's office specifically assigned to trial court security. Generally a bailiff is not a fully empowered police officer. In states with a nonunified court system using inferior courts, the bailiff may be a member of the local police agency or a specially appointed functionary without general police authority. At the federal level, the bailiff may be assigned by the U.S. Marshals Service.

**bailiwick.** *n.* (1) Originally, the geographical area within which a bailiff had jurisdiction. In contemporary usage, the geographical area within which an officer has jurisdiction. (2) A metaphor for any area of responsibility.

**bail reform.** A system of bail allowing those charged with offenses to post only 10 percent of the full amount of the bail bond, 90 percent of which is returned after the defendant appears in court at the appointed time and date. See *Illinois plan.*

**Bail Reform Act (1984).** An act providing for the denial of bail for federal offenders if " . . . no conditions or combination of conditions [of bail] will reasonably assure . . . the safety of any other person and the community." 18 USC § 3142(e) (1985).

**ballistics.** *n.* The science (physics) of the motion and impact of projectiles, including velocity, mass, and trajectory.

**banc.** *(Fr.)* Bench; the permanent location of a sitting court. Courts sitting *en banc* are those using the full bench—all the judges, as distinguished from a court using only one judge or a partial panel of the full appellate court.

**banishment.** *n.* A sanction placed on convicted defendants demanding their expulsion from a sovereign state for a specified time, including life. See *deportation.*

**Bank of Commerce and Credit International (BCCI).** The BCCI paid a $15 million settlement as a result of an international drug money laundering scheme uncovered by the USDOJ in 1989. This international bank is headquartered in Luxembourg and has offices in approximately seventy other nations.

**bar.** *n.* In its strictest sense, the court sitting in full term. Figuratively, the entire corpus of attorneys and counselors collectively. The bar is separated from the "bench," which implies the entire body of judges and justices.

**barbiturates.** *n.* Drugs inducing a depressed state of the central nervous system. Sedatives are light barbiturate doses; heavier doses act as hypnotics and can lead to coma and death.

**barrister.** *n.* In England, a licensed member of the bar who practices law; a counselor-at-law, as distinguished from a solicitor (see that term).

**Bastille.** *n.* A fortress erected in Paris in 1369 that served as a prison until its destruction during the French Revolution of 1789. The prison's demise is celebrated in France, on July 14th, as Bastille Day.

**baton.** *n.* A wooden or plastic nonlethal weapon used by police officers for striking or pushing. See *truncheon.*

**battalion.** *n.* In military usage, a tactical unit composed of three or four companies and a headquarters company; a unit larger than a company but smaller than a regiment or a brigade.

**Battered Child Syndrome.** An affirmative defense employed in cases where children commit crimes as a result of a history of abuse at the hands of parents or overseers.

**Battered Women Syndrome.** An affirmative defense employed in cases where women commit crimes as a result of a history of abuse at the hands of their husbands or partners.

**battery.** *n.* The unlawful use of force upon another; that which follows an assault.

**Baumes's laws.** Punitive legislation endorsed by a committee of the New York State Senate, chaired by Senator Caleb H. Baumes. These 1926 laws mandated an increase in penalty for each successive criminal conviction, with an automatic life sentence upon the fourth conviction. This legislation serves as the model for contemporary habitual offender statutes enacted recently by many states.

**bawdy house.** A brothel; a house of ill fame.

**Bazelon, David (1920–1993).** A federal associate justice, appointed in 1949, to the Fourth Appellate Circuit in Washington, DC, serving until 1985. He was chief justice of the U.S. Court of Appeals 1962–1978. In 1954, as a liberal advocate, he crafted the "Durham Rule," which has served as a standard for legal insanity tests.

**beadle.** *n.* Originally a church figure whose duty it was to bid parishioners to attend the vestry and to carry out its orders. Before the clear separation between ecclesiastical and secular institutions became widely recognized, this church figure was responsible for biding or citing persons to appear in court throughout England.

**beam test.** The identification of crushed marijuana through microscopic examination.

**Bean, Roy (circa 1825–1903).** In 1882, he established a saloon on the Pecos River in Texas. Bean ruled with the blessings of the Texas Rangers as a justice of the peace and coroner, calling himself the "law west of the Pecos."

**beat.** *n.* In municipal-level policing, the geographic area of responsibility for a given policing unit, motorized patrol, or foot-patrol officer.

**Beccaria, Marchese De (Cesare Bonesana) (1738–1794).** Among the early founders of the classical school of criminology, he published the *Essays on Crime and Punishment,* which was later translated into English in 1767. He argued that although most criminals were punished for their criminal intent, they should be punished based on the degree of harm they caused.

**Becker, Howard Saul (1928– ).** Although he never considered himself a criminologist, as a sociologist (Ph.D., University of Chicago, 1951) his research into deviance has had a lasting impact on the field. The 1954 edition of his book *Outsiders: Studies in the Sociology of Deviance* stands as a classic in the literary canon regarding delinquency.

**bedlam.** *n.* (1) *(capitalized)*A well-known London hospital for the mentally ill. (2) Noise and confusion.

**behaviorism.** *n.* A psychological perspective, coined by American psychologist John B. Watson in 1913, holding that empirical psychology can study only human behavior and rejects the mind. That is, consciousness and its processes are not considered subject to scientific inquiry, but rather should be interpreted as covert language activity.

**behavior modification.** The technique of altering behavior by a system of rewards and punishments.

**bench.** *n.* The court itself; the full complement of judges comprising a court "the full bench or *en banc*"; any tribunal empaneled for the administration of justice; the seat of judges.

**bench blotter.** The official record, kept by police, of all arrests and other significant events, sometimes called the sergeant's desk blotter.

**bench trial.** A trial before a judge without a jury; a trial where a jury waiver has been granted.

**bench warrant.** The process of issuing a warrant directly from the bench for the arrest of a person for a crime, or upon indictment or presentment, or for failure to comply with a subpoena.

**benefit of clergy.** A medievally based privilege permitting members of religious societies (and occasionally those of the ruling classes who could read and write) the option of being tried for violations of secular law in the ecclesiastical courts. It does not exist in the United States as a result of the April 30, 1790, act of Congress forbidding it.

**Bentham, Jeremy (1748–1832).** As an English philosopher (utilitarianism) and classical criminologist, he advanced the notion of utilitarianism, that is, the role of pain and pleasure as issues that people factor in when choosing a course of action. He considered criminals to be rational actors driven by the pain–pleasure concept and argued that swift and sure reasonably based punishments were powerful disincentives against crime. He also argued that unnecessarily punitive measures would not help reduce future criminality.

**benzidine test.** A preliminary chemical field test used on stains to detect the presence of blood.

**Berkowitz, David (Son of Sam).** Berkowitz terrorized residents of New York City between 1976 and 1977, killing numerous victims—some with a .44 magnum revolver. A special detective unit was established, called the "Omega Group," charged with finding the ".44 caliber killer" as he came to be known.

**Bertillon, Alphonse (1853–1914).** A French anthropologist who developed an identification system based on the measurement of body parts, eye color, and numerous other physical characteristics. This became known over time as the Bertillon method.

**Bertillon method.** See *Bertillon, Alphonse.*

**best-evidence rule.** Also called the original document rule, this rule requires the original or "best evidence" to be produced in court. Parties in a litigation are required to produce the original unless excused because the original is not available.

**bestiality.** *n.* Sexual acts of any kind between a human being and an animal, historically considered a "crime against nature" and associated strongly with sodomy.

**beyond a reasonable doubt.** That level of proof required for a conviction for the violation of a criminal statute. Proof beyond the doubt that a reasonable person might have after a full and fair examination of the facts at hand, where the facts have been proven by virtue of their probative force. This does not mean proof beyond the shadow of a doubt, as this would place too high a standard for a conviction.

**bias.** *n.* The influence, prejudice, inclination, or predisposition of opinion that does not leave the mind open to fully and fairly consider all facts in a legal controversy.

**bicameral legislature.** A legislative body divided into two distinct parts. In the United States, this equates to the House of Representatives and the Senate. The term was originally coined by Jeremy Bentham.

**biennium.** *n.* A period of two years. Often referred to as the biennial sessions of the various state legislatures.

**bifurcated trial.** A trial divided into two separate parts, that is, a trial to determine legal guilt or innocence, followed by a separate sentencing phase.

**bifurcation.** *n.* (1) The process of dividing into two parts. (2) In fingerprints, the point at which a ridge line forks.

**bigamy.** *n.* The criminal offense of knowingly marrying another while a prior marriage is legally in effect.

**bill of attainder.** Any special legislative act that requires the death penalty, without trial, for treason or other felony, after which all of the defendant's property is forfeited. If less than death is required by this legislation, it is known as a "bill of pains and penalties." Both are expressly forbidden by the U.S. Constitution, Article I § 9, 3.

**bill of exceptions.** A document citing specific objections or exceptions to the judge's ruling or jury instructions at the trial stage of the adjudicatory process. This document then becomes a permanent part of the record for the appellate court to consider during its deliberations.

**bill of indictment.** A legal document of accusation, often drafted by a prosecutor charging an individual with the commission of a crime (usually a felony). The document is then submitted to an empaneled grand jury for consideration. If the grand jury finds sufficient grounds to support the accusation, it hands up a "true bill." Should the grand jury not find sufficient cause to support the accusation, it returns a "no bill" that reads "not a true bill."

**bill of pains and penalties.** A legislative pronouncement or conviction, without trial, that imposes a criminal penalty (not including death) and the forfeiture of property, without recourse. It is similar to an attainder, and like an attainder, is prohibited by the U.S. Constitution, Article I § 9, 3 (Congress), § 10 (States).

**bill of particulars.** A bill expressly citing the particular charges underpinning an accusation. An expanded or amplified version of a proceeding, hearing, or charging document, outlining with specificity the allegations therein.

**Bill of Rights.** (1) The first ten amendments to the U.S. Constitution, constituting the basic civil liberties, added in 1791, after the ratifying committees from the various states objected to the absence of any guarantees against governmental oppression in the original draft of the document. (2) A statement claiming numerous fundamental rights, granted to the people against intrusion or infringement by the government. The English Bill of Rights was passed by Parliament in 1689, and the Virginia Bill of Rights of 1776 incorporated a number of common-law principles. State constitutions generally begin with a bill of rights specifically limiting the authority of the government and guaranteeing certain protections to the people.

**bind-over hearing.** (1) A hearing in which a judge or magistrate requires a person to provide some form of bail assuring appearance for trial. (2) The act of a lower court judge binding over the defendant or transferring of the case to a higher court (sometimes used in a juvenile case that has been sent to adult criminal court). (3) The binding over of the defendant after an indictment by a grand jury and the issuance of a warrant. Bind-over connotes a sending forward; by contrast, a remand connotes a sending back.

**biocriminology.** *n.* See *sociobiology.*

**biological determinism.** A school of criminological thought holding that genetic factors predispose people to certain behaviors. This perspective has its origins in Lombroso's classic works and argues that "born criminals" exist.

**biometry.** *n.* (1) A predictive estimate or calculation of the probable length of human life. (2) An attempt to generate a correlative estimate of crime between parents, children, and siblings. See *Charles Goring.*

**Black.** *n.* The appellate case law reporter for U.S. Supreme Court rulings, spanning 1861–1862. Before the introduction of, e.g., the *United States Reports (U.S.),* and the *United States Supreme Court Reports Lawyers's Edition/Second Edition (L.Ed., or L.Ed. 2d),* a series of lesser-known reports covered the decisions of the High Court; they include *Dallas* (1790–1800), *Cranch* (1801–1815), *Wheaton* (1816–1827), *Peters* (1828–1842), *Howard* (1843–1860), *Black* (1861–1862), and *Wallace* (1863–1874). Today, these early reports have been catalogued in the U.S. Reports and other reporters for the convenience of legal researchers.

**Black Hand Society (*Sp. mano negra*).** Originating in nineteenth-century Spain as an anarchist group, the organization evolved into a Sicilian secret society of blackmailers operating in New York during the early years of the twentieth century.

**Black, Hugo (Lafayette) (1886–1971).** U.S. Supreme Court associate justice appointed by Franklin D. Roosevelt (1937). Before becoming a Supreme Court justice, he served as a U.S. senator from Alabama, supporting Roosevelt's plan to "pack" the Court by adding six justices. He was also a supporter of Roosevelt's New Deal. As a justice, he was an ardent supporter of the civil liberties found in the Bill of Rights.

**black list.** An informal listing of persons to be punished, refused employment, or meant to suffer other deprivations as a result of their unpopular beliefs, values, or activities. See *House Un-American Activities Committee; McCarthyism.*

**blackmail.** *n.* Extorted payment made to prevent the disclosure of information that could bring public disgrace.

**black mariah.** See *paddy wagon.*

**Black Panther Party.** Founded in 1966 by Bobby Seale and Huey P. Newton, the Panthers were originally a militant group demanding full equality for blacks. During their formative years, members were systematically harassed by police; in response they developed a ten-point self-defense program. Among their many demands were the absolute exemption of blacks from compulsory military duty and the creation of all-black juries for blacks accused of crimes. Eventually, the Black Panthers abandoned their self-defense agenda and firearms and focused on black-community-betterment programs.

**blanket search warrant.** One warrant authorizing a search of more than one location and/or the seizure of items found that have not been specifically itemized in the warrant, the latter constituting a violation of the Constitution's Fourth Amendment. See *general warrants.*

**black sites.** Secret prisons operated clandestinely by the U.S. Central Intelligence Agency in numerous foreign countries, including Thailand, Afghanistan, Egypt, Jordan, Morocco, and some eastern European nations, formerly part of the old Soviet Union, where prisoners (usually alleged terrorists) are held incommunicado and without the benefit of counsel, *habeas corpus* relief, or adjudication. Prisoners may be imprisoned for life and under conditions contrary to international law and American constitutional protections. Many of these host nations are noted for permitting the use of torture.

**blasphemy.** *n.* Any vilification of God, the name of the Almighty, or religious societies and ceremonies. During the period of the divine right of kings, it was a high crime punishable by death, as the Crown claimed its right to rule from God, under a doctrine known as the "divine right of Kings." Some criminal justicians claim that as governments evolved, the offense of blasphemy was supplanted by treason.

**blood alcohol level (BAL).** Expressed as a percentage of alcohol in the blood, a BAL of .10 indicates that there is one part of alcohol to 1,000 parts of blood. The BAL can be measured through blood, urine, or breath samples.

**bloodborne pathogens.** The microorganisms that are present in animal blood (including humans') and can infect and cause disease in people who are exposed to blood containing the pathogen. These microorganisms can be transmitted through contact with contaminated bodily fluids, especially the blood.

**blood feud.** A condition between two or more families, tribes, or clans that has led to chronic quarreling and physical confrontations. In the United States, the most notable being the feud between the Hatfields and McCoys.

**Bloods.** *n.* A street gang that serves as a substitute for the traditional family. Members refer to one another as "homeboys," "homies," and "bloods."

**blue curtain.** A metaphor for the solidarity among police officers; a wall of silence; an impenetrable barrier between police and outsiders, including citizens, investigating committees, commissions, and others.

**blue laws.** Originally, a code regulating morality in the New Haven colony of the seventeenth and eighteenth centuries, as a result of the theocratic underpinnings of that closed society. In contemporary usage, blue laws refer to a legal ban on secular activities, such as commerce, athletic contests, and others on Sunday.

**blue-ribbon panel.** A panel, jury, committee, or commission selected carefully for the particular qualifications of its individual members.

**board of pardons.** The generic title for a state-level board granting all forms of executive clemency, e.g., commutations of sentences and pardons. The board may act independently of the governor's office or as an advisory board to the governor, depending on the jurisdiction.

**Boesky, Ivan (1937– ).** The infamous New York stock market manipulator who was the first to be convicted of "insider trading." He was fined $100,000,000, sentenced to three years in federal prison, and banned from the stock market.

**bona fide.** *adj.* Something genuine; without fraud or deceit.

**bona fide occupational qualification (BFOQ).** Any attribute or skill that an employer can demonstrate as a requisite to satisfactory performance in a particular job. This is contrasted against characteristics that have traditionally been required constituting artificial barriers to employment, such as education or gender. See *Griggs v. Duke Power Company*, 401 U.S. 424 (1971).

**bond.** *n.* An obligation imposed by money or other assets, which is deposited with the clerk of the court by the defendant or his or her bonding agent (surety) to secure temporary release from custody. The bond may be forfeited if the defendant fails to appear in court at the specified time and date.

**bondsman.** *n.* One who furnishes surety (bail bond) for another, thereby taking responsibility for his or her appearance in court at the time and date specified. Some states have made the business of bondsmen illegal and have substituted some form of bail reform. See *Illinois plan.*

**Bonger, Willem Adrian (1876–1940).** A Dutch criminologist and author of *An Introduction to Criminology* (1932), an influential book on the emerging field of criminology in Europe. Like Marx, he argued that capitalism was a producer of criminal activity because of the exploitation of workers.

**boodle.** *n.* (1) Anything offered and accepted as a bribe; graft. (2) The money or loot taken in a robbery.

**booking.** *n.* The administrative processing of an arrested person at the police station, often including the taking of fingerprints and mug shots and the entry of the defendant's name and official charge in the desk blotter.

**bookmaking.** *n.* The taking of illegal bets on race horses or other contests.

**boot camp.** (1) In a military context, the initial and basic training of a recruit. (2) In a criminal justice context, a para-militarized and highly disciplined postsentencing program for adjudicated juveniles that is theoretically expected to make a long-term difference in the behavior of offenders. Empirical research does not support this position.

**bootlegger.** *n.* One who sells alcoholic beverages unlawfully.

**Boston police strike.** The September 9, 1919, strike by Boston police officers, where nearly 75 percent of the department walked off the job, as a result of the police commission's refusal to recognize the union. Massachusetts Governor Calvin Coolidge made the famous statement: " . . . there is no right to strike against the public safety by anybody, anywhere, anytime . . . ." This law and order posture largely paved the way for his nomination to the presidency by the Republican Party in 1920.

**bounty.** *n.* An award or premium offered and authorized by the government for the carrying out of a particular act, e.g., the capture of a fugitive or the taking of a varmint.

**bounty hunter.** One who earns his or her living in full or in part by taking into custody those who have a bounty on their heads. Bounty hunters have unusually wide legal latitude in the apprehension of wanted offenders.

**bourgeoisie.** *n.* Originally, that social class found between the nobility and working-class people; the middle class. In contemporary society, the word has taken on a much wider meaning, to include all persons whose interests are in harmony with the owners of the means of production and the generation of capital.

**Bow Street Runners.** An early investigative unit of the London Metropolitan Police Force, established during the last half of the eighteenth century by John and Henry Fielding to prevent crime. Members were to quickly arrive at the scene of the crime by running, thus the title, "Bow Street Runners."

**Brandeis, Louis D. (1856–1941).** Appointed a U.S. Supreme Court justice (1916) by President Woodrow Wilson, he served as an associate justice until his retirement in 1939. Justice Brandeis was famous for his "Brandeis brief," a radical departure from the traditionally drafted lawyer's brief, focusing on narrow points of law. The Brandeis briefs included lengthy and rather scholarly footnoted points concerning economic and social issues relevant to the issue at hand, especially demographic and social science data.

**brassard.** *n.* (1) In military usage, an armband bearing upper-case letters, worn to denote a special position of authority, e.g., a military policeman (MP) or an officer of the day (OD) armband. (2) Any armband bearing an emblem, badge, or symbol of distinction and/or authority.

**breach of peace.** Any violation or interruption of public order or tranquillity.

**breaking.** *v.* The forcible parting of any material or substance. It involves the tearing away and removal of any part of a dwelling place, e.g., locks and latches, in order to gain unlawful entry. See *burglary.*

**Breathalyzer.** *n.* An instrument used to detect the level of blood alcohol. Usually used when subjects are suspected of driving a motor vehicle while intoxicated.

**brethren.** *n.* (1) The plural form of the word "brother." In contemporary legal documents, it includes the female gender. (2) The unofficial title given to the members of the U.S. Supreme Court.

**bribe.** *n.* Anything offered with the intention of inducing another to do something illegal, morally or ethically wrong.

**bribery.** *n.* The giving, offering, or receiving of bribes. The offering or taking of any gift, personal gain, or emolument proffered or promised with the intent of influencing a public official's behavior.

**Bridewell.** *n.* A 1576 act of Parliament requiring each county to establish a "House of Correction," a bridewell. A common nineteenth-century term for the ordinary municipal lockup or county jail.

**brief.** *n.* A written document prepared by an attorney or his/her designee representing a condensed statement regarding a larger document or documents or facts and circumstances. Briefs come in the following forms: (1) legal briefs, often prepared by legal students, about published opinions on a given case or issue; (2) appellate briefs, summary documents required to be provided to the appellate court specifically citing the reasons why the lower court acted either correctly or incorrectly; and (3) trial briefs, documents containing the issues to be tried, an overview of the evidence, and any statutory or appellate law pertaining to issues in the case.

**brigade.** *n.* In traditional military usage, a unit consisting of several regiments and frequently commanded by a brigadier general (one star).

**Brockway, Zebulon R. (1827–1920).** First superintendent of the Elmira Reformatory, Elmira, New York, 1876, credited as the first penologist to employ indeterminate sentencing in the United States; he introduced the use of prison parole. He served as a charter member and first president of the National Prison Association (1898).

**broken windows.** A seminal article written in the 1980s by James Q. Wilson and George L. Kelling, serving as a metaphor for the relationship between community disorder and crime. The notion surrounding the article became the impetus for a paradigm shift in policing practices. As "broken windows" suggests, attention to low-level community problems is the key to crime prevention, as they telegraph crime-promoting signals, which in turn lead to major crime. Broken windows has become a metaphor for the crime syndrome associated with rundown communities.

**Broken Windows Hypothesis.** The premise that neighborhood deterioration telegraphs crime-promoting signals. That is, neglect suggests an absence of concern, and this in turn promotes community disorder, which in turn promotes crime. Community-wide attention to low-level community problems can have an ameliorating impact on criminal behavior.

**buggery.** *n.* See *sodomy.*

**bugging.** *n.* The placing of secreted electronic surveillance equipment. See *wiretapping.*

**bullet.** *n.* The lead projectile located at the front of a cartridge that is discharged from a rifle or handgun (revolver or automatic pistol). Bullets come in various styles including wad cutters, armor-piercing, semijacketed, fully jacketed, hollowpoint, and so on.

**bullet drift.** The lateral movement (deviation) of a firearm projectile while in flight.

**bullet yaw.** The deviation from a projectile's intended course, a swinging back and forth on a vertical axis, in a fashion wherein the longitudinal axis forms an angle from the line of intended flight.

**bunko game.** A nefarious act intended to gain the confidence of a victim with the intent of defrauding him or her.

**burden of proof.** The legal duty or responsibility to affirmatively establish a fact or facts at issue. In criminal cases, this burden is incumbent on the state.

**bureau.** *n.* A department or subdivision of a department under the executive or the various administrative branches of government, e.g., a detective bureau within a police department.

**bureaucracy.** *n.* A type of rational organization, usually associated with government, although adapted by many other entities that is hierarchical in its structure and administered through a complex series of inflexible rules and routines intended to improve organizational efficiency.

**Bureau of Alcohol, Tobacco, Firearms, and Explosives (BATFE).** Originally the United States Bureau of Alcohol, Tobacco, and Firearms (see that term), an agency under the umbrella of the Treasury Department, the BATFE was transferred to the Department of Justice (from the Treasury Department) on January 24, 2003, following a major federal reorganization of intelligence, security, policing, and law enforcement agencies, as a result of the Homeland Security bill on January 24, 2003, under the U.S. Department of Justice. The agency is responsible for the investigation of arson, explosives, and firearms violations. The Bureau has field offices in key foreign cities across the globe.

**Bureau of Indian Affairs (BIA).** The federal bureau that oversees the administration of American Indian reservations. Policing on some reservations is accomplished under the aegis of the BIA, on others under tribal police arrangements.

**Bureau of Justice Assistance (BJA).** Established in 1984, the BJA dispenses block grants to state and local governments with the express purpose of improving the criminal justice system, especially with regard to the way the system handles violent and other serious criminal offenders.

**Bureau of Justice Statistics (BJS).** That arm of the U.S. Department of Justice responsible for the dissemination of nationwide crime statistics and the publication of the *National Crime Victimization Survey,* the most widely used victimization survey in America.

**Bureau of Land Management (BLM).** Established in 1946 through the merger of the General Land Office (established 1812) with the Grazing Service (created 1934), the BLM manages some 450 million acres of national resource lands across the nation. The BLM also oversees the mineral resources on lands that are submerged off the Outer Continental Shelf; the agency has an enforcement arm.

**Burger, Warren Earl (1907-1995).** Appointed in 1969 by President Richard Nixon, he served as fourteenth chief justice of the High Court from 1969 to 1986. He had earlier been named assistant attorney general by President Eisenhower in 1953 and placed on the U.S. Court of Appeals for the District of Columbia. Considered a staunch conservative, Burger took exception to many of the liberal reforms undertaken by the Warren Court.

**Burgess, Ernest Herbert (1919-1977).** Along with his colleague Robert Park of the University of Chicago, he contributed greatly to the field of criminology in their studies of urban social disorganization, leading to the development of the concentric zone theory of urban crime.

**burglary.** *n.* (1) Under common law, the offense of burglary consisted of three elements: (a) the unlawful breaking and entering of the dwelling of another, (b) in the nighttime, (c) with the intent to commit a felony therein. More modern statutes generally comport with the following definition: the unlawful entry, or remaining therein, of the dwelling place of another, with the intent of committing a crime therein. Further, many jurisdictions distinguish between residential and commercial burglary or create various degrees of burglary. Burglary may include vehicles and public places. In all cases, the offense of burglary is a felony. (2) The unlawful entry into a building or other structure with the intent to commit a felony or a theft (FBI Uniform Crime Reporting Definition).

**burglary tools.** Any devices or implement s that may be used to effect a burglary, despite the fact that they were designed and intended for legitimate use, the possession of which constitutes an independent offense if accompanied by a knowing intent to employ them for illegal purposes.

**Burns International Security Services, Inc.** Originally founded as a detective agency by William J. Burns (1909), it is one of the largest private contract security agencies in the world.

**bus sweep.** The warrantless and suspicionless searches of buses, trains, planes, and city streets are permissible as long as officers ask individuals for permission, no coercion is used, and they do not convey that the search is mandatory. See *Florida v. Bostick,* 111 S.Ct. 2382 (1991).

# C

CAD, computer-aided dispatch
CALEA, Commission on Accreditation for Law Enforcement Agencies
CCRB, civilian complaint review board
CGIS, Coast Guard Investigative Service
CIA, Central Intelligence Agency
CID, Criminal Investigation Division
CJAIN, Criminal Justice Archive and Information Network
CJC, *Corpus Juris Canonici*
CJS, *Corpus Juris Secundum*
CLETS, California Law Enforcement Telecommunications System
CN, chloroacetophenone
CODIS, Combined DNA Index System
COMPSTAT, Computer Comparison Statistics
COP, Community-Oriented Policing
CS, O-chlorobenzalmalononitrile

---

**cadaver.** *n.* In law, a dead human body; a corpse.

**cadet, police.** A nonremunerated police assistant; usually a person under the statutory minimal age at which one may become a sworn police officer.

**cadre.** *n.* The basic core of highly trained and dedicated people within an organization who train others for membership positions.

**caliber.** *n.* (1) The size of a firearm projectile, bullet, or shell casing according to its diameter. (2) The bore diameter of a firearm.

**California Law Enforcement Telecommunications System (CLETS).** The computerized teletype system for California state, county, and local police and law enforcement agencies.

**Calley, William L., Jr.** The U.S. Army lieutenant in charge of the platoon that shot and killed a large number of Vietnamese civilians at the hamlet of My Lai, on March 16, 1968. Some of his soldiers refused to participate in what has now become known as the "My Lai Massacre," claiming the order to execute the Vietnamese was unlawful and therefore not actionable. Calley was court-martialed and sentenced to life imprisonment. His defense was premised on the argument that he was only following orders, a defense that had failed Nazi war criminals following World War II. Later, his life sentence was commuted.

**call girl.** A slang term for a prostitute dispatched to a man who has requested her sexual services, usually by telephone.

**calumny.** *n.* An intentionally false and malicious accusation intended to damage someone's reputation.

**Camorra.** *n.* A secret criminal society originating in Naples, Italy, about 1830 and continuing its activities until approximately 1922. The organization was notorious for the terror it inflicted as well as for its blackmail and violence.

**campus police.** The duly established police department of any postsecondary educational institution. The designation of campus police, whether it be located at a private or public institution, denotes the police authority or power of the sovereign state, as opposed to a security department (composed of nonsworn members), which has no such authority. Some jurisdictions have police departments for public school districts, and they too may be classified as campus police.

**Campus Unrest, President's Commission (1970).** A panel commissioned to determine the causes of campus violence nationwide and to proffer possible remedies. The panel was commissioned by Pennsylvania governor William Scranton on June 13, 1970. See *Kent State University incident.*

**cannabis.** *(Lat.)* Hemp; a plant of Asiatic origins yielding both hemp and hashish.

**canon.** *n.* (1) A law, rule, ordinance, statute, standard, or norm of an organization, especially that of an ecclesiastical organization; church law. (2) The official listing of fundamental publications within a specific academic or professional discipline.

**canonical court.** A church court ruling on issues pertaining to canon law.

**canon law.** Generally known as church or ecclesiastical law, compiled during the years spanning the twelfth through the fourteenth centuries in Rome, from among other sources, the decrees of the General Councils and bulls of the Holy See.

**Canon of Police Ethics.** Known as the Law Enforcement Code of Ethics, it is the official code of ethics for policing compiled by the Executive Committee of the International Association of Chiefs of Police in 1989. It replaces the code adopted by the IACP at Louisville, Kentucky, in 1957.

**capacity.** *n.* A legal qualification, ability, competency, or disability. Criminal capacity often involves that accountability associated with the age of the accused; e.g., children under certain ages (ranging from seven to fourteen) lack the capacity to make their behaviors actionable under the criminal law.

**capias.** *(Lat.)* "That you take." (1) The common name for writs that are generally addressed to the county sheriff commanding the arrest, either civilly or criminally, of the individual therein named. (2) In many jurisdictions, this writ is used for the civil arrest of persons, often because they have failed to satisfy the damages or debts stemming from a judgment for debt against a creditor. The person so named is deprived of his or her liberty until the debt or damages are paid, technically known as a *capias ad satisfaciendum.*

**capital offense.** Generally any offense punishable by death, although some jurisdictions include offenses providing a sentence of death or imprisonment for life.

**capital punishment.** A sanction issued by a court of competent jurisdiction imposing a sentence of death by means provided by statute. Methods of administering a death sentence internationally have included beheading, stoning, crucifixion, gassing, electrocution, hanging, lethal injection, and firing squad. By 1972, the U.S. Supreme Court had placed a moratorium on capital punishment, but by 1976 the High Court in *Gregg v. Georgia,* 428 U.S. 153, 96 S.Ct. 2909, 49 L.Ed.2d 859 (1976) sustained the constitutionality of the newly revised state capital punishment statutes.

**CAP-STUN.** A nonlethal inflammatory agent containing oleo resin capsicum, found in hot peppers. The product has proven to be less than effective on subjects with reduced sensitivity to pain or under the influence of drugs or alcohol.

**captain.** *n.* A military rank; the highest ranking commissioned officer of the company-grade category. A captain is immediately above a 1st lieutenant but below a major (a field-grade officer). In naval usage, a captain is the equivalent of an army full-colonel. Among police agencies, captain is an administrative rank used widely by mid-range or larger agencies.

**carbine.** *n.* A lightweight, .30 caliber, semi-automatic rifle with a short barrel.

**carbineer, *carabiniere.*** *n.* The term derives from French and historically denoted a mounted soldier equipped with a carbine rifle. A carabiniere is a national-level police officer, who is a member of the *Arma dei Carabiniere,* a branch of the Italian military.

**Cardozo, Benjamin N. (1870–1938).** Admitted to the New York state bar in 1891, he was educated at Columbia University. He served as a trial court judge in New York from 1914 to 1917 and the New York Court of Appeals (the highest appellate court in that state) from 1917 to 1932. In 1932, he succeeded Oliver Wendell Holmes as an associate justice of the U.S. Supreme Court. His liberal orientation influenced other Supreme Court justices regarding acceptance of the New Deal.

**career criminal.** A habitual offender; repeat offender; professional criminal; a person with a history of criminal arrests and convictions for various offenses. Some states have statutes that increase the penalty, upon conviction, for persons so designated by the prosecution.

**carelessness.** *n.* The absence of care. See *negligence.*

**carnal abuse.** The depraved act of a male with the sexual organs of a female falling short of penetration. Carnal abuse, in some jurisdictions, includes any injury to the genital organs of a female while attempting, but failing, penetration. See *carnal knowledge.*

**carnal knowledge.** The act of a male having sexual bodily contact with a female; coitus; sexual intercourse.

**Carriers Case.** A 1483 English law precedent that favored the interests of carriers, merchants, and traders in larceny cases by changing its definition.

**Carroll Doctrine.** The doctrine posits that the lawful warrantless search of a motor vehicle on the public ways by police officers having probable cause to believe that the vehicle holds items subject to seizure is not unreasonable under the Fourth Amendment of the U.S. Constitution and, thus, creates the "automobile exception" to the warrant requirement; *Carroll v. United States,* 267 U.S. 132, 45 S.Ct. 280, 69 L. Ed. 543 (1925). The High Court has revisited and reaffirmed the doctrine in several cases, e.g., *California v. Acevedo,* 500 U.S. 565 (1991).

***carte blanche.*** *(Fr.)* "White card." A blank sheet of white paper containing only the signature of a person, thus allowing the person in possession to fill in whatever he or she wishes. A *carte blanche* grants full authority, latitude, and discretion.

**cartographic school.** A nineteenth-century contribution to the study of criminology, begun by Adolphe Quetelet and Andre-Michel Guerry, employing social statistics. The cartographic school primarily used demographic data on the European population, including density, gender, distribution of wealth, and religious affiliation.

Quetelet, e.g., studied data collected in France in order to determine the relationship between social factors and the inclination to violate the law.

**case law.** That body of jurisprudence created by appellate decisions on specific issues, distinguished from statutory or constitutional law. See *Stare Decisis*.

**caseworker.** *n.* A professional social worker who assists disadvantaged individuals.

**causality.** *n.* The act or agency without which an effect would not have been produced. See *proximate cause*.

**cause célèbre.** *(Fr.)* A case that has drawn wide public attention, controversy, and resistence, e.g., the *Sacco and Vanzetti* case (circa 1927).

**caveat.** *(Lat.)* "Let him beware." A special warning, condition, or stipulation.

**caveat emptor.** *(Lat.)* "Let the buyer beware." A rule or maxim warning that the buyer must examine and evaluate for himself or herself.

**cease-and-desist order.** A formal order issued by a court or administrative agency forbidding a person, persons, organization, or business to continue a specific act, action, or course of conduct.

**celerity.** *n.* The swiftness of the entire criminal justice process, including detection, arrest, prosecution, adjudication, and sanctioning of criminal offenders. Adherents to the concept of deterrence strongly consider celerity a central factor in determining the effectiveness of the criminal justice process.

**censorship.** *n.* The act of suppressing or controlling the exposure of various art forms, symbolic speech, ideas, values, beliefs, and ideologies found in books, the media, plays, and films on the grounds that they are objectionable to the common morals, values, and customs of mainstream society.

**censure.** *n.* (1) The blaming, condemnation, or criticism of an opinion, position, or judgment. (2) A formal resolution made by a legislature, administrative agency, or other entity against an individual or government officer, or agency, or one of its own members or former members for a specific act or omission.

**Center for Criminal Justice.** Established at Harvard University in 1969, the center studies criminal justice policy issues that impact juvenile justice; it also publishes the *Annual Report of the Center for Criminal Justice.*

**Central Intelligence Agency (CIA).** The primary intelligence organization of the federal government, created under the National Security Act of 1947; the CIA reports to the National Security Council. It is not to be confused with a law enforcement agency.

**Central Intelligence Agency (CIA) secret prisons.** See *black sites*.

**Centre for Criminology Library.** Created in 1963 under the authority of the University of Toronto, this research library has comprehensive holdings related to virtually all issues in criminology.

**ceremonial rank.** Nonpermanent rank that is not cited within the official organizational rank structure, the insignia of which is displayed for the purpose of ceremony only. Authorized rank, often called hard or permanent rank, may be limited, e.g., to the rank of major, yet the organization allows certain individuals to wear the insignia of a lieutenant colonel, without necessarily awarding any additional authority or salary. In some circumstances, the rank comes with additional authority and salary; however, the rank is not permanent.

**certification hearing.** A hearing at which the court rules whether a juvenile offender's case may be extracted from the juvenile court (a court of exclusive jurisdiction) in order to have the case heard in adult criminal court. If the juvenile is certified, he or she is remanded to the trial court for adjudication. See also *transfer, bind over,* or *waiver hearing.*

**certiorari.** *(Lat.)* "To be informed of." A writ issued by a superior court ordering up a certified record of the trial transcript from a lower court. The writ has historically been used by the U.S. Supreme Court to select the cases it wishes to hear.

**chain gang.** A group of prisoners literally chained together while working, often on the highways or at other public places.

**chain of command.** In military and paramilitary organizations, the formal organizational hierarchy through which information and orders flow. Because the chain of command is vital to the efficient operation of a bureaucratized organization, "skipping" any one stratum of the chain of command is strictly forbidden, as doing so would create an inefficiency in the organization and leave those skipped uninformed. Skipping the chain of command is a punishable offense.

**chain of custody.** Also known as the "chain of evidence," it is a formal accounting for the security of evidence to be used by the prosecution at trial. Nearly always, a formal log is kept, carefully documenting the times, places, and persons to whom custody of evidence has been entrusted.

**chain of evidence.** See *chain of custody.*

**challenge for cause.** A challenge, by way of a request to the judge, made regarding a specific juror's ability to render a nonbiased verdict for a specific reason. The number of challenges for cause while empaneling a jury is unlimited, whereas the number of peremptory challenges is strictly limited in all jurisdictions, usually to about five.

**chambers.** *n.* The room or office exclusively used by a judge or justice; any place a judge or justice does business pertaining to that office, when not overseeing a session of the court.

**Chambliss, William Joseph (1933– ).** A Marxist criminologist holding that traditional criminologists focus too much on official crime data provided via government records and reports. In doing so, criminologists mask the criminality of government itself. In his examination of governmental bureaucratic involvement in crime in the *Sociological Analysis of the Law of Vagrancy,* he cogently outlines the government's involvement; it stands as one of his most celebrated publications in criminology.

**chancery procedure.** The procedure that existed in England's Chancery Courts where the king's chancellor adjudicated cases involving persons unable to protect themselves (usually women and children). In contemporary American legal proceedings, these responsibilities have been absorbed by the juvenile court, which assumes the guardianship of delinquent, neglected, and abandoned children.

**change of venue.** The movement of a case from one judicial venue to another, often within the same court circuit or district, but always within the borders of the charging sovereignty. In criminal cases, a change of venue is often granted when one of the parties to the case demonstrates to the court's satisfaction that a fair and impartial rendering of the facts cannot be had in the originating venue.

**character evidence.** Evidence concerning one's reputation or moral standing in the community. The general rule is that the prosecution cannot present character evidence against the defendant unless the defense first "opens the door" by presenting character evidence on the defendant's behalf.

**charge.** *n.* An allegation of a criminal act or acts against an individual or individuals, specifying what statutes have been violated and usually appearing as a formal complaint in misdemeanor cases or information or an indictment in felony cases.

**charge sheet.** The written record, usually maintained by the desk sergeant at a police station, recording the names of persons taken into custody, the accusations against such charged person(s), and the accuser(s). See *police desk blotter.*

**charging document.** The formal written document, submitted to the court, citing the specific offenses to which the defendant must respond.

**charter.** *n.* A document issued by the sovereign, granting to an entire people, or portion thereof, permission to form a corporation or a dependent government, along with certain rights, liberties, or powers, e.g., the Magna Charta, or a specific charter issued to a municipal corporation granting special privileges, e.g., a home-rule charter.

**Chase, Salmon Portland (1803–1873).** American statesman; U.S. senator from Ohio (1849–1855); chief justice of the Supreme Court of the United States (1864–1873); he also presided over the impeachment trial of President Andrew Johnson.

**Chase, Samuel (1741–1811).** American statesman; signer of the Declaration of Independence; associate justice of the U.S. Supreme Court from 1796 to 1811.

**chattel.** *n.* Any animate or inanimate personal property, excluding real property.

**check kiting.** The practice of issuing a check from an account for which the endorser knows sufficient funds are not available to cover the encumbrance, but with the faith that funds will become available to pay the amount by the time the check clears. It is essentially a fraudulent method of obtaining credit by kiting.

**chemiluminescence.** *n.* The production of light as a result of a chemical reaction at ambient temperatures.

**Cherry Hill.** The nickname given to the historic Eastern Penitentiary, located in Philadelphia, Pennsylvania. The original penal philosophy of this correctional institution was centered on individual solitary confinement.

**Chicago Area Project.** Pioneered by celebrated criminologist Clifford R. Shaw of the University of Chicago's School of Sociology, this project garnered the attention of juvenile justice functionaries across the nation and was replicated by a number of cities throughout the nation. The premise upon which the project was based was that high crime rates were closely associated with neighborhoods lacking cohesiveness and a concomitant lack of concern for youth. The project developed self-help programs leading to neighborhoods that generated neighborliness, civic responsibility, and neighborhood pride. As early as 1959, the Illinois Youth Commission replicated the program throughout the state, and by the mid-1970s communities across the nation had instituted the program.

**Chicago Boy's Court.** A court begun in 1914 expressly to deal with delinquent boys between the ages of seventeen and twenty, who were ordinarily not within the purview of the juvenile court.

**Chicago School.** The cartographic school of the Sociology Department of the University of Chicago that came to prominence during the 1920s. Referred to as the "concentric zone (ring) theory" of criminology, it was heavily influenced by the researchers' academic backgrounds in biology and took into account the socioeconomic factors that contributed to criminality.

**Chicago Seven.** The 1970 trial of seven defendants who faced federal charges of crossing state lines to incite riots during the 1968 Chicago Democratic Convention. During the trial, federal Judge Julius Hoffman had some of the defendants bound to their chairs and gagged. All seven defendants and their attorneys were found guilty of contempt of court.

**chicanery.** *n.* Legal trickery where a plausible but false argument is proffered.

**chief deputy.** The position, title, or rank within a sheriff's office immediately below the sheriff, which is sometimes synonymous with the title of undersheriff. The chief deputy is considered to be the chief operational officer of the agency, second in command only to the sheriff.

**chief executive.** See *chief magistrate.*

**chief justice.** The principal judge (justice) of the highest appellate court in a given jurisdiction, as in chief justice of the Supreme Court. Generally, the chief justice is the senior member of the highest appellate bench.

**chief magistrate.** (1) In politics, the head of the executive branch of any nation, state, or local-level government, i.e., president, governor, or mayor. (2) In juridical usage, the head judge or justice of a given court.

**chief of police.** The generic title for the chief administrative officer of a police department; generally an appointed position; sometimes known as superintendent or director of public safety. An administrative title not to be confused with permanent rank, e.g., a captain may apply and be appointed to the chief's position, while retaining his or her rank as captain. Further, the chief of police need not necessarily be a sworn officer of the department and need not necessarily hold permanent rank in some departments.

**child abuse.** Acts or omissions endangering a child's physical or emotional well-being. Child abusers are frequently caretakers in some capacity, e.g., parents, babysitters, or childcare workers, who physically or psychologically injure a child or in someway neglect a child. Physical abuse can include beatings and sexual abuse. Neglect may come in many forms, including inadequate supervision and emotional deprivation.

**child molester.** One, often a pedophile, who in some capacity knowingly assaults a child sexually.

**child neglect.** The willing failure to adequately provide a minor child with the basic necessities of life, including but not limited to nutrition, clothing, housing, education, and adult supervision.

**child savers.** A group of progressive-era people, dating from the late-nineteenth century through the early-twentieth century, focused on creating new institutions through social engineering, intended to address the special problems posed by juvenile delinquency. As a result, a special system for juvenile offenders, including juvenile courts, probation, child guidance, and reformatories, was created.

**child welfare board.** In some jurisdictions, a locally elected board of citizens having the responsibility and authority to investigate and adjudicate matters concerning juveniles. Such boards have both a policing and an adjudicatory function.

**Children's Defense Fund.** A privately funded organization serving in an advocacy role in children's rights issues. It funds research concerning the processing of children in both social welfare and juvenile justice settings.

**chivalry hypothesis.** A perspective holding that women are treated differentially by criminal justice officials, who are predominantly males.

**chloroacetophenone.** *n.* See *CN.*

**chop shop.** Slang term for an automotive garage where stolen vehicles are stripped in order to sell their parts or use them in the repair of damaged vehicles.

**Christopher Commission.** The commission, chaired by former Judge Warren Christopher, to report on the causes of the Los Angeles riots. Formally known as the Independent Commission on the Los Angeles Police Department (LAPD), it focused on the 1992 beating of motorist Rodney King and the excessive use of force by LAPD officers.

**chromatography.** *n.* The process by which chemists can analyze chemicals, compounds, and substances by vaporizing them into a gaseous form. Used heavily in arson investigations for the detection of accelerants.

**chromosomal aberration.** A genetically based criminological perspective positing that some males have an extra Y chromosome (XYY), predisposing them toward violent antisocial behaviors. There has been ongoing research into this controversial assumption since the early 1960s. See *Richard Speck.*

**chronic offender.** One who continues to violate the law for a long term. For some offenders, there is a pathologically driven need to violate the law, whether it be for felony or misdemeanor offenses. For others, the causation may not be pathological, but rather functionally motivated; nonetheless, an extended history and pattern of law violation exists.

**circa.** *(Lat.)* About, approximately, around; frequently used before a date that is in question, as in circa 1860.

**circuit court.** (1) In many states, e.g., Illinois, the court of general jurisdiction or trial court; (2) in other jurisdictions, e.g., the federal judiciary, the intermediate appellate court. In the state judiciaries, e.g., Illinois, a circuit is often, although not always, made up of more than one county, and at the federal level, of a number of U.S. court districts.

**circumstantial (indirect) evidence.** Evidence, often testimonial, establishing facts from which a jury may make inferences regarding other facts at issue. Often, this type of evidence comes in the form of evidence not based on first-hand knowledge, but rather other facts from which deductions are made, indirectly supporting primary facts intended to be proven.

**citation.** *n.* (1) A written order executed by a police agency (usually for minor violations) to appear before a magistrate at a specified date and time, sometimes known as a "notice to appear." (2) An order issued by a court commanding the person therein named to appear before the issuing court at a specified time and date.

**citator.** *n.* A set of legal reference books providing, in abbreviated form, the precedents, interpretations, and legal histories of various issues and cases applicable to statutes at issue. The process of using citators is commonly known as "shepardizing" a case, and legal researchers often use *Shepard's Citations.*

**citizen oversight.** The process providing outside, citizen-based oversight of a public institution or agency, a civilian complaint review board (CCRB), e.g., overseeing allegations of police misconduct.

**citizen's arrest.** A warrantless arrest executed by a private citizen, other than a bona fide police officer or other law enforcement agent, for the violation of a serious breach of the peace. In most jurisdictions, the crime must have been committed in the presence of the person affecting the apprehension, although some jurisdictions waive this requirement.

**civil commitment.** A civil detention or confinement of individuals who are disordered, alcoholically or chemically dependent, or insane. Most jurisdictions provide for the temporary emergency civil commitment by various classes of public officials for a specified period of time before a full adjudication can determine whether a long-term commitment is warranted. Emergency civil commitments are limited to about ninety-six hours.

**civil contempt.** Contempt of court that arises from purposeful failure to comply with an order of the court, out of the court's immediate presence.

**civil death.** In many jurisdictions, persons convicted of felony violations undergo a period where they lose certain civil rights or privileges, outlined by statute, including the right to vote, litigate, hold public office, and others. In addition, some civil liberties may also be lost, e.g., the protection against unreasonable search and seizure. These losses are considered "collateral consequences" that attach upon conviction, independent of the criminal sanction imposed. The time span under which these losses occur may last for the natural life of the offender or may be restored after the sentence has been served, depending on the jurisdiction.

**civil disabilities.** See *civil death.*

**civil disobedience.** A method of drawing attention to a perceived injustice, condition, or law by purposely breaking another law. For example, persons may block traffic, requiring the police to intervene and arrest them. Civil disobedience is generally passive or nonconfrontational and has deep roots in American culture; consider Henry David Thoreau (1817–1862), for example.

**civilianization.** *n.* The process of having civilian (nonsworn) personnel perform certain duties historically done by sworn or commissioned police officers. Popular responsibilities that have been civilianized in recent years include parking enforcement, communications, and animal control.

**civilian complaint review board (CCRB).** See *civilian review board.*

**civilian review board.** An advisory public board operating externally to the police department reviewing complaints lodged against the department or any one of its members regarding improper activities. Also known as civilian complaint review boards (CCRB), they generally serve in an advisory capacity, recommending to the chief of police or police commission the sanction to be imposed upon conviction. These boards are generally granted subpoena power for investigative purposes. See also *citizen oversight*.

**civil law.** That body of law dealing exclusively with tort issues (private wrongs) sharply differentiated from criminal law (public wrongs). The level of proof at a civil trial is a preponderance of the evidence, whereas at a criminal trial it is proof beyond a reasonable doubt.

**civil liberties.** Those liberties (protections) enumerated in the first ten amendments to the U.S. Constitution, i.e., the Bill of Rights, expressly stating what the government cannot do to its people. Clarification of those liberties can be found in case law. Civil liberties are also found in sections of the various state constitutions and protect citizens against unreasonable governmental intrusions in state action. Civil liberties, e.g., specify when, where, and why the government may search our homes—a Fourth Amendment protection. Civil liberties must not be confused with civil rights, as civil rights are those things to which the government must provide affirmative assistance. For example, the government must protect citizens' right to vote. Unlike civil liberties, civil rights have nothing to do with criminal law, criminal evidence, or criminal procedure.

**civil process.** Any activity in the furtherance of a civil law case, e.g., the issuance of a summons by a court and the serving of that summons by a sheriff's deputy. Sheriffs' deputies often differentiate between civil process and criminal law enforcement.

**civil rights.** Those rights cited in the U.S. Constitution, the constitutions of the various states, and statutory enactments enumerating those privileges to which a citizen may lawfully request affirmative governmental assistance, e.g., the right to vote. Congress has passed numerous civil rights acts dating from the post–Civil War era to the late 1960s, i.e., the Civil Rights Acts of 1866, 1870, 1871, 1872, 1875, 1957, 1960, 1964, and 1968. The latter, e.g., gave protection to civil rights workers, disallowed discrimination in most housing, and provided sanctions against those who attempted to interfere with protected civil rights via interstate commerce for the purpose of creating a riot. Civil rights must not be confused with civil liberties, which limit governmental authority, especially in criminal evidentiary procedures.

**Civil Rights Act.** A series of federal statutes dating from the post–Civil War era, intended to protect personal rights found in the Constitution, to which individuals may claim affirmative governmental assistance. These statutes prohibit discrimination based on national origin, race, age, gender, and so forth. See the *Civil Rights Acts* of 1866, 1870, 1871, 1872, 1875, 1957, 1960, 1964, and 1968.

**civil service.** A generic phrase connoting public employment via a merit system based on competitive examinations and involving due process driven employment rights; a meritocracy.

**Clark Bavin National Fish and Wildlife Forensics Laboratory.** See *wildlife forensic laboratory*.

**class action suit.** A suit brought in the name of a class or group of affected individuals, sharing some common injury or grievance.

**class characteristics.** Characteristics that constitute a defined category or class.

**classical criminology.** Developed in the eighteenth century largely by Cesare Beccaria, it is a theoretical criminological perspective (theory) holding that (1) people have the free will to choose between criminal and acceptable behaviors; (2) people are rational actors, choosing whether to become involved in criminal activities for personal gain; and (3) crime is best controlled by deterrence growing from the fear of apprehension, conviction, and punishment.

**classical penal theory.** A perspective posited by Beccaria, Bentham, and Feuerbach during the eighteenth century, arguing that the sanctions for crimes should be meted out swiftly and in proportion to their degree of social harm.

**classification of crimes.** The categorization of criminal offenses into numerous strata in a descending order. In most U.S. jurisdictions, criminal violations are categorized as follows: treason, felonies, and misdemeanors. Some argue that a fourth class can be added for quasi-criminal infractions of municipal and county ordinances, although, technically, they are not crimes, as they are generated by nonsovereign legislative bodies, i.e, municipal and county councils and boards.

**classification of prisoners.** The initial process involved the placement of new inmates in the proper security level and treatment program available in a given prison system. In large penal programs, this is done at a separate diagnostic facility, e.g., the federal correctional facility located in Springfield, Missouri.

**clearance.** *n.* Any instance where a known *Uniform Crime Report* violation is cleared to the satisfaction of the police or other law enforcement agency. A clearance may result from the following: a formal arrest; a station adjustment; a suspect has been identified but an arrest is not possible; an arrest is made but the prosecutor declines to prosecute; an arrest is made and the case is adjudicated but a conviction is not obtained; or, finally, where multiple suspects are involved and one is arrested and the others remain at large, the case is said to be cleared by arrest.

**clearance rates.** The number of known offenses that have been cleared divided by the total number of offenses known to the police. The "dark" figure of crime is likely higher than officially recognized, thereby attenuating the clearance rate.

**clear and convincing evidence.** An evidentiary standard (concerning the level of proof) with a somewhat unclear definition. Some case law describes it as evidence lying beyond a mere preponderance but short of what is required for a criminal conviction, i.e., proof beyond a reasonable doubt. Some definitions, however, equate it with proof that is beyond a reasonable or well-founded doubt.

**clear and present danger.** A court-generated test generally applied to free speech during times of crisis. The test, promulgated by Supreme Court Justice Oliver Wendell Holmes following World War I, holds that speech can be legally sanctioned if there exists an imminent danger that can result in illegal action, injurious to the collective well-being of the community. Despite the fact that the First Amendment protects free speech, the court has attempted to balance that protection against the community's best interest, holding that speech tending to incite lawlessness falls outside the First Amendment's protections. See *Schenck v. U.S.*, 249 U.S. 47, 39 S.Ct. 247, 63 L.Ed. 470.

**clemency.** *n.* A form of final nonjudicial relief for alleged crimes, generally issued by the chief magistrate (a governor in issues of state law and the president in issues of federal law) or a clemency board within the executive branch of government. Some forms of legislative clemency are also available, although far more rare than executive clemency. Clemency comes in various forms, including pardons (full and conditional), commutations, reprieves, remissions of fines and forfeitures, and general amnesties.

**clink.** A commonly used slang term for prisons, jails, and lockups, deriving from the well-known London-based prison that formerly existed on the south bank of the Thames, not far from the London Bridge during the time of Charles Dickens.

**closing argument.** A final summarizing statement made first by the prosecution and followed by the defense to the jury, or to the judge in bench trials, citing evidence supporting their respective positions and pointing out weaknesses in the other's. The closing argument is made before the judge charges or instructs the jury.

**Cloward and Ohlin's *Delinquency and Opportunity.*** A perspective (theory) of differential opportunity envisioned over forty years ago by criminologists Richard Cloward and Lloyd Ohlin. The theory combines principles found in both strain and social disorganization theories, leading to a thoughtful description and explanation of gang-sustaining delinquent subcultures.

**Cloward, Richard A. (1926– ).** A criminological scholar known primarily for his copublishing of the influential piece on subcultural delinquency, *Delinquency and Opportunity* (1960). See *Cloward and Ohlin's Delinquency and Opportunity.*

**CN.** chloroacetophenone, a tear-producing chemical used in "tear gas" and other aerosol irritants.

**Coast Guard Investigative Service (CGIS).** That department within the U.S. Coast Guard charged with the responsibility of investigating criminal violations perpetrated against the U.S. Coast Guard or any of its members. A parallel agency to the U.S. Army Criminal Investigation Division (CID), the U.S. Naval Criminal Investigative Service (NCIS), or the U.S. Air Force Office of Special Investigations (OSI).

**Coast Guard jurisdiction.** The physical jurisdiction and legal authority of the U.S. Coast Guard to conduct inquiries, inspections, searches, seizures, and arrests on the high seas and other navigable water of the U.S. proper, its territories, vassal states, protectorates, and possessions.

**cocaine.** *n.* An illicit drug (a crystalline alkaloid) derived from the dried leaves of the coca plant.

**code.** *n.* (1) A body of law covering one specific area, e.g., the criminal code of a given state or the traffic code of a municipal corporation. (2) A compilation of all laws for a given government, organized by area, e.g., criminal law, municipal government, and school law. Codes may represent either a privately or governmentally published compilation of the laws for a particular government, categorized by subject area, for easy reference.

**codefendant.** *n.* One charged in the identical complaint or indictment with the same criminal offense as another.

**codeine.** *n.* An opiate derivative (an alkaloid produced from the head of the poppy plant) resembling morphine, but milder and less habit forming. Codeine is a legal drug used as a sedative for the relief of pain, but illegal if not properly prescribed by a licensed physician.

**code of criminal procedure.** In many jurisdictions across the United States, the code consists of case law regarding criminal procedural issues handed down by the appellate courts and supplemented by rules of court. In some states and the federal courts, it is codified; e.g., 18 USCA § 3001. These formalized codes are supplemented by the *Rules of Evidence* and the *Rules of Criminal Procedure* and largely supplant case law.

**code of ethics.** An official statement of an organization, occupation, or profession regarding its purpose, mission, and values. Most comprehensive codes for the established professions also explicitly cover expectations concerning professional conduct and practices.

**Code of Hammurabi.** A body of laws created during the twenty-second century B.C. for Babylon; one of the oldest extant legal codes.

**code of silence.** In law enforcement and policing, an informal understanding between police and law enforcement officers that they will not divulge unfavorable information against a fellow officer or agent.

**codicil.** *n.* An addition, supplement, provision, addendum, or appendix to a will.

**codification.** *n.* The process of formally and systematically collecting and arranging various bodies of law or procedure, e.g., the *Code of Federal Regulation* or the *California Evidence Code.* The collected corpuses may be variously titled, revised codes, revised statutes, compiled statutes, or titles.

**coercion.** *n.* Any compulsion or constraint, whether physical, psychological, direct or indirect, that compels one to act against his or her will.

**cohabitation.** *n.* The act of living together as husband and wife, implying a sexual relationship.

**Cohen, Albert Kircidel (1918– ).** As a result of his longevity in academics, he has become one of the modern-day synthesizers of the theoretical propositions of earlier criminologists. His works focus primarily on theories of subcultures, the culture of gangs, and the concept of criminal organizations, e.g., *Delinquent Boys: The Culture of the Gang* (1955).

**COINTELPRO.** *n.* A controversial FBI program of surveillance and counterintelligence (1956–1971) that targeted and harassed suspected subversives and others of nonconformist political persuasions.

**coitus.** *n.* The act of sexual intercourse; the penetration of the vagina with a penis.

**Coke, Sir Edward (1552–1634).** An influential English lawyer and judge, he is credited with developing the common-law system in England.

**cold blood.** A phrase denoting a crime of violence perpetrated without passion.

**collar.** *n.* Police jargon for a physical arrest by an officer, commonly used by officers from police agencies in the northeastern region of the United States.

**collateral.** *n.* (1) Something that is indirect or parallel, as in a collateral attack, that is, an attack that does not address the central issue or problem directly, but rather an ancillary issue; (2) something that accompanies something else and which is unintended, as in a collateral consequence; (3) property set aside and designated as surety for the satisfaction of a debt.

**collateral attack.** In law, an attack that does not go directly to the issue at hand, but rather deals indirectly with the matter or with a side issue.

**collateral consequence.** An unintended consequence resulting from an action expressly directed against something or someone else.

**collateral estoppel doctrine.** A legal doctrine applicable to both civil and criminal law (the underlying doctrine for double jeopardy) barring the relitigation of an issue previously adjudicated; that is, the finding of a verdict presents an estoppel to future litigation.

**collective bargaining.** A procedure and process established by the National Labor Relations Board (NLRB), intended to foster binding collective agreements between employers and employees. See *National Labor Relations Act,* 8(5), § 29 USCA § 158(5).

**collusion.** *n.* An agreement between at least two parties to defraud or act against another's interest.

**colonel.** *n.* The highest ranking commissioned officer of the "field grade"; above a lieutenant colonel but below a brigadier general; the military draws distinction between types of colonels, dividing them into lieutenant colonels (the lower rank) and colonels "full colonels" (the higher rank); only the very largest police agencies use either of these ranks.

**color of law.** The misuse of the sovereign's legal authority. Acting with the appearance of authority without the legal right to do so.

**Colquhoun, Patrick (1745–1820).** Author of the noted manuscript *A Treatise on the Police of the Metropolis,* which addressed issues concerning various types of criminal behavior, the establishment of highly trained and active police agencies, a public register for criminal offenders, and improvements in the relationship and forms of communication between urban and rural courts.

**Colt, Samuel (1814–1862).** Inventor and founder of Colt Firearms, he is especially well known for his invention of the revolver (1836), later adopted by the U.S. Army (1847) and the .45 caliber Automatic Colt Pistol (ACP), also developed for the army.

**Combined DNA Index System (CODIS).** The FBI's digital database, formally established in 1998 under the authority of the *Identification Act of 1994* (Public Law 103–322). The CODIS system generates a profile for each of those convicted of serious offenses, e.g., rape, sexual assault, murder, and various personal crimes against children. The system, also known as the National DNA Index System (NDIS), holds the DNA of unknown offenders.

***comes stabuli.*** *(Lat.)* A uniformed mounted law enforcement officer during the medieval period in England. His primary purpose was to organize citizen efforts to track down wanted criminals.

***comity.*** *(Lat.)* A legal courtesy granted out of respect or deference but not as a matter of right. See *full faith and credit clause.*

**command.** *n.* In a military or policing context, an order issued by a person holding higher rank or legal authority than that of another. Within military organizations, commands are of two types: (1) direct commands or orders that come from an officer of the commissioned ranks; and (2) indirect commands, orders issued by noncommissioned officers. Refusal to obey a legal command is punishable as insubordination.

**commander.** *n.* (1) In American police organizations, especially municipal-level police organizations, it is an appointment, generally made by the chief of police, outside the permanent rank structure sanctioned by the civil service or merit commission; a supervisory position for one in charge of a given shift or unit, which would otherwise be filled by a sergeant or a lieutenant. (2) In American military usage, a commissioned officer in charge of a military unit; a descriptive functional title, but not a recognized formal rank. (3) A naval rank equivalent to a lieutenant colonel in the U.S. Army, Air Force, or Marine Corps.

**commission.** *n.* (1) The authority granted by a government or any of its departments empowering the person or persons so named to carry out certain tasks and to take on specific powers. In the case of a police officer, this grants the right of the state to conduct police business and make criminal arrests. (2) A panel authorized by law to conduct certain affairs, e.g., a police and fire commission of a municipality. (3) In the military, it is the official authority to act for another and an official document placing a specific rank upon an officer, e.g., a colonel.

**commissioner.** *n.* (1) In American government, one holding a seat on a board or commission overseeing a political function, e.g., commissioner of public health. (2) In American policing, especially at the local level of government, one holding a seat on the police commission. It must be noted that the commission is only an oversight body, leaving the hands-on and day-to-day operation of the department to the appointed administrators, i.e., the chief of police and his or her assistant(s). Thus, the term "police commissioner" is generally not synonymous with the title, position, or function of chief of police. (3) At the state, federal, and international levels, one in charge of a public department, e.g., the commissioner of highways, the commissioner of communications, or the high commissioner for refugees. (4) The lowest judicial classification for a trier of law, as with U.S. commissioners; a low-level judge below a magistrate.

**Commission on Accreditation for Law Enforcement Agencies (CALEA).** A private accrediting agency for police organizations, brought about as a result of the high cost of lawsuits against the police throughout America. Established in 1979, it published its first set of standards in 1983, but only a little over 500 (out of nearly 18,000) police agencies nationwide had garnered accreditation by 2001.

**commitment.** *n.* A warrant (warrant of commitment) or a judicial order commanding an officer to transport and place a defendant in a penal or custodial institution. See *mittimus.*

**commodore.** *n.* In the U.S. Navy, a commissioned officer ranking above a captain (the equivalent of an army full colonel) but immediately below a two-star rear admiral (the equivalent of an army major general); a commodore is the parallel rank to an army brigadier (one-star) general. This rank fell into disuse by 1899 but was reinstituted during World War II. Today, the closest naval rank is that of a rear admiral (two stars) of the lower division.

**common law.** (1) The unwritten law of early England, derived solely from customs and usages found in antiquity and from the rulings of judges before the American Revolution. In its strictest sense, it does not involve formal written law generated by a legislature (positive law). However, in its broadest sense, common law may include both unwritten law before the American Revolution and all positive law generated by a sovereign legislature (within a common-law system) that is universally in force. (2) A system of law, as contrasted against, e.g., socialist law, civil law, and Islamic law systems, found across the globe.

**common-law crime.** A crime occurring at common law; a crime not necessarily recognized by statute.

**common-law marriage.** An unofficial and nonceremonial marriage between two adults, consummated by an agreement to marry and followed by cohabitation. Most states do not legally recognize such marriages.

**commonwealth.** *n.* The body politic constituted by persons bound by a compact or charter under a recognized form of government instituted for the common good, e.g., a state within the United States of America or a nation state.

**community-based corrections.** Correctional programs provided within an open community setting, e.g., a half-way house, as opposed to a closed institutional setting, e.g., a penal facility.

**community-oriented policing (COP).** A philosophy of policing that centers on the collective well-being of the community being policed, where a partnership is forged between the formal police agency and the community. As an open institution, the police department enters into a dialogue with the community and focuses its efforts largely on low-level community concerns that impact quality-of-life issues. The more invasive law enforcement approach, found in "professional-model" and "zero-tolerance policing, for example," is de-emphasized as a last resort. A major principle in COP is that once a police or community partnership is begun and an agenda developed, the police act proactively to deal with the root causes of community problems before they lead to crime. COP promotes organizational strategies addressing both the root causes of crime and fear of crime by implementing problem-solving tactics grounded in a community partnership. By empowering service-level officers, COP calls for organizational decentralization and structural change from a paramilitarized hierarchy to a more flattened democratized organizational format.

**community policing.** See *community-oriented policing.*

**community property.** Property owned collectively by a marital couple, where each party has a legal one-half interest by virtue of the marital contract.

**community service dispositions.** A judicial sanction and correctional practice whereby a convicted offender performs work that is of service to the community, in lieu of incarceration.

**community service officer.** Generally a nonsworn officer who handles non-emergency, low-priority calls for the department not requiring a sworn officer.

**community treatment.** Treatment programs for offenders that take place in a community setting, as opposed to those within the confines of a correctional institution, e.g., programs sponsored by half-way houses.

**commutation.** *n.*  A form of executive clemency where a judicially prescribed sentence is reduced by the chief executive (or a clemency board), i.e., the governor in state cases or the president in federal cases. Sometimes known as a "partial pardon," commutations are generally granted under exceptional circumstances, e.g., where the guilt of the defendant is clearly in question but a definitive determination is unlikely. For example, a death sentence may be commuted to life imprisonment.

**comparative analysis.**  A process wherein items are analyzed for both class and individual characteristics to determine whether those items originated from a known source. For example, a bullet may be microscopically examined to see whether it is first from the same class as a known bullet (by caliber and weight) and, secondly, to determine whether its individual characteristics (striations) match the known source (the comparison bullet or the gun barrel from which it was fired).

**comparison microscope.**  A microscope used by forensic scientists and technicians, enabling them to view two separate objects at one time. Through prisms, the two objects are brought together in order to determine whether they are one and the same, or in the case of firearms evidence, for example, if two bullets were fired from the same gun barrel.

**compelling interest.**  The legal justification underpinning the basis for suspicionless searches of certain classes of employees, both public and private, e.g., mandatory urinalysis tests for locomotive engineers and airline pilots, where public safety is a compelling issue. See *Skinner v. Railway Labor Executives' Association* (1989) and *National Treasury Employees Union v. Von Raab* (1989). The High Court held, through these cases, that the issue of public safety may provide a compelling interest sufficient to delimit one's right to privacy, under some circumstances.

**compensatory damages.**  A damage award that simply compensates the injured party for injuries sustained only.

**competency.** *n.*  In evidentiary law, those factors that make a witness legally qualified or disqualified to give testimony or evidence to be admitted or excluded from trial; the state of being competent.

**competent evidence.**  The antithesis of incompetent or inadmissible evidence. Relevant evidence that has been lawfully gathered, supporting the allegation to be proven.

**compiled statutes.**  The codified statutes of a sovereign government, usually a state in the United States, where the laws are arranged systematically. See *code, codification.*

**complaint.** *n.*  In criminal law usage, a formal written accusation, made under oath and providing the facts required to support a criminal charge. The complaint is made before a magistrate, in a court of competent jurisdiction, alleging that an individual or a group has violated a specific law; it constitutes a formal request for a prosecution. A complaint is sometimes synonymous with information, but usually used for misdemeanor offenses.

**complicity.** *n.*  The state of being involved in some capacity in a crime or criminal conspiracy; an accomplice.

**compounding a criminal offense.**  An offense committed by the victim of a felony who was injured as a result of that felony, who enters into an agreement with the offender not to prosecute him or her, with the stipulation that the offender make reparations, or after receiving a bribe not to prosecute.

**Comprehensive Crime Control Act of 1984.** A substantial revision of the *Omnibus Crime Control and Safe Streets Act* of 1968 (Title 18 of the *United States Code*) and various other relevant federal statutes and codes.

**compulsion.** *n.* A defense claiming that a criminal act was the product of a clear, present, and imminent apprehension of death or serious bodily harm. See *coercion* and *duress.*

**compurgation.** *n.* Meaning to purge or purify, it was an accepted ancient defense strategy against an accusation of criminal conduct, whereby the defendant attempted to establish his or her innocence by introducing a sufficient number of individuals to the court, who would testify to their belief in his or her innocence. Some scholars suggest that the origins of the jury system may be linked to this historic practice.

**computer-aided dispatch (CAD).** An automated system comprised of computer and radio communications hardware and software that aids emergency dispatch centers in efficiently and effectively dispatching calls for service for first responders, i.e., police, fire, rescue, and ambulance.

**Computer Comparison Statistics (COMPSTAT).** A method for holding mid-level police managers or administrators accountable for the crime rates in their areas of responsibility, created by the New York City Police Department. Computer-generated data on crime rates and arrest rates are compared for each 24-hour period; police managers are expected to explain their efforts to counter the crime data.

**computer crime.** Generally classified as a high-tech white-collar crime, computer crime is divided into five general categories: (1) theft of services, (2) illegal use of computer data for personal gain, (3) improper use of computers for numerous types of financial processes, (4) use of a computer to damage another's assets, e.g., planting a damaging virus to destroy data, (5) the theft of software via unlawful copying.

**concordat.** An agreement, compact, or covenant between two or more separate and independent governments, not necessarily sovereign governments.

**concurrent jurisdiction.** (1) A condition existing when more than one sovereignty or court has jurisdiction over a case. It often occurs in criminal cases when an offense is both a state and federal violation. (2) A condition existing when more than one police or law enforcement agency has jurisdiction over a geographical area or legal issue.

**concurrent sentence.** In criminal law, sentences that are served simultaneously, as opposed to those that are served consecutively (one after the other).

**condemn.** *v.* (1) To pass judgment and pronounce guilty (to sentence); (2) to determine to be unfit or unsafe; (3) to disallow for public use.

**condemnation.** *n.* (1) A legal process whereby property is condemned and seized by state authority for the violation of a law; (2) the process used to enforce the state's right of eminent domain whereby property is seized for public use, with adequate compensation.

**conditional pardon.** A form of executive clemency where a condition or stipulation is placed or added to the pardoning document.

**conditional release.** A form of executive clemency where a prisoner is released, under specified conditions, before his or her sentence has run its course. The conditional release serves as a virtual contract that must be fulfilled and where certain behavioral rules are stipulated for the continued early release, before the date when the sentence is completed.

**Condorcet, Marquis de. (1743–1794).** A French philosopher who held that as man and society evolved to a state of near perfection, there would be no need for an organized formal police presence. Concomitantly, Condorcet's ideal form of corrections included an emphasis on rehabilitation as opposed to the warehousing of inmates.

**confabulation.** *n.* The act of communicating would-be life experiences in story form. Persons with psychopathic tendencies are inclined toward confabulatory behavior.

**confession.** *n.* A statement that is usually recorded in some fashion, being composed of a number of admissions concerning the commission of a crime or crimes. In order for a confession to be admissible in court, the person giving the confession must do so knowingly and voluntarily.

**confidence game.** The vernacular for any false representation employed in order to gain things of value via a deception whereby the victim's belief in the offender's statement or promise causes him or her to be swindled.

**confidential communications.** See *privileged communications.*

**confinement.** *n.* A state of physical restriction of a person to a specified place, resulting from a legal process or sanction. Defendants are generally confined in a jail or penal facility.

**confiscation.** *n.* The authorized seizure or forfeiting of property and/or other assets or emoluments by the state without compensation, e.g., the confiscation of contraband. Confiscation may occur under state or federal civil seizure provisions or asset forfeiture statutes. Assets may be confiscated if (1) they were used as instrumentalities of a crime; (2) they were the fruits of a crime; (3) they were lawful property used contrary to the law; or (4) they are assets legally proscribed.

**conflict model.** A model that attempts to explain criminal behavior as a result of the conflict between various groups, caused by the inequitable social and economic stratification generated by capitalism.

**conflict of interest.** A condition arising from decisions and actions by officials when they have a vested interest in the outcome of a controversy and cannot, therefore, act in a neutral capacity.

**conflict resolution.** A process that attempts to find ways of eliminating disagreements in order to reach an equitable settlement over a given controversy. Often a conflict mediator or arbitrator is called in to help settle disputes via compromise.

**conflict theory.** A social or criminological perspective (theory) holding that conflict is to be expected when societies do not have a functional system for producing social justice. Often associated with Marxism, this perspective looks at what is wrong with the state (collective society) as opposed to what is wrong with the individual accused of violating a statute.

**conjugal visitation.** Formally introduced in 1963 in the Mississippi correctional system, the program allows for "cohabitation" of prisoners with their wives under controlled circumstances during their period of incarceration. Later, the program was advocated by the National Advisory Commission on Criminal Justice Standards and Goals and has become commonplace throughout the nation, for both male and female prisoners.

**connivance.** *n.* The passive cooperation in a crime providing a fabricated ignorance.

**consecutive sentence.** A sentencing scheme where, upon conviction, one or more sentences run sequentially; i.e., a defendant receiving a twenty-year sentence and a ten-year sentence would first have to complete the twenty-year sentence, whereupon the ten-year sentence would begin, adding up to thirty years of incarceration.

**consensus theory.** A theory of law generation holding that laws are created by a consensus of the citizens for the public good, largely eschewing the notion that powerful groups may actually influence legislation.

**consent search.** A warrantless search conducted by police or law enforcement officers after receiving permission from the subject of the search or another with the legal authority to wave the Fourth Amendment right, e.g., a wife granting permission to a search of the family home, when her husband is the subject of the investigation. The waiver of rights must have been done voluntarily, knowingly, intelligently, and without coercion.

**consolidated laws.** A codification and compilation of all the laws of a given sovereign jurisdiction arranged by subject. See *compiled statutes* and *codes.*

**conspiracy.** *n.* An agreement or plan between two or more people to commit a crime. It is one of the few *inchoate* (incomplete) offenses not requiring full *actus reus* as a necessary element. In addition to the criminal plan, there must be some overt act in the furtherance of the crime, short of the commission of the crime itself, to make the conspiracy chargeable. Some jurisdictions abide by the Wharton Rule in charging a conspiracy, where conspiracy cannot be charged if the illicit agreement to commit a crime requires the full participation of the two involved parties, e.g., adultery.

**constable.** *n.* A term that has commonly been applied to all classes of police officers; however, it applies directly to a municipal officer whose duties are virtually identical to those of a county sheriff, only being carried out at the municipal-level of government (often the township). He or she is a conservator of the peace who executes the writs of a magistrate's (inferior) court. The office has fallen into dormancy throughout most of the United States, as a result of the reorganization of the state court systems; the state of Texas, however, is an exception.

**constitution.** *n.* The organic law of a sovereign state (nation) organizing the government and establishing certain legal principles upon which all statutory enactments are based and assessed.

**constitutional entities.** Those entities created and mandated under constitutional (organic law) authority; i.e., the office of the sheriff is a constitutional office in thirty-five states, and as such is not a department created under statutory law, like most other policing organizations.

**constitutional law.** (1) The organic law of a given sovereign to which all other internal statutory and ordinance laws must conform. The constitution is virtually the "yard stick" by which all other laws of or within the sovereign must measure up. (2) The fundamental law of a nation or state that sets forth the organization, authority, and structure of the government and the rights and duties of individual citizens in relation to the state. (3) A statute or ordinance that is in accord with the constitution.

**constitutional officer.** An official holding an office or position that is explicitly authorized in the organic law (constitution) of the sovereign. An officer with state authority that cannot be delimited or altered by legislative action, e.g., the office of the county sheriff, in thirty-five of the fifty states.

**constitutional right.** A right (more correctly a protection that is not absolute) granted to the citizens of the commonwealth in the organic law (constitution) of the sovereign. There are two broad categories of constitutional rights. The first category, and arguably the most important, is found in the Bill of Rights, and is known as civil liberties. These constitute a list of things the government cannot do, protecting the people against oppressive governmental intrusion into their lives, especially in the area of criminal process. Civil rights are more properly constitutional protections against governmental oppression and are not absolute. The second category holds privileges granted to the people, such as the right to vote and assemble peaceably, i.e., civil rights. Assistance in the latter category may be gained by petition to the responsible governmental agency.

**construct.** *n.* A concept, idea, or perception emanating from the careful arrangement of facts, inferences, and impressions.

**constructive contempt.** Sometimes called consequential or indirect contempt, this category of contempt arises when a person(s), outside the immediate presence of the court, in some material way obstruct(s) or make(s) impossible the intent of a lawful court order, usually by failure to comply. Also known as civil contempt of court.

**constructive intent.** Intent that exists when a reasonable person should have reasonably anticipated a particular outcome.

**contact surveillance.** Surveillance by means of a material that attaches to the surface of the hands or other body parts or clothing once one comes in contact with it, e.g., a fluorescent powder that can be detected under an ultraviolet lamp.

**containment.** *n.* In criminal justice usage, an effort by police to confine homeless persons to one area of a given community in order to bolster the perception of order and to keep the homeless from public view.

**containment theory.** A criminological perspective (theory) holding that delinquency and criminality occur as a result of a breakdown of the inner (moral, religious, or superego) and outer (social control agencies and the family) constraining negative forces found in society.

**contempt of Congress.** A misdemeanor criminal offense, dating from 1857, arising from a refusal to appear when lawfully subpoenaed or a refusal to respond to questioning from congressional committees or their various members. Such contempt is punishable by fine and/or incarceration for up to one year. The process requires a simple majority vote on a resolution in either house, whereupon the matter is dispatched to the U.S. attorney for presentation to a sitting grand jury. If a true bill is handed up, the case is processed for prosecution in federal court.

**contempt of court.** (1) Any intentional obstruction of the administration of justice. (2) An intentional vilification of the court calculated to offend its dignity or lessen its perceived authority.

**contiguous.** *adj.* To immediately border upon; in physical contact with one another.

**continuance.** *n.* The postponement of a court proceeding for cause.

**continuous crime.** An offense that is virtually uninterrupted and ongoing.

**contraband.** *n.* Any property, material, object, or substance that is unlawful to possess, transport, or manufacture.

**contract policing.** (1) Policing services that are provided under the terms of a negotiated contract between two or more political subdivisions of a state or between a political subdivision and the state. (2) A form of police unification or consolidation, e.g., a municipality contracts for its police services, in full or in part, to be conducted by the county sheriff's office. When all elements of police service are contracted, it is said to be a contract of total unification or consolidation. When only a portion of the police service is contracted, e.g., only communications under a countywide system, the contract is said to be a functional unification or consolidation.

**contract system.** A system of contracting for the employment of prisoners that was popular at the end of the eighteenth century; today fewer than 1 percent of all prisons participate in the system. Under the contract, the private employer provides a reasonable standard of care, food, clothing, and supervision. Labor unions have been instrumental in the demise of this system.

**control theory.** A criminological perspective (theory) centering on a specific aspect of socialization and social learning, i.e., the learning of self-restraint. The study of the social mechanisms under which socialization takes place is of great importance to social control theorists.

**Controlled Substances Acts.** Acts found at the federal and state level modeled after the Uniform Controlled Substances Act. See Title II of The Comprehensive Drug Abuse Prevention and Control Act (1970) as amended (1984).

**contumacious.** *adj.* The obstinate resisting of authority in an overtly insubordinate manner.

**conversion.** In law, the unlawful appropriation of the property of another for one's own use and/or benefit.

**convict.** *n.* (1) An inmate in a state or federal penal facility for a felony violation. *v.* (2) To find one guilty of an offense, criminal or quasi-criminal.

**conviction.** *n.* The affirmative determination or judgment of a court arising from a jury verdict, the decision of a judge or magistrate at a bench trial, or the guilty plea or *nolo contendere* plea by a defendant.

**convict labor.** Labor performed by prisoners of penal institutions either for the state or for private contractors.

**Cooley, Charles H. (1864–1929).** The noted social psychologist who coined the term "looking glass self" in 1902, to demonstrate how one's self-concept is produced through interaction and responses to others. His work had an important impact on the interactionist school of criminology.

**Cooper, D. B.** The name used by the person who, on November 24, 1971, hijacked a Northwest Orient Airlines jet, receiving $200,000 in ransom and who later parachuted to escape, some think to his death.

**copycat syndrome.** The committing of an act, often criminal, in imitation of what others have recently done.

**copyright.** *n.* The right and protection of ownership to literary property recognized by statutory law for a specified period.

**coram nobis.** *(Lat.)* "Before us." A writ of error that was formerly used as a vehicle for appeal directly to the original trial court, requesting that the conviction be set aside for some alleged error not appearing on the official record.

**coram vobis.** *(Lat.)* A writ of error, likened to a *coram nobis*, but directed from the court of review to the original trial court.

**coroner.** *n.* An elected county-level criminal justice official charged with the duty of determining, through an inquest, the cause of death where suspicion of foul play is present or a physician was not present at the time of death. Not to be confused with a medical examiner, who is by definition a medical doctor. In many parts of the United States, the coroner is a part-time position, frequently filled by funeral directors. The coroner is the only criminal justice official with the authority to arrest the sheriff in most states.

**coroner's inquest.** An inquisition by a jury empaneled via the authority of the coroner to look into the death of a person or persons under suspicious circumstances.

**corporal.** (1) In a military context, the lowest noncommissioned officer of the enlisted ranks, one step below a sergeant and one grade above a private first class. (2) In a police organizational context, the lowest rank of the supervisory grade, one step below a sergeant. Many police departments simply skip the rank of corporal and ascend from patrol officer to sergeant.

**corporal punishment.** Punishment that is physical in nature.

**corporate crime.** Criminal offenses chargeable to a corporate entity that result from the activities of its officers or employees.

**corps.** *(Lat., pronounced core.)* (1) A body of individuals organized under a common purpose. (2) In a military context, a large specialized branch within the armed forces providing a unique function, i.e., the Military Police Corps or the Signal Corps; a subdivision of the army, commonly overseen by a lieutenant general being comprised of two or more divisions and other auxiliary service units; the Marine Corps within the U.S. Department of the Navy.

**corpus.** *(Lat.)* "The body." A body of people, laws, rules, regulations, or articles; the physical mass of something as opposed to an intellectual concept.

**corpus dilecti.** *(Lat.)* "The body of the crime." (1) In a derivative context, all the substantial facts supporting the conclusion that a crime has occurred. The *corpus dilecti* generally consists of two elements: the criminal act itself and the agency behind the act. (2) The material substance against which the criminal act was perpetrated, e.g., the corpse of a murdered person.

**corpus juris.** *(Lat.)* A body of law; a book or books that constitute a body of law; they include the *Corpus Juris Civilis* and the *Corpus Juris Canonici*. In the United States, there is also a collection known as the *Corpus Juris Secundum,* an encyclopedia covering the principles of American jurisprudence.

**Corpus Juris Canonici.** *(Lat.)* "[The] body of the canon law." The law, decrees, and canons of the Roman Catholic Church until 1918.

**Corpus Juris Civilis.** *(Lat.)* "[The] body of the civil law." That body of law compiled and promulgated during the reign of Justinian (A.D. 528–534); it has served as the underpinning for most European (civil law) legal systems.

**Corpus Juris Secundum.** *(Lat.)* A legal encyclopedia covering the principles of American law.

**correctional institution.** A prison; a facility dedicated to administering the sanctions pronounced by the criminal courts following guilty verdicts. These institutions are responsible for the custody, control, treatment, and rehabilitation of inmates. In all reality, the phrase is little more than a politically correct euphemism for prison, since very little treatment or rehabilitation exists in prisons in the United States today.

**corrections.** *n.* That branch of the criminal justice system dealing with the custody, control, treatment, and rehabilitation of inmates. The term is largely a euphemism for incarceration, since little if any treatment or rehabilitation exists in American prisons today.

**correlates of crime.** The variables most strongly associated with criminal activity, e.g., age, sex, and race.

**corroborating evidence.** Evidence that supports, enhances, or supplements evidence previously proffered. Evidence deriving from a separate source that supports or adds to the credibility of the original evidence.

**corruption of blood.** The collateral consequences under English common law that automatically attached after a conviction for treason or a felony. They included the inability of the convicted person to own, inherit, or bequeath through inheritance any property, rank, or title. Corruption of blood is forbidden by the U.S. Constitution, Article III § 3, 2.

**corruption, police.** A form of police misconduct involving the misuse of authority for the personal gain of the officer or another.

**counsel.** *n.* See *attorney, attorney-at-law,* or *counselor.*

**counselor.** *n.* In legal usage, a licensed member of the legal profession who renders legal advice on issues of law; an attorney or lawyer.

**count.** *n.* A synonym for "charge" in criminal proceedings stemming from an information or indictment. For a single charge, the counts come from the four elements of the *mens rea.*

**counterfeiting.** *v.* The making of imitation currency or negotiable instruments with the intent to deceive or defraud by the passing of the forged copy. See 18 USCA § 471 *et seq.*

**countermand.** The express or implied change, revocation, or annulment of an order or command previously issued.

**counterpunching.** *n.* Police jargon for the act of calling the police regarding the behavior of another, as a means of diverting attention away from the caller's own behavior.

**county.** *n.* In the United States, a local administrative subdivision of a state, usually divided into townships and generally consisting of two or more municipalities. In most states, counties are technically not considered municipalities. Many states distinguish between municipal corporations and counties, holding that counties are political subdivisions of the state created by state government for the purposes of administering state services and functions, and not like cities, towns, and villages, incorporated by a petition of local residents for the conveniences associated with local self-government.

**county court.** The administrative board overseeing the physical and fiscal responsibilities of county government, also called a county board, and board of supervisors. It is not to be confused with the trial court, located at the county seat, associated with the state judiciary.

**county police.** An anomalous form of county-level policing wherein an appointed chief of police oversees a countywide police department that by statute supplants the office of the sheriff, or adds a separate police department to the existing sheriff's office. Only about 1 percent of police agencies are of this type.

**county seat.** The municipality chosen to host the county government and its administrative offices, e.g., the office of the sheriff and the county jail.

**court.** *n.* That organ of government established to administer justice in issues of controversy and consisting of at least one judge and sometimes a jury and other such officers as designated by law.

**court administrator.** A nonjudicial officer charged with the responsibility of administering efficiently the court's budget, calendar, and other nonjudicial personnel as provided by law.

**court-martial.** (Plural form is "courts-martial"). A military or naval court proceeding established under the authority of the Uniform Code of Military Justice (UCMJ), 10 USCA § 801 *et seq.* The process is used primarily for trying alleged offenders who are active members of the armed forces (or others under military jurisdiction) for violations of the UCMJ or the USCMJ. All appeals go directly to the Court of Military Appeals, a court from which no further appeal is available. Three types of courts-martial exist; they are the "summary" court-martial for petty infractions; the "special" court-martial, used for offenses equivalent to a misdemeanor in the civilian criminal justice system; and the "general" court-martial, used for the equivalent of a felony offense in the civilian criminal justice system. Military courts are not considered part of the federal judiciary, as they were not created under the authority of the Judiciary Act of 1789. Rather, they were established under the authority of Congress to regulate the armed forces of the United States.

**court of claims.** A court of original and exclusive jurisdiction in all claims against the sovereign at both the federal and state level. At the federal level, this court was originally established in 1855 under 10 Stat. 612; 28 USCA 171, 1491–1506 but abolished in 1982, and reconstituted into the U.S. Claims Court, with its appellate jurisdiction transferred to the new Court of Appeals for the Federal Circuit. At the state level, e.g., in Illinois, the Court of Claims is presided over by a commissioner appointed by the governor who hears cases without a jury. Appeals may be made to the full court of three commissioners, from which no further appeal is possible. When a verdict is rendered in favor of the plaintiff, the full court has the right to reverse or modify, and the settlement, which is limited to $100,000, is sent to the state general assembly for payment. The general assembly has three years to consider the settlement and act accordingly if no economic exigency arises.

**court of common pleas.** An English court of original jurisdiction for cases arising out of common law.

**court of general sessions.** In some jurisdictions, a court of general and original jurisdiction (the state-level trial courts).

**court of last resort.** (1) The highest court of appeals in a sovereign jurisdiction, i.e., a state supreme court or the federal Supreme Court. (2) A metaphor used for any entity of last appeal.

**Court of Military Appeals.** Established in 1950 under 10 USCA § 867, it is the court of last resort in court-martial appeals for all of the armed ser vices. Consisting of three civilian judges, the court is appointed by the president and reviews cases involving criminal matters. Its decisions may not be appealed to the U.S. Supreme Court.

**court of record.** A trial court at the state or federal level, where a complete formal written record of all official proceedings are kept, usually in verbatim stenotype format.

**court of the star chamber.** An English court intended to prevent the obstruction of justice by uncooperative witnesses and defendants. Conducting its business in a building with a domed roof upon which stars were emblazoned on the interior, it became known as the star chamber, where defendants and witnesses were subjected to cruel punishments like the rack until they told the king's prosecutor what he demanded. Because of its abuses, the court was abolished in 1641. The term has become synonymous with, and a metaphor for, any court proceeding that is perceived as abusive and lacking in due process protections. Some legal critics argue that the grand jury system is a modern-day star chamber.

**court order.** Any order, command, or directive issued under the authority of a judicial officer.

**court packing.** The process attempted by President Franklin D. Roosevelt to alter the composition of the Supreme Court by adding six additional justices (all of his political inclination). The packing of the Court was attempted in order to shield his National Recovery Act legislation from appellate disapproval, as conservative members of the High Court had previously found such legislation unconstitutional, much to the advantage of their Republican big-business supporters.

**court reporter.** The person responsible in courts of record to record verbatim all official proceedings, usually in stenographic format.

**coverture.** *n.* The situation, condition, state, or status of a married woman, in the eyes of the law.

*Cranch.* *n.* The appellate case law reporter for U.S. Supreme Court rulings, spanning (1801–1815). Before the introduction of the *United States Reports (U.S.),* and the *United States Supreme Court Reports Lawyer's Edition/Second Edition (L.Ed., or L.Ed. 2d),* a series of lesser-known reports covered the decisions of the High Court; they include *Dallas* (1790–1800), *Cranch* (1801–1862), *Wheaton* (1816–1827), *Peters* (1828–1842), *Howard* (1843–1860), *Black* (1861–1862), and *Wallace* (1863–1874). Today, these early reports have been catalogued in the *United States Reports* and other reporters for the convenience of legal researchers.

**credit card fraud.** A burgeoning form of fraud and theft stemming from the illegal appropriation of another's credit card, credit card number, or identity. See the *Credit Fraud Act of 1984.*

**crime.** *n.* (1) In a natural law sense, any act, even without a statute prohibiting such behavior, that a reasonable person would or should have known intuitively was an egregious wrong and an offense against nature itself. (2) In a positive law context, any act committed or omitted in violation of a written criminal statute of a legitimate sovereign government. (Note that since a municipal government is not a sovereign entity, its laws [ordinances] are by definition not criminal laws; they are civil laws, and as such, a conviction does not constitute a crime.) (3) A crime is an offense that constitutes a public wrong, proscribed by law, and made punishable by the state in a criminal proceeding in its own courts and in its own name; any legislated act or omission that involves harm to the peace and dignity of the collective people of a state, as opposed to an act or omission that causes harm only to an individual (a tort offense), where restitution rather than punishment is sought. Criminal acts generally require the proof of both *mens rea* (criminal intent) and *actus reus* (an overt criminal act). Crimes are categorized as *mala prohibita* (not intrinsically bad, only bad because they are defined so) or *mala in se* (bad intrinsically in and of themselves). Crimes are divided into the following categories: treason, felonies, and misdemeanors.

**crime clock.** A graphically depicted clock, found in the FBI's *Uniform Crime Reports*, representing the estimated number of known crimes committed in the United States, on average, in a twenty-four-hour period.

**Crime Control Act of 1984.** This act pertains to the federal government exclusively. The act established the U.S. Sentencing Commission to address perceived sentencing disparity problems. Recommending split-sentence models, the commission and its recommendations took effect in 1987.

**crime control model.** A model for dealing with crime focusing on the efficient and equitable processing of offenders through the criminal justice system. The crime control model is a conservative approach to dealing with society's thorny crime problem, based largely on the perspective of classical criminology, especially the swift and sure punishment component.

**crime fighter.** An operational style of policing that fits nicely with Wilson's "legalistic" police officer perspective and work style, where officers see their role primarily as law enforcement officers, where arrest is the preferred first option.

**crime index.** Those crimes noted in the *Uniform Crime Reports* (UCR), submitted voluntarily by participating police organizations and law enforcement agencies across the United States to the FBI, indicating the volume and distribution of crime by political and geographical venue. Index offenses include murder, nonnegligent manslaughter, forcible rape, robbery, aggravated assault, burglary, larceny, theft, motor vehicle theft, and arson.

**crime laboratory.** A forensic laboratory where police and law enforcement agencies send evidence to be identified and analyzed for use in subsequent criminal adjudications. Crime laboratories may be found at the federal, state, and local level. The FBI, e.g., operates a major crime laboratory that is available to federal as well as to state and local enforcement agents. Very large municipal police departments sometimes operate a forensic laboratory. However, the preponderance of crime laboratories are found at the state level and are generally part of a statewide system of crime laboratories available to all police agencies within a particular region of a given state. A crime laboratory must not be confused with a medical examiner's laboratory where deceased crime victims are sent for autopsies. See also *wildlife forensic laboratory.*

**crimen.** *(Lat.)* Crime, or an accusation of a criminal violation.

**crime of passion.** A crime committed during the heat of passion where the defendant acts so quickly and impulsively that the requisite criminal intent (*mens rea*) is clearly attenuated and criminal culpability is reduced as a result of an irresistible impulse. In many jurisdictions worldwide, if a crime is committed during the heat of passion, the penalty is reduced statutorily.

**crime rates.** The rate of crimes reported to the police as a ratio per 1,000 or 100,000 persons.

**criminal.** *n.* (1) In a strictly positivist legal sense, one convicted of a criminal offense in a court of law. (2) One who is guilty of committing a crime. *adj.* Having the characteristics or nature of crime or criminal behavior.

**criminal anthropology.** The criminological perspective (theory) evinced through Lombrosian criminology, holding that there exist distinctive types of criminals with identifiable physical characteristics. See *atavistic anomalies.*

**criminal contempt.** The willful vilification of the court in the presence of the court.

**criminal culpability.** The liability and blameworthiness of a criminal actor, requiring the demonstration of his or her knowing, purposeful, reckless, or negligent act or actions.

**criminal, endogenic.** A term used mainly by European criminologists, denoting a type of offender whose criminality is largely predetermined by heredity.

**criminal, exogenic.** A term used mainly by European criminologists to identify a criminal whose behavior is largely determined by situational and other contextual factors.

**criminal, habitual.** (1) One whose criminal behavior has become such a permanent mode of operation in his or her life that it becomes an embedded personality pattern. (2) One who is a recidivist.

**criminal intent.** An element inherent in all crimes (*mens rea*), save those of absolute liability, that along with *actus reus* must be proven in order to achieve a criminal conviction. It is the state of mind that must be inferred from the facts at hand, usually through circumstantial evidence. The intent may be either general or specific and includes the consequences representing the express purpose for which the criminal act was attempted or completed.

**Criminal Investigation Division (CID).** That organization within the U.S. Army responsible for conducting criminal investigations, involving felony violations; misdemeanor violations are investigated by the military police. Originally, the CID was little more than the detective division of the Military Police Corps (MPC); today the CID is a separate division, albeit under the aegis of the Provost Marshal General's Office. CID special agents are commissioned warrant officers and are part of the larger United States Army Criminal Investigation Command (USACIDC). The other armed services have similar investigative organizations, e.g., the U.S. Navy's Naval Criminal Investigative Service (NCIS).

**criminal investigator.** A sworn member of a police department organized at any level of government or a law enforcement agency at any level of government whose primary duty is to investigate crimes. In the military, criminal investigators are members of a special organization, e.g., in the army, the Criminal Investigation Division (CID). The CID investigates all felony-level offenses, whereas the military police investigates misdemeanor-level offenses. See *police detective* or *law enforcement agent*, e.g., FBI agent. Under some arrangements, an arson investigator employed by a local fire department may be classified as a criminal investigator, as may an inspector from the fire marshal's office.

**criminalist.** A forensic scientist, usually one holding the highest academic degree, a Ph.D., in one of the natural or physical sciences, e.g., chemistry, who is employed by a municipal, state, or federal crime laboratory. His or her duties involve, and are generally limited to, the identification and analysis of materials and substances delivered to the crime laboratory, often via the postal system. A criminal justice functionary is not a sworn police or law enforcement officers, and he or she does not have the official state power to make criminal arrests; nor does he or she have the legal authority to conduct criminal investigations in the field. A civilian assigned to the crime laboratory as a scientific technician. A criminalist should not be confused with the medical examiner who is employed by the county coroner's office or the county medical examiner's office.

**criminalistics.** *n.* The application of the various sciences and professions to the detection of crime. Generally, a criminalist is a chemist working in a municipal, state, or federal crime laboratory, who supports and assists criminal investigators (detectives) by analyzing items sent to the crime lab for identification and analysis purposes. Criminalists are not sworn police or law enforcement officers and, as such, do not accompany police to a crime scene and do not make criminal arrests. The collection of physical evidence, in larger departments, is generally done by a crime scene or evidence technician (generally a patrol officer) who is employed by the police department, not the criminalistics laboratory, unlike what is portrayed by the images shown by popular culture, e.g., television.

**criminal justice.** (1) That branch of the justice system dealing expressly with the administration of the criminal law, its processes, and institutions, i.e., the criminal code, the criminal process including investigation, arrest, detention, adjudication, sentencing, and corrections, i.e., the police, courts, and corrections. (2) The organized study of the administration of the criminal justice system and its component parts. An interdisciplinary academic field of study found in colleges and universities, including, but not limited to, police, prosecutors, courts, corrections, criminology, and criminal law.

**Criminal Justice Archive and Information Network (CJAIN).** A division within the U.S. Department of Justice, Bureau of Justice Statistics, established in 1978, providing data regarding victimization, juvenile delinquency, and the overall American criminal justice system. The CJAIN publishes the *Criminal Justice Data Directory* and *Criminal Justice Archive and Information Network.*

**criminal justice system.** The network of institutions, processes, and agencies comprising that portion of the justice system devoted to the prevention, suppression, and control of crime and delinquency. The phrase is not to be construed as a literal system, but as a network of loosely coupled institutions, processes, and agencies with differing objectives, which in one form or another deals with criminal offenders and the social conditions leading to crime. The greater justice system includes the civil justice system, the administrative justice system, and the criminal justice system.

**criminal justician.**  One holding or having held a faculty position within a department of criminal justice or a closely related discipline at an institution of higher learning, who investigates the processes and dynamics of the criminal justice system. Criminal justicians nearly always hold the terminal degree, i.e., a Ph.D., in criminal justice or a related discipline, e.g., sociology, and they teach as well as conduct social science research; an academic title closely paralleling that of a criminologist.

**criminal law.**  That portion of the law dealing exclusively with crime and criminals, their treatment and control, and being divided into two primary areas, i.e., the substantive and procedural law. Criminal laws (in a positive law system and as public documents) are assembled at the state level as revised or compiled statutes by chapters, whereas under federal law they are organized into titles. They may also be organized into such privately available publications as annotated statutes.

**criminal mischief.**  The illegal and intentional destruction or attempted destruction of the property of another.

**criminal offense.**  Any violation of a criminal statute created by the legislative arm of a sovereign government, whether a misdemeanor or felony. Note that the violation of a municipal ordinance is not a criminal offense, as laws passed by a nonsovereign government cannot be classified as crimes.

**criminaloids.**  (1) A label applied by noted criminologist Cesare Lombroso to those criminals considered career criminals and criminals of opportunity who did not possess atavistic features. He attributed their criminal proclivities to greed, passion, and other issues. (2) A label applied to corporate "white-collar" offenders by criminologist E. A. Ross.

**criminal organization.**  Any organization, whether formal or informal, created expressly for the purpose of facilitating criminal acts, especially those for profit.

**criminal procedure.**  The legal processes and methods used in the investigation through adjudication of criminal suspects. Criminal procedure and criminal evidence are areas that heavily overlap, dealing with the applicability of the substantive criminal law.

**criminal statistics.**  Statistics regarding crimes, crime patterns, and criminals from both official and unofficial sources, used mostly by criminological and criminal justice researchers.

**criminal syndicalism.**  A unique phrase found in American jurisprudence to describe the activities of labor unions, especially the Industrial Workers of the World (IWW) to curb their growth during the first twenty-five years of the twentieth century. Labor organizations were said to unlawfully advocate the destruction of private property and to unlawfully appropriate it for un-American ends.

**criminal typologies.**  Criminologist Stephen Schaffer developed a life-trend classification of criminal types including abnormal, habitual, occasional, and professional criminals.

**criminogenesis.** *n.*  The origins of criminal behavior; patterns of behavior that are inclined to lead to criminal acts.

**criminogenic.** *adj.*  Crime-producing elements, characteristics, or features.

**criminologist.** *n.*  A scholar who studies the causation of crime. Criminologists have traditionally been trained and educated in the academic discipline of sociology, although criminology has to some degree become an independent discipline; it also includes those from other social and behavioral sciences like psychology. Others are sometimes trained and educated in the ancillary field of criminal justice. Criminologists generally hold the highest academic degree in their field, a Ph.D., and focus their efforts on the causation of crime. They should not be confused with criminalists or criminal investigators. Most often, criminologists are employed by large universities and conduct research, publish, and teach in departments of sociology, criminology, psychology, and criminal justice.

**criminology.** *n.* The scientific study of the causation, treatment, and control of crime and criminal behavior in individuals, groups, organizations, cultures, and societies. Sociology has historically dominated the study of crime, although other social science and behavioral disciplines have substantially contributed to our under-standing of crime. The origins of criminology can be traced to the age of Enlightenment during the eighteenth century and to such noted figures as Cesare Beccaria and Jeremy Bentham. It was, however, not until the nineteenth century that the scientific study of crime and criminal behavior began in earnest.

**critical criminology.** A criminological perspective (theory) known variously as Marxist, conflict, or radical criminology; affiliated perspectives or branches include, e.g., peacemaking, radical feminism, left realism, postmodernist, or deconstructionist criminology. Conflict theorists see crime as the result of class struggles and the inequitable distribution of limited resources within a society, leading to social conflict. Central concerns for critical criminologists include, e.g., the role of government in creating a criminogenic environment, the relationship of capitalism and crime rates, and the relationship of political power and the genera-tion of criminal law.

**Croften, Sir Walter. (1815–1897).** As director of the Irish Prison System in 1854, he was an apologist for Alexander Maconochie's graduated release system.

**cross-examination.** The reexamination of a witness, on a matter within the scope of the preceding direct examination, by a party other than the original (direct) examiner.

**Crown Attorney.** The official title for a prosecuting attorney in Canada.

**cruel and unusual punishment.** Punishment prohibited by the Eighth Amendment of the U.S. Constitution and as defined by case law. This federal constitutional pro-hibition is made applicable to the states in state action via the Fourteenth Amendment (the due process clause) under the "selective incorporation" doctrine.

**cryptographer.** *n.* One who produces or deciphers secret writings (cryptograms).

**CS.** O-chlorobenzalmalononitrile, a white powder mixed with a dispersal agent, often methylene chloride, used to propel the CS particles through the air; it is generally more stable and less toxic than a CN agent. CS causes severe burning of the eyes, burning of the nose and throat, and a general shutting down of the vascular system. Police and military manuals suggest that CS should be used out of doors, while CN should be used indoors.

**culpability.** *n.* Liability and blame; blameworthiness; responsibility for a situation involving moral blame. Criminal culpability necessitates a showing that the perpe-trator acted purposely, knowingly, recklessly, or negligently in each material element of the charged offense. See *Model Penal Code,* § 2.02(1).

**cultural lag.** A condition that exists when a culture changes, but ideas, values, and behavioral patterns lag behind, causing some consternation.

**cultural relativism.** A perspective holding that the cultural values of one culture cannot be universally imposed on all cultures at all times, and that simply because the values of one culture offend the cultural sensitivities of another, they are not necessarily morally wrong or inherently evil.

**cultural transmission theory.** A criminological perspective (theory) holding that norms of conduct are passed from one generation to the next (through a process of social learning) and thus become reasonably stable within a given locale and its attendant culture. Should these cultural values be in conflict with conventional social norms, crime and conflict often result. See *Shaw, Clifford R.* and *McKay, Henry D.*

***curators urbis.*** *(Lat.)* The title for Roman magistrates during the reign of Augustus (27BC).

**curfew.** *n.* A law, rule, or regulation (often a municipal ordinance) establishing a time at which all persons of a specified age or class must be off the streets or out of public places. Curfews may be imposed by law or during times of military occupation or under emergency circumstances.

**curtilage.** *n.* The area immediately surrounding a house or domicile including all structures within that area having the same constitutional protections as the house or domicile itself.

**custodial arrest.** A full-custody arrest; an arrest where the offender is placed under physical as well as legal arrest for the purpose of criminal prosecution, as opposed to a technical arrest where the person arrested may only be temporally detained and is not placed in custody for the purpose of prosecution. That is, any detention constitutes a technical arrest but may not necessarily be considered a full-custody arrest.

**custodial care.** (1) That level of care accorded to persons who are in need of personal assistance in performing basic human functions. (2) The level of reasonable care afforded prisoners in a custodial facility (jail).

**custodial interrogation.** See *Miranda warnings*; interrogation of a suspect by sworn police or law enforcement officers following an arrest or in formal custody or otherwise having been deprived significantly of his or her freedom. *Miranda v. Arizona,* 384 U.S. 436, 86 S.Ct. 1602, 16 L.Ed.2d 694.

**custodial officer.** (1) An officer with the responsibility of maintaining the custody and/or transportation of a prisoner or prisoners. (2) An officer responsible for the safety and security of the county jail and its inmates. (3) An officer not actively or directly involved in treatment or correctional programs but rather the simple custody of prisoners, as opposed to a correctional officer.

**custody.** *n.* (1) The physical care and control of a person or thing. (2) The legal detention of a person or thing.

# D

DA, district attorney; Doctor of Arts
DARE, Drug Awareness Resistance Education
DCL, Doctor of Civil Law
DEA, Drug Enforcement Administration
DHS, Department of Homeland Security
DIA, Defense Intelligence Agency
DIS, Defense Investigative Service
DLEA, Directory of Law Enforcement Agencies
DNA, deoxyribonucleic acid
DNR, Department of Natural Resources
DOB, date of birth
DOJ, Department of Justice
DRC, day reporting center
DUI, driving under the influence
DWI, driving while intoxicated

---

**DA.** (1) See *district attorney*; (2) Doctor of Arts; a terminal degree, a doctorate in an academic field similar to a Ph.D., with a pedagogical component. See *doctorate*.

**dactylogram.** *n.* A fingerprint, whether latent or plastic.

**dactylography.** *n.* See *dactyloscopy*.

**dactyloscopy.** *n.* The study of or science of fingerprints as a means of identification.

**Dallas.** *n.* The appellate case law reporter for U.S. Supreme Court rulings, spanning 1790–1800. Before the introduction of the *United States Reports (U.S.)*, and the *United States Supreme Court Reports Lawyer's Edition/Second Edition (L.Ed., or L.Ed., 2d),* a series of lesser-known reports covered the decisions of the High Court; they include *Dallas* (1790–1800), *Cranch* (1801–1815), *Wheaton* (1816–1827), *Peters* (1828–1842), *Howard* (1843–1860), *Black* (1861–1862), and *Wallace* (1863–1874). Today, these early reports have been catalogued in the *United States Reports* and other reporters for the convenience of legal researchers.

**Darrow, Clarence Seward (1857–1938).** A Chicago law partner of the venerable John Peter Altgeld (a former governor of Illinois, famous for pardoning the Haymarket anarchists), he represented numerous unpopular individuals and causes as an apologist for a legal philosophy known as "legal realism." Among his clients were Eugene V. Debs, the American Railway Union (after the Pullman strike, when he championed the cause of organized labor), Leopold and Loeb, John T. Scopes, and the Scottsboro Boys of 1932.

**date of birth (DOB).** One's official date of birth.

**Davis, David (1815–1886).** Associate justice of the Supreme Court (1862–1877). An old Eleventh Circuit (IL) colleague of Lincoln. His ruling in *Ex parte Milligan* (1866), criticizing the arbitrary use of military power, enhanced civil liberties in the United States; instrumental in Lincoln's presidential campaign.

**day reporting center (DRC).** A nonresidential community-based treatment program that represents a relatively recent expansion of the residential community corrections concept. Various types of correctional clients are assigned to a single consolidated location where they are supervised and where treatment programs are carried out.

**DCL.** Doctor of Civil Law; an honorary degree conferred by colleges and universities to scholars for significant contributions to jurisprudence.

**deadly force.** That level of force likely to cause death or great bodily harm. It is never justified in making an arrest for a misdemeanor violation, *Holloway v. Moser,* 193 N.C. 185, 136 S.E. 375 (Supreme Court of North Carolina, 1927). Even in felony situations, officers who use deadly force do so at their own peril and may be held civilly and criminally liable. See *Model Penal Code,* § 3.07(2)(b) and *Tennessee v. Garner,* 471 U.S. 1, 85 L.Ed. 2d 1, 105 S.Ct. 1694 (1985). Unless the suspect poses a significant threat of death or serious physical injury to the officer or another, deadly force cannot legally be used.

**deadly weapon.** Any weapon, instrument, tool, object, material, or substance used in a manner intended to cause death or great bodily harm. See *Model Penal Code,* § 210.0.

**death penalty.** The imposition of the sanction of death upon a criminal conviction for a small band of criminal offenses that generally must meet special circumstances, for the purposes of social defense. A controversial criminal penalty that few first-world nations still allow, with the notable exception of the United States.

**death-qualified jury.** The Supreme Court ruled in *Witherspoon v. Illinois,* 391 U.S. 510 (1968), that jurors who are philosophically opposed to capital punishment may legally be excluded during jury selection.

**death warrant.** A warrant issued by the appropriate executive authority, after receiving a judicial finding condemning the defendant to a sanction of death, specifying the time, date, and place for the execution to be conducted.

**Debs, Eugene V. (1855–1926).** A celebrated pacifist and socialist advocate for organized labor at the turn of the nineteenth century, he was an unsuccessful presidential candidate who was arrested for his breach of the federal injunction at the Pullman strike and, as a result, was incarcerated in 1895. He was imprisoned again in 1918 for an offense in violation of the federal Espionage Act.

**decedent.** *n.* The deceased or dead person.

**declarations against penal interest.** Statements made out of court that are in conflict with one's innocence.

**decoy.** *n.* A person or thing that lures another into danger or entrapment.

**decree.** *n.* A judgment, sentence, or order by a court, declaring the legal rights of those involved in a suit and legal implications of the facts found relevant to that case.

**decriminalization.** *n.* A legislative action removing a type of conduct, formerly deemed criminal, from the jurisdiction of the criminal justice system. Note that the decriminalization of an act does not mean that it is condoned by the state, simply that the act has been removed from the jurisdiction of the criminal justice system.

**deduction.** *n.*  A reasoning process where an inference or conclusion is drawn from stated general principles. Known as a syllogism, deductive reasoning consists of three elements: a major premise, a minor premise, and a conclusion.

*de facto.* *(Lat.)*  A legal term indicating that a matter must be accepted and recognized in all practicality, despite the fact that it may be improper, illegal, illegitimate, or immoral, the opposite of *de jure.*

**defamation.** *n.*  A slandering or defaming.

**defame.** *v.*  To attack one's reputation or to slander.

**default.** *n.*  (1) A failure to comply with a court order or to appear when directed; a general failure to take part; any nonperformance of a required act. (2) A position to which something automatically falls, as a matter of course.

**defendant.** *n.*  The defending party; one who is civilly sued or criminally accused.

**defense.** *n.*  (1) The defendant and his or her attorney collectively. (2) A legal argument proffered by the defendant (usually through his or her lawyer).

**defense attorney.**  The licensed lawyer defending the party who is either civilly sued or criminally charged.

**defense counsel.**  See *defense attorney.*

**Defense Intelligence Agency (DIA).**  The national agency charged with the responsibility of disseminating defense intelligence data to the secretary of defense, the Joint Chiefs of Staff, and other components of the Department of Defense.

**Defense Investigative Service (DIS).**  The national agency charged with the responsibility of conducting personnel investigations for all components for the Department of Defense.

**defensible space.**  The principle, based on environmental design, holding that crime prevention is attainable via modification of the physical surroundings, thereby reducing the opportunity to commit crimes.

**defounding.** *n.*  The act of reducing unsolved felonies to misdemeanor status or reducing reported offenses to not credible.

**defraud.** *v.*  To cheat, deprive, or hold back something of value (usually property) of another.

**degree.** *n.*  (1) In a legal sense, a ranking of crimes by their seriousness. (2) In an academic context, an academic degree awarded by an institution of higher education, e.g., a B.A. (Bachelor of Arts). Two broad categories of degrees may be earned: (a) academic degrees, e.g., B.A, M.A, and Ph.D., and (b) professional degrees, e.g., JD, LLM, and SJD.

*Dei gratia.* *(Lat.)*  By the grace of God.

**deindividuation.** *n.*  A process through which an individual, acting within a group, loses his or her individual identity and accountability for his or her actions while a member of the group.

**deinstitutionalization.** *n.*  The process of removing wards of the state from treatment or custodial facilities into open society or community-based programs.

*de jure.* *(Fr.)*  According to the law; legitimate; lawful; as a matter of right.

**delinquent.** *n.* (1) A juvenile offender, adjudicated a delinquent by a court of competent jurisdiction for an offense, sometimes an infraction, deemed less serious than if committed by an adult. (2) One who commits antisocial conduct generally considered less serious than the type designated as criminal.

**delirium tremmens.** *(Lat.)* A severe reaction experienced by chronic alcoholics who have drunk excessively for many years, where tremors of the hands, sweats, and fever are experienced, followed by a deep sleep lasting several days. After lapsing into the deep-sleep mode, death often follows.

**demeanor.** *n.* Conduct or outwardly observable behavior, bearing, or deportment.

**demography.** *n.* The collection, description, and analysis of population variables and other vital statistics, e.g., age, sex, or social status.

**demonstrative evidence.** Evidence (usually real or physical evidence) that virtually speaks for itself by addressing directly the senses, independent of explanation or testimony, e.g., a knife admitted as evidence at a murder trial.

**demur.** *(Fr.)* To object or take exception to the adequacy or sufficiency in a point of law.

**denizen.** *n.* One who inhabits or regularly frequents a foreign state, not holding citizenship therein, but who is granted some of the fundamental rights of citizenship under the domestic law of that foreign sovereign. A political and legal status used largely by the British, for a person other than a natural or naturalized citizen who inhabits a British commonwealth or former commonwealth nation.

**de novo.** *(Lat.)* As new; anew; a second time. In a trial *de novo,* a case is heard for the second time (as new) as if it had never been previously adjudicated. This occurs when a case is heard in an inferior court—that is, not a court of record—when the defendant insists that the case be heard in a superior court. States using nonunified court systems, e.g., justice of the peace courts at the municipal level, sometimes have cases sent for rehearing in the state trial court system after they have first been heard in the inferior courts. This does not constitute an appeal, as there is no record to hand up to the appellate court, a requirement for an appeal. Further, it does not constitute double jeopardy.

**deoxyribonucleic acid (DNA).** A nucleic acid found in the center of cells, metaphorically known as a DNA fingerprint. A primary component of chromosomes, involved in the structures transmitting hereditary characteristics.

**department.** *n.* A separate subdivision of the executive branch of government, e.g., a police department.

**Department of Homeland Security (DHS).** The DHS was created under the authority of the Homeland Security Act of 2002 (Public Law 107–296) and the National Security Act of 1947 (amended 50 USC 401 et seq.), as a result of an executive order following the terrorist attack on the Twin Towers in New York City. Numerous federal policing and law enforcement agencies, as well as various other federal agencies, were placed under the control of the DHS in an effort to coordinate effective terrorist prevention efforts at the federal level, creating one of the largest reorganizations of the national law enforcement or intelligence or security apparatus in the nation's history.

**Department of Justice (DOJ).** The umbrella department, headed by the attorney general of the United States, under which a number of federal law enforcement and correctional agencies are housed, e.g., the Federal Bureau of Investigation, Drug Enforcement Administration, U.S. Marshals Service, and the U.S. Bureau of Prisons.

**Department of Natural Resources (DNR).** An umbrella agency of state government having numerous dependents and agencies operating under its purview, e.g., the Department of Conservation, the State Department of Environmental Protection, and others. Game wardens and conservation police have, in recent years, been relocated within the newly developed DNRs of the various states and have experienced a widened scope of responsibilities as a result.

**deponent.** *n.* A witness or affiant who gives sworn testimony regarding a controversy at issue. The testimony is transcribed for the record by a certified court reporter.

**deportation.** The banishment of a person to another nation state, often accompanied by confiscation of properties and the withdrawal of civil rights and liberties. A listing of the grounds for deportation can be found in 8 USCA § 1251, §§ 1252–1254. See *banishment.*

**deportment.** *n.* The manner in which one presents one's self; bearing; demeanor.

**depose.** *v.* To make statements under oath in response to interrogatories.

**deposition.** *n.* A discovery process where one party asks questions (found in interrogatories) orally of another who, testifying under oath, has his or her responses transcribed verbatim for later use in court.

**deputize.** *v.* To appoint as a deputy, especially in matters of law enforcement. The empowerment of an individual to act for another in the capacity of an officer of the law.

**deputy sheriff.** A person appointed to conduct activities and discharge responsibilities in place of the sheriff. A deputy sheriff (the equivalent in rank to a patrol officer in a municipal police department) is a general deputy, one authorized to carry out all requisite ordinary duties of the sheriff, without special authorization to do so. A special deputy is an officer *pro hoc vice,* appointed for a particular service, occasion, activity, or responsibility only, and, as such, acts under a special appointment and authority that does not extend to general duties.

**dereliction of duty.** The neglect and subsequent failure to perform legally mandated duties and responsibilities.

**derivative evidence.** (1) Evidence resulting from information gained through a previous act or statement. (2) Evidence obtained from other illegally gained evidence, which becomes inadmissible as a result of the primary taint. See *tainted evidence,* the *exclusionary rule,* and *fruit of the poisonous tree doctrine.*

**despecialization.** *n.* A movement among municipal-level police to replace specialized police units with neighborhood officers. The underlying assumption is that generalist officers who are permanently assigned to the neighborhood are more knowledgeable about the area and are more likely to find creative remedies for local problems that lead to crime.

**detain.** *v.* To restrain, to delay, keep in custody, arrest. In its strictest sense, the detaining of a person constitutes a technical arrest, although a more passive and less invasive form, as opposed to a full-custody arrest.

**detainee.** *n.* The one being detained.

**detainer.** *n.* A lawful restraint on one's liberty against his or her will.

**detective.** *n.* (1) A sworn police officer, assigned to the detective bureau or criminal investigative unit of a police department. In most American police departments, the position of detective is an assignment (albeit a prestigious one) to the detective bureau, where one carries his or her permanent rank. After leaving the detective bureau, the officer resumes work at the same rank in another bureau, e.g., juvenile or patrol. Thus, one may be a detective sergeant, where his or her rank is sergeant, not detective. This comports with the paramilitary system used by most police agencies. In only a few departments is the position of detective considered a rank, making lateral transfer into other bureaus problematic and ill advised. In agencies that are not police agencies, but rather law enforcement agencies, e.g., the FBI or the army CID, they do detective work, but are known as special agents or criminal investigators. See *criminal investigator.* (2) One whose occupation involves investigative matters, whether in civil or criminal law areas, or other areas having nothing to do with the law. See *private detective/investigator.*

**detention.** *n.* (1) In a policing or law enforcement context, a noninvasive technical arrest, where one is only temporarily detained, pending some other action; an enforced delay where the decision to formally charge has not been made. (2) In correctional usage, detention connotes a custodial sanction following an adjudication or a form of custody pending a trial.

**detention center.** A secure facility for the purpose of detaining juveniles.

**detention hearing.** A formal hearing before a judicial officer of the juvenile court for the purpose of determining whether a juvenile should be detained, remain in custody, or be released awaiting future proceedings. A hearing that seeks to determine the lawfulness of the detention, if it is to continue for longer than forty-eight hours, in most jurisdictions. In this capacity, the hearing serves the same purpose as a *habeas corpus* hearing in the adult criminal justice system.

**determinate sentencing.** A sentencing model wherein the offender is given a fixed sentence that may be reduced for either prior earned time or good behavior. As a justice model of sentencing, it renders the same sanction to all offenders for the same offense. See *fixed sentencing.*

**deterrence.** *n.* A primary goal of both the criminal law and the criminal justice system seeking to restrain, inhibit, or stop criminal behavior through fear of swift and sure punishment.

**detoxification center.** A short-term treatment facility for chronic alcohol and drug users, functioning as an alternative to incarceration.

**Devil's Island.** A penal colony for French convicts (1852–1947) located in French Guiana. It serves as the archetypal criminal justice banishment program.

**devolve.** *v.* To pass or transfer a duty, responsibility, title, right, or liability to another. For example, in policing, when a lieutenant is incapacitated, his duties devolve to the sergeant.

**diagnostic and classification center.** That part of a correctional system where prisoners are sent for classification purposes. Parolees determined to have violated their parole contracts are also sent to these facilities for reclassification purposes.

In some instances, these centers are used for the evaluation of persons who have not yet been adjudicated, to determine if criminal proceedings should continue.

**Dicennial Digests.** An integral part of West's *National Reporter System,* digests constitute a compilation of reported appellate cases spanning a ten-year period, indexed according to subject matter and identified by a "key number."

*dicta. (Lat.)* The shortened plural form of *obiter dictum,* the opinions of a judge or justice that go beyond the facts or issues of the case before the court and that are not binding in future cases.

*dictim dicta. (Lat.)* An opinion offered by a judge or justice on some element in a case under review that is not essential to the court's decision.

*dictum. (Lat.)* The shortened singular form of *obiter dictum* "a remark by the way" constituting an unnecessary observation made by a judge or justice that is not binding on the case before the court.

*dies non. (Lat.)* A day or days on which the court is not in operation, e.g., holidays.

**differential association theory.** A criminological perspective (theory) based on learning theory and developed by Edwin Sutherland and Donald Cressey during the 1930s and 1940s, holding that criminal behavior is related to one's exposure to an excess amount of antisocial attitudes and values within one's circle of close acquaintances. The theory has five primary principles: criminal behavior is learned, learning is a by-product of interaction, learning occurs within intimate groups, criminal techniques are learned, and perceptions of the legal code influence motives and drives.

**differential response.** The screening of calls to 911 with the intent of providing appropriate responses.

**differentiation.** *n.* The segmentation of an organization into discrete categories or ranks; three primary forms of differentiation exist within organizations, vertical (ranks), horizontal (functions), and diagonal (movement both up or down and across). In a police agency, for example, the height (vertical differentiation) of the organization is determined by the number of formal ranks, whereas the number of separate bureaus with unique functions, like the detective bureau, is a measure of horizontal differentiation. If one moves up in rank in order to fill a position in a different bureau, there is diagonal movement or differentiation, as both vertical and horizontal movement is required.

**dilatory.** *adj.* Causing intentional delay.

**diminished capacity defense.** A phrase used to connote the absence or reduction in capacity necessary to attaining the state of mind (*mens rea*) needed to be criminally liable for the violation of a criminal statute. Also known as partial insanity, it allows the jury (or judge in a bench trial as trier of fact) to consider the defendant's state of mind in mitigation of the sanction imposed upon conviction.

**diplomatic immunity.** The immunity enjoyed by diplomats, their ligations, and immediate family members while in a foreign state. Diplomatic immunity was formalized in the Vienna Convention on Diplomatic Relations (1972). Diplomatic immunity is rooted in the common practices of nations and is fully reciprocal. Diplomatic persons have immunity from the legal jurisdiction of the host state, arrest, trial, police, and ecclesiastical jurisdiction. When diplomats or their subordinates commit a serious criminal offense they may, however, be deported.

**direct evidence.** Evidence proving the existence of facts at issue without inference or presumption, deriving from the testimony provided by a witness to first-hand perceptions about things from his or her senses. Clearly distinguished from circumstantial evidence, also known as "indirect" evidence.

**direct examination.** The first examination of a witness by the party who summoned him or her.

**directed verdict.** A verdict of acquittal in favor of the defendant issued by the judge without allowing the jury to render a verdict, because the state (in criminal cases) has failed to establish a *prima facie* case.

**Directory of Law Enforcement Agencies (DLEA).** Formally, the *National Directory of Law Enforcement Administrators, Correctional Institutions, and Related Agencies,* published by the National Public Safety Information Bureau, PO Box 365, Stevens Point, WI 54481–9896. The directory is organized by states into three sections: (1) municipal law enforcement chiefs of police and city sheriffs; (2) county law enforcement sheriffs, jails, and county police; and (3) coroners and medical examiners, county, and precinct.

**disavow.** *v.* To repudiate any knowledge or approval of any thing, act, or agency to act, and a denial of a granting of authority to act.

**discovery.** *n.* A legal process used in the ascertainment of facts or things previously not known, as in a deposition.

**discretion.** *n.* A legally recognized prerogative granted to public functionaries, e.g., police officers, to make their own judgments and to act in an official capacity in situations or under conditions that are ambiguous requiring a decision that is proper and just under the totality of the circumstances.

**discrimination.** *n.* The act of showing a discernable favoritism or bias in services or treatment; making or perceiving inaccurate differences and distinctions.

**disfranchisement.** *n.* An act of deprivation against a person or group, causing a loss or hindering advancement in occupation, the political sphere, and so forth.

**disorderly conduct.** Conduct loosely defined as any act against public morals, peace, and safety. Unless given specificity by statute, the term is one of ambiguous meaning. According to the *Model Penal Code,* § 250.2, disorderly conduct occurs when one engages in activity causing a public inconvenience, alarm, or annoyance, (a) engages in making unreasonable noise, utterances, or gestures, uses coarse and abusive language; (b) becomes involved in fighting, threatening, or other tumultuous behavior; or (c) generates a hazard or other physical condition offensive to the public peace serving no legitimate purpose.

**disorderly house.** A building where people engage in activities damaging to the public welfare, health, or morals, e.g., a gambling house or house of prostitution.

**displacement.** *n.* A phenomenon occurring when crime has been displaced and thus prevented in that specific locale, but resulting in the commission of similar crime at a different time and place.

**district attorney (DA).** The official title for a licensed attorney serving as a state prosecutor, who is selected in a countywide election to represent the various police and law enforcement agencies of the state in criminal and quasi-criminal prosecutions within a specified county. While a district attorney works within a specified state trial court circuit or district, his or her authority to prosecute is limited to his or her county, within that given state trial court. (State trial court circuits or districts often include more than one county.) A district attorney is the equivalent to a state's attorney or prosecuting attorney found in other states. New York and Louisiana, for example, use the title "district attorney" for their county-level prosecutors.

**district court.**  A court with jurisdiction over a specified venue at either the trial or appellate level, depending on the jurisdiction. On the state level, it is usually a court of appellate jurisdiction, e.g., Illinois. On the federal level, a district court is a trial court of general jurisdiction.

**diversion.** *n.*  The suspension of judicial proceedings against an alleged offender after intake but before judgment, followed by the referral of the subject to a treatment program administered by an agency separate and apart from the justice system. A diversion constitutes a release without referral within the official system.

**division.** *n.*  In traditional military usage, a unit consisting of several regiments and/or brigades, commanded by a major general (two stars).

**Dix, Dorothea Lynde (1802–1887).**  An American humanitarian who devoted nearly half of her life to fight for the protection of the mentally ill. Her efforts led to reform legislation for the mentally ill in her home state of Massachusetts and others, resulting in the establishment of state asylums and treatment programs and the abandonment of the practice of placing the mentally ill in state prisons.

**dizygotic (DZ) twins.**  Fraternal twins; twins developing from two separate eggs that are fertilized simultaneously.

**DNA fingerprinting.**  A metaphor for the unique identification rendered through the DNA analysis process, where comparisons are made on a probability estimate.

**DNA, mitochondrial.**  (*mitochondria*, singular: *mitochondrion*) DNA (deoxyribonucleic acid) is a molecule used to encode genetic data concerning all life on the planet. The DNA responsible for most aspects of one's physical makeup is known as nuclear DNA, whereas mitochondrial DNA are those present in the mitochondria, which are energy-producing organelles located in body cells. Mitochondria have DNA molecules separate from nuclear DNA. Unlike nuclear DNA, inherited from both the mother and father, mitochondrial DNA derives from the mother only, with each cell having approximately 500 to 1,000 copies. In forensic usage, mitochondrial DNA is far less common and more vulnerable to legal challenges. It is used, for example, in cases where hair is found at the scene of a crime, but does not include the root.

**DNA, nuclear.**  See *deoxyribonucleic acid (DNA).*

**DNA profiling.**  A process employing biological residue found at a crime scene for a genetic comparison leading to the eventual identification and arrest of a suspect. The FBI now has a nationwide DNA database from which to compare samples.

**docket.** *n.*  The formal register in which the proceedings of the significant acts done in a court of justice are recorded. The terms "docket" or "trial docket" are sometimes used for the official listing of the court calendar of cases to be tried during a particular term of the court.

**doctorate.** *n.*  (1) The highest attainable (terminal) degree in an academic field, e.g., the doctor of philosophy (Ph.D.). The doctorate in this sense is a research-oriented degree, generally held by college and university professors, and many university-based law school and medical school professors, as they are required to conduct research. (2) The lowest entry-level professional degree granted (as opposed to a terminal academic research degree) to those who graduate from a professional school as practitioners, e.g., a juris doctor (JD) or a medical doctor (MD). In the professional sector, advanced graduate degrees are available, although few pursue them; they are in law, e.g., a master of law (LLM) and the doctor of juridical science (S.J.D). Some who go on for a doctorate in law seek a Ph.D. in legal philosophy or legal history; these are doctorates in the academic and research context.

**documentary evidence.** Evidence provided via written instruments and documents of any type. This category of evidence must be distinguished from testimonial evidence made orally by witnesses.

**document examiner.** A recognized expert in the field of handwriting, typewriting, word processing, inks, and so forth.

**Doe, John.** The fictitious name given to a party in a legal action where his or her actual name is unknown or where he or she wishes to remain anonymous.

**domain.** *n.* (1) The absolute ownership of a parcel of land. (2) The sovereign authority of a state, allowing for the public control, usage, or ownership of private property, known as the "right of eminent domain." (3) The national domain consists of the aggregate of all property owned by a nation state.

**domestic battery.** The physical abuse occurring between intimates. This abuse involves married couples and unmarried couples living in intimate relationships.

**domestic disturbance.** A dispute involving two or more people engaged in an intimate relationship whether they be married, divorced, or live-in lovers. The term also includes problems between adults and children or between adults and their elderly parents.

**domestic relations court.** An inferior court, generally found at the municipal-level of government, with jurisdiction over matters concerning the care of children and other family related matters.

**domestic violence.** An assault or a battery upon a member of the household including a spouse, parent, child, other blood-related family member, or others domiciling in the house.

**domicile.** *n.* One's legally established and fixed residence to which he or she intends to return. Despite the fact that one may own and occupy more than one residence, he or she may have only one domicile.

**donnybrook.** *n.* A rowdy free-for-all fight.

**double jeopardy.** A prohibition found in common law and the U.S. Constitution (Fifth Amendment) against a second prosecution for the same offense by the same sovereign.

**double marginality.** A phrase for the position in which minority police officers find themselves when dealing with citizens who are members of their own ethnicity; i.e., department culture expects attitudes and behaviors on the part of the officer that comport with organizational expectations, while minority citizens expect the officer to be understanding, sensitive, and lenient. The phrase was coined by Nicholas Alex in his 1969 book *African American in Blue.*

**Douglas, William O. (1898–1980).** A "legal realist" who was appointed to the U.S. Supreme Court by President Franklin D. Roosevelt to succeed Louis Brandeis.

**Dred Scott case.** The case in which Chief Justice Tanney of the U.S. Supreme Court wrote the Court's opinion claiming that descendants of Africans who were sold as slaves, whether emancipated or not, were not considered citizens under the Constitution. Further, they had only those rights that the government specifically might grant them. See *Dred Scott v. Standford,* 60 U.S. (19 How.) 393, 15 L.Ed. 691. Tanney's decision in the Dred Scott case pushed the nation toward war.

**drivers' records.** A database including license suspensions and revocations of licensed drivers from participating states, available through the National Driver Register, a Washington, DC- based organization.

**driving under the influence (DUI).** A vehicle code violation for the offense of driving under the influence (of alcohol, drug[s], or any controlled substance); a phrase used as a rubric for this statute in many states. See *driving while intoxicated.*

**driving while intoxicated (DWI).** A vehicle code violation for the offense of driving while intoxicated (from alcohol, drug[s], or any controlled substance); a phrase used as a rubric for this statute in many states. See *driving under the influence.*

**drug.** *n.* A narcotic or any other chemical substance used legally or illegally for its bodily and psychic effects.

**drug addiction.** A state of chronic drug intoxication caused by repeated dosages of a drug, whether natural or synthetic, producing the following pattern of characteristics or symptoms: (1) a powerful compulsion to continue consumption; (2) a proclivity to increase dosages as a result of increased bodily tolerance; and (3) a psychological dependence followed generally by a physiological dependence.

**Drug Awareness Resistance Education (DARE).** A program begun in 1984 by the Los Angeles Police Department, under the leadership of Chief Darryl Gates. Uniformed police officers are sent into elementary schools to help students ward off the temptation to use drugs. The program has since spread across the United States. Critics of the program suggest DARE is largely ineffective as the program's effects wear off quickly.

**Drug Enforcement Administration (DEA).** A federal law enforcement agency established in 1973 within the U.S. Department of Justice operating throughout the nation and selected parts of the globe. Publishes quarterly the *Drug Enforcement Magazine.*

**drug paraphernalia.** The various articles, equipment, utensils, implements, tools, and trappings associated with drug use.

**drug registration.** A function of the Registration Branch of the DEA, requiring every person, company, or corporation that manufactures, distributes, or dispenses any narcotic drug or other controlled substance to register with the DEA on a yearly basis.

**drunkenness.** *n.* Drunkenness (voluntary) in a public place is considered a misdemeanor in many jurisdictions, if the drunken person poses a danger to himself or herself or others, although many states have decriminalized the offense. Depending on the jurisdiction, the state of drunkenness may either mitigate or aggravate a crime. In some states, drunkenness may serve as a defense for some crimes under certain situations.

**dual citizenship.** The holding of citizenship in two sovereign states simultaneously. Dual citizenship may be held in two nation states, or, as in the United States, in both the National Union and the state in which one resides. See *Fourteenth Amendment, U.S. Constitution.*

**duces tecum.** *(Lat.)* "Bring with you." A writ commanding the person so named therein to appear in court and to bring with him or her various items to be inspected by the court. The sweeping subpoena commonly used by grand juries.

**duel.** *n.* A prearranged formal fight between two combatants armed with deadly weapons (usually firearms) at a specified locality and witnessed by at least two persons (known as seconds). Dueling is a crime in common law and in statutory law; it becomes murder if one of the contestants dies from wounds inflicted at the duel. Seconds witnessing the event are considered abetters and are punishable as principals.

**due process clause.** Found in the Fifth and Fourteenth Amendments to the U.S. Constitution, the first applying to the national government and the latter to the states in state action. Two principles are involved: procedural due process, where individuals are guaranteed fundamental fairness in legal procedures, and substantive due process preventing unfair governmental interference.

**due process model.** A philosophical perspective within criminal justice holding that one is legally presumed innocent and that the state has the full burden of proving a defendant's guilt. The prosecution must carefully follow applicable case law and the rules of evidence protecting private citizens from arbitrary governmental abuses. The model assumes that justice cannot be carried out without faithful adherence to due process, despite its inherent inefficiency and high costs. It stands as the anthesis of a crime control model, with its absence of due process, a more highly efficient and streamlined processing of offenders, and lower operating costs.

**due process of law.** The processes and procedures of law providing for "fundamental fairness" in legal proceedings for all parties in a dispute. Due process is addressed twice in the U.S. Constitution, first in the Fifth Amendment and later in the Fourteenth Amendment. Essentially, the due process protections found in the Fifth Amendment (1791) apply to the federal government, whereas those found in the Fourteenth Amendment (added to the Constitution in 1868) deliver due process to the states and have been the source of most federal constitutional challenges in state action. Progenitors to American due process can be found in article 29 of the Magna Carta (1215) and the Statute of Edward III (1354). Due process is divided into two areas: (1) procedural due process and (2) substantive due process. Procedural due process involves the safeguards embodied in the Fourteenth Amendment, which is the vehicle by which any of the guarantees found in the Bill of Rights are delivered to the states, under the "selective incorporation" doctrine. Substantive due process is broadly interpreted as the general constitutional guarantee providing that no person shall be deprived of life, liberty, or property by arbitrary and unreasonable action on the part of the government.

**dumdum bullet.** A bullet having a projectile made of unjacketed lead that, as a result of its design, expands to cause greater bleeding and trauma to tissue than would a standard bullet. Often, the lead projectile has a hole in the center intended to increase its expansion upon impact. The etymology of the name "dumdum" derives from the town in India (Dumdum), where the bullet was originally produced. This type of bullet has become popular with some police and law enforcement officers because of its tremendous stopping power; it is proscribed, however, in military use by international law recognized by most nations.

**duquenois reaction.**  A chemical test employed to detect marijuana.

**duress.** *n.*  The unlawful influence inducing one to commit an act or crime otherwise not contemplated by the actor. See *compulsion.*

**Durham rule.**  The "irresistible impulse" test for criminal responsibility promulgated in 1954. The rule holds that defendants suffering from mental disease or defect are not criminally responsible if a jury finds, beyond a reasonable doubt, that there was a linkage between the act and the mental condition existing at the time of the commission of the act.

**Durkheim, Emile David. (1858–1917).**  The most eminent French sociologist of the twentieth century who posited that crime is normal, given that no society can be found without it. Durkheim argued that religion and morality are a social construction made in the collective mind of society. He pioneered the concept of *anomie* and conducted seminal research on suicide.

**dyathanasia.** *n.*  A form of euthanasia (mercy killing) that is denoted by its passivity. For example, it may involve only the withdrawal of any extraordinary life-support systems, causing a natural death.

**Dyer Act.**  The National Motor Vehicle Theft Act (1919) making the interstate or foreign transportation of stolen motor vehicles a federal offense. See 18 USCA § 2312.

**dying declaration.**  A statement made by the victim of a homicide who is *in extremis* and without any hope of recovery regarding the facts and circumstances under which the fatal injury was inflicted.

# E

EEOC, Equal Employment Opportunity Commission
EM, electronic monitoring
EMT, emergency medical technician
EPA, Environmental Protection Agency

**Eastman gang.** An Irish-American gang organized in New York City about the turn of the nineteenth century; it was among the earliest gangs to emerge in the United States.

**eavesdropping.** *v.* (1) The act of knowingly, unlawfully, and surreptitiously intercepting and/or recording either the oral or electronically transmitted conversation of others. (2) The installation of any device outside or within a private place, for the purpose of amplifying, broadcasting, recording, or transmitting the private conversations of others without their knowledge or permission. (3) In common law, the act of listening next to walls, windows, or the eaves of houses with the intent of promulgating slanderous tales.

**ebriety.** *n.* The state of drunkenness; alcoholic intoxication.

**ecclesiastical council.** A church tribunal having the dual functions of a judicial court and an advisory board determining issues concerning church discipline, doctrine, and orthodoxy in early New England, before a clear separation of secular and church functions developed.

**ecclesiastical courts.** The name given to a religious or church court, especially among Christian churches in the occidental world. In England, they were given the authority of the sovereign, as well as that of the church, and had jurisdiction over religious rituals, rights, duties, and the discipline of ecclesiastical functionaries.

**ecclesiastical law.** That corpus of jurisprudence developed by the church and administered through the ecclesiastical courts. In England, it derives largely from canon law and secular civil law. In modern usage, it deals largely with issues concerning church doctrine, worship, and the discipline of church officials within a given denomination.

**ecology.** *n.* (1) That part of the biological sciences dealing with the relationship of living organisms and the environment. (2) In the social sciences, the relationship between social groups and the distribution of resources and resulting social and cultural behavioral patterns.

**edict.** *n.* A formal public decree, order, or proclamation issued under the authority of the government.

**Edmunds Act (1882).** The federal act making polygamy a punishable offense.

**effigy.** *n.* An image or likeness, usually of a person; a crude representation of a person held in contempt.

**Egan's Rats.** A criminal gang in St. Louis, Missouri, organized by Jellyroll Egan, which later became dominated by Irish elements; it evolved into an organized crime network in that city.

**egress.** *n.* An exit or way out. An accepted path leading out of an area, for either pedestrians or vehicles.

**Eighteenth Amendment (1919).** The 1919 amendment to the Constitution proscribing the manufacture, sale, transportation, importation, and/or exportation of alcoholic beverages in the United States and its various territories. Repealed in 1933 through the Twenty-First Amendment.

**Eighth Amendment (1791).** Among the first ten amendments to the Constitution, collectively known as the "Bill of Rights," this amendment prohibits excessive bail, fines, and cruel and unusual punishment. It is the amendment under which capital punishment was successfully challenged during the 1970s. "Excessive bail shall not be required nor excessive fines imposed, nor cruel and unusual punishments inflicted."

**electrocution.** *n.* In a criminal justice context, a method of administering capital punishment for the purpose of state protection, where the offender is strapped in a wooden chair and connected to electrodes at the top of the head, forearms, and lower legs. The modern trend is to abandon electrocution and replace it with the more humane lethal injection option.

**electronic monitoring (EM).** An electronic monitoring device that is attached to an offender's body, transmitting a signal to the monitoring agency's computerized tracking system. First used in Florida in 1984, it has become a popular alternative to incarceration.

**electrophoresis.** *n.* Somewhat similar to thin-layer chromatography, electrophoresis is used by forensic scientists to separate unknown substances according to their unique migration rates. This process is especially useful in identifying and characterizing proteins found in dried blood, as many substances in blood are electrically charged and react predictably to this process.

**Elmira Reformatory.** The first reformatory prison to employ indeterminate sentences, based on the concept of earned early release, opening its doors in 1876 under the direction of Zebulon Brockway. Accepting first-time offenders only, between the ages of sixteen and thirty, Elmira required mandatory schooling and a minimal level of acceptable deportment. Despite high expectations, the reformatory proved to be somewhat of a disappointment to its apologists, like Theodore W. Dwight and Enoch C. Wines.

**emancipated minor.** One under the age of eighteen who is living an independent life, separate and apart from parents or guardians, and who is self-supporting.

**embargo.** *n.* (1) Any legal restriction placed on commerce. *v.* (2) To place an embargo upon or around a place or unit of commerce.

**embezzlement.** *n.* The unlawful appropriation and/or conversion of money or other assets placed in one's care to his or her gain.

**embracery.** *n.* The act of unlawfully attempting to influence or instruct a judge or a jury.

**emergency medical technician (EMT).** One who has replaced the former ambulance attendant of years past, and who today is required by all fifty states to have successfully completed state-mandated emergency medical training and certification. Generally, this type of first responder is dispatched by the 911 operator or other such dispatcher, along with fire, rescue, and police personnel. Following a strict protocol, an EMT renders appropriate medical aid and transportation to a hospital or other authorized medical treatment center. An EMT who has undergone advanced training (a paramedic) is authorized to render treatment on the scene to victims with minor injuries. Emergency treatment may also be rendered by a paramedic, under a doctor's direction (via radio), while transporting victims to the hospital. EMTs are categorized into four tiers by the National Registry of Emergency Medical Technicians (NREMT): (1) Responder, (2) EMT-Basic, (3) EMT-Intermediate, and (4) EMT-Paramedic.

**eminent domain.** A legal doctrine granting the state, any of its subordinate political subdivisions, persons, or private corporations the right to seize private property (generally real estate) for public interests with adequate compensation. See *condemnation* and *expropriation.*

***en banc.*** *(Fr.)* A term indicating that the entire panel of jurists will participate in a decision, as opposed to a simple quorum; the whole appellate court; the full bench.

**endogenous criminal.** A term employed mainly by European criminologists to classify a type of offender whose criminality is predetermined by heredity.

**enforcement.** *n.* Any act or process used to gain compliance with law, rules, regulations, or policies.

**Enforcement Acts.** A series of three federal acts legislated between 1870 and 1871, granting the federal government the legal authority to directly intervene in election trickery, fraud, or disfranchisement. The last such law, passed in 1871, provided for the suppression of the Ku Klux Klan and other such organizations flourishing in the South at that time, by authorizing the president to suspend the privilege of *habeas corpus* and to use the militia or the U.S. Army for its enforcement.

**entrapment.** *n.* The act of government agents or functionaries (usually police or law enforcement officers) inducing one to violate a criminal statute for the express purpose of arresting and criminally prosecuting him or her.

**Environmental Protection Agency (EPA).** Created in 1970 by an act of Congress, the agency is intended to protect the environment by coordinated and effective governmental action. The various states have agencies nearly identical to the federal EPA.

**episodic criminal.** A person, not normally inclined toward criminality, who commits a criminal offense while experiencing extreme emotional distress, e.g., a man who immediately kills his wife and lover when caught *flagrante delicto.* A solitary act committed in the heat of passion while in the course of otherwise normal activity.

**Equal Employment Opportunity Commission (EEOC).** The EEOC was established under Title VII of the Civil Rights Act of 1964 (78 Stat. 241; 42 USCA § 2000), although it was not in force until July 2, 1965. Its purpose focuses on ending discrimination based on race, religion, sex, age, or national origin in employment.

**equal protection.** That part of the Constitution (Section I of the Fourteenth Amendment) that protects one's civil rights and prohibits discrimination. The provision found in the Constitution was enacted in 1868 and was interpreted by the High Court to mean that a state could not discriminate against persons within its jurisdiction; however, in 1954 the Court expanded its interpretation to include the responsibility of a state to make a reasonable attempt to eradicate discrimination. In 1964, the Court held that should a state not make a reasonable effort to eradicate discriminatory practices, a court decree would follow.

**equity.** *n.* The administration of justice according to fundamental fairness, independent of strictly formulated common-law rules.

**equivocate.** *v.* To hedge; to be purposively ambiguous; to mislead.

*erratum. (Lat.)* An error noted in printing or writing.

**error in fact.** An error in a judicial proceeding unknown to the court, which depending on its seriousness could make the subsequent ruling voidable as a nullity.

**error in law.** An error by a judge in applying the law to a particular case, establishing grounds for an appeal.

**escape.** *v.* The unlawful absenting of one's self from lawful custody, by either passive or forceful means.

**Escobedo, Danny.** A celebrated murder defendant whose conviction was overturned by the Supreme Court, because the police had denied him access to his attorney during interrogation, where he gave a confession that was later admitted in evidence at his trial. A progenitor case to *Miranda v. Arizona* (1966), the *Escobedo* case (1964) developed the "focus test" for police questioning. That is, when a subject became the focus of a criminal investigation, *Miranda*-type warnings were required or the evidence would become tainted. See *Escobedo v. Illinois*, 378 U.S. 478 (1964).

**espionage.** *n.* The act of spying on a sovereign state, usually to illegally obtain military or state secrets. It is a crime at both the federal and state level.

**Espionage Act (1917).** A federal act that limited certain civil liberties during America's engagement in World War I. The act provided for imprisonment for as much as twenty years for certain forms of disloyalty and opposition to the military draft. In 1918, the Sedition Act was passed, extending disloyalty offenses to published writings.

**estop.** *v.* To prevent; preclude, obstruct, impede; or stop. See *estoppel.*

**estoppel.** *n.* A barrier or impediment militating against or disallowing an allegation or denial of a fact(s) involved in a pervious accusation, allegation, or admission in a final adjudication of a matter.

*et al. (Lat.)* And others; or another in the singular form.

**ethnocentrism.** *n.* A factually unsupported attitude, holding that one's own group, race, culture, society, or region is superior to that of others.

**ethnography.** *n.* (1) That branch of anthropology dealing with the description of various primitive cultures. (2) A qualitative data collection methodology involving interviews and participant observer techniques.

**etiology.** *n.* The study and assignment of causes or origins, as in the origins of a folkway or law.

*et seq. (Lat.)* A common abbreviation in law for *et sequentes*, "and the following." Also abbreviated "et sqq." when more than one page follows.

**eunuch.** *n.* A castrated human male.

**euthanasia.** *n.* An act or method of bringing about a reasonably painless and easy death, usually to end suffering; mercy killing.

**evidence.** *n.* Something presented at trial with probative value, providing information to the court regarding matters in controversy, including documents, objects, substances, and testimony. The law of evidence, sometimes codified, determines when evidence is admissible at trial. Numerous forms of evidence exist, including, e.g., direct evidence, indirect evidence, and real evidence.

**examination.** *n.* (1) In an investigatory context, an investigation, search, or interrogation of a suspect. (2) In a judicial or procedural context, the questioning of a subject charged with a crime and aided by counsel, in order to determine whether sufficient grounds exist to bind him or her over for trial, by setting bail and/or sending such person to jail to await trial, if bail cannot be procured.

**examining trial.** See *preliminary hearing.*

**ex cathedra.** *(Lat.)* "From the chair." Generally used in relation to a decision or statement of a sitting pope. Used variously to evince a decision of great authority, where the pontiff is thought to be speaking for God himself.

**exception.** *n.* In a legal context, formal objection (noted in the official court record) regarding some activity, action, or statement.

**excessive bail.** Prohibited by the Eighth Amendment to the U.S. Constitution, it is bail that is greater than is reasonable and that is disproportionate to the purpose of ensuring the defendant's appearance at trial for an alleged criminal offense.

**excited utterance.** See *res gestae declaration*; a spontaneous utterance.

**exclusionary rule.** A court-generated rule holding that evidence obtained in violation of the protections granted by the U.S. Constitution becomes tainted and, thus, inadmissible at trial. First developed in *Weeks v. United States,* 232 U.S. 383, 34 S.Ct. 341, 58 L.Ed. 652 (1914), it applied only to federal officers involved in federal action. Later, through a number of appellate cases, the rule was expanded and made applicable to the states, through the Fourteenth Amendment. See *Wolf v. Colorado*, 338 U.S. 25, 27–28, 69 S.Ct. 1359, 1361, 93 L.Ed. 1782, 1784 (1949) and *Mapp v. Ohio*, 367 U.S. 643, 655, 81 S.Ct. 1684, 1691, 6 L.Ed.2d 1081, 1090 (1961).

**exclusive jurisdiction.** (1) In a judicial context, the authority that a court or other tribunal has over a matter, person, or venue to the exclusion of all others. (2) In a policing or law enforcement sense, the legal right and power to exercise enforcement action in a particular locale, a particular area of law, or against a particular individual or class of people.

**exculpate.** *v.* To distance or separate from blame; to declare or prove guiltless.

**exculpatory.** *adj.* Exculpating, as in a vindicatory statement.

**execution.** *n.* (1) In law, the carrying out of a legal obligation, command, or procedural course of conduct. (2) The lawful putting to death of a person so sentenced.

**execution of warrant.** The lawful service or carrying out of a warrant (whether arrest or search) by the proper class of officer and during the time period stipulated by law.

**executive branch.** That branch of government (separate and apart from the judicial and legislative branches) charged with the responsibility of carrying the laws into effect and the execution and enforcement of court writs, orders, and decrees. Thus, policing and law enforcement functions fall directly under this branch of government.

**executive clemency.** The power vested in the chief executive (governor or president) of a sovereign state (or a clemency committee or pardoning board) to pardon, commute, or grant a reprieve in criminal cases. See Article II § 2, U.S. Constitution.

**executive order.** Any order or regulation issued by the president or an administrative agency of government via the president's authority to interpret, carry out, or effectuate a constitutional provision, law, or treaty. When intended to have the effect of law, executive orders must be published in the *Federal Register.*

**executive privilege.** A privilege or immunity stemming from the constitutional doctrine of the separation of powers, under which the chief executive is exempt from the required disclosures expected of ordinary citizens. Usually, the privilege involves matters concerning military, diplomatic, and state secrets, necessary for the secure and effective administration of government. The privilege does not, however, establish an absolute immunity from judicial process, as some circumstances warrant disclosure by court order, especially a definitive order from the U.S. Supreme Court. See *United States v. Nixon,* 418 U.S. 683, 94 S.Ct. 3090, 3106, 3107, 41 L.Ed.2d 1039.

**exemplar.** *n.* A form of nontestimonial evidence taken from or produced by the defendants, e.g., handwriting samples, fingerprints, blood, hair, and so forth; sometimes called nontestimonial evidence.

**exhibit.** *n.* Any physical object offered in evidence at trial.

**exhibitionist.** *n.* One who indulges in exposing parts of his or her body (usually to members of the opposite sex) that conventional social norms and law require to be concealed.

**exhumation.** *n.* The disinterment of a corpse.

**exigent circumstances.** Conditions calling for an emergency response; urgent circumstances calling for immediate action; an emergency situation.

***ex officio.*** *(Lat.)* "By virtue of the office." One serves on a committee, e.g., simply because of his or her rank or standing in a particular organization. In many instances, the *ex officio* member does not have voting privileges, or may only vote when a tie occurs. The vice president of the United States is an *ex officio* member of the Senate, casting a vote only when a tie occurs.

**exogenic criminal.** A term used mainly by European criminologists to classify a type of criminal whose etiology is, in the main, situationally determined.

**exonerate.** *v.* To free one from the imputation of culpability or guilt; to exculpate or show as blameless.

***ex parte.*** *(Lat.)* (1) Something done for or on the behalf of one side or one party only. (2) An application made without notice given to the opposing party in a litigation.

**expatriation.** *n.* The knowing and voluntary separation and abandonment of one's citizenship from his or her country, and the taking of citizenship or becoming a subject of another nation.

**expectation of privacy.** The right of citizens to be protected against unreasonable governmental intrusion into their right to privacy, especially in terms of their property; a reasonable expectation of privacy is the controlling element in lawful searches and is the underpinning of the warrant requirement of the Fourth Amendment. See *Katz v. United States,* 389 U.S. 347, 88 S.Ct. 507, 19 L.Ed.2d 576 (1967).

**expert testimony.** Testimony given by an expert (opinion) witness in a deposition or in open court. Expert testimony, unlike that of lay witnesses, is in regard to his or her opinion, as an expert. See *expert witness.*

**expert witness.** A witness who by virtue of his or her specialized knowledge, credentials, research, and/or experience is allowed to testify as to his or her opinions on highly technical or esoteric matters, in order to assist the jury in forming more accurate judgments and conclusions about facts at issue, when dealing with subjects not normally within the knowledge of the laity.

**expiation.** *n.* (1) To make atonement for one's wrongdoing. (2) A position historically holding that the purpose of punishment for human criminal acts lies in the fact that the acts angered the gods against the entire community. As a result, the best way to appease the gods was to destroy the offender. A more contemporary usage involves a turning of the anger of the community toward the offender, and, as such, is nearly synonymous with retribution.

**explosive bullet.** A bullet (projectile) containing an explosive element detonated on impact or by timed fuse.

**explosive-ordnance disposal unit.** Commonly called a bomb squad, it is a specialized unit within a police or law enforcement agency charged with the responsibility of safely removing or neutralizing explosive devices.

**ex post facto law.** *(Lat.)* (1) A law providing for the punishment of persons for an act done before a law proscribing its commission was enacted. (2) A law providing enhanced sanctions for an offense greater than that under the law in effect at the time of commission of the criminal act. (3) A law that changes the rules of evidence allowing for the admission of evidence not allowed under the rules in place at the time of the offense. (4) A law of any kind, which in relation to an offense or its consequences, in some way changes the legal situation to the disadvantage of the person charged. *Ex post facto* laws are forbidden by Article I § 10 of the United States Constitution.

**expropriation.** *n.* A synonym for *eminent domain*; the term is used largely by the state of Louisiana.

**expungement.** *n.* The process of removing a criminal record under court order. Although the court expungement order calls for the destruction or obliteration of the official record, many criminal justice agencies do not fully comply with the order in its literal sense.

**ex rel.** *(Lat.)* The shortened form of *ex relatione* (upon relation or information). A legal proceeding instituted by the state (usually by the attorney general or other official) in the name and on the behalf of the state but through the information provided by one having a vested interest in the case. Such cases are commonly entitled *"State ex rel. Smith v. Jones."*

**extort.** *v.* To exact something wrongfully by threats, violence, or misuse of authority.

**extortion.** *n.* The exacting of something of value from another through threats, violence, or under color of law. See *blackmail, Hobbs Act, shakedown, 18 USCA § 871 et seq.*

**extradition.** *n.* The process of formally surrendering a person wanted on criminal charges by one nation to another, assuming that the offense for which he or she is wanted is an offense punishable under the law of the asylum state. Note that the extradition of an offender from one state to another within the United States is properly known as "rendition." See U.S. Constitution, Article IV § 2; 18 USCA § 3181.

**extrajudicial.** *adj.* That which lies outside the jurisdiction of a court or a procedure outside the customary course of justice.

***extra judicium.*** *(Lat.)* See *extrajudicial.*

**extralegal.** *adj.* That lying outside of legal authority and control.

**extraordinary rendition.** Also known as "rendition to torture," it is the act of knowingly delivering a suspected criminal or terrorist, against his or her will, to foreign intelligence authorities, with the knowledge that torture will more than likely be inflicted during an incommunicado interrogation. Given that U.S. agents routinely engage in this ethically and legally questionable tactic (because both domestic and international law forbid torture) it has commonly been referred to as "torture by proxy." The very act constitutes kidnapping in the foreign state where the abduction and rendition was initiated without proper legal process.

**extraterritorial abductions.** See *irregular rendition* and *extraordinary rendition.*

***extremis* (also *in extremis*).** *(Lat.)* Beyond any reasonable expectation of recovery; near death.

**extremist group.** Any group or organization that attempts to bring about radical change in the government or general society through illegal, violent, and/or unconventional means.

**eyewitness.** *n.* One offering direct testimony concerning something that he or she observed first-hand.

# F

*F. Federal Reporter,* First Series
*F.2nd. Federal Reporter,* Second Series
*F. Supp., Federal Supplement.*
FBI, Federal Bureau of Investigation
FCC, Federal Communications Commission
FDA, Food and Drug Administration
FDIC, Federal Deposit Insurance Corporation
FEMA, Federal Emergency Management Agency
FIPS, Federal Information Processing Standards Code
FISA, Foreign Intelligence Surveillance Act
FIST, Fugitive Investigative Strike Team (United States Marshals Service)
FLETC, Federal Law Enforcement Training Center
FOP, Fraternal Order of Police
FTC, Federal Trade Commission
FTO, field training officer

**facsimile.** *n.* An exact copy.

**facts.** *n.* In law, findings (evidence) regarding specific occurrences or alleged incidents; events or happenings actually occurring in time and place, the quality of actual existence, as in events or physical objects; a truth separated from fiction and/or error.

**false arrest.** The unlawful detention of a person restricting his or her personal liberty. Given that the unlawful arrest restrains the subject, it also constitutes unlawful imprisonment and may constitute both a crime and a tort.

**false imprisonment.** The unlawful detention or incarceration of a person.

**fasces.** *n.* A symbol indicating authority and justice, commonly displayed on official buildings and agencies of criminal justice, consisting of a bundle of rods bound around an ax, having at its top, a protruding blade. The origin of the fasces dates to the ancient Roman magistrates.

**fascism.** *n.* An anti-democratic political orientation or system of government denoted by a one-party police state rule. Originating in Italy in 1922, it was later adopted by Germany under Adolph Hitler, who referred to Benito Mussolini as his "teacher."

**feasance.** *n.* The performance of an act, condition, or obligation, not to be confused with malfeasance, misfeasance, or nonfeasance.

**Federal Aviation Act (1958).** The federal law (49 USC 1473) making it a crime to attempt to board, or the actual boarding of, an aircraft with a concealed weapon. See paragraph 902 of the act.

**Federal Bureau of Investigation (FBI).** Its progenitor agency (the Bureau of Investigation) was created in 1908 and later evolved into the FBI (1924). It is charged with the enforcement of virtually all federal laws that are not the exclusive jurisdiction of other federal police and law enforcement agencies. Beyond criminal law enforcement, the bureau is responsible for internal intelligence conducted within the United States, espionage investigations, and the monitoring of other subversive activities. The bureau also operates the National Academy, an advanced training center for state and local police administrators, the FBI Crime Laboratory, and the National Crime Information Center (NCIC).

**FBI Academy.** Located in Quantico, Virginia, the academy provides programs for recruited FBI agents, in-service training for field agents, and a separate program for the training of senior police administrators from state, county, and local police agencies (the National Academy).

**FBI Laboratory.** A forensic laboratory used by police and law enforcement agencies at all levels of government in the United States and its territorial possessions. The laboratory is divided into three basic sections: the document section, analysis section, and the special projects section.

**FBI National Academy.** A special training program within the FBI Academy for senior police and law enforcement administrators from state, county, and local agencies, located in Quantico, Virginia.

**Federal Communications Commission (FCC).** The federal agency charged with the responsibility of regulating interstate communications nationwide, including telephone, telegraph, radio, cable, and television.

**Federal Deposit Insurance Corporation (FDIC).** Established under the purview of the Banking Act of 1933, the FDIC provides insurance for depositors and makes bank robbery, bank embezzlement, and bank theft federal offenses.

**Federal Emergency Management Agency (FEMA).** Originally created to act as an arson training center (Arson Resource Center) in 1983, it has evolved to include the management and coordination of national disaster relief efforts, including earthquakes, floods, hurricanes, and other large-scale disaster-related events.

**Federal Firearms Act.** A federal statute (1938) proscribing interstate commerce of firearms and ammunition by unlicensed persons.

**Federal Information Processing Standards (FIPS) codes.** Codes developed by the National Institute for Standards and Technology of the U.S. Department of Commerce for data storage, retrieval, and analysis on "places" in the United States (coverage includes unincorporated places as well as incorporated).

**Federal Judicial Center.** Created by Congress in 1967, in response to a public outcry concerning poorly managed court calendars, the agency is charged with investigating judicial problems and developing relevant training programs.

**Federal Law Enforcement Training Center (FLETC).** The federal multiagency training center, providing training for agents from numerous federal police and law enforcement agencies. FLETC is located in Glynco (Brunswick), Georgia.

***Federal Register.*** Established under the Federal Register Act of 1935, the *Register* publishes presidential proclamations, executive orders, and reorganization plans. The *Register* provides both citizens and businesses a timely overview of new federal rules applicable to them.

***Federal Reporter*** *(F. and F.2nd).* The published opinions of selected federal courts. See *Federal Supplement (F.Supp.).*

**Federal Rules of Criminal Procedure.** Promulgated by the U.S. Supreme Court in 1945, this codification provides procedural rules governing criminal proceedings in all U.S. district courts.

*Federal Supplement (F.Supp.).* The published opinions of selected federal courts. See *Federal Reporter (F. and F.2nd).*

**Federal Tort Claims Act.** The Federal Tort Claims Act (1946), which largely waved the blanket immunity for the federal government under the doctrine of sovereign immunity. Formerly, the U.S. government could not be sued without its consent. That consent was given under the specific provisions of the 1946 act. However, the federal government preserves governmental immunity in some traditional categories of intentional torts. It also reserves the immunity for acts or omissions falling under the discretionary function or duty of any federal agency or employee.

**Federal Trade Commission (FTC).** The federal agency established in 1914 with the express purpose of promoting free and fair competition in interstate commerce. See the *Clayton Act*, the *Robinson–Patman Act*, and the *Sherman Antitrust Act.*

**felon.** *n.* One found guilty of having committed a felony by a court of competent jurisdiction.

**felony.** *n.* A crime of greater gravity than a misdemeanor; one punishable by death or incarceration in a penitentiary (as opposed to a jail) and for a period of one year or more.

**felony murder doctrine.** A rule of common-law origin, claiming that one whose conduct results in the unintended death of another during the course of a felonious act is guilty of murder. Some states still follow the rule, whereas others have generally limited its application.

**femicide.** *n.* The unlawful killing of a woman.

**fence.** *n.* One who deals in stolen property as a receiver and seller.

**fencing.** *n.* In law, the act of dealing in stolen property.

**Ferri, Enrico (1856-1928).** A disciple of the noted Italian criminologist Cesare Lombroso, Ferri expanded on Lombroso's theory arguing that socioeconomic and political as well as biological factors were important causal variables in criminality. He published *The Criminal Sociology.*

**fetal alcohol syndrome.** Congenital anomalies present in newborns of women who have consumed large quantities of alcohol during pregnancy.

**feticide.** *n.* The intentional and unlawful destruction of a fetus; see *abortion, criminal.*

**fetishism.** *n.* An abnormal psychological condition in which erotic emotions and sexual gratification are experienced, in association with nonsexual objects, often women's undergarments or shoes.

*fiat. (Lat.)* "Let it be done." (1) A legal and authoritative command to act originating from a competent and authoritative source. (2) Under church law, it is often a command issued by a sitting pontiff.

**fiduciary.** *n.* A person holding a position of public trust, as in a trustee of a public institution. *adj.* A public trust responsibility.

**Fielding, Henry (1707-1754).** A lawyer and novelist appointed principal magistrate of Westminster, England (near London) in 1748. In 1750, he published *An Inquiry into the Causes of the Late Increase of Robberies.* With his brother John, he established the Bow Street Runners, the first detective unit that ran to the scene of crimes.

**field training officer (FTO).** A senior police officer assigned to the field training component of a recruit police officer's training regime. Generally, only large- to mid-range police agencies have formal FTO programs.

**Fifth Amendment (1791).** One of the original "Bill of Rights," this amendment provides that no person shall be required to answer for a capital or infamous crime without an indictment or presentment from a grand jury, except in military cases; that no person shall suffer double jeopardy; that no person shall be compelled to be a witness against himself or herself; that no person shall be deprived of life, liberty, or property without due process of law; and that private property shall not be taken for public use without just compensation.

**fighting words.** Words directed toward a specific person or group having a tendency to cause acts of violence by the person or persons to whom the words are directed. In some states, fighting words may be used as the basis for a defense against assault and/or battery.

**filing.** *n.* The formal initiation of a criminal charge via a charging document, e.g., a complaint or indictment, alleging that a person or persons have violated some criminal statute against the peace and dignity of the people of the said state.

**finding.** *n.* A decision on a question of fact by a jury, court, or other tribunal. See *judgment* or *verdict*.

**fine.** *n.* A sanction imposed by a court on a convicted person stipulating a specific sum of money to be paid to the court.

**fingerprint classification.** A standardized system for classifying fingerprints by the ridge patterns found on the tips of the fingers. See *Bertillon method*.

**Fireman's rule.** A rule dating to 1892, restricting recovery for injuries that police officers and firefighters incur during the course of their duties, as a result of negligently inflicted injuries by third parties. Essentially, the rule has a number of underlying assumptions that make suits by police and firefighters difficult to win as a result of the inherent dangers in their positions, which they willingly assume when they accept those positions.

**fire marshal.** A public official operating at the state, county, or local level of government, charged with the responsibility of supervising, firefighting, fire prevention, and arson investigation. In many jurisdictions this official has police or law enforcement authority in the investigation of arson cases and the enforcement of fire codes.

**First Amendment (1791).** "Congress shall make no law respecting an establishment of religion, or prohibiting the free exercise thereof; or abridging the freedom of speech, or of the press; or the right of the people peaceably to assemble, and to petition the Government for a redress of grievances."

**first responders.** A term used to collectively join all individuals and agencies who are officially dispatched to the scene of an emergency. The group includes police, fire, rescue, hazardous materials specialists, and ambulance personnel.

**fishing expedition.** A metaphor for the discovery of evidence based on vague notions that are not legally actionable where, for example, the police cast a wide net in order to find evidence of a crime.

**fixed sentencing.** See *determinate sentencing.*

**fleeing-felon rule.** A legal doctrine overturned in *Tennessee v. Garner*, 41 U.S. 1, 105 S.Ct. 1694, 85 L.Ed 2d. 1 (1985) as unconstitutional. The rule originally allowed police officers to use deadly force in the apprehension of a subject who was fleeing the scene of any felony.

**flight.** *n.* The act of knowingly and voluntarily escaping or fleeing from justice. The act of flight can be used as presumptive evidence of guilt at trial.

**Floyd, Charles Arthur.** "Pretty Boy Floyd." Born in 1901 in Atkins, Ohio, he was credited with eight robberies and thirteen murders in various Midwestern states. In a robbery in Kansas City, Missouri, he killed six people with a machine gun.

**fluorescence.** *n.* The characteristic of a substance to produce light or glow after it is acted upon by some form of radiant energy, similar to the characteristic of an ultraviolet lamp.

**folk crime.** A term applied by criminologist H. Lawrence Ross to conduct that was traditionally noncriminal and nonviolent but that later became codified as a public wrong as a result of social complexity. Generally speaking, folk crimes are more correctly considered folk offenses, as they do not usually rise to the seriousness of crime.

**folkways.** Informal traditions sanctioned by a culture, the breach of which is punished informally by avoidance, ridicule, or exclusion. For example, the good manners requiring a man to open a door for a lady.

**Food and Drug Administration (FDA).** A federal regulatory agency with law enforcement authority established in 1907, under the Public Health Service of the Department of Health, Education, and Welfare. The agency's responsibilities are conducted within six internal bureaus.

**foot patrol.** A patrol modality whereby police officers make rounds on foot within a specific neighborhood or patrol beat. Despite the fact that it is very expensive, proponents argue that it enhances community relations better than other patrol modalities.

**foot rail.** A robbery signaling device used by commercial establishments allowing the cashier to activate the alarm by placing a foot under the rail and lifting it.

**forcible entry.** The unlawful entry onto the property of another or into the buildings or secure place of another, by the use of force or threat and without the voluntary consent of the owner.

**forcible felony.** Any felony offense involving the use or threatened use of violence or actual physical force against a victim. Examples include, but are not limited to, treason, murder, aggravated criminal sexual assault, rape, kidnapping, arson, and aggravated battery.

**forcible rape.** (1) That aggravated form of rape, where sexual intercourse with a female is gained by the use of force or threatened use of force, generally with a weapon of some sort. (2) The carnal knowledge of a person forcibly and/or against that person's will; or not forcibly or against the person's will where the victim is incapable of giving consent (FBI Crime Reporting Definition).

**Foreign Intelligence Surveillance Act (1978) (FISA).** The federal act Foreign Intelligence Surveillance Act of 1978, Public Law 95–511, 92 Stat. 1783 (codified as amended under 50 USC 1801–1811, 1821–1829, 1841–1846, and 1861–1862) providing legal authority to intelligence and law enforcement agencies to conduct foreign intelligence within legal parameters notably wider and more relaxed than those conducted under ordinary law enforcement circumstances. The act draws a sharp distinction between the lawful activities of criminal law enforcement and those of counterintelligence operatives. As a result, a special FISA Court has been established to deal with issues of legal conduct by federal agents conducting foreign intelligence investigations. See *Foreign Intelligence Surveillance Court (FISA Court)*.

**Foreign Intelligence Surveillance Court (FISA Court).** A special court established under the authority of the FISA legislation of 1978 to rule on the lawfulness of FISA-authorized investigative techniques like electronic eavesdropping. The court is composed of seven federal district judges who are appointed by the Chief Justice (50 USCA 1803). The court reviews the U.S. attorney general's applications to electronically conduct surveillances intended to gain foreign intelligence data. The court's records are sealed and are not discoverable, even to defendants who are the target of a federal criminal investigation, except under narrowly specified circumstances, as determined by the court's rulings on motions to suppress, 50 USC 1803c. Critics argue that the court's powers are overly broad and lack specificity. Coupled with its secrecy and immunity from discovery, the FISA Court is susceptible to abuse.

**foreign jurisdiction.** The jurisdiction of another sovereign state or nation.

**foreman.** *n.* A member of a grand or petit jury who presides over the panel and who signs the jury's decision form and speaks to the court on the jury's behalf.

**forensic.** *adj.* Belonging to or applied to the courts of law.

**forensic medicine.** The entire science of medicine as applied to the courts of law; e.g., medical examiners and coroners make use of forensic medical evidence in determining the cause of death.

**forensic odontology.** The science of dentistry as applied to the courts of law. Forensic odontologists examine the structure, growth, and diseases of the teeth and mouth for purposes of identification in criminal investigations.

**forensic pathologist.** A medical doctor practicing that branch of medicine addressing diseases and disorders of the body for legal purposes. Medical examiners are frequently forensic pathologists.

**forensic psychiatry.** That branch of medicine dealing with mental disorders for legal purposes. It should be noted that a psychiatrist is a medical doctor specializing in psychiatry; he or she is not a psychologist.

**forensic sciences.** The sum of the hard sciences as applied to the courts of law, e.g., chemistry, biology, and physics. Generally, forensic science is practiced in a crime laboratory at the local, state, or federal level.

**forensic scientist.** A scientist, generally employed by a university or state or federal crime laboratory. Although he or she may hold a doctorate in any of the hard sciences, chemistry is generally the preferred discipline.

**forfeiture.** *n.* The seizure of things or rights lost as a result of criminal or alleged criminal behavior. See *asset forfeiture proceeding*.

**forgery.** *n.* The unlawful act of imitating or counterfeiting documents or personal sig-
natures for the purpose of deception with the intent to knowingly injure or defraud
another. See *Model Penal Code,* § 224.1.

**Fosdick, Raymond Blaine (1833–1972).** Fosdick earned a BA in 1905, an MA in
1906, and an LLB in 1908. Considered an early expert on policing, he studied both
American and European policing systems, claiming the European system to be far
superior. He wrote *American Police Systems* in 1920, and in 1922 called the
Cleveland Police Department lethargic and ineffective.

**Fourteenth Amendment (1868).** Known as the "due process" amendment, it is the
vehicle through which the U.S. Supreme Court can make its decisions regarding
federal due process applicable to the states in state action. This process of the High
Court making applicable fundamental protections found in the U.S Constitution in
state action is called the doctrine of "selective incorporation."

**Fourth Amendment (1791).** The specific amendment to the U.S. Constitution
providing the right of the people to be secure in their homes against unreasonable
searches and seizures. The amendment provides that warrants will issue on
probable cause only, naming the places to be searched and items to be seized.

**Frankfurter, Felix (1882–1965).** Graduating from Harvard University Law School
with highest honors in 1914, he later became an associate justice of the Supreme
Court and an ardent apologist of the doctrine of judicial restraint.

**frankpledge.** *n.* Literally meaning "peace pledge," it was a system under which each
man in a tithing was responsible for the actions of others within the tithing, in early
England.

**Fraternal Order of Police (FOP).** America's oldest and largest police association, representing several hundred thousand police officers nationwide, through a series of
lodges. Most lodges serve as police unions in collective bargaining arrangements.

**fratricide.** *n.* The act of unlawfully killing one's brother or sister.

**fraud.** *n.* The knowing and unlawful deception of another with the intent to cause
him or her to unwittingly surrender property, rights, emoluments, or pecuniary
interest.

**freedom of assembly.** A fundamental right guaranteed by the First Amendment
of the U.S. Constitution. The freedom to assemble peaceably is restricted by
numerous variables and, like all constitutional protections, is not an absolute right.

**Freedom of Information Act (1967).** Signed by President Lyndon B. Johnson, the act
supercedes the Disclosure of Information Act of 1966, allowing for greater access by
the public to government data. Under the provisions of the 1967 act, disclosure allows
for refusal in only nine categories, including national defense, law enforcement files
on specific individuals, some personnel files, and other areas prohibited by law.

**fresh pursuit.** The common-law right of police to make warrantless entries into
homes and buildings while in fresh pursuit of suspects and to cross jurisdictional
lines (including sovereign borders) to make an apprehension for a felony violation
while engaged in hot pursuit of an offender. Many states have adopted the Uniform
Extra-Territorial Arrest on Fresh Pursuit Act (UETAFPA), allowing police officers
of the state in which the felony occurred to enter another state that has also entered
into the UETAFPA, or a similar compact, in order to make an arrest. Officers from

the initiating state have the same arrest powers and authority to hold in custody the fleeing subject as do police officials of the foreign state. The provision authorizing interstate pursuit found in the Uniform Act on Fresh Pursuit, § 852.2 reads, "Any peace officer of another state, who enters this State in fresh pursuit, and continues in this State in fresh pursuit, of a person in order to arrest him on the ground that he has committed a felony in the other state, has the same authority to arrest and hold the person in custody as peace officers of this State have to arrest and hold a person in custody on the ground that he has committed a felony in this State."

**Freud, Sigmund (1856–1939).** An Austrian physician or psychiatrist and founder of the school of psychoanalysis. While all concede that Freud was a famous psychologist and theorist of the human personality, his influence has been notable far beyond psychology, as a man whose thought revolutionized the thinking of his age, even into disciplines as far removed as criminology.

**friction ridges.** The capillary ridges found on the palm side of the hand and fingers (as well as on the feet and toes), providing the friction necessary to grasp objects effectively and from which fingerprint identification is made possible.

**frisk.** *n.* A noninvasive precautionary pat down search of the outer clothing of a suspect (including articles and property under his or her immediate control) for the purpose of protecting the officer and others from possible violence in situations where the officer has reason to believe that crime is afoot. A frisk follows a stop and is predicated on a separate set of justifications. The justification for both a stop and a frisk were clearly outlined by the High Court in *Terry v. Ohio,* 392 U.S. 1, 88 S.Ct. 1868, 20 l.Ed.2d 889 (1968).

**fruit of the poisonous tree doctrine.** Evidence derived from illegal interrogations or searches is inadmissible in a subsequent adjudication against the criminal defendant, even when such evidence is gained indirectly, as a result of a violation of his or her constitutional rights. Sometimes called "derivative" or "secondary" evidence, the fruit of which is also referred to as "tainted" evidence, it is generally ruled inadmissible at a suppression hearing. There are a growing number of exceptions to the rule, e.g., the admission of tainted evidence under the "independent source" or "inevitable discovery" doctrine exception or the use of tainted evidence by a grand jury in issuing an indictment.

**fruits of the crime.** Currency, material objects, or other gains obtained through criminal means.

**frustration aggression theory.** Emerging in the 1940s and 1950s out of general learning theory, this social-psychological perspective (theory) of crime causation was largely promulgated by John Dollard and Neal Miller. They argued that as one's aspirations became impeded, frustration ensues, often leading to aggression and violence. Originally, the theory held that the venting of frustration and aggression, which built up over time, led to a reduction in violent behavior or a cathartic effect, a safety-valve concept. Later research has proven this assumption wanting, but has left the remainder of the theory largely intact.

**fugitive.** *n.* One who knowingly and intentionally flees from justice.

**Fugitive Felon Act (1932 and 1934).** A federal law making interstate flight across state lines to avoid prosecution or incarceration for the violation of a state felony or attempted felony or the avoidance of testifying in a felony case a federal offense. See 18 USCA § 1073.

**fugitive from justice.** One who has fled one state to avoid prosecution, incarceration, or testifying in a felony case.

**Fugitive Investigative Strike Team (FIST).** A team of United States Marshals Service (USMS) deputy marshals who can quickly assemble to respond to the apprehension of federal fugitives. The team coordinates its efforts with state and local police and law enforcement agencies located within the federal court district where the fugitive is located. The program was initiated in the 1980s as a result of the transfer of responsibility, ordered by the U.S. attorney general, for apprehending federal fugitives from the FBI to the USMS.

**fugitive slave laws.** Federal statutes passed between 1798 and 1850 requiring that asylum states and territories return slaves who had fled from a slaveholding state.

**full faith and credit clause.** Article IV § 1 of the Constitution providing for the various states to recognize the public laws and judicial decisions of all other states within the Union.

**functional specialization.** A type of horizontal differentiation in police organizations where employees are assigned specific duties based on their expertise, allowing less critical tasks to be assigned to nonsworn personnel.

**fundamental fairness.** Due process of law, as required under the Fifth and Fourteenth Amendments to the U.S. Constitution.

**fundamental law.** (1) The organic law of a sovereign state under which all statutory laws must comport in order to be legally viable, i.e., constitutional law. (2) Natural law, argued to be both morally and legally above positive (statutory) law.

**furlough.** *n.* (1) In military usage, a leave of absence for more than three days. (2) In a correctional setting, a leave during a period of incarceration.

E
F

# G

GAO, Government Accountability Office (Formerly the Government Accounting Office)
GOVID, Government Division Codes
GSR, gunshot residue

---

**gag order.** (1) An order issued by the court to attorneys and witnesses, preventing them from discussing the case with the media, in an attempt to assure the defendant a fair trial. (2) The gagging and sometimes restraining of an unruly defendant during the course of the trial. For example, in the infamous trial of the "Chicago Seven" (1969–1970), all seven defendants were ordered gagged and bound to their chairs by the presiding federal judge.

**Galton, Francis (1812–1911).** As an English scientist and one of the early criminologists, he was a pioneer in the emerging study of fingerprinting.

**gambling.** *v.* The act of placing a bet; gaming; game of chance; wager or bookmaking.

**gaming.** *n.* The practice of gambling. See *gambling*.

**gang.** *n.* (1) A group (usually of males) that develops in face-to-face relationships spontaneously and that achieves a degree of solidarity stemming from the perception of conflict in its immediate social environment. (2) A group of criminals or delinquents operating as a supportive unit in the furtherance of criminal matters.

**Garofalo, Raffaele (1852–1934).** An Italian criminologist who aided in the development of the concept of natural crime. According to Garofalo, natural crime involves behaviors offending fundamental moral values and the respect expected for the property rights of others. In his treatise *Criminology,* he creates a scheme of sanctions calling for the banishment or confinement of those disinclined to adapt to civil society.

**Garrity rule.** A rule holding that police officers can be disciplined and/or suffer employment termination for refusing to answer questions from the internal affairs unit. However, information disclosed cannot be used against officers in a subsequent criminal prosecution.

**garrote.** *n.* (1) An instrument for the execution of the condemned, used primarily by the Spanish, whereby the subject is strangled with an iron collar that is tightened by a screw. (2) Any disabling by strangulation.

**gas chromatography.** A chemical analysis used by forensic scientists to determine the identity of an unknown chemical substance. Technically known as gas–liquid chromatography, the process is conducted via the use of a gas chromatograph, a scientific device that analyzes a vaporized sample of the unknown substance by injecting it into a chromatographic column. There are a number of chromatographic methods, including gas chromatography, high-performance liquid chromatography, and thin-layer chromatography.

**Gatling, Richard Jordan (1818–1903).** The inventor of the Gatling gun, a gun mounted on wheels like a cannon, with multiple barrels firing as the gunner turns a crank; it was the forerunner to the modern-day machine gun.

**gauge.** *n.* In firearms usage, a term describing the size (inside diameter or bore) of a shotgun, e.g., 410, 28, 20, 16, 12, or 10 gauge.

*gemeinschaft.* *(Ger.)* Commonly contrasted against *gesellschaft*, and translatable as fellowship, community, or society in general. Utopian communities serve as a useful conceptual model.

*gendarme.* *(Fr.)* Originally a French cavalryman in command of a squad; in modern usage, an armed French police officer; in popular culture, any police officer.

*Gendarmerie Nationale.* *(Fr.)* In France, a military unit operating under the aegis of the minister of the armed forces, used primarily to police rural venues. See *gendarme.*

**general** The highest rank (category) of commissioned officers in the military; the naval counterpart is that of admiral. The military divides generals into five separate ranks: brigadier general (one star), major general (two stars), lieutenant general (three stars), general (four stars), and general of the army (five stars and an honorary rank no longer in use). Police organizations do not use the rank or title of general (with the notable exception of the Military Police Corps, where the provost marshal general usually holds the rank of major or lieutenant general).

**general deterrence.** One of the goals of criminal sentencing that seeks to prevent or inhibit criminal behavior through fear of punishment, directed at those who have not been arrested but who are tempted to commit a crime.

**general intent.** In criminal law, the intent to do what the law forbids; i.e., it is not necessary to prove that the defendant intended the specific harm or result that occurred because of his or her behavior (specific intent), simply that he or she intended to commit a specific act proscribed by law.

**general warrants.** See *writs of assistance.*

**genetic marker.** A metaphor for substances produced by the body that identify a specific individual, as a result of reproductive instructions transmitted by one's DNA.

*gesellschaft.* *(Ger.)* A German word frequently contrasted against *gemeinschaft* and meaning secular society.

**ghetto.** *n.* (1) Originally a sector of a European city where Jews were forced to live. (2) Any area of a city where disfranchised ethnic or racial minority groups live.

**Giambattista della Porta (1536–1615).** Considered by some scholars to be the first criminologist; an adherent of physiogonomics, he made detailed anthropometric measurements to create a typology of offenders.

**Gideon, Clarence Earl.** An indigent defendant erroneously charged with the burglary of a pool hall in Panama City, Florida; he sought an appeal on the grounds that he did not enjoy assistance of counsel because of his indigent status, as the state of Florida did not provide counsel in such cases. He was convicted and sentenced to five years in the state prison in 1961. In 1962, he appealed his case to the Supreme Court through an *in forma pauperis* petition. The High Court issued certiorari and assigned the case to Washington, DC, attorney Abe Fortas (who later became an associate justice of the High Court). Fortas argued that the assistance of counsel in a criminal trial constitutes a fundamental right protected by the Sixth Amendment and made applicable to the states in state action under the Fourteenth Amendment. The Court, ruling unanimously for the defense, overturned the conviction and remanded it for retrial. In 1963, Gideon was retried and acquitted. During the subsequent retrial, it was found that one of the witnesses against him in the first trial was in fact the actual perpetrator of the crime. See *Gideon v. Wainwright*, 372 U.S. 335, 83 S.Ct. 792, 9 L.Ed.2d 799 (1963).

**Glueck, Sheldon (1896–1980).** A celebrated American criminologist and jurist, he was instrumental at the Nuremberg War Crimes Trials (1945–1946); he and his wife Elinor became formative figures in American sociological and criminological thought.

**goal displacement.** A perspective developed by criminologists Chambliss and Seidman (1971), holding that goal displacement " . . . occurs when the expressed and agreed-upon goals of an organization are neglected in favor of some other goals." For example, although a hospital's formal goal may be to render aid to those in need of medical attention, that goal can easily be substituted by a drive to make a profit.

**Goffman, Erving (1922–1982).** Although not a criminologist in the strictest sense of the term, his contributions to the field are legendary. Among his areas of interest that influenced criminological thought was the notion of the face-to-face domain as an "interaction order," which he studied using microanalysis. His observational approach to investigating social interactions was concerned with process and adhered to no one theoretical proposition. His works use the dramaturgical perspective, incorporating this approach to everyday life. The works most important to criminology include *Presentation of Self in Everyday Life* (1956), *Asylums: Essays on the Social Situation of Mental Patients and Other Inmates* (1961), and *Stigma: Notes on the Management of Spoiled Identity* (1963).

**good faith exception.** An exception to the exclusionary rule holding that if an officer conducts a search or seizes evidence in good faith, believing that he or she is operating according to established legal standards, but later discovers that a mistake had been made (for example, in the search warrant application process), the evidence may still be admitted at trial. See *United States v. Leon,* 468 U.S. 897 (1984).

**good samaritan doctrine.** A protection from liability, recognized by law, under which a rescuer cannot be held civilly liable for attempting to assist another in imminent peril, who was placed there through the negligence of himself or herself or another, unless the rescuer worsens the distressed person's situation as a result of his or her reckless attempt at intervention.

**good time.** That time deducted from the official judicially imposed penal sentence as a result of good behavior or an automatic awarding via statute or correctional regulation.

**Goring, Charles Buckman (1870–1919).** A British physician and researcher who published *The English Convict,* arguing that criminal proclivities are correlated with mental deficiencies and related psychological problems as opposed to physical characteristics as suggested by Lombroso.

**Government Accountability Office (GAO).** The official watchdog-investigative agency for Congress, based in Washington, DC. The GAO is an independent nonpartisan federal investigative agency conducting, among other things, accounting audits on the various federal agencies. Formerly known as the Government Accounting Office, operating since 1921, its name was changed under the provisions of the *Human Capital Reform Act* (2004) PL 108–271, 118 Stat. 811 (2004).

**governmental immunity.** See *sovereign immunity* and *Federal Tort Claims Act*

**Government Division Codes (GOVID).** Codes developed by the U.S. Census Bureau, identifying the jurisdictional authority of various governments at the local and county levels and their corresponding police agencies throughout the nation.

**government secrets.** Recognized in evidence law as a privilege protecting governments from revealing "state secrets" or other information that would be damaging to state security and the public interest. See *state secrets*.

**governor's warrant.** See *rendition*.

**graffiti.** *n.* The willful defacing of property by the painting or drawing of symbols. It is often perpetrated by gang members in order to mark the parameters of their territory against the intrusion of other gangs.

**graft.** *n.* The act of obtaining money, personal gain, or advantage through means proscribed by law, by taking advantage of one's public office. For example, the illicit profit gained from a decision by a public official, influenced by received or promised personal advantages. See *bribery*.

**grandfather clause.** A proviso in a rule, policy, regulation, or legislation exempting those already vested under a preexisting rule, policy, regulation, legislation, or lack thereof, to continue to do what the new rule, policy, regulation, or legislation disallows.

**grand jury.** A group of citizens judicially empaneled for the purpose of determining whether there is sufficient cause to bind a criminal defendant over for trial. The grand jury was originally intended to be a buffer between the government and accused citizens and was commonly known as the "peoples' panel"; however, the grand jury has become a powerful investigative tool for law enforcement over the past several decades, using the sweeping powers of the subpoena *duces tecum* and the use of forced immunity. Generally consisting of twenty-three members, many grand juries function with as few as eighteen. There are two types of grand juries: (1) the standing grand jury, empaneled to hear cases unrelated to one another for a specified period, and (2) the special (investigative) grand jury that is empaneled for the express purpose of hearing a particular case or series of cases that are related (see 18 USCA 3331 *et seq.*). When a grand jury votes to indict a suspect, it issues a true bill; if it votes not to indict, it returns a no bill. In either case, the grand jury is guided by the prosecutor who asks for the indictments. In some instances, the grand jury may issue an indictment not requested by the prosecutor by way of a grand jury presentment. In a small number of instances, the grand jury may decide to investigate something the prosecutor is not interested in pursuing. In such cases, the grand jury is referred to as a "runaway" grand jury. Grand juries are also charged with some administrative oversight responsibilities, e.g., reporting on the condition of the county jail annually, in some jurisdictions.

**graphology.** *n.* The science of handwriting analysis.

**grass eaters.** Police officers who accept gratuities and/or protection moneys passively when voluntarily offered to them. Sometimes, recruit officers are offered protection money garnered by veteran officers, whether they desire it or not.

**gratuity.** *n.* The most commonly occurring form of police corruption involving gifts and favors offered to officers, generally out of self-interest on the part of the provider, with the implied expectation of improved police services, or the non- or under enforcement of various offenses.

**Green River Task Force.** A task force comprised of federal, state, and local police and law enforcement officials, charged with investigating the serial murder of forty-nine women in the area surrounding Seattle, Washington, during 1984.

**grid search.** A crime-scene search method that divides the area to be searched (usually a large outdoor scene) into a grid, formed by perpendicular lanes.

**grievance.** *n.* A formal complaint filed by the proper union representative with an organization regarding an issue covered under a collective bargaining agreement. Ideally, formal grievance procedures are instituted to protect officers against unfair discipline and to ensure due process. See *police officers' bill of rights.*

**grooves.** *n.* The depressions found in the rifling pattern in the barrel of a firearm; the inverse of lands (the raised portion of the rifling).

**guardian ad litem.** *(Lat.)* A special court-appointed guardian for juvenile offenders (infants) or those found to be incompetent.

**Guardian Angels.** A New York–based citizen protection organization (organized in 1979) that rides public transportation as a self-appointed peacekeeping group; the Guardian Angels also patrol other crime-prone hot spots and have received official recognition from some major American cities.

**guillotine.** *n.* An instrument used primarily by the French during the French Revolution to carry out capital punishment by beheading. It consists of a large weighty blade that is dropped between two channeled pillars.

**guilty.** *adj.* Legally adjudged an offender, blameworthy; culpable criminally.

**gumshoe.** *n.* Colloquialism for a detective (often a private detective), deriving from "gum" (rubber) and "shoe" (sneaker). *v.* To sneak around quietly.

**gun control laws.** Laws at the federal, state, and local level regulating firearm ownership, purchasing, manufacturing, distribution, sale, and possession.

**gunshot residue (GSR).** Residue resulting from the discharge of a firearm, composed of residues found in the primer, gunpowder, and projectile.

# H

**habeas corpus.** *(Lat.)* "You have the body." The shortened form of the writ of *habeas corpus ad subjiciendum.* The writ is a procedural device used to challenge the lawfulness of the detention of a person who has been taken into custody. The origins of *habeas corpus* can be traced to English common law that was formalized by an act of the British Parliament in 1679 and the American Constitution Article III, § 9, which reads: "The privilege of the writ of *habeas corpus* shall not be suspended, unless when in a case of rebellion or invasion the public safety may require it."

**Habeas Corpus Act.** *(Lat.)* See Article I, § 9, U.S. Const.; 28 USC § 2241.

**habeas corpus ad subjiciendum.** *(Lat.)* A writ directed to one detaining another (usually the county sheriff), demanding the production of the body for the purposes of judicial examination, in order to determine the lawfulness of the detention, commonly referred to as a writ of *habeas corpus.*

**habeas corpus ad testificandum.** *(Lat.)* A writ to the official having legal custody of a jail or prison inmate ordering him or her to deliver the prisoner to court for the purpose of being present at the hearing or to testify before it.

**habitual criminal laws.** Laws increasing the penalties for repeat offenders that have been instituted by various state legislatures and some national legislatures. See *Baumes's laws.*

**habitual offender.** One sentenced under the authority of a statute providing a more severe sanction than would be normally imposed for the violation of the committed offense alone, as a result of numerous prior felony convictions. Under this sentencing scheme, offenders are eligible for life imprisonment on the third or fourth conviction, depending on the jurisdiction. See *Baumes's laws.*

**habituation.** *n.* A psychological dependence on a given substance, not necessarily a controlled substance.

**halfway house.** (1). A treatment center whose origins date to 1845, where criminal offenders, i.e., prisoners or probationers, reside while conditionally released from confinement within a penal institution; (2) a center assisting mental patients in their readjustment to open society; and (3) a supervised living center assisting those with alcohol and drug addictions.

**haloperidol.** *n.* A substitute drug used in the treatment of those suffering withdrawal from heroin and methadone addiction; it is nonnarcotic and nonaddicting.

**hands-off doctrine.** A long-standing judicial policy of nonintervention in the administration and management of prisons, adhered to by American courts until the 1960s. For nearly four decades following, judicial intervention has notably increased, although there is a growing trend toward a new hands-off doctrine, as a result of the conservative shift in American politics.

**hanging.** *n.*  A method for carrying out a death sentence. In its original form, death from hanging was a result of a slow strangulation; today, however, death is faster, caused by an abrupt stop, after a seven-foot fall from the gallows.

**hangman.** *n.*  The executioner in charge of a hanging.

**Harlan, John Marshall (1833–1911).**  An associate justice of the Supreme Court of the United States, appointed by Rutherford B. Hayes in 1877, he was known for his dissent in rulings supporting racial discrimination and segregation. During his lifetime, he underwent a complete reversal regarding his attitude toward slavery and the enforcement of the fugitive slave laws, becoming a proponent of civil rights. He was opposed to the ruling in *Plessy v. Ferguson,* 163 U.S. 537 (1896), establishing the separate-but-equal doctrine.

**harmless error rule.**  A judicially generated rule holding that an error in not applying a federal constitutional protection can sometimes be of such insufficient magnitude as to not demand a reversal on appeal. See *Chapman v. California,* 386 U.S. 18 (1967).

**Harrison Narcotics Act (1914).**  The first major antidrug legislation in the United States at the federal level, restricting those dealing in opium, morphine, heroin, and cocaine to members of the medical profession. Illegal drug traffickers were subject to a $2,000 fine and as many as five years in prison.

**hashish.** *n.*  A drug produced from the leaves and stalks of the hemp plant.

**Hatch Act (1939).**  A federal act forbidding the intimidation, threat, or coercion of any person for the purpose of influencing his or her vote in a federal election. It further prohibits federal, state, county, and local employees from participating in specified types of political activities.

**hate crimes.**  (1). Acts of violence or intimidation intended to victimize, terrorize, or frighten unpopular groups or individuals as a result of their ethnic origin, religion, ideology, or sexual orientation. (2) A criminal offense committed against a person or property that is motivated, in whole or in part, by the offender's bias against a race, religion, disability, ethnicity or national origin, or sexual orientation (FBI Uniform Crime Reporting Definition).

**Hauptmann, Bruno Richard (1899–1936).**  The person convicted of the kidnapping and murder of the son of Charles Lindbergh; he was electrocuted at the state prison of New Jersey on April 3, 1936.

**Hawes-Cooper Act (1929).**  The federal law mandating that prison-made items involved in interstate commerce be subject to the same laws of the various states and territories of the United States as prison-made items from those states and territories. This federal law was passed largely as a result of political pressure from trade unions in response to the economic depression of that era.

**Hawthorne effect.**  George Elton Mayo was responsible for conducting behavioral research on employees at the Hawthorne Works of the Western Electric Company, in Chicago from 1924 to 1927. His findings have shed light on many of the dynamics of human relations and motivation theory. Among his numerous findings was the discovery that workers became more productive when they were aware that they were being observed, a phenomenon known as the "Hawthorne effect."

**Haymarket massacre.** The May 4, 1886, bombing incident by striking workers of the McCormick Reaper factory in Chicago. The Haymarket protest was called that evening by August Spies, a well-known journalist and anarchist. After the meeting, the commander of a 180-officer unit of the Chicago Police Department (CPD) ordered the attendees to disperse. Suddenly, a bomb was thrown into the police formation, and both sides fired handguns, resulting in the death of seven officers and numerous civilians, with many more police and civilian injuries. The riddle of who threw the bomb is unknown to this day. The CPD arrested a number of Chicago-based anarchists, all of whom were convicted at trial in Cook County. Seven defendants were sentenced to hanging, of which four were eventually hanged. The venerable Governor John P. Altgeld, a progressive reformer and learned constitutional jurist, pardoned the remaining survivors, writing a sixty-page pardon justification, claiming that both the judge and jury were responsible for judicial murder. This largely cost Altgeld his reelection in 1897.

**hearing.** *n.* A proceeding, generally coming before a formal trial, where facts, evidence, witnesses, and arguments are reviewed or heard by a judicial officer or an administrative body or officer (i.e, an administrative law judge) without a jury. Hearings, while technically formal proceedings, are actually noted for their informality.

**hearsay.** *n.* Out-of-court statements offered with the intent of proving the truth of the matter found in such statements. They become hearsay only when they are offered to prove that the statements themselves are true. There are numerous exceptions to the hearsay rule. See, e.g., *Federal Rules of Evidence* 803 and 804.

**hearsay evidence.** Hearsay that has been admitted into evidence, either by way of error on the judge's part, or as a result of one of the many exceptions to the hearsay rule. See *hearsay.*

**hematoporphyrin test.** A chemical test used to confirm the presence of blood.

**hemolysis.** *n.* The rupture of red corpuscles, causing an infusion of hemoglobin into the ambient blood fluid, upon exposure to lower concentrations of salts than commonly found in blood plasma.

**Henry system.** A fingerprint classification system developed in 1901 by Sir Edward Richard Henry. The system separates fingerprints into four categories: arches, loops, whorls, and composites.

**heroin.** *n.* A habit-forming narcotic; a white crystalline form of a morphine derivative and one of the most widely used narcotic drugs in the United States.

**Herzberg's motivation-hygiene theory.** A perspective postulated by Frederick Herzberg, claiming that a set of extrinsic job conditions exist and that when these conditions are not present, dissatisfaction among employees results. Dissatisfying (hygiene) factors include job security, salary, working conditions, quality of technical support, status, company policies, and work-related interpersonal relations between peers, supervisors, and subordinates. Intrinsic job conditions also exist that satisfy employees; they include achievement, recognition, the work itself, responsibility, personal growth, advancement, and development.

**hierarchy rule.** When UCR data are submitted to the FBI, by contributing police and law enforcement agencies across the United States for index offenses, only the most serious crime for any single criminal incident is reported, assuming the incident involves more than one crime. For example, if a convenience store is robbed, and the clerk is killed during the robbery, only the homicide is reported. Arson, however, is an exception to this rule, as arson is often used in an attempt to cover up another crime and constitutes a separate and distinct offense in and of itself.

**high crimes and misdemeanors.** A phrase mentioned in the Constitution meaning criminal offenses sufficient to warrant an impeachment by the lower house of Congress, the House of Representatives. An impeachment is tantamount to an indictment, the trial of which rests with the upper house of Congress, the Senate.

**higher-law doctrine.** A juridic position claiming that the law of nature, i.e., natural law, is intrinsically superior to man-made positive (statutory) law.

**high misdemeanor.** A misdemeanor rising to the level approaching a felony; a misdemeanor of the highest category. Many states categorize misdemeanors according to a severity scale, with lesser offenses being at the bottom of the paradigm and more severe offenses located at the top, e.g., offenses A–D or 1–4. Some high misdemeanors may also be chargeable as felonies and may be dealt with by a grand jury, as they constitute "bastard" offenses.

**high-seas law enforcement.** Law enforcement conducted by the U.S. Coast Guard within the territorial waters of the nation, its protectorates and vassal states, contiguous zones, and special interest areas of the high seas, including federal law and various international agreements.

**High Sheriff.** The modern-day office of the sheriff in England, having derived from the original reeve of the shire (county). The sheriff's office in England no longer has any real policing or enforcement responsibilities. Thus, the office of the High Sheriff is little more than a ceremonial appointment.

**high-speed pursuit.** See *hot pursuit, vehicular.*

**highway patrol.** A less intrusive form of state-level policing that followed the development of state police, as a more traffic safety-oriented organization, without the full range of law enforcement and police authority inherent in a state police organization. The trend today is to expand the authority of highway patrol organizations to a more state police-like model.

**hijacking.** *v.* A popular term used to describe a variety of statutorily proscribed behaviors including the taking control of any vehicle and/or the driver and passengers through the use of force (unlawful restraint, kidnapping, and/or robbery), or threatened use of force or by intimidation, stealth in order to steal the vehicle or its contents or both (theft or larceny).

**Hirschi's control theory.** A criminological perspective (theory) developed originally by Travis Hirschi and later integrated with social bond, social control, and strain theories with colleague Michael Gottfredson, to explain criminal behavior as a failure to exercise self-control as an intervening variable. Eventually this perspective became a general theory of crime.

**Hirschi, Travis (1935– ).** Known for his formulation of Social Bond Theory, set forth in his 1969 book *Causes of Delinquency*; he posits that social bonds (an element found in Control Theory) largely determine whether one engages in a licit life or one of crime. The theory's four bonds include attachment, commitment, involvement, and belief.

**hit and run.** The unlawful flight by the operator of a motor vehicle from the scene of a vehicular accident resulting in death, injury, or damage to the property of another.

**Hobbes, Thomas (1588–1679).** A celebrated English social philosopher and author of the *Leviathan*, he was an apologist of utilitarian punishment for criminal offenders; i.e., punishment must be proportional to the offense, not carried out for the purpose of retribution; it must follow a public condemnation and be dispensed by the proper public authority in order to persuade people to obey the law.

**Hobbs Act (1947).** An act of Congress intended to suppress labor racketeering by imposing additional penalties on those convicted of robbery or extortion when they obstruct or impede the course of interstate commerce.

**Holmes, Oliver Wendell, Jr. (1841–1935).** Appointed to the High Court by President Theodore Roosevelt, he served as an associate justice of the Court from 1902 to 1932, where he was known as the "great dissenter." He graduated from Harvard Law in 1866 and wrote the *Common Law* in 1881.

**holograph.** *n.* An unattested will or deed constructed entirely by the person (testator or grantor) in his or her own hand. State laws vary as to the legally binding status of such self-made wills. Under the *Uniform Probate Code,* § 2–503, such "holographic" wills are valid given that the signature and content are in the handwriting of the testator.

**Homeland Security.** See *Department of Homeland Security (DHS)*.

**homerule.** *n.* A constitutional provision or legislative action resulting in a degree of autonomy in self-government for some municipalities, e.g., cities and towns, if the local government formally accepts the terms of the enabling legislation offered by the sovereign state. In some states, certain counties may also enjoy homerule status.

**homestead.** *n.* The house and adjoining land and buildings encompassing the primary house in which the head of the family resides. Under modern homestead statutes, the homestead is an artificial estate in land, constructed to protect the possessions and use of the owner against his or her creditors by creating a homestead exemption, wherein the property is excluded from an execution and forced sale, as long as the land is occupied as a domicile.

**Homestead strike and massacre (July 6, 1892).** A confrontation between strikers and Pinkerton guards at the Carnegie Steel Corporation, of Homestead, Pennsylvania. Ten people were killed, including strikers and guards; the union was broken, and the state militia was called in to restore order. This and other labor conflicts like it eventually led to "anti-Pinkerton legislation" and the emergence of the state police.

**homicide.** *n.* (1) The killing of a human being by another, e.g., the lawful killing in the performance of a duty (justifiable homicide) or the unlawful and/or intentional killing of another (murder). (2) Murder and nonnegligent manslaughter are defined as the willful (nonnegligent) killing of one human being by another (FBI Uniform Crime Reporting Definition). Note that not included in the UCR definition are deaths caused by negligence, suicides, or accidental deaths; attempted murders are classified as aggravated assaults.

**Hooton, Earnest Albert (1887–1954).** An American physical anthropologist and biological determinist.

**Hoover Commissions.** A series of commissions over which Herbert Hoover was the chairman, spanning 1947–1949 and 1953–1955 (Commission on the Reorganization of the Executive Branch). His unshakable reputation for trustworthiness and his status as a former president made him the likely choice to chair these commissions, where he was focused on uncovering inefficiency.

**Hoover, John Edgar (1895–1972).** Appointed the first director of the newly formed Federal Bureau of Investigation (FBI) in 1924, he held the position for forty-eight years. Presidents were literally afraid to replace him and deferred to him on matters that a bureaucrat had no legitimate authority to demand. He was the only chief bureaucrat to have a state funeral in the national rotunda. Expanding the espionage authority granted him by President Franklin D. Roosevelt, he largely changed the mission of the FBI from a law enforcement agency into an internal intelligence and espionage agency, where his personal ideological persuasions were followed. Failing to take a stand on organized crime in its nascent stages, he allowed the mob to gain strength during its formative years. Heavily criticized after his death, he remains at once the bright light in law enforcement and a bureaucrat who took the bureau into the troubled waters of ideological policing.

**hostage.** *n.* One confined or offered as a pledge for the attainment of specified agreements or conditions. Under international law the use of hostages is expressly forbidden. See *Geneva Convention (1949).*

**hot pursuit doctrine.** Officers in fresh pursuit of a fugitive need not seek a search warrant to continue their chase into buildings and homes, and items found pursuant to the incident are admissible at trial. See *fresh pursuit.*

**hot pursuit, vehicular.** Also known as high-speed pursuit or police vehicle pursuit, it is the vehicular pursuit of an offender by police officers, where the subject knows the police intend to stop him or her, and where the offender either increases his or her speed or drives in an evasive manner to avoid apprehension. A controversial and invasive police practice, argued by many opponents to contravene the primary mission of the police, i.e., the protection of public safety.

**hot spots.** Areas demanding a disproportional number of calls for service from police and/or an area having an extremely high crime rate.

**house arrest.** The monitored restriction of a subject to his or her residence or another venue before an adjudication or hearing. House arrest has been imposed legally and extralegally throughout history.

**housebreaking.** *v.* The unlawful breaking into a house or dwelling place of another with the intent to commit a crime therein. See *burglary.*

**House Un-American Activities Committee (HUAC).** A congressional committee headed by Wisconsin Senator Joseph McCarthy to ferret out those disloyal to the United States and who had communist connections. In the name of internal security, the committee proceeded to hunt Communists to advance the individual careers of its members. HUAC's investigation of Hollywood led to blacklisting many who were called to testify during the 1950s. See *McCarthyism.*

**Howard.** *n.* The appellate case law reporter for U.S. Supreme Court rulings, spanning (1843–1860). Before the introduction of the *United States Reports (U.S.),* and the *United States Supreme Court Reports Lawyer's Edition/Second Edition (L.Ed., or*

*L.Ed. 2d),* a series of lesser-known reports covered the decisions of the High Court; they include: *Dallas* (1790–1800), *Cranch* (1801–1815), *Wheaton* (1816–1827), *Peters* (1828–1842), *Howard* (1843–1860), *Black* (1861–1862), and *Wallace* (1863—1874). Today, these early reports have been catalogued in the *U.S. Reports* and other reporters for the convenience of legal researchers.

**Howard, John (1726–1790).** An early prison reformer in England, his efforts resulted in the passage of the Penitentiary Act of 1779. Earlier in his career (approximately two decades), Howard had been sheriff of Bedfordshire. He wrote *State of Prisons,* based on his first-hand experiences with the English prison system. Today, the John Howard Association is active in prison monitoring and reform initiatives.

**hue and cry.** In early England, a system under which an alarm was sounded by the shouting of citizens pursuing a felon. All able-bodied men were expected to join in the pursuit. See *frankpledge.*

**hulks.** *n.* Unseaworthy sea-going vessels, used in England during the eighteenth century as detention centers for criminal offenders.

**hundred.** *n.* The Saxon organization of England, which divided the nation into shires (counties) subdivided into hundreds, with each hundred having ten tithings (groups of ten families of freeholders or frankpledges). Each hundred was overseen by a high constable and operated its own court. The actual size of a hundred was likely derived from one hundred hides of land, a unit of measure still in use in the state of Delaware.

**hung jury.** A jury that is so irreconcilably divided as to be unable to come to a decision. If the judge is satisfied that the hung jury cannot produce a verdict, the trial is terminated. Generally, the case is sent back for retrial; however, charges are sometimes dismissed at this juncture.

**hydroplaning.** *v.* A skimming along the water's surface. Automobile tires sometimes skim along the water's surface, thus reducing or eliminating the coefficient of friction necessary to steer or stop the vehicle.

*hyperlexis. (Lat.)* The excessive creation of laws.

**hypoglycemia.** *n.* A low blood sugar condition that can cause behavioral problems in some people, e.g., anxiety, severe headaches, confusion, fatigue, and aggressive behavior.

# I

IAATI, International Association of Auto Theft Investigators
IACP, International Association of Chiefs of Police
IAD, Internal Affairs Division
IAPP, International Association of Police Professors
IAU, Internal Affairs Unit
ICAP, Integrated Criminal Apprehension Program
ICC, Interstate Commerce Commission
ICE, Immigration and Customs Enforcement
ICMA, International City Management Association
ICPI, Insurance Crime Prevention Institute
ICPSR, Inter-University Consortium for Political and Social Research
IG, inspector general
ILEIA, International Law Enforcement Instructors Agency
ILETA, International Law Enforcement Training Agency
INS, Immigration and Naturalization Services (United States)
INSLAW, Institute for Law and Social Research
INTERPOL, International Criminal Police Organization
IPS, Intensive Probation Supervision
IRS, Internal Revenue Service

---

**identification record.** The official criminal record, kept by the bureau of identification of a public police or law enforcement agency, generally including arrest details, demographic data, convictions, dispositions, and fingerprints.

**Identi-Kit.** An identification device invented by a former Los Angeles Police Department officer, consisting of over 500 transparencies, allowing an officer to create a likeness of a suspect by overlaying combinations of facial features until an approximate likeness is produced.

**ignorance of the law.** A legal principle holding that a law violator cannot raise a viable defense because he or she was not aware that such behavior was legally proscribed.

**ignorantia legis non excusat.** *(Lat.)* A legal principle holding that the wrongdoer does not escape criminal responsibility simply because he or she was not aware that his or her actions constituted a violation of the law. See *ignorance of the law.*

**illegal detention.** Any detention not sanctioned by law, legal process, or procedure; a detention made under color of law. Confessions made under such circumstances may not be admissible at trial.

**ill fame.** Of notoriously bad character, e.g., houses of ill fame or houses of prostitution.

**Illinois plan.** A bail procedure developed for pretrial defendants, whereby the defendant is required to post only 10 percent of the full amount of the bail bond. After appearing in court at the appointed time and date, 90 percent of the bond is returned to the defendant. See *bail reform.*

**Immigration and Customs Enforcement (ICE).** Combining the former departments of Immigration and Naturalization Service (INS) and the U.S. Customs Service, the Homeland Security bill's federal reorganization section created ICE in March of 2003. The newly formed federal law enforcement agency attempts to better coordinate the targeting of illegal immigrants, and people, materials, and money used in the support of terrorist activities against the United States, in what the Department of Homeland Security calls a "layered defense" approach.

**Immigration and Naturalization Service (INS).** This federal agency, first begun as the U.S. Bureau of Immigration under the Treasury Department, evolved to embrace the broader function of naturalization services in 1933; it eventually became part of the Justice Department in 1940 and later part of the newly formed Department of Homeland Security (2003), under the title of Bureau of Immigration and Customs Enforcement (ICE), see that term. The organization is charged with the administration of immigration and naturalization statutes of the United States, including admission, exclusion, expulsion (deportation), and the naturalization of aliens.

**immigration laws.** A set of laws disallowing entrance into the United States. Various classes of peoples are denied entry, including beggars, felons, prostitutes, physically or mentally diseased persons, and contract laborers. See *Immigration and Naturalization Act,* 8 USCA 1101.

**immunity.** *n.* Exemption, release, or freedom from legal obligations, duties, and requirements; special privilege. Several types of established immunities are recognized by law, e.g., sovereign immunity, governmental tort immunity, and diplomatic immunity.

**Immunity Act (1954).** A federal statute granting the authority to Congress to compel testimony that may be self-incriminating by a grant of immunity to the witness, in cases of national security. The attorney general must first be notified in order to present any objections. Congressional committees and the federal district courts as well as federal grand juries may compel testimony under the provisions of the act; a process known as use or forced immunity.

**immunity bath.** (1) A granting of immunity to witnesses who may give self-incriminating testimony that bathes them in immunity from any future prosecution based in whole or in part on the testimony produced. Forced or use immunity was later introduced to end the abuses of immunity baths. Under forced or use immunity, the witness must testify, despite possible self-incrimination; however, if the government can build a case against him or her independent of the immunized testimony, a trial may proceed. (2) The term is sometimes used to depict an excessive number of potential defendants who have been granted absolute immunity from prosecution.

**immunization.** *n.* The process of being immunized; the condition or status of being immunized; being protected from criminal prosecution.

**impanel.** *v.* To select and impanel a jury (either a petit or grand) that will hear or investigate a case. The term is also used for the selection and emplacement of various nonjuridical tribunals, commissions, and committees.

**impeach.** *v.* (1) To discredit a witness in open court. (2) To charge a public official with wrongdoing, through a process where the lower house of the legislature issues articles of impeachment. Note that an impeachment is the equivalent to a grand jury indictment in a criminal proceeding and not a conviction.

**impeachment.** *n.* A criminal inquisitory proceeding conducted to determine whether a public officer should be charged (by the lower house, i.e., the House of Representatives) and tried by the upper house of the legislature, i.e., the Senate, which functions as the jury. The House of Representatives functions much like a grand jury, determining whether to file articles of impeachment (the functional equivalent of an indictment or true bill) against a public official. The impeachment trial is conducted by the Senate, and in the federal government is overseen by the chief justice of the Supreme Court. In the federal system, the power of impeachment is provided under Article II § 4 of the Constitution.

**impersonation.** *n.* The unlawful imitation of a public official or an employee or one licensed by the state to provide some professional practice or skilled trade.

**implied consent law.** Any law requiring one to submit to something, a blood alcohol test, for example, as a condition to accepting the privilege of driving. Concomitant with the implied consent requirement of the given statute is a rebuttable presumption provision.

**importation model.** A correctional perspective used to explain prison culture and prisoner behavior as a result of values and attitudes imported from the outside world, as opposed to the culture and behaviors generated within the prison environment.

**impossibility, defense of.** A defense that contends that the act was one that the defendant could not perform, under the following categories: physically impossible; relatively impossible (impossibility in fact); practically impossible; legally or juridically impossible; or logically impossible.

**impoundment.** *n.* The confiscation or seizure by police or law enforcement authorities of evidence, materials, booty, and/or instrumentalities used in the commission of a crime.

**imprisonment.** *n.* (1) The lawful and involuntary placement of a person in a prison. (2) The forcible (and sometimes unlawful) confinement of a person in or at any location.

**impulse.** *n.* A sudden proclivity, inclination, or urge to act.

**impunity.** *n.* The exemption or freedom from consequences, penalty, punishment, harm, or loss.

**in absentia.** *(Lat.)* Literally meaning "in the absence of." It is commonly used for a trial where the defendant is not present. The defendant's absence is generally a result of his or her fleeing the jurisdiction either before or after the trial has begun. Under U.S. law, the defendant waives his or her constitutional protection to face his or her accuser(s) when he or she flees.

**inadmissibility.** *adj.* Unacceptability; the inability to gain admittance into evidence for trial, under recognized rules of evidence and procedure, e.g., evidence gained from an unconstitutional search and seizure becomes inadmissible.

**inalienable rights.** Those rights that are not capable of surrender or transfer without the express consent of the person in possession of such rights. Originally, those rights conferred by God; not human-made rights; those rights recognized under natural law.

*in articulo mortis. (Lat.)* At the point of death.

*in camera. (Lat.)* In chambers (of the judge); in private. See *in camera inspection.*

*in camera* **inspection.** An inspection of a document, item, witness, or other person by the judge in private, usually in his or her chambers, or with the courtroom cleared.

**incapacitation.** *n.* The condition or status of being in want of capacity; the lack of legal, physical, moral, or mental capacity.

**incarceration.** *n.* An imprisonment or confinement in a penal, correctional, or custodial facility.

**incendiary.** *n.* (1) A person who knowingly and willfully damages or destroys property by fire or a fire-producing mechanism. *adj.* (2) The type of device used to set a fire.

**incest.** *n.* The act of unlawful sexual intercourse between a man and a woman who are so closely related to one another as to prevent a legal marriage. See *Model Penal Code,* § 230.2.

**inchoate.** *adj.* Incomplete; unfinished; incipient; rudimentary. An inchoate crime substantially lacks the necessary *actus reus* element required for an act or omission to be classified as a crime, e.g., a conspiracy to commit a crime never carried to its fruition.

**incite.** *v.* To foment or instigate a criminal action.

**included offenses.** Generally referred to as "lesser included offenses," they are offenses composed of a combination of other offenses considered less serious; e.g., robbery inherently includes the offense of theft, a lesser offense.

**incompetent evidence.** That evidence not permissible under the accepted rules of evidence and procedure.

**incorrigibility.** *n.* In juvenile justice, the unmanageable and often uncontrollable behavior of a minor child, which by definition constitutes juvenile delinquency.

**incorrigible.** *adj.* That which is incapable of being corrected, improved, or reformed. In juvenile justice usage, a child who is unmanageable.

**incriminate.** *v.* To blame, accuse, or suggest culpability in crime.

**inculpate.** *v.* To blame, incriminate, accuse, or suggest guilt in crime.

**inculpatory.** *adj.* That which tends to incriminate and suggest involvement or culpability in crime.

**incumbrance (encumbrance).** *n.* A hindrance; a claim, lien, or liability against property.

**indecent exposure.** The unlawful, knowing, and intentional exposure to the sight of others, in a lewd or indecent manner, those parts of the body that are considered private and that a reasonable person would attempt to keep covered from public view.

*in delicto. (Lat.)* At fault; responsible.

**indemnification.** *n.* A protection from loss, harm, or damage; a compensation for loss.

**indeterminate sentence.** A sentencing scheme where an offender is sentenced to a nonfixed range of incarceration, e.g., from three to six years as opposed to a determinant sentence of five years.

**index offenses.** The specific eight crimes found in the FBI's *Uniform Crime Reports* that constitute Part I offenses: willful homicide, arson, forcible rape, robbery, burglary, aggravated assault, larceny over fifty dollars, and motor vehicle theft.

**indicia.** *n.* Indications; indices; characteristic marks; circumstances supporting or suggesting the existence of a fact as probable; denoting facts giving rise to inferences, as opposed to inferences in and of themselves; likened to circumstantial evidence.

**indictment.** *n.* A formal written accusation presented to the court by a grand jury, charging one or more persons with the violation of a statute(s) after an examination of the facts. The indictment comes in the form of a bill of indictment (a true bill) or a presentment and may charge numerous counts. See *charging document, filing, information,* or *presentment.*

**indigent.** *adj.* (1) Destitute; needy; poor. (2) In law, the financial inability to retain counsel.

**indirect evidence.** Evidence inferring, suggesting, or supporting but not directly proving facts at issue. See *circumstantial evidence.*

**individualized treatment.** A correctional philosophy holding that individuals differ in the causation underlying their criminality. As such, treatment should take into account the unique issues involved and engineer a treatment program crafted to the individual offender's deficiencies.

**industrial school.** A dated name for a juvenile institution for boys, where industrial training was given; a reform school.

**inebriate.** *n.* (1) One who is frequently intoxicated with alcohol. *v.* (2) To intoxicate.

**inevitable discovery doctrine.** Evidence made admissible, despite the fact that it had been garnered as a result of an illegal search and seizure or some other governmental misconduct; e.g., a warrantless search and seizure of evidence that would have inevitably been discovered. Given attenuation of the connection between the official misconduct and its exclusion (as a result of suppression), such suppression would not serve as a substantial deterrent to such conduct in the future by agents (police and law enforcement officers) of the state or federal government; thus, the evidence is admitted into evidence at trial. See *Nix v. Williams,* 467 U.S. 431, 448 (1984); see also the *attenuation doctrine.*

**in extremis.** *(Lat.)* In the last stages or extremities; the last illness; near death, although not necessarily *in articulo mortis.*

**infamous punishment.** Imprisonment at hard labor, generally in a state prison or penitentiary.

**infancy.** *n.* The condition or state of a person who is "chronologically" less than the age of majority, at common law twenty-one, but in contemporary criminal justice usage seventeen or eighteen years of age, depending on the jurisdiction.

**infanticide.** *n.* The murder of a baby.

**inferior court.** (1) A court functioning at the municipal level of government and, as such, not a part of the state trial court system and not a court of record. A court located in a nonunified court system and overseen by a judge who is generally an elected official, often with no law degree or license to practice law. Given that this type of court does not keep a record and the fact that it is not part of the state trial court system, no appeal is possible to the state appellate court. A trial *de novo* (as new) must be sought in the state trial court system. (2) A court subordinate to appellate courts in a given judicial system, e.g., a state trial court.

**in flagrante delicto.** *(Lat.)* In the commission of the act or crime; caught red-handed.

**informant.** *n.* (1) One who provides information and is used as a source. (2) In an undercover investigative context, a person, officer, or agent in a clandestine activity who is rewarded in some way for his or her services. Under federal law, rewards are provided under 18 USCA § 3059.

**in forma pauperis.** *(Lat.)* The permission given to an indigent by the court to proceed in a matter without concern for costs and fees.

**information.** *n.* A formal criminal accusation against a person(s) prepared by the prosecutor and presented to the court without an indictment. Many states provide for the information processing of a complaint without the use of a grand jury; however, in federal courts a grand jury indictment is required in all felony prosecutions.

**informer's privilege.** The right of the police not to reveal the identity of informants in order to protect them from retaliation and for use as future confidential sources. Cautious judges, however, often require the informant to appear for an *in camera* inspection in his or her chambers to ensure police veracity.

**infra.** *(Lat.)* That which follows; found within or under; the reverse of *supra*.

**infraction.** *n.* A lesser offense, carrying a sanction of fine only; many times these include municipal ordinance violations, like overtime parking. Some statutory offenses for which the only available sentence is a fine and which is specifically noted as an infraction.

**infrared light.** Light in the range of approximately 8,000 to 9,000 angstroms and having a wavelength greater than visible red. Not to be confused with ultraviolet light, which is at the opposite end of the light spectrum. Infrared light is used by criminalists to read erased or obliterated markings.

**infrared motion detector.** An electronic sensor used to detect changes in the infrared light radiated from things within a protected area.

**ingress.** *n.* An access or place of entrance for people or vehicles.

**in initio.** *(Lat.)* In the beginning, at the initial stages.

**initial appearance.** The first judicial appearance by the accused.

**injunction.** *n.* A judicial order directed to a person(s), requiring that person(s) to do (a mandatory injunction) or refrain from doing (a preventive injunction) a particular act or thing. Injunctions may be temporary, as in preliminary or interlocutory injunctions, or permanent. Injunctions are made enforceable through the contempt authority of the issuing court.

**in loco.** *(Lat.)* In place of; in lieu of.

**in loco parentis.** *(Lat.)* In the place of the parent(s).

**in nomine.** *(Lat.)* In the name of.

**in pari delicto.** *(Lat.)* Equal culpability in criminality.

**in personam.** *(Lat.)* Legal action directed against the person, as distinguished against *in rem* (against the thing, "property").

*in primis.* *(Lat.)* In the first place or instance.

**inquest.** *n.* An investigation or inquiry under the authority of a coroner or medical examiner, often with the aid of a jury, into the death of a person where foul play is suspected.

**inquisitorial system.** The criminal justice system used by most continental European nations, as well as various other civil law countries. An investigative magistrate is assigned to investigate a criminal case, unlike the common-law arrangement where the judge is a neutral actor during the trial only.

*in re.* *(Lat.)* "In the affair of." Usually used as a method of entitling a proceeding, where no adversary is present or in a situation where a party makes a motion in his or her own behalf, although this type of proceeding is commonly titled "*ex parte*_____."

*in rem.* *(Lat.)* A term denoting a proceeding or legal action against the thing, as opposed to a person; an asset forfeiture proceeding is an *in rem* action, as it is instituted wholly against the property.

**insanity.** *n.* In legal usage, a term indicating the necessary degree of mental illness or capacity to negate one's legal culpability, responsibility, or capacity.

**insanity defense.** An affirmative defense, claiming that the defendant was not sane, therefore, not criminally culpable, as the *mens rea* requirement is absent. The *Model Penal Code,* § 401, reads, "A person is not responsible for criminal conduct if at the time of such conduct as a result of mental disease or defect he lacks substantial capacity to either appreciate the criminality (wrongfulness) of his conduct or to conform his conduct to the requirements of the law." See *diminished capacity*; *diminished responsibility*; *Durham rule*; *irresistible impulse*; the *M' Naghten rule*; and *substantial capacity.*

**Insanity Defense Reform Act (1984).** The act establishes the affirmative defense of insanity where more than mere mental disease or defect is at play; that is, the defense must prove that as a result of a severe mental disease or defect the accused was unable to recognize either the nature or quality of the wrongfulness of his or her act(s).

**insider trading.** The illegal use of nonpublic financial information for the purpose of gaining an unfair advantage in securities trading, a Federal Trade Commission (FTC) violation.

**inspector general (IG).** That government official charged with the oversight, inspection, and auditing of a particular public service agency, e.g., the Inspector General of the Los Angeles Police Department. Inspectors general are found at nearly all levels of government in the United States and serve in an important watchdog capacity.

**inspectional services.** That bureau within a bureaucratized police organization responsible for internal affairs, inspections, adherence to the standard operating procedures of the department, and intelligence gathering.

**instanter.** *adv.* Immediately, forthwith, and without delay; when appearing on a writ it means that the officer or class of officer to whom the writ is directed must execute it as soon as practicable (this has generally been interpreted to be within 24 hours).

**Institute for Court Management (ICM).** An educational and research-oriented professional organization established in 1971, the institute has two primary purposes: to educate those directly involved in the court system and to research issues of concern regarding the management, administration, and effectiveness of American courts. It publishes the *Justice System Journal* three times yearly and is located in Denver, Colorado.

**Institute for Criminal Law and Procedure.** Founded (1965) at Georgetown University, it provides empirically based research data on criminal law–related issues including plea bargaining, bail, pretrial release, and repeat-offender statutes.

**Institute for Law and Social Research (INSLAW).** A nonprofit research-based institution focused on investigating issues of social concern within the sphere of legal process. INSLAW researchers engineered the Prosecutor's Management Information System (PROMIS), and INSLAW publishes the *Promis Newsletter* on a quarterly basis. Located in Washington, DC, INSLAW was founded in 1973 and became a nonprofit organization in 1981.

**institutional capacity.** The official maximum number of inmates for which a confinement or residential facility is rated or intended to house.

**institutionalized personality.** A commonly used term to denote a personality so accustomed to life within an institutional (penal) environment so that life outside its confines seems daunting.

**instrumentalities.** *n.* Those things used in the commission of a crime.

**insubordination.** *n.* The act of being disobedient; the act of not submitting to authority.

**insularity.** *n.* The state of existing on an island, thus, narrow-mindedness; prejudice.

**Insurance Crime Prevention Institute (ICPI).** Established in 1971 and located in Westport, Connecticut, the institute is funded by a group of over 400 insurance companies. The ICPI's mission is to seek criminal prosecutions against those who attempt to defraud the industry. The institute publishes *The ICPI Report*, a quarterly newsletter.

**insurgency.** *n.* The rebellious rising up against governmental authority.

**insurrection.** *n.* A rebellion or revolt against governmental authority.

**intake.** *n.* (1) The initial processing stage at which a juvenile offender is received by probation officials where a classification decision is made, i.e., whether to proceed with formal processing (issuing a petition to the juvenile court), referral to another agency, or diversion. (2) The general term used for initial receiving of subjects into any of the processes or institutions of criminal justice.

**Integrated Ballistics Identification System (IBIS).** A digital ballistics fingerprinting database developed by the Bureau of Alcohol, Tobacco, Firearms, and Explosives (BATFE) in 2000, which is employed in the identification of firearms and ammunition suspected of being used in criminal incidents. IBIS is an adjunct of the National Integrated Ballistics Information Network (NIBIN), a ballistics fingerprinting database also operated by the BATFE.

**Integrated Criminal Apprehension Program (1976).** This ICAP-sponsored program, established in 1976, was originally focused primarily on improving police patrol methods but was later expanded to include criminal investigations, warrant service, as well as other areas. The program's goals focus on increasing the clearance rate for violent crime cases through improved police practices.

**intelligence.** *n.* In criminal law usage, the acquisition of information relative to crime; intelligence is of two basic types: (1) strategic intelligence (gathered and stored for its potential value) and (2) tactical intelligence (information used in-the-field in a law enforcement capacity).

**Intensive Probation Supervision (IPS).** A form of probation supervision requiring frequent face-to-face interactions between the probationer and the probation officer, often resulting from nonscheduled visits.

**intent.** *n.* The state of mind behind a criminal act. The determination under which one acts; inferred from his or her behavior; one of the parts of the *mens rea*. Not to be confused with motive, the reason for carrying out the criminal act, which need not be proven at trial.

**interactionist school of criminology.** Closely linked with labeling theory, it has its roots in the work of two early pioneers of the twentieth century: Charles H. Cooley (1864–1929) and George Herbert Mead (1863–1931). Essentially, the school's perspective posits that one's self-image comes from the perspectives of others or from how one perceives how others see one's self. Also known as the school of symbolic interactionism.

**Interactionist Theory.** A criminological perspective (theory) holding that crime is often created by agencies of social control as a result of the stigmatizing effects of the process itself, as people tend to act according to the labels they are given (Labeling Theory). This approach led to the noninterventionist perspective of the 1960s. See *Edwin Shur.*

**inter alia.** *(Lat.)* "Among other things." An abbreviation used to indicate a shortened version of something, when not citing an entire body of literature.

**inter arma silent leges.** *(Lat.)* Translated as "during war the law is silent," and deriving from Cicero's maxim *silent enim leges inter arma* ("when arms speak, the laws are silent"). This political/legal doctrine is frequently invoked during times of national emergencies and diminishes the civil liberties, due-process safeguards, and other constitutional protections of citizens in the name of national security. Abraham Lincoln, e.g., suspended the writ of *habeas corpus* during much of the American Civil War. Civil libertarians fear that this doctrine looms ominously in twenty-first century America, given the "war" on terrorism worldwide. See *Ex Parte Milligan* 71 U.S. 2(4 Wall) (1886) and *Korematsu v. United States* 323 U.S. 214 (1944).

**intercept order.** A type of search warrant specifically authorizing a police or law enforcement agency to legally wiretap or "intercept" telephone and other forms of electronic communications.

**interlocutory.** *adj.* In legal usage, something pronounced during the course of a legal action, pending the final decision; a temporary court order or appellate court ruling.

**interlocutory appeal.** A review regarding a prejudgment decision, requested by the lower court (judge) to the appropriate appellate court, concerning an issue of law or decision about some point of law or evidentiary procedure not clearly addressed in existing case law, during the course of the trial.

**intermediate court.** Any court having general jurisdiction, whether at trial or appeals, but which is situated below the court of last resort in that specific sovereign state.

**intern.** *v.* (1) To confine or restrict any person or group, e.g., the internment of American Japanese during World War II. *n.* (2) An advanced student undergoing a hands-on practical or clinical experience as a requirement for graduation or receipt of professional license.

**Internal Affairs Division (IAD).** That unit within a police agency charged with investigating police wrongdoing, whether a criminal offense or an infraction of departmental policy, rules, or regulations. In larger departments, the IAD unit is an investigative unit reporting directly to the chief of police. In smaller police departments, this function is generally carried out by the chief of police or through some other external police organization, e.g., the state police, at the request of the chief. Usually, these investigators are seasoned officers with former detective experience, and many times they are volunteers and in the last years of their policing careers. The IAD should not be confused with the Civilian Complaint Review Board system, which may have nonsworn agents conducting its investigations who report directly to the board itself. An assignment to the IAD is generally not a popular one and can sometimes be problematic to an officer's assent up the departmental career ladder.

**Internal Affairs Hearing.** The official review of an internal affairs investigation for the purpose of determining whether charges will be brought and sanctions sought against an officer for violation of departmental policy, professional standards, or municipal or statutory law. The process is nearly identical to a military article 32 hearing and is insulated from civilian trial court jurisdiction.

**Internal Affairs Unit (IAU).** See *Internal Affairs Division (IAD).*

**Internal Revenue Service (IRS).** The tax collecting agency for the federal government that maintains a criminal investigation unit to aid in its enforcement of the federal tax code. The Criminal Investigation (CI) unit is composed of approximately 2,900 special agents with investigative jurisdiction involving criminal violations of the Internal Revenue Code, money laundering, and Bank Secrecy Act violations.

**International Association of Auto Theft Investigators (IAATI).** The private international organization, established to assist auto theft investigators from police and law enforcement agencies, along with those from insurance companies, car rental companies, and the National Insurance Crime Bureau in the apprehension and prosecution of auto thieves and chop-shop operators.

**International Association of Chiefs of Police (IACP).** Originally established in 1893, it has undergone a number of name changes including the National Chiefs of Police Union, the National Association of Chiefs of Police, the Chiefs of Police of the United States and Canada, and eventually the International Association of Chiefs of Police. The contemporary name reflects the organization's evolving worldwide scope. The IACP's objectives are to "advance the science and art of police service; to develop and disseminate improved administrative, technical, and operational practices and promote their use in police work; to foster police cooperation and the exchange of information and experience among police administrators throughout the world; to bring about recruitment and training of qualified persons; and to encourage adherence of all officers to high professional standards of performance and conduct." Currently, the IACP claims over 12,000 members from fifty-four nations; it publishes the *Police Chief* and is located in Arlington, Virginia.

**International Association of Police Professors (IAPP).** A professional and scholarly society formed in 1963 to meet the expanding higher-educational needs of police officers. The IAPP eventually changed its name to the Academy of Criminal Justice Sciences (ACJS), reflecting the expanding scope of academic curricula at American colleges and universities from police administration or police science to criminal justice.

**International City Management Association (ICMA).** Originating in 1914, the ICMA is a professional association of city and county managers dealing with numerous local governmental issues, including police management. ICMA publishes *Target,* a monthly newsletter, and *Municipal Police Administration,* a well-regarded text; it is located in Washington, DC.

**International Court of Justice (ICJ).** Currently known as the World Court, it was pre-dated by the League of Nation's Permanent Court of Justice created during the 1945 conference at San Francisco. The Court's existence is mandated by the United Nations charter, citing all member states of the United Nations as members of the ICJ. The court sits at The Hague and has fifteen judges, elected by the General Assembly and the Security Council of the United Nations. The court's orders and judgments are enforced by the Security Council. Judgments of the court are final without the possibility of appeal, as no appellate branch exists. Judges serve nine-year terms; nine judges form a quorum, and rulings require a majority vote of nine judges only.

**International Criminal Police Organization (INTERPOL).** INTERPOL was created in Vienna in 1923, expressly to aid police and law enforcement agencies worldwide in the fight against international crime and criminal organizations. The headquarters were moved to Paris in 1938; today it consists of 126 member nations. The General Secretariat headquarters of INTERPOL is staffed by French police officers, and it aids in the coordination of member police and law enforcement agencies worldwide by providing information on vehicles, persons, and various goods involved in criminal enterprises. Although INTERPOL functions as a worldwide clearing house for criminal justice information and coordination, it conducts no investigations in and of itself and has no independent arresting powers. Joining INTERPOL in 1958, the United States established its National Central Bureau (the national headquarters) at Washington, DC, and it is located within the U.S. Department of Justice. INTERPOL publishes monthly the *International Crime Police Review,* and biennially, the *International Crime Statistics* in Saint-Cloud, France.

**Interpol "red notices."** Although commonly considered "international arrest warrants," they are actually not warrants *per se.* Red notices are internationally dispatched Interpol alerts, usually regarding persons who have outstanding warrants for their arrest, issued by sovereign nation states or international tribunals regarding specified criminal offenses. There are two types of red notices:

(1) notices issued for defendants for whom there are active arrest warrants, and (2) notices issued in conjunction with judicial determinations and sanctions, e.g., indictments and sentences. Many red notices are issued for those tried *in absentia*; this group of defendants is being sought for the purpose of satisfying their court-ordered sanctions. Red notices are issued to assist domestic police and law enforcement agencies in the identification and apprehension of wanted persons who are avoiding apprehension through international flight.

**International Law.** The law of nations regulating relationships between sovereign nation states. Not statutory in nature, this corpus of law has its origins in international treaties, customs, and decisions handed down by such courts as the International Court of Justice.

**International Law Enforcement Instructors' Agency (ILEIA).** Founded in 1976, the agency strives for the development of uniform professional training standards for criminal justice personnel. ILEIA publishes a monthly newsletter, the *Torch and Tome,* and is located in Concord, Maryland.

**International Law Enforcement Training Agency (ILETA).** Established in 1976 as the Police Defensive Tactics Study Group, it was housed at the Royal Marines' Commando Depot and was responsible for training numerous British constabularies in military tactics. The organization underwent a number of name changes and became an international police training center in 1980.

**international police force.** The combined armed forces of member states of the United Nations authorized under the United Nations charter to preserve the peace and to prevent aggression by rogue states or insurgent forces.

**interrogation.** *n.* A forceful questioning or examination of a suspect in a criminal investigation. Such questioning is more invasive than that carried out in an interview of subjects regarding a crime and is focused on a likely suspect.

**interrogatory.** *n.* A discovery device; a written question by a party in a legal proceeding dispatched to the opposing party, which is to be answered in writing and under oath.

**interstate.** *adj.* Among and between states or sovereigns within a federated system, i.e., states within the United States.

**Interstate Commerce Commission (ICC).** The organization expressly created by Congress to regulate carriers subject to the Interstate Commerce Act (49 USCA § 1 et seq.) involved in interstate commerce and the transportation of goods. The ICC has regulatory authority over railroads, trucking, buses, freight handlers, water carriers, pipelines, transportation brokers, and others.

**interstate compact.** A voluntary agreement between two or more states (within the United States) concerning mutual problems. Major compacts must, according to Article I § 10 of the Constitution, receive congressional approval before ratification.

**Interstate Compact for the Supervision of Parolees and Probationers (1937).** Entered into by all fifty states by 1951, this compact provides for the supervision of parolees or probationers in a state other than the one wherein they were convicted. The customary formal procedural requirements of extradition (rendition) are waived under its provisions.

**interstate extradition (rendition).** (Properly, it is "rendition" between the various states and "extradition" between nation states). The U.S. Constitution, other acts of Congress, and numerous state statutes provide for the rendition of an accused person charged in one state with the offense of treason, or other felony, or misdemeanor who has fled from justice in one state to another. In order for a person to be legally surrendered, (1) one must be charged with a crime in the demanding state through a valid indictment, information, or complaint; (2) one must have physically been in the demanding state (no flight could have occurred without this condition); and (3) there must be a similar offense in the asylum state. It must be noted, however, that if the person sought left the demanding state for reasons other than flight to avoid prosecution, he or she may still be surrendered legally to the demanding state.

**Inter-University Consortium for Political and Social Research (ICPSR).** An organization founded in 1962 to coordinate and share social science research with member universities. The organization provides "a central repository and dissemination service for machine-readable social science data; training facilities in basic and advanced techniques of quantitative social analysis; and resources that facilitate the use of advanced computer technology by social scientists." ICPSR is based at the University of Michigan, Ann Arbor, Michigan.

*in toto. (Lat.)* Wholly; completely; on the whole.

**intoxication.** *n.* A condition caused by drinking intoxicants (usually alcohol), where a person loses the normal use of his or her physical and mental faculties to a point that he or she fails to act as an ordinary prudent and cautious person. See *Model Penal Code*, § 2.08.

**intrastate.** *adj.* Within a state as opposed to interstate (among and between states).

**intrinsic evidence.** That evidence garnered from a document needing no explanation, as it speaks for itself.

**inventory search.** A cataloging of the contents of an impounded vehicle by officers pursuant to departmental procedures or a standing custom. The intent is to safeguard valuables found in the vehicle, protect officers and the public, and protect officers from liability regarding any alleged disappearances. Evidentiary items found pursuant to such a search may be admissible in a subsequent criminal prosecution. See *South Dakota v. Opperman,* 428 U.S. 364, 96 S.Ct. 3092, 49 L.Ed.2d 1000 (1976).

**investigating magistrate.** A judge (in an accusatorial system used by many European nations) assigned to investigate a crime. See *juge d' instruction.*

**involuntary manslaughter.** An unlawful homicide committed unintentionally, albeit under circumstances where a disregard for the probable harmful consequences of one's actions rises to the level of actionable negligence.

**involuntary servitude.** A condition under which one is compelled by force, coercion, or imprisonment to conduct labor for another; whether one is paid for his or her services is neither an issue nor a defense. The Thirteenth Amendment forbids both slavery and involuntary servitude.

**iodine.** *n.* A chemical used in forensics to raise fingerprints from paper.

*ipse dixit. (Lat.)* He himself/she herself said it.

***ipso facto.*** *(Lat.)* By the mere fact itself.

***ipso jure.*** *(Lat.)* By the law itself.

**Irish system.** An early correctional system designed by Sir William Crofton, providing for successive stages through which the prisoner had to progress before eventual release under supervision, followed by termination of sentence.

**irregular rendition.** The practice of illegally and often forcibly abducting a person on foreign soil, without his or her consent and absent any formal extradition process, for the purpose of detaining, interrogating, and/or adjudicating him or her in the demanding jurisdiction—a legal euphemism for judicially sanctioned kidnapping. The practice takes three basic forms: transnational forcible abductions, informal surrenders, and luring through trickery. Despite the widespread use of this extralegal practice by agents of the U.S. Government, it has been highly criticized by scholars of international law worldwide. See the *Ker–Frisbie* rule (doctrine), *Kerr v. Illinois,* 119 U.S. 436, 7S.Ct. 225 (1886), *Frisbie v. Collins,* 342 U.S. 519, 72 S.Ct. 509 (1952), *United States v. Toscanino,* 500 F.2d. 267 (2nd Cir., 1974), and *United States v. ex rel Lujan v. Gengler,* 510 F. (2d Cir., 1975).

**irresistible impulse.** An affirmative defense claiming that as a result of one's mental condition, an overwhelming urge to do a particular act was beyond his or her ability to resist, and thus he or she is either not criminally culpable or should be given a lesser sentence as a result.

**issue of fact.** A question within the domain of the jury, as the trier of fact (or the judge in a bench trial).

**issue of law.** An issue within the purview of the court (judge) only (not the jury) to be decided by the court.

# J

**jail.** *n.* A custodial or detention facility generally located at the county seat and administered by the sheriff's office or a county jail administrator; it must not be confused with a correctional facility, as a jail is a temporary or short-term custodial facility with no correctional programs. Usually intended for adult offenders, it sometimes temporarily houses juvenile offenders. In some anomalous situations, e.g., St. Louis, Missouri, a city jail is used, as the city does not lie within a county; thus, it is a city jail functioning as a county jail. Most jail inmates are detained pending the posting of bond, a grand jury hearing, or a petit trial, or are awaiting transportation by the sheriff's office to the state prison for felony convictions, or are serving sentences for a criminal conviction with a sentence of less than one year.

**jailer (jailor).** *n.* An official responsible for the operation of a jail, usually a member of the county sheriff's office assigned to jail operations, and frequently not a sworn deputy.

**jailhouse lawyer.** An inmate who has become knowledgeable about criminal law and procedure and who assists other inmates in filing briefs, appeals, and other legal processes.

**jail time.** The time credited to an inmate's sentence for time spent in jail awaiting trial before his or her conviction.

**James, Jesse Woodson (1847–1882).** The leader of the infamous outlaw gang comprised of Frank James, Cole Younger, and several others. Known for its proclivity to rob banks and trains, the gang terrorized bankers and railroad executives throughout Missouri and the Midwest. Eventually, Jesse James was shot and killed for a $5,000 reward by Robert Ford, a member of his own gang.

**Jay, John (1745–1829).** The first chief justice of the U.S. Supreme Court (1789–1795), he previously served as the state of New York's representative to the Continental Congress (1774–1779). Jay also authored five essays in the *Federalist,* supporting the ratification of the Constitution; was active in foreign affairs for the new republic; and later served as governor of New York from 1795 to 1801.

**jeopardy.** *n.* Exposure danger, i.e., legal process, criminal conviction, and punishment. Jeopardy technically begins, in most jurisdictions, when the petit jury is impaneled and sworn, or in the case of a bench trial, when the first witness is sworn.

**Jim Crow laws.** The common label given to legislation passed in southern states (whether ordinances or statutes) during the 1880s giving legal status to de facto segregation.

**job action.** An activity undertaken by employees, often union members, to place pressure on the employer to meet workers' demands. Job actions generally take place after "good faith" bargaining has failed. Police job actions have taken the form of strikes, the blue flu, and work slowdowns.

**John Birch Society (1958).** A right-wing extremist organization begun by Robert Welch in 1958 to oppose communism. The organization opposes moderate and liberal political efforts and disapproves of internationalism. The organization has traditionally been supportive of traditional law enforcement practices and has fought against civilian review boards to oversee police practices.

**John Howard Association (1901).** Based on the principles evinced by John Howard (1726–1790), an early English prison reformer, the organization works for penal reform in the United States and publishes a bimonthly newsletter. The organization is based in Chicago.

**joinder.** *n.* The combining of multiple defendants and/or charges during any single legal proceeding. In criminal law, the citing of multiple defendants or the citing of multiple charges on the initial charging document.

**judge.** *n.* A judicial officer presiding over a judicial tribunal. See also *court, justice,* and *magistrate.*

**judge advocate.** A lawyer and commissioned officer in the Judge Advocate General's Corps within the various branches of the armed services. See 10 USCA § 801.

**judge advocate general (JAG).** The general (Army or Air Force) or admiral (Navy and Marine Corps) who serves as the senior legal officer and advisor within a given armed service.

**judge-made law.** The law of judicial precedent created by case law from appellate justices. See *stare decisis.*

**judge *pro tem* (judge *pro tempore*).** A judge appointed to fill the term or partial term of another judge, exercising all the functions and powers of the regularly appointed judge.

**judgment.** *n.* A judicial or other legal decision, decree, order, sanction, or sentence.

**judicial act.** The act of a judge exercising his or her authority in trying a case and rendering a decision.

**judicial authority.** The legal and official authority pertaining to the office of a duly appointed judge, including the legal right to hear and settle questions in controversy. Authority is the legal right to direct and command, whereas power is the force by which the state compels others to comply with its authority; thus, in the strictest sense of the word, there is no judicial power. The power to enforce a court's authority (orders) is a function of the police power of the state, exercised through the executive branch of government.

**judicial college.** A training institute for the instruction of newly elected judges in most states. The National Judicial College at the University of Nevada, Reno, was established in 1963 for the express purpose of preparing newly elected state judges nationwide.

**judicial days.** The days during which the courts are functioning.

**judicial error.** Any error made by the court when rendering an erroneous judgment.

**judicial immunity.** A long-standing protection from civil liability for acts done in the course of a judge's official capacity. The immunity is nearly absolute and applicable even when acts are conducted in bad faith.

**judicial notice.** A judicial act wherein the judge takes notice of commonly known facts having a bearing on the case at hand without requiring formal proof. Examples include facts concerning the laws of the states, the Constitution, and geographic features.

**judicial officer.** Any judge, justice, or magistrate. One who exercises the judicial function and is vested with the state's authority to decide cases of controversy before the court.

**judicial powers.** See *judicial authority.*

**judicial process.** Any proceeding undertaken in a legally constituted court in order to gain a remedy allowed by law.

**judicial reprieve.** In earlier times, it served as a form of suspended sentence, allowing a defendant the opportunity to seek some form of clemency from the Crown.

**judicial restraint.** A judicial doctrine largely adhered to before the activist court of the 1960s, holding that the Supreme Court would not actively pursue social issues in and of its own accord, but, rather, would hear cases on those issues only as they were appealed to it for final review. The antithesis of judicial activism.

**judicial review.** A review of the actions taken by the executive branch of government by the court in common-law countries. Refer to Article III of the Constitution. The scope of judicial review is limited, however, allowing the administrative processes to take their proper course before intervention by the judiciary. At the federal level, a federal statute provides the scope of judicial review over administrative agencies. See the *Judicial Review Act*, 28 § USCA 2341–2351; see also *Marbury v. Madison*, 5 U.S. 137 (1803).

**judicial system.** Collectively, the entire system of courts used throughout the United States, including local-level inferior courts (where they still exist), state trial and appellate courts (including the court of last resort, generally known as the state supreme court), and the federal trial and appellate courts, including the U.S. Supreme Court. The system also includes a number of specialized courts, e.g., the Customs Court, the Court of Claims, and the Court of Military Appeals.

**judiciary.** *n.* That part and function of government charged with the responsibility of administering justice through a system of courts, which at the federal level is arranged as a three-tiered system. Most state courts are also arranged accordingly, having at the bottom trial courts, at the appellate level intermediate courts of appeals, and a court of last resort, generally known as the state supreme court. Some states allow for a nonunified system having inferior courts at the local level of government, with the three-tiered system superimposed.

**Judiciary Act (1789).** The act establishing the blueprint for the federal court system at the time of the creation of the nation's first constitution. It originally provided for a Supreme Court having a chief justice and five associate justices, who also served on the thirteen appellate (circuit) courts along with a trial (district) court, a system notably different from what exists today. The structure, composition, and jurisdiction of the original federal judiciary reflected the controversy concerning a federal judiciary and federal powers in general at the time of the act's creation. One faction envisioned a forceful federal court system administering a uniform federal code of justice, whereas another faction envisioned the existing state courts as the enforcers and interpreters of federal law.

**juge d' instruction.** *(Fr.)* In France, the investigating magistrate. He investigates the alleged crime along with the police to determine whether a prosecution should follow. There is no common-law system counterpart.

**Jukes family.** The Jukes family gained notoriety through the research and publications of R. L. Dugdale and A. H. Estabrook, when they reported in 1875 that they had traced the genealogical records of over 2,100 people of the Jukes bloodline, claiming that 171 were categorized as criminals, 458 were considered educationally mentally retarded, while hundreds of others among them were paupers, drunkards, or prostitutes. Given the family's propensity toward aggressive behavior against the Kallikak family (a protracted blood feud), the researchers concluded that heredity was the primary factor accounting for the family's poor social development and criminal proclivities. These findings have been seriously challenged by contemporary criminologists claiming that social influences were not adequately controlled for in the study.

**jural.** *adj.* Pertaining to jurisprudence; founded in law and recognized and sanctioned by positive law and its rules for the recognition and protection of societal rights and duties.

**jural postulates.** The juridical propositions promulgated by the well-known jurist Roscoe Pound, holding that the law reflects shared societal needs that make society and coexistence workable. Pound's postulates support the notion that the law can serve as a vehicle with which to engineer the social structure in order to produce certain beneficial outcomes, e.g., property rights inherent in theft statutes that support a capitalist society.

**jurat.** *n.* Official certificate of a public officer before whom a writing was sworn; a clause at the foot of an affidavit indicating when, where, and before whom the affidavit was sworn.

**jurisdiction.** *n.* (1) In policing or law enforcement, the authority and power to apply specific types of law (federal, state, and local; criminal and quasi-criminal, administrative, or civil) and the geographic area in which the legal authority and power is applicable. (2) In a juridical context, the authority under which courts and their officers function; the legal right under which judges exercise their authority; the scope and right of the court to adjudicate various legal issues, i.e., subject matter. For the jurisdiction of the federal judiciary see 28 USCA § 1251.

**jurisdiction in general.** As a general rule, states have jurisdiction only over offenses committed within their borders, and crimes must be prosecuted within the county in which they were committed. In the federal system, offenders are to be tried within the U.S. court district in which the alleged offense occurred.

**juris doctor(JD).** The lowest entry-level professional degree granted to law school graduates, replacing the former bachelor of laws (LLB) during the 1950s. The actual doctorate in law is the doctor of juridical science (SJD), earned after first completing the JD and a master's degree in law—the master of laws (LLM). Only a handful of attorneys nationwide hold the SJD, and virtually all of them are legal scholars (researchers), not legal technicians (practicing lawyers).

**jurisprudence.** *n.* The philosophy of law or the study of law regarding the principles of positive law; the science of law, ascertaining the principles upon which legal rules are anchored. Jurisprudence seeks to answer what effect various legal rules might have on the social order and which among them brings about the greatest good for the greatest number of the community at large.

**jurist.** *n.* One who is a legal scholar; learned and skilled in the law.

**juristic.** *adj.* Relating to law; of jurists or jurisprudence.

**juror.** *n.* One who takes an oath as a member of a jury panel.

**jury.** *n.* A group of citizens, selected according to law and sworn to hear evidence in a legal trial and to render a decision based on that evidence. Several types of juries exist, e.g., petit, grand, and coroner's.

**jury nullification.** The act of a jury finding the law to be a nullity. Throughout history, American juries have occasionally found a defendant not guilty, despite the fact that the prosecutor proved his or her case according to the law, as it existed at the time of trial. The jury, which has the right to find a person not guilty for any reason or no reason whatsoever, has found that despite the defendant's technical violation of a statute, he or she is to be found not guilty because they (the jury) disagreed with the law or its application in the instant case.

**jury panel.** A pool of prospective jurors summoned by the court to appear on a specified date. It is from this group that a petit or grand jury is selected.

**jury poll.** A poll conducted after a verdict has been rendered and entered into the official record, requesting each juror to state his or her vote regarding the verdict.

**jury trial.** A trial by a jury of one's peers, generally, although not always, consisting of twelve members. Some jurisdictions allow for as few as six jurors, although a Supreme Court decision requires a unanimous decision for conviction under such circumstances. Twelve-person juries are not necessarily required to have a unanimous decision for a conviction. See *Williams v. Florida,* 399 U.S. 78 (1970).

**jury wheel.** A random selection device used to determine which jurors will attend a particular trial.

***jus cogens.*** *(Lat.)* The "compelling or higher law," not to be violated by any nation state. Customary international law of such fundamental importance that even treaties cannot derogate them, e.g., laws on slave trafficking, torture, or genocide.

***jus gentium.*** *(Lat.)* Seen by legal scholars as the progenitor to the principles underpinning international law, it was originally a corpus of law originating in Rome to settle disputes between Roman citizens and foreigners by medieval judges.

**justice.** *n.* (1) The lawful use of authority to uphold what is right and just through the inherent police power of the state. (2) The quality of being fundamentally fair, impartial, and righteous. (3) The proper title for an appellate court judge. In the U.S. Supreme Court and the various state high courts (highest courts of appeal), a chief justice presides over a specified number of associate justices. Intermediate appellate court judges also hold the official title of justice.

**Justice Fellowship (1983).** A Christian-based organization established in 1983 supporting a systemwide reform of American criminal justice, based on the biblical principles of reconciliation, restitution, and restoration. The fellowship publishes *The Justice Report,* a monthly newsletter.

**justice of the peace.** A judge who presides over an inferior court in states having a nonunified court system. These judges rule on minor criminal offenses and local ordinance violations, sending serious law violations to the state trial court. They have authority in some civil issues and perform marriages. Most states have abolished the office by unifying their court systems.

**justifiable homicide.** (1) The intentional and legally condoned killing of another in self-defense under circumstances involving the imminent probability or the perception of imminent probability of death or grave bodily injury. (2) Any act sanctioned by law permitting one to perform an execution upon conviction for a capital crime, or to prevent a serious crime, or to prevent an escape by a duly appointed officer.

**justification.** *n.* A term used to demonstrate sufficient reason why a defendant acted in the way he or she did in the cause for which he or she is to answer before the court; a lawful reason for acting or failing to act.

**Justinian Code (529).** The Roman codification of law during the reign of Justinian I (A.D. 483–565), the emperor of the Byzantium.

**juvenile.** *n.* In legal usage, a person under a statutorily specified age (usually between seventeen or eighteen years of age) who is potentially under the jurisdiction of the juvenile court.

**juvenile court.** A special court that has original jurisdiction over persons under a statutorily specified age, usually between seventeen and eighteen years of age, dealing with matters involving delinquency, neglect, or dependency. The first juvenile court emerged in Chicago in 1899, under the authority of the Illinois Juvenile Court Act of that same year.

**juvenile delinquency.** The state or condition of being involved in delinquent acts. Delinquent acts are committed by juvenile offenders (persons of a statutorily specified age) involving crimes and status offenses (activities deemed wrongful as a function of one's age, e.g., smoking).

**juvenile facility.** A secure detention and/or treatment facility for juvenile offenders.

**Juvenile Justice and Delinquency Prevention Act (1974).** A federal act originally passed in 1974 but amended in 1977 and again in 1980, providing funds to states to support prevention and treatment programs. The act focused on the de-institutionalization of status offenders and the funding of research on juvenile delinquency. Additionally, the act included the Juvenile Justice, Runaway Youth, and Missing Children's Act Amendments (1984) and established the Office of Juvenile Justice and Delinquency Prevention (OJJDP) and the Missing Children's Assistance Act.

**juvenile justice system.** A system of justice somewhat paralleling the adult criminal justice system for delinquent, abused, and neglected youth (those under a statutorily specified age). The system consists of a network of agencies and functionaries including juvenile police officers, juvenile probation officers, the various juvenile courts, juvenile detention facilities, juvenile probation services, and treatment centers. Stemming from the original 1899 Illinois Juvenile Court Act, the system is a complex of agencies intended to redirect troubled youth.

**juvenile offender.** In most jurisdictions, a juvenile who has committed an offense that if committed by an adult would be a crime; however, some states classify juveniles who have committed a status offense as a juvenile offender. Note that a juvenile delinquent is one who has been adjudicated a delinquent.

**juvenile petition.** The charging document filed with the juvenile court, alleging delinquency, dependency, or a status violation and seeking court jurisdiction over the youth so named in the document. The document occasionally requests that the delinquent be transferred to the adult court for prosecution.

# K

**kangaroo court.** A metaphor commonly applied to any legal or extralegal proceeding wherein a person's civil liberties and due process rights are not procedurally protected, leading to a foregone conclusion resulting from the bias of the judge or tribunal.

**Kansas City Gun Experiment.** A federally funded experiment conducted in Kansas City, Missouri, between July 1992 and January 1993, with the intention of reducing violent crime incidents through the seizure of illegal guns. Intensive police activity focused on an 80-block area of the city that was a hotspot for gun-related homicides; the homicide rate was twenty times the national average. Searches in traffic stops were found to be most effective in finding illegal guns, with a ratio of one gun found for every twenty-eight stops. All varieties of gun-related crimes dropped precipitously during the experiment's time frame; drive-by shootings dropped from seven to only one. Overall, gun-related crimes dropped 49 percent, and criminal homicides dropped 67 percent. Perhaps most interesting was the fact that no displacement effect was noted.

**Kansas City Preventive Patrol Experiment (1972).** A Police Foundation–funded study spanning 1972 and 1973, investigating whether conventional wisdom regarding the effectiveness of police patrol was correct, produced findings that virtually shook the theoretical foundations of American policing. The experiment divided sectors of the city into three different levels of preventative patrol including normal, proactive, and reactive sectors. Following a one-year observation, researchers concluded that the changes in patrol strategies had no appreciable effect on the amount of crime reported, the crime perceptions of citizens as measured by citizen surveys, or citizens' fear of crime. Supporters of professional-model (law enforcement-oriented) policing intensely criticized the study methodologically; nonetheless, the study has had lasting effects on the use of police resources nationwide.

**Kefauver Committee (1950).** A committee chaired by Senator Estes Kefauver and empaneled to investigate organized crime in the United States. It developed the nation's first overview of the interconnections and hierarchy of interstate organized crime. Given little assistance in its investigation by the FBI, the committee, nonetheless, raised public awareness of the problem of organized crime.

**Kellor, Frances Alice (1873–1952).** After completing her LLB degree in 1897, she went on as a graduate student in the Department of Sociology at the University of Chicago; she studied under W. I. Thomas, Albion Small, and Charles Henderson between 1898 and 1900, all the time living at Hull House. Although she did not complete her graduate degree, her research in criminal anthropology did contribute significantly to the growing discipline of criminology. Perhaps her most notable contribution was as research director for the Progressive Party (1912).

**Kemmler, William. (1860–1890).** The first person executed via electrocution in the United States. His execution took place at the Auburn Prison in New York State on August 6, 1890. Kemmler was convicted of the hatchet murder of his wife in 1889.

**Kent State University incident (1970).** On May 4, 1970, the Ohio National Guard, in response to several days of demonstrations, involving criminal damage to property and arson, opened fire on Kent State University students who were protesting the U.S. incursion into Cambodia, which had further expanded the unpopular Vietnam War. In all, four students were killed by guardsmen gunfire; nine others were wounded. Criticism over the handling of the incident by the Guard led to a grand jury investigation of the incident and a movement to upgrade campus policing nationwide.

**keratin.** *n.* A protein found in animal life necessary in the production of keratinized epidermal tissue, e.g., hairs, nails, horns, and feathers.

***Ker-Frisbie* rule (doctrine).** A legal doctrine evinced by the U.S. Supreme Court in two similar cases decided decades apart, i.e., *Ker v. Illinois,* 119 U.S. 436, 7S.Ct. 225 (1886) and *Frisbie v. Collins,* 342 U.S. 519, 72S.Ct. 509 (1952), which posit that even when a defendant is forcibly and extralegally abducted against his or her will (kidnapped) from a foreign jurisdiction to stand trial in an American court, either state or federal, such extralegal abduction does not divest an American court of jurisdiction. The Second Circuit Court of Appeals imposed a limitation on the otherwise sweeping abuses allowable under the *Ker–Frisbie* rule, in the case of *United States v. Toscanino,* 500 F.2d. 267 (2nd. Cir. 1974). In that case, the appellate court refused to affirm American court jurisdiction, as a result of the "totality of the unconscionable treatment" of the defendant, which "shocked the conscience." However, only a year later in the *United States v. ex rel Lujan v. Gengler,* 510 F.2d 62, 66 (2nd. Cir. 1975), the same court trimmed the applicability of the *Toscanino* decision, positing that absent brutality by the U.S. federal agents, which rises to the level of "shocking the conscience," the *Ker–Frisbie* rule was to remain in force. See also *irregular rendition.*

**Kerner Commission (1968).** Formally known as the National Advisory Commission on Civil Disorders, the Kerner Commission studied the growing number and scope of civil disorders in the United States. Heading the commission was chairman Otto Kerner, then a federal judge and a former governor of Illinois. A follow-up report was issued in 1969 by the Urban Coalition and Urban America largely echoing and expanding the findings of the original 1968 report. Each found a nation polarized by the prolonged Vietnam War and suffering from the domestic inequalities inherent in a racist America.

**Kevorkian, Jack.** Known as "Dr. Death," he was a physician who in the mid-1990s was an advocate for physician-assisted suicide; he spent time in jail yet was found not guilty twice.

**Khadi justice.** The arbitrary law practiced by Islamic courts, described by Max Weber as being based on religious precepts as opposed to procedural rules, as found under English common law. Weber posits that Khadi justice is but one of three types of justice systems, including empirical and rational justice.

**kidnapping.** *n.* The unlawful, intentional, and felonious taking of a human being by force against his or her will. To be found guilty of the charge of kidnapping, one must take the subject a substantial distance from the area in which he or she was originally located, or one must hold the victim in a place of isolation for any of the following purposes: (1) to hold as a hostage or shield for ransom or reward; (2) to aid in the furtherance of the commission of a felony or flight; (3) to terrorize or inflict physical injury; or (4) to prevent the performance of a governmental or political function. See *Model Penal Code,* § 212.1.

**kilogram.** *n.* The equivalent of 2.2046 pounds.

**King, Martin Luther, Jr. (1929–1968).** A Nobel Peace Prize winner in 1964 and an inveterate apologist for the American civil rights movement and social justice. Best known for his support of the Montgomery bus boycott from 1955 to 1956, in the fight against institutionalized racism, from which he gained national attention. Active in the Southern Christian Leadership Conference, he pressed for peaceful nonviolent civil rights efforts to better the plight of black Americans. He and his followers were a potent force behind the passage of the Civil Rights Act of 1964. He was assassinated on April 4, 1968, in Memphis Tennessee, allegedly by James Earl Ray.

**kiting.** *n.* The kiting of funds or check kiting is a system of fraud wherein the perpetrator deposits balances in a number of accounts and writes checks from one account to another, knowing there does not exist sufficient funds to cover the draft at the time the first draft is issued, but intending to cover the overdraft with other funds before it clears.

**kleptomania.** *n.* A compulsive proclivity to steal, often without any economic motive driving the urge. Frequently, kleptomaniacs are women who steal impulsively without any rational plan or purpose and who take no effective steps to avoid capture. Many times, kleptomaniacs steal for some underlying symbolic sexual purpose and often steal the same items repeatedly. In cases of juveniles, especially boys, kleptomania is often linked to some type of emotional deprivation during the formative years of development.

**Knapp Commission (1971).** A commission chaired by Percy Whitman Knapp, which was an evolutionary iteration of the original Rankin Committee empaneled by New York Mayor Lindsay, to probe the corruption problems besetting the New York Police Department. The Rankin Report was about to be made public by the *New York Times* in April of 1970. The Knapp Commission was fueled largely by the extraordinary efforts of plainclothes officer Frank Serpico, who refused to become involved in the endemic corruption of the department and who broke the code of silence. Serpico found the department's administration reluctant to investigate his charges and went outside the department to the Knapp Commission for relief. The televised hearings of the commission's work stunned the nation, revealing over 15,000 officers who were found to be involved in some form of corrupt practice.

**knowingly.** *adv.* With knowledge; done consciously, intelligently, intentionally, and willfully. See *Model Penal Code,* § 2.202.

**Know Nothings (1852).** After the collapse of the Whig Party, the Know Nothings, who became the American Party, filled the vacuum. This new party was dedicated to opposing the great wave of Catholic immigration. So dedicated were the Know Nothings to their ideals of American purity that a secret regulation required members to say they "knew nothing" when questioned. When in 1854 the American Party voted to support the Kansas–Nebraska Act, most of its southern members joined the Democratic Party, while those in the Northeast moved to the Republican Party.

**Kretschmer, Ernst (1888–1964).** Known as the father of psychopharmacology, the science of the relationship between drugs and human behavior, this German psychiatrist posited that various types of mental disorders and criminality were correlated; thus, treatment and not punishment should follow the adjudication of criminals.

**Kropotkin, Peter (1842–1921).** Russian philosopher and anarchist, positing that property constitutes crime.

**Ku Klux Klan (1866).** A vigilante organization established in Tennessee in 1866 to reimpose white supremacy throughout the South. Klan members originally rode on horseback at night terrorizing blacks who voted and conducted themselves in ways contrary to conventional white social standards prior to the Civil War. In 1871, Congress passed the Ku Klux Klan Act and the Force Act pressuring the Klan to largely abandon its more violent methods of attaining its goals of black social, political, and economic suppression. A number of Klan-like organizations reemerged in American life in 1915, but were focused on the suppression of a wider audience than that of the original Klan; they directed their efforts against Catholics, Jews, immigrants, and blacks. Masquerading under different names, the Klan still exists in modified form throughout the contemporary United States, e.g., the various white supremacist organizations like the White Socialist Party and the Aryan Brotherhood.

# L

LEAA,  Law Enforcement Assistance Administration
LEEP,  Law Enforcement Education Program
LEMAS,  Law Enforcement Management and Administrative Statistics
LETN,  Law Enforcement Television Network
LHD,  Doctor of Humane Letters
LLB,  bachelor of laws (this degree has been supplanted by the JD, *juris doctor*)
LLD,  doctor of law (today an honorary degree, the modern doctorate in law is the SJD, *doctor of juridical science*)
LLM,  master of laws
LSD,  lysergic acid diethylamide

**K**
**L**

**labeling theory.** A criminological perspective (theory) originating in the school of symbolic interactionism, pioneered by post–World War II criminologists Charles Horton Cooley, William I. Thomas, and George Herbert Mead. Expanding on their work were criminologists of the 1940s through the 1960s, including Edwin Lemert, Kai Erickson, and Edwin Schur. In sum, labeling theory explains deviance in terms of the processes by which one acquires a negative social identity and corresponding self-image. According to Edwin Schur, "Human behavior is deviant to the extent that it comes to be viewed as involving a personally discreditable departure from a group's normative expectation, and it elicits interpersonal and collective reactions that serve to 'isolate,' 'treat,' 'correct,' or 'punish' individuals engaged in such behavior."

**laches.** *n.* A legal doctrine holding that equity supports the vigilant and not those who procrastinate. The neglectful nonassertion of one's claim, combined with the attendant circumstances, creates a legal prejudice to the opposing party, operating as an impediment to successful litigation of the issue in controversy.

**lachrymator.** *n.* A chemical substance that causes intense tearing of the eyes.

**La Guardia Report (1938).** A report regarding the study of marijuana use in New York City requested by then Mayor Fiorello La Guardia, carried out by the New York Academy of Medicine, under the cosponsorship of the New York Police Department. The study's final report largely debunked prevailing conventional wisdom supporting the slippery slope hypothesis, namely that marijuana use leads to a host of serious associated problems including social, psychological, and medical problems.

***laissez-faire.*** *(Fr.)* (1) A policy of noninterference by government in matters of economics and business, including the related issues of competition, labor relations, and other associated matters. (2) A metaphor for a hands-off policy.

**landmark decision.** A term applied to any appellate court decision (usually a Supreme Court decision) that is considered a turning point in legal thinking, reflecting changing social values or standards and significantly changing the course of evidentiary or procedural law, e.g., *Mapp v. Ohio,* 367 U.S. 643, 655, 81 S.Ct. 1684, 1691, 6 L.Ed.2d 1081, 1090 (1961).

**Lanham Act (1946).** The federal act (15 USC) providing for the registration and protection of official trademarks expressly used in commerce. The act provides for the enforcement of the provisions of specified international conventions regarding trademark protection.

**lanyard.** *n.* In military or police usage, a short cord, usually affixed around the shoulder epaulet, where a pistol or whistle is attached.

**larceny.** *n.* A general term for various forms of theft, defined as the unlawful and intentional taking of another's property, without his or her consent and with the intent to permanently deprive.

**laser light.** High-energy light with an extremely thin beam, having very little divergence. That is, the light is collimated, where all of the light waves flow in the same direction. This pure wavelength light produces luminescence in certain objects, minerals, or chemical compounds; it is used by forensic scientists to expose biological fluids such as semen or fibers, for example.

**latency theory.** A Freudian concept holding that urges, drives, and needs not manifested in overt behavior, but which exist at the unconscious level, will likely surface as overt behaviors, if not redirected via therapeutic intervention.

**latent print.** A hidden or undeveloped print, e.g., a finger, palm, toe, or footprint, not visible to the naked eye. The opposite of a patent or plastic print.

**latent fingerprint.** One present yet not visible to the naked eye. Police evidence technicians "raise" the print using various methods. The opposite of a plastic print, one left visible to the naked eye, e.g., one left in fresh paint or clay.

**lateral entry.** In organizational theory, the moving from one agency to another at either the same or higher position or rank. State law generally prohibits lateral transfer or entry for policing agencies.

**laundering money.** The movement of illicit monies to legitimate business practices or financial instruments in an attempt to make the money appear to have been garnered legally.

**Lautenberg Amendment (1996).** A federal law amending the Gun Control Act of 1968 (18 USC 921, 922 and 925), disallowing anyone with a conviction for domestic violence from possessing a firearm, including security, police, law enforcement, and military personnel.

**Lavater, Johan Casper (1741–1801).** The author of *Physiognomical Fragments,* a tome on the relationship between facial features and human behavior. This Swiss scholar's writings served as the springboard for the physically based body-type criminological theories that followed.

**law.** *n.* (1) In its broadest sense, the entire body of rules of social conduct promulgated and enforced under the authority, legislation, and custom of a given community. (2) The entire corpus of positive law (formally legislated, written, and codified law), including constitutional law, statutory law, appellate decisions, executive orders, and ordinances of a given jurisdiction. (3) The entire body of laws, whether positive law, common law, unwritten natural law, or international law, based on commonly accepted jural principles used in their enforcement.

**law and order.** A popular phrase used by conservative elements in the "war on crime" and the suppression of crime and violence in contemporary American life, implying a "get tough on crime" approach for criminal justice policy makers. In recent years this has translated into, among other things, a shift from community-oriented policing to a zero-tolerance policing modality as well as a shift from indeterminate to determinate sentencing.

**law encyclopedias.** Encyclopedias dedicated to subjects involving jurisprudential matters and controlling case law. Leading contemporary law encyclopedias include the *Corpus Juris Secundum* (*CJS*) and *American Jurisprudence* (*Am. Jur.*). The *Corpus Juris Secundum* is the successor to the *Corpus Juris* (*CJ*), which itself supplanted the *Encyclopedia of Law and Procedure* (*Cyc*).

**law enforcement.** (1) The reactive activity of enforcing the statutory law (both criminal and administrative) created by the legislative branch of a sovereign state, i.e., the enforcement of the state's criminal code. Note that sheriffs' offices may enforce civil court orders and some civil code provisions. (2) The enforcement of the ordinances of municipal- and county-level government. The processes involved in the detection, apprehension, and adjudication of criminal offenders. Law enforcement is often viewed as a negative function of the state, intended to deter violators and others through the imposition of negative criminal sanctions upon conviction. Nonetheless, law enforcement can involve a degree of negative proactivity through the use of sting and undercover operations. Technically, law enforcement should not be used as a synonym for policing, as only a small part of the police function involves the enforcement of the law, as policing involves a great deal of positive proactivity, having nothing directly to do with the enforcement of the law, unlike law enforcement.

**law enforcement agency.** A public agency (or private agency holding the public police power of the state through some specific legal arrangement) whose mandate is to enforce the criminal code. The Federal Bureau of Investigation (FBI) serves as a clear example of a public law enforcement agency. Note that the FBI is not charged with general policing responsibilities involving non–law-enforcement-related tasks.

**Law Enforcement Assistance Administration (LEAA).** The predecessor agency was created by an act of Congress in 1965, under the Law Enforcement Assistance Act, the Office of Law Enforcement Assistance (OLEA). The Law Enforcement Assistance Administration (1968), which replaced the OLEA formed under the Law Enforcement Assistance Act, funneled large amounts of federal money into crime fighting efforts in the United States spanning the late 1960s through the early 1980s, especially state and local policing agencies. Police and law enforcement agencies nationwide received technical assistance and new crime-fighting hardware, including weapons and communications equipment; the program ended in 1982.

**Law Enforcement Education Program (LEEP).** A federally funded program made available under the provisions of both the OLEA of 1965 and the LEAA of 1968, providing financial assistance to in-service officers as well as students interested in the study of police science, police administration, and criminal justice. The operation of the LEEP expended nearly $200 million in financial assistance to college students enrolled in police science, police administration, and criminal justice programs between 1965 and 1976.

**Law Enforcement Management and Administrative Statistics (LEMAS).** The federal entity responsible for the collection and dissemination of statistical data regarding American policing and law enforcement agencies. LEMAS is a part of the Bureau of Justice Statistics, which falls under the organizational umbrella of the U.S. Department of Justice (DOJ), located in Washington, DC.

**law enforcement officer.** An official vested with the arrest authority or power of the state. As a general rule, an agent of a bona fide public law enforcement agency (e.g., the FBI or a state investigative bureau like the Georgia Bureau of Investigation, GBI) or an agent of a private entity (e.g., a railroad employing special agents as railroad police) granted the police authority or power of the state under some legal arrangement, whether that be via a statutory provision or some other contractual arrangement. The term has been misused by popular culture to refer to all police officers, although this is technically incorrect and misleading, as a police officer's role involves much more than reactive law enforcement. Thus, the terms "police officer" and "law enforcement officer" are not synonymous. Law enforcement agents do not perform police work, although police officers do conduct some law enforcement work. Research shows that a police officer's day consists of somewhere between seventy and ninety non–law enforcement activities.

**Law Enforcement Television Network (LETN).** A for-profit police and law enforcement telecommunications training institute located near Dallas, Texas.

**law of nations.** See *international law.*

**law of precedent.** A legal principle not to deviate from former rulings established under prior appellate case law on the same issue. See *stare decisis, "let the former decision stand."*

**law reform.** The alignment or adjustment of legislative enactments with changing social values, conventions, and conditions. The reformation of law (statutes) can take place at a number of levels within a society and its government. For example, the police may simply avoid making apprehensions for the violation of certain offenses by using their discretion not to arrest or to arrest for another lesser included offense. The prosecutor may decline to prosecute or may prosecute for a lesser included offense. The legislature may pass new legislation and replace the old law. The appellate courts may reinterpret the Constitution and find the law unconstitutional. Juries may nullify the law, thereby making it a nullity. Some political action groups may form a coalition to reform the law in a specific area, e.g., making abortion legal.

**law reports/reporters.** They are the published rulings and opinions of the appellate courts, both state and federal. (Federal district/trial court decisions are published in the *Federal Supplement*, no such supplement is available for state trial court rulings). The West Publishing Company publishes seven regional reports for state appellate courts in the United States; they are the (1) *Atlantic Reporter* (A) and *Atlantic Reporter, Second Series (A. 2d),* (2) *Pacific Reporter (P)* and *Pacific Reporter, Second Series (P.2d),* (3) *North Eastern Reporter (N.E.)* and *North Eastern Reporter, Second Series (N.E.2d),* (4) *North Western Reporter (N.W.)* and *North Western Reporter, Second Series (N.W.2d),* (5) *South Eastern Reporter (S.E.) and South Eastern Reporter, Second Series (S.E.2d),* (6) *South Western Reporter (S.W.)*

and *South Western Reporter, Second Series (S.W.2d)*, and (7) *Southern Reporter (S.)* and *Southern Reporter, Second Series (S.2d)*. Two anomalies to the above system developed early on; they are the *New York Supplement (N.Y.S.)* and *New York Supplement, Second Series (N.Y.S2d)* and the *California Reporter (Cal. Rptr.)* and *California Reporter, Second Series (Cal. Reptr.2d)*. The federal courts are reported, e.g., in the *United States Reports (U.S.)* and the *United States Supreme Court Reports Lawyer's Edition, Second Edition (L.Ed., or L.Ed.2d)*.

**lay judge.** A judge (magistrate) who is not a licensed attorney in the jurisdiction; (2) usually a justice of the peace.

**lay witness.** A nonexpert who must testify to facts based on his or her ability to observe or recall. These facts, to which he or she is testifying, are facts based on first-hand knowledge, gained directly through his or her own senses.

**leading question.** A question suggesting the desired answer to the witness.

**learning theory.** Learning theorists hold that criminal behavior is learned behavior. Through the process of socialization, people may learn to be criminals and accept the values associated with the criminal lifestyle. As a result, family members and peers are seen as powerful influences on one's development toward a law abiding life or a life of criminality. See *differential association theory.*

**leftist criminology.** See *radical criminology.*

**left-realist criminology.** A criminological perspective (theory) that emerged during the mid-1980s in response to the conservative "neoliberal" crime control model with its emphasis on punishment, so popular during that era. Left-realist criminology argues that in contravention to conventional "cosmetic" criminology that treats crime as a problem that can be treated and removed from the body politic, an otherwise healthy organism, crime is an endemic social problem inherent in the social fabric of many modern industrial capitalistic societies. Crime is viewed as a natural result of flawed social institutions based on core social values undergirding a class-stratified society, gender discrimination, and a competitive individualist ethos. One of left-realist criminology's primary theoreticians is British criminologist Jock Young.

**legal aid.** A generic phrase used for a nationwide system providing legal services to those who cannot afford to hire private legal counsel; most legal aid services and societies are administered at the local and county level. See *legal services corporation; public defenders*, and so forth.

**legal ethics.** In most jurisdictions, the Code of Professional Responsibility of the American Bar Association, which has promulgated the canon of ethics for the practice of law. Legal ethics consist of usages and customs among and between members of the legal profession, involving the moral, legal, ethical, and professional responsibilities expected to be extended to other members of the profession, clients, and the court.

**legal evidence.** A term used to include all admissible evidence and implying that such evidence must be of sufficient trustworthiness and character to substantially prove relevant facts, i.e., not to merely raise suspicion or stimulate conjecture.

**legal fiction.** The use of an assumed fact, created by the court, as a means for deciding a question.

K
L

**legal opinions.** The general name given to opinions concerning an issue of law, e.g., an attorney general's opinions rendered to the governor or any state agency upon request regarding an interpretation of law, especially when no case law exists as a guide.

**legal person.** The legal standing granted a company, corporation, or other entity, extending to it the right to hold property, file suit in court, and take on the legal liabilities of a human being.

**legal provocation.** The provocative act, sufficient to incite another to act, based on passion as opposed to sound rational judgment; the level of legal provocation necessary to reduce murder to manslaughter, e.g.; it must be sufficient in the mind of the average reasonable person to fuel enough resentment to lead to violence. Further, the criminal act must be carried out within a brief window of time, i.e., without the time necessary to allow a cooling of passion, whereupon a reasonable person would regain control of his or her emotions.

**legal realism.** A philosophy of law focusing on the actual workings of legal procedure and court-generated rules of litigation, as it is created and carried out by and through human beings and the various legal institutions of their making. This approach to understanding law goes beyond the abstract and focuses on the social factors that account for its creation and processing, and the law's failure to keep pace with changing social values. It is founded on the methodology found in empirical inquiry used in the social and behavioral sciences in order to uncover and evaluate the factors underlying the law's creation and its social consequences; that is, the individual proclivities and ideologies of legal functionaries, e.g., the judge in appellate rulings—not the formal abstract legal system or process itself.

**legalistic service style.** A police officer's service style emphasizing an aggressive crime-fighting and law-and-order approach to policing, i.e., an officer who uses a by-the-book law enforcement-oriented approach to policing.

**legation.** *n.* (1) An individual (or group of diplomats) and his/her or their assistants (e.g., attachés, interpreters, ministers, and secretaries) representing his/her or their government in a foreign country, in a capacity as or like an embassy. (2) A foreign diplomatic entity, immediately below that of an embassy.

**legislative immunity.** (1) The immunities granted to legislators at both the federal and state level, making them privileged from legal arrest during the legislative session. (2) The immunity extends also to any speech or debate made or conducted during the various sessions of either house. For federal legislative immunities see Article I, § 6, cl. 1 of the Constitution.

**legislative power.** The lawful right and power of a legislative body to create legislation. Legislative power includes the right to generate, alter or amend, and repeal laws within the purview of the given legislative body. Such bodies may delegate rule-making authority to regulatory and administrative agencies; however, under no circumstances may the legislature of a sovereign state delegate its authority to created criminal law. This has become a particularly knotty and unsettled area, given that some administrative laws carry a criminal sanction.

**legitimacy.** *n.* In legal usage, a lawful birth, or being born within the state of wedlock.

**Lemert, Edwin M. (1912–1996).** A well-known sociologist or anthropologist who expanded the symbolic interactionists' perspective in criminology. Among his contributions to the interactionist school was his introduction of the concepts of primary and secondary deviance.

**Leopold and Loeb.** Nathan Leopold, Jr., and Richard Loeb abducted and murdered Bobby Franks (fourteen years of age) on May 21, 1924, and demanded payment of $10,000 for his release from Bobby's father, Jacob Franks, a wealthy Hyde Park resident of Jewish extraction, even though young Bobby was already dead. Much to the credit of two investigative journalists for the *Chicago Daily News,* James Mulroy and Alvin Goldstein, the crime was quickly solved. Considered the crime of the century and a thrill-slaying, Leopold and Loeb thought they had committed the perfect murder, largely for the purpose of committing the perfect crime. Defended by the best legal counsel of the time, life sentences were secured for both Leopold and Loeb by Clarence Seward Darrow; Loeb was later murdered in prison.

**lesser included offense.** Any separate offense that is necessary to the definition or completion of a greater criminal offense; e.g., in the case of burglary, the offense of trespassing must be accomplished and is a separate and lesser included offense thereof.

**lethal chamber.** The room within a prison where those convicted of capital crimes and sentenced to death are put to death by any of the existing authorized legal means, including, in the United States, hanging, firing squad, electrocution, gassing, or lethal injection.

**letters rogatory.** The formal request of a court in one jurisdiction to the court of an independent (sometimes foreign) jurisdiction to permit and assist in the examination of a witness within its jurisdiction in response to interrogatories appended to the request.

**leuco-malachite test.** A preliminary field test for the presence of blood. This test is used less frequently today, as a result of other more sophisticated blood identification methods that have been introduced in recent years.

**lewd and lascivious cohabitation.** In criminal law usage, the living together of a man and woman, while not married, as husband and wife. Sometimes known as "illicit cohabitation"; such statutes are only infrequently enforced.

*lex. (Lat.) Leges* (plural), "law." (1) The body of various laws recognized during medieval jurisprudence, but not constituting a legal code that was systematized; the aggregation of laws regarding a particular subject. (2) In contemporary jurisprudence, any body of laws formal or informal applicable to a specific issue considered peculiar to a given jurisdiction and differing from other established rules or laws on the same matter applicable in other venues.

*lex fori. (Lat.)* "The law of the forum." The law of the jurisdiction in which a given court resides and whose law it uses procedurally to settle matters before it.

**Lexow Commission (1894).** A New York State General Assembly committee, bearing the name of the New York State senator who chaired the committee; it was mandated to investigate corruption in the New York City Police Department.

*lex talionis. (Lat.)* "The law of the claw." The ancient law of retaliation; an eye for an eye and a tooth for a tooth.

**LHD.** Doctor of Humane Letters; an honorary degree conferred on distinguished scholars by colleges and universities. See *doctorate.*

**liberty.** *n.* The sum total of the rights, privileges, and exemptions held in common by the various peoples of a political entity, e.g., civil liberties, political liberties; freedom from slavery, captivity, or other capricious and arbitrary controls.

**license.** *n.* (1) The formal and often legal authorization to do something, e.g., to practice medicine, one of the characteristics of a profession. (2) The authorization permitting a specified activity, e.g., a driver's license. Note that a license is a legal abstraction, not to be confused with the physical sheet of paper reflecting the state's authorization, e.g., a driver's license certificate.

*lictores.* *(Lat.)* See *vigiles.*

**lie detector.** The common name for a polygraph, an instrument measuring a number of biological responses under autonomic control (brain waves, heart rate, blood pressure, blood flow, respiration, and galvanic skin response) reflecting the body's responses to attempted deception.

**lieutenant.** *n.* A military rank (also used by many police agencies); a company grade officer in the military; the military draws distinction between 2nd lieutenants (the lower grade) and 1st lieutenants (the higher grade); lieutenants are the lowest grade of the commissioned officers in the military, the next highest rank being that of captain. In police agencies, the rank of lieutenant is the line of demarcation between supervisors (sergeants and corporals) and administrators (lieutenants and above). Note that police agencies, unlike the military, have only lieutenants (no distinction between 1st and 2nd lieutenants). Further, in contravention to military conventions, police agencies use gold insignia to denote the higher or highest rank, whereas the military uses silver to indicate the higher or highest rank; note that a general sports silver stars, and a lieutenant colonel (one grade above a major) has silver oak clusters as opposed to the major's gold oak clusters.

**lieutenant colonel.** A military rank (also used by some very large police agencies); a field-grade officer, above a major but below a full colonel.

**ligature marks.** Marks left on the body as a result of some form of binding, as with a rope or other binding material.

**lighthorse.** *n.* (1) The Cherokee nation's rudimentary form of policing found on reservations a few decades before the Civil War to control horse theft. These warriors were assigned to mounted "regulating" companies. A lighthorse company consisted of two officers and four privates. (2) In military usage, a lightly armed cavalry unit.

**Lindbergh Act (1934).** The federal statute proscribing kidnapping for ransom or reward if the victim is taken to a foreign jurisdiction (state or nation). A rebuttable presumption is created if the victim is not released within twenty-four hours of the kidnapping. See 18 USCA § 1201.

**line function.** In police or law enforcement usage, any function, activity, or duty carried out by and within the sphere of responsibilities of line officers (those officers who actually provide the basic services of policing, e.g., patrol work, making arrests, and providing non–law enforcement services to the community); distinguished from staff functions, where supervisory and administrative functions are carried out.

**lineup.** A police investigative technique wherein a suspect is placed in a line with others known not to have been involved in the crime, in order to have a witness or witnesses identify the suspect out of the group. The suspect has the right to have his or her attorney present during the lineup, if he or she so requests, as a result of *U.S. v. Wade,* 388 U.S. 218, 18 L.Ed.2d 1149, 87 S.Ct. 1926 (1967) and *Gilbert v. California,* 388 U.S. 263, 18 L.Ed.2d 1178, 87 S.Ct. 1951 (1967).

**link-network diagram.** A visual representation (a flow chart) of the relationship of people, instrumentalities, and organizations to a given crime or series of related crimes.

**liquor laws.** The category within the FBI's *Uniform Crime Reports* (UCR), where alcohol-related violations (with the exceptions of public drunkenness and driving while intoxicated) are cited.

**Liszt, Franz von (1851–1919).** Known for his comprehensive theory on the global science of criminal law, Franz von Liszt was a cousin of the well-known musical composer bearing the same name. Coining the phrase the global science of criminal law, Liszt envisioned the division of criminals into two typologies: occasional offenders (*Augenblicksverbrecher*) and chronic offenders (*Aussandverbrecher*).

**litigation.** *n.* A suit; a judicial controversy; a judicial contest; a legal action, inclusive of all inherent proceedings, whether civil, criminal, or administrative.

**litigiousness.** *adj.* A predilection to settle issues through the courts. See *litigation.*

**lividity.** *n.* Known properly as postmortem lividity, it is a condition created by the movement of the blood to the lowest parts of the body after death, via the force of gravity, where the parts of the body touching the surface upon which the body rests are discolored. The discoloration caused by this phenomenon looks a good deal like bruising. Should the body be moved after lividity has occurred and placed in a different position, evidence of lividity will remain.

**Livingston, Edward (1764–1836).** One of America's most celebrated penologists, who was also influential in the writing of the state of Louisiana's original criminal code.

**LLB.** Bachelor of laws degree; the predecessor to the JD (juris doctor); the entry-level law degree for legal practitioners. See *doctorate.*

**LLD.** Doctor of letters and law, an honorary degree granted by universities to distinguished scholars. See *doctorate.*

**LLM.** Master of laws; the specialized graduate degree in law following the JD (juris doctor), required to practice some legal specialities, e.g., admiralty law.

**loan shark.** One who makes illegal loans at extraordinarily high rates of interest, rates that are considered usury under most state codes.

**Locke, John (1632–1704).** A celebrated philosopher from the age of Enlightenment who posited the "social contract" theory, whereby those governed surrender some of their individual rights to judge and sanction to the collective community (the sovereign state) for the higher good of the commonwealth. He posited that should the government violate the social contract, the community had the right to nullify the government's authority by withdrawing from it.

**lockup.** *n.* A temporary detention cell usually located in a police station or court house for people unable to post bail bond awaiting a judicial hearing. The maximum time one can be legally detained in a lockup is limited by law; in many jurisdictions one may not be confined for more than two hours or a reasonable amount of time, after which the subject must be taken before a magistrate for a *habeas corpus* hearing.

**logistics.** *n.* In military or police usage, the efficient movement of troops and equipment. In a larger sense, the science of the coordinated movement of people, supplies, and materials.

**Lombroso, Cesare (1835–1909).** Known as the "father of criminology," Lombroso served a good deal of his life as a physician in the Italian army, where he had ample opportunity to study the physical characteristics of soldiers who had been convicted and later executed for crimes. The Lombrosian criminological perspective consists of a number of fundamental beliefs; it holds that (1) serious criminal offenders have inherited criminal traits, (2) because of these inherited traits, "born criminals" are literally impelled into a life of crime, and (3) the criminogenic traits of born criminals consist of atavistic anomalies—physical throwbacks to more primitive human forms. His vision regarding criminal behavior was later expanded upon by a school of thought known collectively in modern criminology as biological determinism.

**London Metropolitan Police Act (MPA).** An act of Parliament establishing the London Metropolitan Police in 1829, as a result of the collapse of nineteenth-century policing. The Gordon riots of 1780 initiated a fifty-year debate concerning the need for a better system of public safety in London, culminating in the MPA. The task of creating a modern, full-time, paid, public police department fell on the shoulders of the British home secretary, Sir Robert Peel, who introduced three elements that have become hallmarks of modern policing in England and later the United States: mission, strategy, and organizational structure (based partially on the military model) and the notion of crime prevention.

**lower court.** (1) A term generically applied to any of the trial courts by courts of appellate jurisdiction. (2) A term specifically intended to describe those courts of limited jurisdiction in a state with a nonunified court system, i.e., states providing for a system of courts operating at the municipal- or township-level of government. These courts are not courts of record, and generally do not have judges who are licensed attorneys; contested verdicts from these courts are sent for retrial in the state trial courts, courts of general jurisdiction (sometimes known as superior courts). These initial lower courts are, therefore, often referred to as inferior courts. As a result, some states title their trial courts superior courts, e.g., California.

**luminescence.** *n.* A type of "cold light"; i.e., which derives from a nonthermal source. Luminescence is created by the absorption of radiant or corpuscular energy; that is, light generated by bioluminescence, e.g., foxfire.

**luminol.** *n.* A chemical reagent spray used at crime scenes to identify the presence of blood. Blood stains not visible to the naked eye fluoresce a white-blue color, with the application of ultraviolet light after application of luminol spray, even after deliberate attempts to sanitize the area by cleaning with detergents.

**lunge doctrine.** A doctrine deriving from *Chimel v. California*, 395 U.S. 752 (1969), announcing that in searches incident to a lawful arrest, officers may lawfully search the area immediately around the subject, giving rise to the "arm's length" doctrine.

Expanding on that doctrine, most courts have liberally construed the findings in *Chimel* to any area to which a subject under arrest may reasonably lunge.

**lynching.** *n.* The unlawful act, usually by a mob, of punishing an accused person, usually by hanging, in defiance of legal authority. The term derives from Captain William Lynch (1742–1820), a member of a vigilante committee in Pittsylvania, Virginia, during the 1870s.

**lysergic acid dielthylamide (LSD).** A semisynthetic psychedelic hallucinogenic drug commonly known as acid, derived from ergot, a fungus grown on rye.

K
L

# M

**Mace.** *n.* (1) In modern criminal justice usage, a trade name for a nonlethal aerosol-propelled eye and respiratory irritant used by police to temporarily disable offenders; (2) a heavy club with a spiked metal head used as a symbol of authority; or (3) a staff-like object used as a symbol of authority by official justice agencies.

**Machiavelli, Niccolo (1469–1527).** An Italian (Florentine) statesman, political philosopher, and writer. In his book *The Prince*, he posits that the ruler must present himself as a role model and example of moral purity. However, in achieving positive political goals, he argues that the ends can justify the means.

**Mack, Julian W. (1866–1943).** As a pioneer in the field of juvenile justice, he was elected to a judgeship in Illinois' Cook County Circuit Court, where he presided over Chicago's Juvenile Court, during its nascent years. He was supportive of the founding of the National Probation Officers' Association, and in 1907 he was placed on the Illinois Court of Appeals. In 1911, President William H. Taft appointed him to a seat on the U.S. Court of Appeals for the Seventh Circuit, from which he retired in 1941, after a thirty-year legal career.

**Maconochie, Alexander (1787–1860).** Overseer of the British penal colony located at Norfolk Island, he pioneered the "ticket-of-leave" system as part of an early form of parole in the 1840s. Under his ticket-of-leave system, good behavior earned inmates marks allowing them to progress through a series of reduced confinement settings, leading to a conditional release (ticket-of-leave or parole) and eventually to complete freedom from incarceration. His ticket-of-leave system was based on a correctional perspective holding that punishment should be intended to reform and not for the purpose of revenge, and that sentences should be indeterminate, giving the prisoner both the carrot and the stick.

**Mafia (Maffia).** *n.* Also known as the Black Hand, La Cosa Nostra, and the Commission, this organized crime syndicate is the largest in the world. Originally intended to be an unofficial policing system instituted in Sicily to protect the landed classes and their estates against the lawlessness caused by the French occupation during the 1860s, it evolved to become a syndicated and federated criminal organization with much of Italy under its grip. Unofficial reports place the Mafia's beginnings in the United States (New Orleans) from about 1869. Today, the organization's influence is found in many regions of the United States and many governmental entities at every level. Many "families" make up the Commission, with its estimated 17,000 operatives.

Familiar family names include Gambino, Lucchese, Salerno, Genovese, Corallo, Rastelli, Bonanno, Columbo, and numerous others. Among the criminal revenue-producing activities of the Mafia are drugs, loan sharking, prostitution, extortion, and gambling.

**magistrate.** *n.* (1) In politics, a generic title given to public civil officers vested with executive or judicial authority, e.g., the governor is often referred to as the chief magistrate of the state. (2) Generally a judicial officer of the inferior courts, or a judge in a state trial court (where such an office still exists) of the lowest rank. (3) A title used generically for a trial court judge. In the federal judiciary, for example, a judicial officer functioning in the U.S. district courts hearing minor civil and criminal offenses and overseeing preliminary or pretrial proceedings, formerly done by U.S. commissioners. See "Rules for Minor Offenses Before U.S. Magistrates." 18 USCA §§ 3401, 3402; 28 USCA §§ 631.

**magistrate's court.** (1) A court of limited jurisdiction in a state using a nonunified court system, at the local level of government; (2) a magistrate's court within a court of general jurisdiction, at the lowest level. Generally, a magistrate's court has jurisdiction delimited to hearing minor offenses, preliminary hearings, and settling small claims.

***magistrature assise.*** *(Fr.)* The formal title for a judge presiding over a French court.

***magistrature debout.*** *(Fr.)* The formal title ascribed to a prosecutor in the French criminal justice system.

***Magna Carta.*** *(Lat.)* The "great charter." This document was signed by King John of England on the plains of Runnymede on June 15, 1215, under pressure from his rebellious barons. This important legal document heavily influenced the "Bill of Rights" found in the American Constitution, and it specifically granted freedoms to certain aristocracy and the church; it also extended a number of rights to the laity, thereby reducing the authority of the Crown and expanding individual freedoms.

**magnetic ink character recognition (MICR).** A computerized method of processing and identifying the origin and routing of checks, bank drafts, and other financial documents that are required by law to be routed through the Federal Reserve System. Printed in magnetic ink, special fields include numeric MICR groupings that identify the Federal Reserve routing code, the American Banking Association transit number, the account number, and the amount of the instrument.

**mail fraud.** The intentional use of the U.S. Mail to defraud another by executing a fraudulent scheme. The elements of the offense include a scheme to defraud and the placement of a letter in the furtherance of the criminal scheme. See 18 USCA §§ 1341 & 1342.

**maim.** *v.* To cripple, mutilate, or disable some necessary part of the body. See *mayhem.*

**major.** *n.* A military rank; the lowest ranking commissioned officer of the "field-grade"; above a captain (the highest company-grade officer) yet below a lieutenant colonel (the next to highest field-grade officer). This rank is also used by some very large police agencies.

***mala captus bene detentus.*** *(Lat.)* "Improper capture but lawful detention." A legal doctrine holding that a person seized extralegally or illegally may, nonetheless, be legally detained. Further, the court having jurisdiction over the alleged offense has the authority to try the defendant, despite his or her "irregular rendition." That is, the unlawfulness of the seizure is not a defense. This juridic principle is becoming increasingly inconsistent with evolving international legal standards regarding human rights, notwithstanding its common use by agents of the U.S. government in the global war on terror.

**maladministration.** *n.* The wrongful or corrupt administration of public affairs; synonymous with misadministration.

**mala fides.** *(Lat.)* In bad faith.

**mala in se.** *(Lat.)* A category of crimes that are said to be immoral and wrong in and of themselves, e.g., murder, rape, arson, and burglary, as opposed to offenses that are wrong merely because the law says that they are wrong. See *mala prohibita*.

**mala prohibita.** *(Lat.)* A category of offenses made wrong only because the legislature has determined that such acts or omissions are wrong, not because they are wrong inherently in and of themselves *(mala in se)*.

**malfeasance.** *n.* In legal usage, the execution of a lawful act in an unlawful manner, thereby creating an infringement on the rights of another or others. Not to be confused with nonfeasance.

**malice.** *n.* In legal usage, the evil active ill will or desire constituting the state of mind (intent) to carry out an unlawful act.

**malice aforethought.** The deliberate and intentional predetermination or plan to commit an unlawful act devoid of legal justification, conceptualized before the scheme was brought to fruition.

**malicious act.** Any unlawful act committed willfully and with the intent to injure another or others, devoid of legal excuse or justification.

**malicious arrest.** An arrest instituted with malice and often without probable cause to support the belief of a reasonable person that the charge or charges can be legally justified.

**malicious mischief.** The willful damaging or destruction of personal property stemming from ill will toward the owner or possessor. See *vandalism*.

**malicious prosecution.** The unlawful prosecution, initiated with malice and without probable cause, to support the belief of a reasonable person that the charge or charges could be lawfully justified.

**malign.** *v.* To maliciously defame, slander, or speak evil of; *adj.* malevolent.

**Mallory Rule.** An appellate rule holding that a confession given by a subject who has been held an unreasonable time before an appearance before a magistrate is inadmissible despite its voluntariness and trustworthiness. See *Mallory v. U.S.*, 354 U.S. 449, 77 S.Ct. 1356, 1 L.Ed.2d 1479; see also *McNabb–Mallory Rule*.

**malpractice.** *n.* The inadequate or injurious practice and/or treatment or culpable neglect of a client by a person vested with fiduciary authority and/or professional responsibility. A failure to provide adequate and competent services and to exercise the degree of skill commonly rendered by prudent and reputable service providers.

**Malthus, Thomas R. (1766–1834).** An English clergyman and political philosopher who posited that the population of the world increases faster than the food supply, and that unless the birth rate is controlled, poverty, crime, and war will result as a natural consequence.

**manacles.** *n.* Physical restraining devices, e.g., handcuffs, shackles, or leg irons.

**mandamus.** *(Lat.)* "We Command." The formal name of a writ issued by a court of superior jurisdiction, and directed to a corporation or any of its officers (whether private or municipal) or an executive, administrative, or judicial officer, or a lower court commanding the performance of a specified act. It is generally considered a drastic remedy used only in extraordinary situations by the federal judiciary to limit and/or compel a lower court to exercise its fiduciary responsibilities, jurisdiction, and authority. See 28 USCA § 1361.

**mandate.** *n.* (1) In law, a command, order, or directive issued by a court demanding that the proper officer enforce a judgment, sentence, or decree. The official method for dispatching the judgment of the appellate court to a lower court, directing that action must be taken or a disposition must be produced in a case pending before it. (2) A public trust responsibility.

**mandatory sentence.** A statutory provision requiring that a specified penalty be imposed for specific offenses upon conviction, despite special circumstances and arguments in mitigation. The discretionary authority of judges was severely and intentionally reduced by the imposition of mandatory sentencing guidelines.

**Manhattan Bail Project (1961).** An experimental project funded by the Vera Institute spanning October 16, 1961 through April 8, 1964, to determine the effectiveness of release-on-recognizance (ROR) programs. A default rate of only .7 of 1 percent occurred, paving the way for other similar programs across the country, like the Philadelphia Common Pleas and Municipal Court ROR program.

**Mann Act (1910).** The federal statute proscribing the interstate transportation of women for immoral purposes. See *The White Slave Traffic Act*, 18 USCA § 2421.

**manslaughter.** *n.* The unlawful killing of another without malice, express or implied. The unlawful killing of a human being without premeditation, in some instances involuntarily, while in the commission of a lawful act but lacking sufficient caution. Criminal homicide can be reduced to manslaughter if the act is committed recklessly or the homicide is committed under the influence of extreme emotional pressure. See *Model Penal Code,* § 210.3.

**Manson, Charles.** Although not directly involved in the killing of seven people, Manson was charged with ordering the "Manson family" to carry out murders on August 8 and 9 of 1969. During those two evenings, members of the Manson family entered the home of Roman Polanski and shot or stabbed to death five individuals, including Mr. Polanski's wife, actress Sharon Tate. The following evening the same group entered the home of Leo LaBianca and murdered Mr. and Mrs. LaBianca. Manson and four of his group were found guilty and sentenced to death; later their sentences were reduced to life following the state supreme court's imposition of a moratorium on capital punishment.

**Marechausee.** *(Fr.)* Established as the Marshals of France in AD 875, they were federal agents responsible for the King's protection.

**marihuana.** *n.* Commonly spelled *marijuana, marihuana, marajuana,* or *mariguana* and referred to as pot, grass, tea, weed, or Mary-Jane; in cigarette form it is known as a joint or reefer. An herb growing as an annual and properly classified as *cannabis sativa.*

**marital communications privilege.** An evidentiary rule found in most American states disallowing private communications between spouses during a valid marriage to be introduced at trial without the consent of the witness spouse. Some jurisdictions disallow the admissibility of this type of evidence even with the consent of the witness spouse. Also known as the husband–wife privilege, there are limitations to the rule, e.g., in the prosecution of an offense by one spouse against the other or their children.

**marshal.** *n.* (1) A federal police/law enforcement official employed by the United States Marshals Service (USMS), formerly the United States Marshals Office (USMO). The director of the USMS is located in Washington, DC, with a U.S. marshal appointed to each of the ninety-four federal court districts, under which there are numerous deputy U.S. marshals. The U.S. marshal is an officer of the federal courts, and, as such, provides the same court-related functions for the federal courts as the county sheriff provides for the state court, within his or her respective county, that is, the protection of the court and its officers, the security and transportation of federal prisoners, the execution of court writs, and the service of court process. (2) A police official at the local level of government with police authority and legal status somewhat below that of a police officer, in states where the office remains. (3) An officer attached to a magistrate's court and acting as a bailiff and in the place of the constable. (4) A police official charged with the security and protection of the state supreme court, sometimes having the authority to enforce the state high court's writs.

**Marshal, United States.** The organizational head (director) of the United States Marshals Service (USMS) and an officer of the federal judiciary with responsibilities and duties similar in many ways to those of a county sheriff at the state level. The Office of the United States Marshal dates from the Judiciary Act of 1789, making the organization the oldest federal police or law enforcement agency in the United States. Unlike any other federal police or law enforcement agency, the U.S. Marshal and those within his office have the legal authority to enforce any federal law or writ, whether criminal or civil. The marshal's responsibilities involve the arrest of those in violation of federal law, the transportation of federal prisoners, the operation of the federal witness protection program, the incarceration of convicted federal offenders, the security of the federal courts, the execution of federal court writs, both civil and criminal, and the service of other federal legal process.

**Marshall, John (1755–1835).** Appointed in 1801 by President John Adams, during the closing days of his presidency, Marshall was titled the "great Chief Justice" by the venerable Benjamin Cardozo, himself an associate justice of the High Court. Marshall fought with a number of presidents over his Federalist interpretation of the Constitution. Over the course of his thirty-four-year tenure as chief justice, he was largely able to control dissent by justices appointed by presidents opposed to his Federalist stance, thus shoring up the role of both the Court and the Constitution in the scheme of American government. He died in office remaining true to his vision of Federalism.

**martial law.** (1) The authority of the military, under orders from the chief executive, to carry on the functions of government by exercising control over civilians and/or civil authorities. Martial law may be declared during times of war or when civil authority has failed to function effectively in the domestic venue, during times of civil unrest, tumult, or insurrection. (2) A system of law and the administration of justice during times of war instituted to respond to the exigencies stemming therefrom in a belligerent venue. During such a period, martial law supplants civil law, all civil authorities, i.e., police, courts, and prisons, which are administered wholly by the military commander, as legislator, judge, and penal administrator. See also *provost* (pronounced "provo") *marshal* and *military government*.

**Marxist criminology.** According to noted criminologist Austin Turk, conflict theory is often misunderstood. It does not suggest that most criminals are innocent or that the socially powerful engage in equal amounts of deviance against the underclasses. What it does point out is that behaviors found among society's underclasses are more likely to come to the attention of the authorities and to be labeled "crime" than the activities and behaviors of the powerful. As a criminological perspective (theory), it identifies social conflict as a fundamental fact of life and the underlying source of discrimination fueling the justice system against classes lacking the power and social status of those who both make and enforce the criminal law. Marxist criminology actually emerged about 1905 under aspiring criminologist Willem Adriaan Bonger with the appearance of his paper "Criminality and Economic Conditions." George Rusche and Otto Kirchheimer contributed to the perspective's recognition with their work in *Punishment and the Social Structure* (1939), although mainstream criminologists paid little attention to the theory until the turbulence of the 1960s. During the decade that followed, Marxist criminology was termed radical criminology, and the evolution of the perspective was further prompted by publication of the *New Criminology* by Ian Taylor, Paul Walton, and Jock Young.

**Marx, Karl (1818–1883).** A political and economic theorist who wrote little about crime, but whose works heavily influenced Marxist criminology, which came many years after his death. Unlike many others who claimed that property is crime (see *Peter Kropotkin*), Marx claimed that the ownership of private property was permissible and that what he was opposed to was the accumulation of private property (capital) to the extent that it allowed the bourgeoisie to oppress the underclasses.

**Maslow's Hierarchy of Needs.** According to Abraham Maslow, human needs can be divided into five basic groups, which in turn are subdivided into lower- and higher-order needs. Among the lower-order needs are (1) physiological needs, e.g., hunger, thirst, shelter, sex, and other bodily needs, and (2) safety needs, e.g., security and protection against physical and emotional danger. Higher-order needs include (3) belongingness, e.g., friendship, acceptance, and affection, (4) esteem needs, e.g., autonomy, achievement, status recognition, and self-respect, and (5) self-actualization needs, e.g., fulfilling one's potential and self-fulfillment. According to Maslow, as each need group is accommodated, the next level becomes a priority.

**mass murder.** The killing of four or more people at a singular location, as one identifiable event, e.g., the sequential murder of eight student nurses in Chicago by Richard Speck in July of 1966.

**mass spectrometer.** *n.* A forensic laboratory instrument often used in tandem with gas chromatography to identify, with more specific certainty than with chromatography alone, the identity of various unknown chemical substances by measuring their mass after chromatographic analysis has been completed. The process is especially useful in the identification of drugs.

**master-at-arms.** In the American Navy, a petty officer (the equivalent of an army sergeant) charged with the responsibility of peace keeping, policing, and the custody of prisoners on naval war vessels; the equivalent of an army or Marine Corps military policeman or policewoman. See *Military Police Corps.*

**Master of Social Work (MSW).** The Master of Social Work degree is the terminal graduate degree in social work practice and often requires forty-five to sixty credit-hours of course work, placing it among the longest master's degree programs in academics.

**material witness.** In criminal law, a witness whose testimony is so important to either the prosecution or defense that he or she may be required to post a bond to ensure appearance or may be held in confinement until he or she testifies; a material witness warrant may be issued for the witness's arrest and detention.

**matricide.** *n.* The unlawful killing of one's mother.

**Matza, David (1930– ).** As a graduate student of Gresham Sykes at Princeton University, he collaborated with Sykes in the development of Neutralization Theory (1957), noting that the underlying feature of delinquent subculture is a value system that represents an inversion of the value system of law-abiding citizens. Matza built upon and expanded Neutralization Theory into what he termed Drift Theory, in *Delinquency and Drift* (1964), arguing that the techniques of neutralization did not actually constitute a theory.

**maximum-security prison.** A penal or correctional institution housing dangerous and violent felons; one maintaining a strict security protocol including high walls, gun turrets, and limited social contacts for inmates with the outside world.

**mayhem.** *n.* In legal usage, the unlawful maiming of a person, in whole or in part, by intentionally mutilating the victim's body; the act of inflicting injury so severe as to deprive the victim of the permanent functional use of that part or organ of his or her body.

**McCarthyism.** *n.* The indiscriminate practice of making sweeping accusations, leading to inquisitorial investigative methods, for the ostensible purpose of weeding out communism. The term (now a metaphor for any accusation or search lacking due process protections) derives from Senator Joseph McCarthy (Republican) of Wisconsin (1946–1957), who was finally censured by the Senate on December 2, 1954, for conducting this conservative witch hunt under the authority of the House Committee on Un-American Activities (HUAC).

**McGregor, Douglas.** The architect of Theory X and Theory Y management styles, holding that Theory X managers manage people under their span of control with the assumption that workers do not like work and that only coercion, threats, and remuneration get them to continue to accomplish work. Theory Y managers believe that employees embrace their work as readily as play, and that the rewards motivating workers include self-actualization, ego satisfaction, and others. He is known for his book *The Human Side of Enterprise* (1960).

**McKay, Henry (1899–1980).** A noted Chicago-based criminologist remembered largely for his study of the spatial distribution of crime, along with his colleague Clifford Shaw. Both Shaw and McKay had been graduate students at the University of Chicago, in the Sociology Department, and although neither completed their Ph.D.s, both later became noted researchers in the university's Institute for Juvenile Research. Their work, both collaboratively and individually, bridged three major areas of contribution: ecological studies, delinquency prevention, and three qualitative life histories of Chicago-area delinquents, i.e, *The Jackroller* (Shaw, 1930), *The Natural History of a Delinquent Career* (Shaw, 1931) and *Brothers in Crime* (Shaw, McKay, McDonald, and Hanson, 1938).

**McLeod Case (1840).** In 1840, New York authorities arrested a Canadian on charges of murder and arson having to do with the destruction of a ship known as the *Caroline.* When the British government, backed by the U.S. government, demanded his release, the state refused; he was tried and acquitted. This international incident led Congress to allow the federal courts to issue writs of *habeas corpus* when aliens are held by state courts on state charges.

**McNabb–Mallory rule (1843).** Also known as the Mallory rule, it is a rule applied to federal courts, and some state courts where a similar rule has been adopted, disallowing any admission or confessions obtained during an unreasonable delay between arrest and an appearance before a magistrate. See *McNabb v. United States*, 318 U.S. 332, 63 S.Ct. 608, 87 L.Ed. 819 (1943) and *Mallory v. United States*, 354 U.S. 449, 77 S.Ct. 1356, 1 L.Ed.2d 1479 (1957).

**McNaughten (M'Naghten) rule (1843).** The primary court decision establishing the clear precedent for acquittal based on an insanity defense. This English case set the legal standard for the insanity defense in common-law nations instituting the "right–wrong" test for criminal responsibility. "If the accused was possessed of sufficient understanding when he committed the criminal act to know what he was doing and to know that it was wrong, he is responsible therefore, but if he did not know the nature and quality of the act or did know what he was doing but did not know that it was wrong, he is not responsible." A 1954 U.S. Court of Appeals for the District of Columbia expanded the McNaughten rule by developing the Durham rule.

**Mead, George Herbert (1863–1931).** A widely acknowledged sociologist whose works later influenced criminologists of the interactionist school. He labeled the group from which one receives his or her concept of self as the "generalized other." He also conceived of the self as being divided into the "I" and "me." "The 'I' is the response of the organism to the attitudes of others; the 'me' is the organized set of attitudes of others which one assumes. The attitudes of the others constitute the organized 'me,' and then one reacts toward that as an 'I.' "

**meat eaters.** Police officers who actively seek and aggressively demand graft and gratuities.

**mechanic's lien.** A lien used as a means of legal recourse to gain a defaulted payment through the attachment of equipment or property in the possession of the defaulted party.

**medical examiner.** A licensed physician, usually a pathologist, holding an appointed position, usually at the county level, who performs autopsies on the bodies of persons who met a violent death, or those who have died under suspicious circumstances, or those who have died when not in the presence of a physician. In some jurisdictions, medical examiners have supplanted coroners altogether.

**medical model.** In criminal justice, it is a rational procedural model seeking to remedy a situation with the least invasive method practicable and where coproduction and prevention are assumed to be fundamental components. Under this model, attention is focused on the underlying causation of crime and not the symptoms of crime, as in a crime-control model.

**medium-security prison.** A penal or correctional facility providing less security than that of a maximum security prison, yet more than a minimum, and generally housing nonviolent offenders and providing increased opportunities for prisoner contact with the outside world.

**megalopolis.** *n.* The statistical area between and among two or more major metropolitan areas that form a de facto metropolis; a "super city" in which a number of municipalities merge together to make a whole urbanized region.

***mens rea.*** *(Lat.)* Evil intent; the criminal state of mind; one of the two necessary elements in criminal offenses (with the exception of strict liability offenses), along with *actus reus* (the overt criminal act itself).

**mercy killing.** See *euthanasia.*

**mere evidence rule.** A rule under the law of search and seizure holding that in a lawful search, an officer has the right to seize all instrumentalities and/or fruits of the crime; however, he or she has no right to seize other items. This rule is no longer in effect.

**merger of offenses.** In criminal law, merger occurs when a serious offense includes a lesser offense or where one crime automatically leads to another.

**merit system.** A competency-based personnel system used by governmental agencies for hiring, rewarding, and promoting employees; instituted in the federal government in 1833 under passage of the Pendleton Act. See also *civil service.*

**Merton, Robert K. (1910–2003).** A celebrated sociologist (criminologist) who developed a number of criminological perspectives (theories), most notably including Anomie Theory and Adaptation Theory. Known widely for his work with Anomie Theory, where he built on and expanded Durkheim's notion in "Social Structure and Anomie" (1938).

**Mesopotamian laws and codes.** The earliest known written legal codes originating in the Mesopotamian region (the area bounded by the Tigris and Euphrates Rivers). Despite the fact that earlier Sumerian codes likely existed as early as 3000 B.C. the Babylonian Code of Hammurabi (discovered by French archeologists in 1902) stands as the most noteworthy of the Mesopotamian codes, as it exists in its entirety. Scholars of legal history speculate that the Code of Hammurabi (circa 1760 B.C.) was predicated on earlier undiscovered codes.

**methadone (Dolophine).** A synthetic opiate used in the treatment of heroin addiction since 1964 and the methadone maintenance experiment at Rockefeller University Hospital in New York.

**methaqualone (Quaalude).** A relatively low potency sedative and hypnotic chemical substance.

**methylphenidate (Ritalin).** A stimulant for the central nervous system, pharmacologically associated with amphetamines; sometimes prescribed for the management of difficult children, upon whom the drug has a calming effect.

**Metropolitan Statistical Area (MSA).** The contemporary acronym for the former Standard Metropolitan Statistical Area (SMSA) of the Office of Budget and Management of the U.S. Census Bureau. A population area of a central city along with its suburban and adjacent areas that comprise a distinguishable metropolitan area; it may include one or more counties. The acronym is commonly used by demographers and social sciences–based researchers.

**microscopy.** *n.* The microscopic investigation of evidence.

**Milgram, Stanley, experiments (1963–1974).** As a noted social psychologist and author of *Obedience to Authority: An Experimental View*, Milgram's work stands as the high-water mark for social or behavioral science research into obedience to malevolent authority.

**military commissions.** Military commissions are military tribunals that serve as special trial courts for offenders charged with crimes allegedly committed against a nation state, or a number of nation states, during war-time hostilities. Defendants thus charged are generally noncitizens, not otherwise subject to the jurisdiction of military law, who have allegedly violated a provision of the Law of War. Typically, criminal charges involve activities that give aid and comfort to the enemy or more direct involvement like terrorist activities directed against a nation and/or its people. The trial is conducted by the military and the jury members are officers from the various branches of the armed forces. In the United States, military commissions, which have taken many different forms and borne different names, and have derived their legal status from a number of sources, including the United States Constitution Article I, Section 8, clause 10, as well as Public Law 107–40, 115 Stat. 224 (Authorization for Use of Military Force), and the Uniform Code of Military Justice Article 21 (10 U.S.C. § 821). One of the first commissions (a council of war) in the United States was convened by General Winfield Scott in 1847, following the close of the war with Mexico. Military commissions must not be confused with courts martial, as commissions hear cases not falling under courts martial, i.e., the Uniform Code of Military Justice; the ruling case law in this matter is *Ex Parte Vallandigham,* 68 U.S. 243 (1863). The president, as chief executive and commander in chief of the armed forces, is constitutionally authorized to convene military commissions under special war-time circumstances. It is important to note that the Supreme Court has ruled that a formal declaration of war is not necessary for the president to convene a military commission in *Madesen v. Kinsella,* 343 U.S. 341, 346 (1952). A classic example of the convening of a military commission occurred when President Franklin D. Roosevelt appointed a military commission to hear a case involving German saboteurs in 1942, under Presidential Proclamation 2561, see *Ex Parte Quirin,* 317 U.S. 1, 63 S.Ct. 1 (1942).

**military government.** (1) Governmental authority and power granted to the military commander by the president during time of war outside the boundaries of the United States or its protectorates. (2) Governmental authority and power granted to the military commander by the president during time of rebellion, insurrection, civil tumult, or belligerency within the borders of the United States or its protectorates.

**military law.** (1) The legal code governing the armed forces of the United States, see the *Uniform Code of Military Justice (UCMJ)*. (2) The legal code governing the armed forces of any sovereign nation state.

**Military Police Corps (MPC).** Originally a corps, now a regiment within the U.S. Army, providing policing services roughly equivalent to those provided by a municipal police department and county sheriff's office at army bases and reservations worldwide. The Military Police provide all of the services associated with civilian policing with the notable exception of felony criminal investigations; these are conducted by the Army Criminal Investigation Division (CID). In addition to its general policing responsibilities, the Military Police serve a vital security function for military courts, military bases, custodial and correctional facilities, and other military assets and interests. In a war theater, the MPC serves prisoner of war, escort guard, scouting, and numerous other duties not associated with civilian police work. The chief administrator of a Military Police command is the provost (pronounced *provo*) marshal, who is overseen by the provost marshal general. A similar system of policing is employed by the Marine Corps, while the U.S. Air Force uses nearly the same arrangement under the rubric of Security Police, formerly the Air Police (AP). The U.S. Navy has an entirely different arrangement, under the banner of the Master at Arms, that functions generally as Military Police on naval vessels. Temporary policing services are provided by the Shore Patrol, when naval personnel are at liberty in ports around the world; they are not, however, the equivalent of the Military Police who have extensive police training and are assigned a permanent military occupational speciality (MOS 95B) as military police personnel.

**military prison.** (1) A penal or correctional facility for those sentenced to prison time by a court-martial under the provisions of the Uniform Code of Military Justice, e.g., the U.S. Disciplinary Barracks at Fort Leavenworth, Kansas. (2) A penal facility managed by the military for those convicted of war crimes, as the facilities maintained in Germany after World War II. (3) A custodial facility for prisoners of war. (4) A custodial facility for the detainment and interrogation of prisoners of war and "enemy combatants."

**militia.** *n.* (1) Any militarylike organization composed of citizens as opposed to "professional" soldiers who are mustered under the authority of the governor of a state during times of emergency. (2) Technically, all able-bodied citizens between the ages of eighteen and forty-five who are not members of the armed forces of the United States, whether active duty or reserve and including the National Guard. In earlier times, a local military unit, composed of volunteers at the local level of government for local defense, these units were considerably less formal than federal or state military units, and their officers were elected by the troops. State militias preceded the National Guard and were voluntary organizations with no connection to the federal armed forces for the satisfaction of compulsory military duty; e.g., Abraham Lincoln was an elected captain of his local militia company in Illinois, during the Black Hawk War.

**millet.** *n.* A socially isolated sectarian and often religious community, having a degree of social, political, and/or legal autonomy through a quasi-theocratic organizational arrangement, and exercising a considerable amount of social control over its members via ecclesiastical authority, while existing within the territorial and jurisdictional authority of a sovereign secular state; a utopian society, e.g., Amish communities.

**minimum-security prison.** The least secure penal or correctional facility housing white-collar and nonviolent offenders. This institutional category maintains a liberal furlough and visitation policy and employs reduced security measures, as compared to maximum-security facilities.

**ministerial act.** An act performed in obedience to the legal commands or requirements of the law, requiring no discretion on the part of the person so performing the act.

**ministerial officer.** An officer who is required by law to perform various acts in obedience to the mandates of legal authorities, without the exercise of his or her independent discretion concerning the act(s) to be performed.

**Minneapolis Domestic Violence Study (1981–1982).** A study to determine the deterrent effect of arrest, mediation, and separation in misdemeanor domestic violence cases, conducted by Lawrence Sherman and Richard Berk. The study found that arrest produced a notably lower repeat violence rate than either separation or mediation. (Arrest reoccurred in only 10 percent of the cases where arrest had been randomly chosen, whereas mediation and separation showed a 19 percent and 24 percent rearrest rate, respectively). Critics of the study claim problems with the study, especially in the area of the random selection of treatment options. Nonetheless, by the late 1990s, 97 percent of all American local-level police agencies had a policy on domestic disputes, and many had adopted a mandatory arrest policy in domestic violence incidents, as many state legislatures created mandatory arrest policies for domestic violence, in response to the study's findings. Replications of the study in other cities failed to show the same pattern of deterrent effect for the arrest option that the original study had.

**Minnesota Multiphasic Personality Inventory (MMPI).** A widely used psychological measurement instrument probing the important aspects of one's personality; the test spans a wide range of issues including psychological health, moral, and social attitudes.

**minor.** *n.* A term deriving from civil law denoting one (an infant) under a prescribed age as set by law, generally eighteen years of age (the age of majority in many states).

**miranda warnings.** The warnings required as a result of the case of *Miranda v. Arizona,* 384 U.S. 436, 444, 478, 479, 86 S.Ct. 1602, 1612, 1630, 16 L.Ed.2d 694 (1966). The warnings must be administered before questioning by a police or law enforcement officer during a custodial interrogation or when the suspect's freedom is significantly deprived. The warnings include (1) the right to remain silent; (2) statements made may be used against him or her at trial; (3) the suspect has the right to an attorney during questioning; and (4) if he or she cannot afford an attorney, one will be appointed prior to any questioning, if he or she desires. Failure to administer the warnings can lead to the suppression of all evidence obtained during the interrogation or interview.

**miscellaneous docket.** The docket citing all *in forma pauperis* appeals before the U.S. Supreme Court.

**miscreant.** *n.* A criminal or otherwise evil person; a wayward juvenile, habitually in trouble with the authorities.

**misdemeanant.** *n.* One who has been found guilty of a misdemeanor offense by a court of competent jurisdiction.

**misdemeanor.** *n.* A criminal code offense falling below a felony, generally punishable by a fine or imprisonment (or both) in a facility other than a penitentiary for a period of less than one year, or a fine not to exceed $500 to $1,000, depending on the jurisdiction. Some states classify misdemeanors into various categories (e.g., A–C) depending on their seriousness. Generally, any criminal offense other than a felony is a misdemeanor. See USCA § 1.

**misfeasance.** *n.* The performance of a lawful act in an unlawful manner, resulting in an unlawful infringement on the rights and liberties of another. Misfeasance must not be confused with "nonfeasance," which is the omission of an act he or she must legally do; or "malfeasance," a wrongful and unlawful act that one has no right or obligation to perform.

**misnomer.** *n.* In criminal law, the application of an incorrect name or title to the accused at the indictment, preliminary hearing, motion, or trial stage. In some jurisdictions, a misnomer provides grounds for a dismissal. However, in most states and the federal court system, a misnomer may be corrected by amending the pleadings.

**misprision.** *n.* The neglectful misconduct of a legal duty; the failure to reveal to the proper authorities that a crime has been committed by another when the subject has knowledge thereof. The term may imply any or all of the following: (1) contempt against the state's administration of justice and the various agencies of justice; (2) the improper administration of a public office; and (3) a failure to report a crime of which an individual has knowledge to the proper authorities and in a timely manner.

**misprision of felony.** The criminal offense of passively concealing a felony perpetrated by another through failure to reveal relevant information to the proper authorities, when the knowing individual has not assisted in the commission of the crime. Under federal law (USCA § 4), a person commits the misprision of a felony when, having knowledge of the commission of a felony, he or she fails to report such criminal activity, in a timely manner, to a judge or other official, i.e., police or law enforcement official, a grand jury, a U.S. attorney, or other federal, civil, or military justice official.

**misprision of treason.** The criminal offense of failing to report to the proper justice authorities, in a timely manner, an act of treason or treasonable plot, when the knowing party has not assisted in the act or conspiracy. See 18 USCA § 2382.

**Missing Child Act (1984).** A later redrafting of the Comprehensive Crime Control Act of 1984, which amended the Juvenile Justice and Delinquency Prevention Act of 1974 to the Juvenile Justice, Runaway Youth, and Missing Children's Act

Amendments of 1984. The act gave rise to the Office of Juvenile Justice and Delinquency Prevention (OJJDP).

**missing persons.** It is generally not a crime to be a missing person, if the person is missing in and of his or her own volition and is an adult. As such, police and law enforcement agencies have no legal obligation to search or return such persons. However, if the person is aged or very young, mentally disturbed, handicapped, or the like, police organizations are generally willing to assist in the recovery of such a person. If the subject is missing under suspicious circumstances, police and law enforcement agencies will conduct searches and investigations. If the missing person has been gone for twenty-four hours or more a formal report is generally taken.

**Missouri plan.** A system designed for the nonpartisan selection of judges, conceptualized at Northwestern University in Evanston, Illinois, by Albert M. Kales (1875–1922), professor of law and one of the founding fathers of the American Judicature Society. State legislatures had been encouraged to incorporate the plan throughout the 1930s; however, it was not until 1940 that the state of Missouri first put the "Kales plan" into use, thus the renaming to the Missouri plan. Under the plan, a commission is empaneled consisting of a judicial officer who serves as a member *ex officio*, attorneys are selected by other lawyers, and laypersons are appointed by the governor. The empaneled commission then nominates three candidates, and the governor appoints one of the three. Once a year elapses, the selected judge goes before a general election whereupon he or she serves the remainder of the term if he or she receives a majority vote.

**mistake of fact.** An error of fact resulting in an act that would not otherwise have been attempted or undertaken. It is an affirmative defense to claim mistake of fact when one commits a legally proscribed act, if done in good faith and in a way a reasonable person would have done it, when such act was based on the belief that certain facts were correct, when in fact they were not. The mistake must have been an honest one, not a negligent act or one done based on shoddy deliberation.

**mistake of law.** The simple ignorance concerning behavior that is legally disallowed does not generally provide a defense for the violation of a criminal statute or ordinance, as "ignorance of the law is no excuse." It must be noted case law suggests that in order for the law to be enforceable, it must first be publically promulgated. See the Supreme Court's ruling in *Lambert v. California,* 355 U.S. 225 (1957).

**mistrial.** *adj.* A trial terminated prior to its fruition, as a result of a want of jurisdiction, an improper drawing of jurors, or some other fundamental shortcoming. An extraordinary event may cause the judge to call a mistrial; so may a prejudicial error that cannot be remedied during the trial, or a hung jury.

**mitigating circumstances.** Those circumstances associated with the commission of a crime that demonstrate extenuating issues reducing the extent of moral culpability of the offender. While mitigating circumstances do not excuse the offense, they can impact the sentencing decision of the judge.

**mitigation.** *n.* The reduction of moral culpability in the interest of fairness and justice; to reduce painful severity; see *abate, ameliorate, assuage, diminish, extenuate, soften,* or *temper.*

**mitochondrial DNA.** See *DNA, mitochondrial.*

**mittimus.** *(Lat.)* A writ issued by a magistrate to the appropriate officer (generally the sheriff) commanding him or her to transport the defendant named therein and place him or her in a custodial (usually the county jail) or correctional institution (prison or penitentiary). See *commitment.*

**M'Naghten, Daniel.** The person whose trial ended in a not guilty by reason of insanity defense (1843) and for whom the "right and wrong" test became the prevailing standard in English and American criminal procedure. M'Naghten, who lived in London during the 1840s, was delusional and thought that Sir Robert Peel was involved in a conspiracy to kill him. M'Naghten shot and killed Edward Drummond, the private secretary of Peel, when he mistook him for Peel. M'Naghten's defense argued that it was his mental delusions that had caused him to act, not a rational mind. See *Mews' Dig.* i. 349; iv. 1112.S.C. 8Scott N.R. 595; 1C. and K. 130; 4St. Tr. N.S. 847 May 26–June 19, 1843.

**M'Naghten rule.** See *M'Naghten, Daniel.*

**mob.** *n.* The assemblage of a number of people (usually defined as at least three people by statute) conducting themselves in either a violent or disorderly way. Often, the mob has unlawfully assembled in its nascent stages and in defiance of law in committing, or threatening to commit, property damage or violence to individuals. Nearly synonymous with the term "riot," mob is the legally preferred usage.

**mobile command post.** A van-type vehicle used by police or law enforcement agencies at the scene of serious criminal or other emergency situations, being generally equipped with sophisticated communications equipment. In a hostage situation, e.g., a mobile command post is frequently used to coordinate communications and personnel.

**mobile crime laboratory.** More correctly a mobile criminal evidence van, used to store and provide sophisticated evidence collection tools, materials, and instruments for field testing at the scene of a serious criminal incident. The van also serves as the repository for evidence that has been gathered, in order to provide secure storage and protection. This is important in establishing a clear chain of custody for the evidence, which will likely be challenged by the defense at suppression.

**Mobile Digital Terminal (MDT).** A digital terminal located in an emergency vehicle, allowing the operator to communicate with and receive messages from transmitting sources in digital or printed format. The advantage of the MDT system is that it reduces the use of the congested radio channels for emergency workers, like police officers, while reducing the necessity for the officer to stop his or her vehicle in order to hand copy a long text message.

**model act.** A proposed model statute created by the National Conference of Commissioners of Uniform State Laws intended for adoption by the various state legislatures, e.g., the *Model Traffic Code* or the *Model Penal Code.* Often states adopt these model codes as they exist, modify them, or selectively adopt portions of them.

**Model Penal Code (MPC).** A proposed compilation of statutes crafted by the National Conference of Commissioners of Uniform State Laws as a model, ready for adoption by state general assemblies, e.g., the *Model Traffic Code* or the *Model Penal Code.* States may adopt the code in toto, modify it, or adopt only selected parts.

**Model Sentencing Act.** A suggested model document for proposed model-sentencing guidelines, drafted by members of the Advisory Council of Judges from the National Council on Crime and Delinquency (NCCD).

**modes of policing.** Policing styles employed by police agencies underpinning a department's policing orientation, e.g., professional or traditional model policing, team policing, problem-oriented policing, community-oriented policing, or zero-tolerance policing.

***modus operandi.*** *(Lat.)* Method of operation (MO) is a term used by justice officials for the habits, patterns, operating practices, and methods of various criminals.

***modus vivendi.*** *(Lat.)* (1) Within the context of international law, a *modus vivendi* is a legal instrument that formally acknowledges some agreement between various international actors, e.g., states or organizations, that is provisional and intended to be replaced by a permanent instrument, e.g., a treaty, at a later date. (2) A way, method, or pattern of living, i.e., a lifestyle.

**molding.** *n.* The process of producing a mirror image of an impression left at the scene of a crime, generally done with plaster of paris, e.g., the molding of a footprint or tire impression.

**Mollen Commission (1994).** Headed by Milton Mollen, a retired New York judge, the commission was established outside the NYPD to independently investigate and report on corruption within the department. As one of the many anticorruption committees established in New York City over the past century, the Mollen Commission argued that a new form of corruption had emerged during the 1980s and 1990s, that is, the confluence of corruption and brutality by police officers, where officers severely beat drug dealers, took their drugs and money, and resold the drugs on the streets, sometimes to other officers.

**Molly Maguires.** A group of militant labor radicals, active in the anthracite coal region of Pennsylvania (circa 1860–1878). A secret order comprised of Irish members and headquartered in Pittsburgh and New York City, they resorted to labor radicalism and strikes in response to economic and social oppression. The organizations's radicalism led to a series of murders of mine officials and the intimidation of judges and police officials alike. When the activities of the Molly Maguires threatened mining operations to the point of collapse, Franklin B. Groves, president of the Philadelphia and Reading Railroad and its subsidiary, the Coal and Iron Company, attempted to neutralize the Molly Maguires by hiring the Pinkerton Detective Agency. Through an undercover operation, James McParlan (a Pinkerton agent masquerading as a Molly Maguire) infiltrated the organization, garnering sufficient evidence to successfully prosecute Molly Maguire members in a series of murder trials spanning 1875 and 1878, resulting in nineteen court-ordered hangings.

**Molotov cocktail.** A homemade firebomb consisting of a glass bottle filled with a flammable liquid, usually gasoline, with a rag as the wick.

**money laundering.** See *laundering money.*

**monozygotic (MZ) twins.** Identical twins; twins developing from the same (single) fertilized egg, later dividing into two separate embryos.

**Montesquieu (1689–1755).** (Charles Louis de Seconat, Baron de la Brede et de Montesquieu). A French philosopher and lawyer during the Enlightenment, who was committed to improving the plight of humanity. His publications debunked the French penal code and called for reforms leading to reasoned punishments for violation of the code. His publications include *The Spirit of the Laws* and the essay "Persian Letters."

**moot.** *adj.* In legal usage, a subject, issue, or action that is unsettled. A point becomes "moot" because it has become merely academic or dead as a legal issue.

**moot court.** A mock court assembled for the purpose of practicing one's legal skills, often in a law school setting, using a hypothetical case.

**moot question.** A question no longer being viable, as something has intervened to make the question irrelevant.

**moral.** *adj.* Related to or involving the distinction between right and wrong; in accord with the principles of right and wrong.

**moral development.** A theory of cognitive development promulgated by Lawrence Kohlberg, somewhat paralleling Piaget's Theory of Cognitive Development. Kohlberg's theory involves three levels of moral maturity, the preconventional, conventional, and postconventional stages. In the preconventional stage, or the stage of concrete operations, children do not actually think in moral terms. During the conventional stage, children shift their thinking to accommodate what others approve. During the last stage, postconventionalism, adults (only some) base their thinking of morality on a clear awareness of the rights of individuals and the importance of critical thinking. At this stage, the morally mature person develops a clear grasp of the rights of others in relative terms.

**moral evidence.** See *circumstantial evidence.*

**moral law.** See *natural Law.*

**moral turpitude.** Behavior seriously impinging on widely accepted rules, conventions, or standards of moral conduct and accepted behavior owed by individuals to other members of society or society as a whole. A crime is said to be one of moral turpitude when it involves an incursion into the moral values of a community, thus distinguishing it from crimes that are merely *mala prohibita* in nature.

**More, Sir Thomas (1478–1535).** The venerable British political figure and author of the book *Utopia,* who was beheaded for his moral stand on religious freedom that would only be secured if King Henry VIII was not given ultimate authority over religious matters in England, needed for his divorce from the queen.

**mores.** *n.* Social customs and folkways that are nearly universally complied with for the welfare of the social order, enforced informally but effectively.

**morgue.** *n.* A facility where dead bodies of unknown persons are held for identification purposes and eventual disposal. Generally, morgues are operated by the county coroner or medical examiner.

**morphine.** *n.* A crystalline alkaloid, bitter to the taste and white in color, deriving from the opium plant and cited as a controlled substance in all American criminal codes.

**mortis causa.** *(Lat.)* By reason of, or in contemplation of, death.

**Mosaic code.** The ancient legal code of the Hebrews, deriving from Moses, contained primarily in the Pentateuch (the first five books of the Old Testament).

**motion.** *n.* An application, request, or petition made to a court, tribunal, or other decision-making authority with the intent of receiving a favorable decision.

**motion to suppress.** In criminal law, a formal petition to the court requesting the elimination of evidence allegedly gained illegally. See *exclusionary rule.*

**motivation.** *n.* The drive or impetus compelling action.

**motive.** *n.* The causative factor or combination of factors moving the will and inducing action.

**motor vehicle theft.** (1) The unlawful taking (larceny) of a motorized vehicle or other motorized road vehicle of another with the intent to permanently deprive. A lesser included offense is joyriding, which involves the unlawful taking with the intent to temporarily deprive (a theft of services). (2) The theft or attempted theft of a motor vehicle, including joyriding (FBI Uniform Crime Reporting Definition).

**Motor Vehicle Theft Act (1919).** The congressional act, formerly known as the Dyer Act, making it a federal offense to transport a vehicle, known to have been stolen, across state lines.

**Motor Vehicle Theft Law Enforcement Act (1984).** A federal act mandating automobile manufacturers to mark fourteen major components in autos classified as high-risk for theft with an identification number consisting of seventeen characters, beginning with the 1987 model year. Additionally, all original manufacturer equipment replacement parts are required to have some unique marking or the letter "R" for trademark to aid police officials in tracing parts from "chop shops."

**moulage.** *n.* The practice of making a mold of an object or imprint (e.g., a footprint or tire impression), usually with plaster of paris, for the purpose of criminal identification and subsequent legal process.

**movant.** *n.* The petitioner making a motion or application for a ruling or order.

**muckraker.** *n.* A journalist who muckrakes, especially a newspaper reporter. Muckraking is a term first coined by President Theodore Roosevelt as an allusion to those who "muck rake" so intently that they lose sight of their "heavenly crown" (see Bunyan's *Pilgrim's Progress*). Muckraking journalists during the "Gilded Age" used the technique to expose the abuses of entrenched power in exposes about corruption among public officials and businessmen. One of the tools used by Progressive reformers to enlighten the masses about abuses that needed public attention.

**mug shot** A photograph, usually taken at the booking stage, showing both sides of the head and a frontal shot showing the head and upper chest.

**multicide.** *n.* The murder of numerous people. See *mass murder.*

**municipal charter.** The organic document of a municipality granted by the sovereign state, upon successful application by the inhabitants of a specified area within a given state, providing the authority to establish a municipal corporation for the purpose of local self-government and its attendant duties, responsibilities, and conveniences.

**municipal corporation.** A local-governmental body authorized by the sovereign state through a prescribed legislative or constitutional process, incorporating the municipality for the purpose of local self-government, as a political appendage (political subdivision) of the state. Typically, a municipal corporation (a city, town, borough, hamlet, burgh, village, or township) petitions the state for incorporation. Counties, however, are technically not considered municipalities, as they do not petition the state for establishment; the state establishes counties expressly for the local or regional administration of state responsibilities and functions, and counties are considered administrative appendages of the state.

**municipal court.** An inferior court with jurisdiction over municipal ordinance violations and generally headed by a justice of the peace or municipal court judge. Often, this judge is not a licensed attorney, and an appeal from the court's rulings is not possible, as no record of the proceedings can be served up to the superior (trial) court. Additionally, because a state trial court is not an appellate court, no appeal is possible. In the event that a case is to be readjudicated in state trial court, the case is heard *de novo* (as new). Such courts are found in states having a nonunified court system or in states having independent cities, i.e., cities that do not lie within a county, e.g., Saint Louis, Missouri; these municipal courts, however, function as state trial courts, albeit at the city level.

**municipal home rule.** A plan under which a state constitutional provision provides greater political autonomy to a municipality eligible for home rule than is generally granted to municipal corporations. A home-rule charter cannot, however, contain any elements contravening the federal or state constitution, federal or state law, or any treaties to which the nation is a signatory. A similar arrangement is available to counties of a certain class in many states. Generally, the county must be one of a million residents or more (a class-one county) to qualify for home-rule status.

**municipal law.** (1) The civil (ordinance) law passed under the legislative authority of a municipality's charter granted by a sovereign state. While many ordinances look like criminal laws, and function similarly, they are considered quasi-criminal and technically are categorized as civil law. Because only a sovereign entity has the authority to generate criminal law and cannot delegate that authority, a municipality is technically disallowed to create criminal law per se. That task can legally be undertaken only by the legislative branch of the various states or national government. (2) In centuries past, the term meant a "public act" or law of a state or nation, generated under the supreme authority of the sovereign, as in the Northwest Ordinance of 1787.

**municipal-level police.** The largest single component of the policing apparatus in the United States. This category of police agency is responsible for the overwhelming majority of arrests nationwide. Police at the municipal level, as well as employees of a municipality, operate under the police authority or power of the state.

**municipality.** *n.* See *municipal corporation*.

**municipal officer.** Any officer representing a municipal corporation, e.g., a mayor, treasurer, or chief of police.

**municipal ordinance.** See *municipal law*.

**municipal reform.** A term associated with the reform efforts of the Progressive reformers spanning approximately 1880 to 1920. Reform efforts at the state and local level of American government began around 1880; federal Progressive reform began about 1900 and lasted until about 1920, although many historians place the end of Progressive reform abruptly at 1917, at the end of World War I when American idealism was shattered. These reform efforts attempted to eliminate corruption and inefficiency and to bring about rationality to the administration of public affairs, as a result of the abuses suffered under entrenched power during the "Gilded Age." Such reform initiatives included, e.g., the referendum, the city-manager form of government, proportional voting representation, the land-grant state university, and police reform.

**murder.** *n.* The unlawful and intentional killing of a human being; in some instances the killing of another while in the commission or attempted commission of another crime. See *felony murder rule.*

**mutiny.** *n.* A capital offense under military law, it is an insurrection by those enlisted in the armed forces against the lawful authority of their superiors; it stands as the military's most serious criminal offense.

**mutual aid.** An agreement, sometimes in the form of a formal document, outlining the duties, responsibilities, and procedures for the assistance rendered among police, law enforcement, and firefighting agencies in a given area under emergency circumstances, when inter-jurisdictional assistance is requested.

**mutual transfer.** The theory holding that when two or more objects come into contact with one another, there is a transference of trace evidence.

**muzzle blast.** The expanded gases produced by the ignition of gun powder in a firearm that forcefully follows the projectile out of the gun barrel. At close range, this blast can tear and burn the skin, leaving an atomized blood-spatter spray.

M
N

# N

NAA, neutron activation analysis
NACJD, National Archive of Criminal Justice Data
NATB, National Automobile Theft Bureau
NCCANI, National Clearinghouse on Child Abuse and Neglect
  Information
NCCD, National Council on Crime and Delinquency
NCIC, National Crime Information Center
NCIS, Naval Criminal Investigative Service
NCVS, National Crime Victimization Survey
NDIS, National DNA Index System
NIBIN, National Integrated Ballistics Information Network
NIBRS, National Incident-Based Reporting System
NIC, National Institute of Corrections
NICB, National Insurance Crime Bureau
NIJ, National Institute of Justice
NLRB, National Labor Relations Board
NOBLE, National Organization of Black Law Enforcement
  Executives
NOP, neighborhood-oriented policing
NRS, National Reporter System
NSA, National Security Agency
NSA, National Sheriffs' Association
NYS, National Youth Survey

---

**nalline test.** A test administered to determine whether or not one has recently used narcotics.

**Napoleonic Code.** The civil law of France dating from 1804 when Napoleon became emperor. Much of Louisiana's legal system derives from this French civil law code, i.e., a civil law system, as opposed to a common-law system.

**narcotic.** *n.* In criminal law, any substance deriving from an opiate, a drug inducing profound sleep or lethargy or providing relief from pain and a dulling of the senses; an addictive controlled substance under the criminal law of all American states.

**narcotic drug.** In law, as opposed to medicine, any drug produced directly or indirectly from the extraction of substances of a plant, or produced by chemical synthesis or any combination of the preceding; narcotic drugs include (1) opium and opiate derivatives, (2) poppy straw, (3) ecgonine, (4) cocaine, and (5) any mixture or compound containing any quantity of the preceding substances.

**Narcotic Prohibition Act (1909).** The first piece of federal legislation making it unlawful to import opium or any of its derivatives into the United States. It was preceded by a section found in the McKinley Tariff Act of 1890, imposing a tax on the manufacturing of smoking opium produced in the United States.

**nation.** *n.* (1) A sovereign state among the community of nations. (2) The people residing in a given territory under the authority of one overarching government, i.e., a state existing by virtue of its own sovereign right.

**National Advisory Commission on Criminal Justice Standards and Goals (1971).** The committee was appointed by the administrator of the Law Enforcement Assistance Administration in 1971 to produce a set of national standards for the reduction and prevention of crime at the state and local level. By 1973, the commission promulgated its recommended standards for police practices.

**National Archive of Criminal Justice Data (NACJD).** Established in 1978 as an appendage of the Inter-University Consortium for Political and Social Research (ICPSR) and supported by the research arm of the U.S. Department of Justice, Bureau of Justice Statistics (BJS), the NACJD catalogues and disseminates digitized crime and justice data collected from federal and state criminal justice agencies and academic researchers to various consumers for the purpose of secondary statistical analysis.

**National Automobile Theft Bureau (NATB).** The private automobile theft investigative organization funded by an amalgamation of automobile insurance carriers to assist police and law enforcement agencies in the detection and recovery of stolen automobiles and the prosecution of automobile theft rings nationwide. See *National Insurance Crime Bureau (NICB).*

**National Central Bureau (NCB).** (1) Located in Paris, France, the NCB is the clearinghouse for communications with INTERPOL. (2) The INTERPOL headquarters of a participating nation.

**National Clearinghouse on Child Abuse and Neglect Information (NCCANI).** Founded in 1974 under the Child Abuse Prevention and Treatment Act, the NCCANI collects and dispenses data on all areas of child abuse, as a service provided by the Children's Bureau, Administration for Children and Families, U.S. Department of Health and Human Services. The National Clearinghouse on Child Abuse and Neglect Information is located in Washington, DC.

**National Computerized Criminal History System (NCCHS).** Established in 1971 under the umbrella of the National Crime Information Center of the U.S. Department of Justice, the system provides criminal histories through the NCIC system to all states and their respective police and law enforcement agencies.

**National Council on Crime and Delinquency (NCCD).** A nonprofit organization, founded in 1907, promoting humane, fair, and economical solutions to family and community-based criminal-justice–related problems. The NCCD conducts research to promote reform initiatives intended to prevent crime and delinquency.

**National Crime Information Center (NCIC).** The national computerized criminal information center that began service in 1967, under the authority of the FBI; NCIC is available to all police and law enforcement agencies in the United States and Canada, both military and civilian.

**National Crime Survey (NCS).** A statistical program, using data from the Census Bureau, to provide information on the victimization of persons twelve years of age or older who have been the victim of selected crimes. Instituted in 1972, the program is administered by the Bureau of Justice Statistics (BJS).

**National Crime Victimization Survey (NCVS).** An ongoing study of victimization, conducted by the U.S. Department of Justice and the U.S. Bureau of the Census, surveying a carefully selected sample of crime victims about their experiences with law violators.

**National Criminal Justice Reference Service (NCJRS).** See *National Institute of Justice.*

**National DNA Index System (NDIS).** Authorized under the DNA Identification Act (1994), it is a computerized database of DNA profiles for serious criminal offenders. See *Combined DNA Index System (CODIS).*

**National Firearms Act (1934).** A congressional act restraining the importation and interstate transportation of short-barreled (sawed-off) shotguns, silencers, and fully automatic firearms. The act also levies a tax on firearms dealers.

**National Guard.** The voluntary military organization (formerly the state militia) of a state government within the United States, serving as a reserve component within the U.S. Army or Air Forces. The guard serves as a state military force, under the authority of the governor, except when activated (nationalized) into the armed forces of the United States. Members of the guard undergo the same training during their active duty training assignment, alongside regular members of the Army or Air Force, but serve the remainder of their military obligation in a reserve capacity, at the state level. The guard is often called upon to quell civil disorder, when the police power of the state has otherwise been exhausted. The guard also provides state-level relief during natural disasters. The governor has the authority to call upon all able-bodied citizens eighteen years of age or older to serve in the guard, upon his or her command, during exigent circumstances.

**National Incident-Based Reporting System (NIBRS).** An outgrowth of the FBI's *Uniform Crime Reports*, NIBRS requires police agencies to provide a brief account-ing of each reported incident in a twenty-two crime-pattern matrix, providing the basis for a national database on the nature of crime, victimization, and criminals. Presently, only about a third of the states participate in this relatively new program.

**National Institute of Corrections (NIC).** An organization, located within the Bureau of Prisons, U.S. Department of Justice, Washington, DC, lending technical assis-tance and providing training programs for staff members of state prisons and local jails. NIC publishes *Annual Program Plan* and the *Annual Report.*

**National Institute of Justice (NIJ).** As the research arm of the U.S. Department of Justice, the NIJ was instituted in 1972 and serves in the capacity of a national clear-ing house for criminal justice information and the primary grant funding agency for criminal justice research.

**National Insurance Crime Bureau (NICB).** A nonprofit organization funded by nearly 1,000 insurance companies to facilitate insurers, police, and law enforcement agencies in the detection and prosecution of those who perpetrate insurance fraud.

**National Integrated Ballistics Information Network (NIBIN).** A program developed by the Bureau of Alcohol, Tobacco, Firearms, and Explosives (BATF or BATFE) to effectively regulate firearms sales in an effort to reduce the illegal sale and use of firearms by criminals and children alike. The network is linked to the Integrated Ballistics Identification System (IBIS), an electronic ballistic fingerprinting system connecting local- and state-level police and law enforcement agencies for the purpose of identifying firearms and ammunition suspected of being involved in criminal activities.

**National Labor Relations Board (NLRB).** The regulatory board created under the Wagner Act of 1935, the Taft–Hartley Act of 1947, and the Landrum–Griffin Act of 1959. The NLRB has four board members who serve five-year terms and are appointed by the president of the United States. The board's purpose is to remedy unfair labor practices and to maintain fair union representation at all stages of negotiations.

**National Magistracy School.** A French school attended by those who have completed formal legal educational programs and who intend to become either judges or prosecutors; the school lasts three years.

**National Narcotics Act (1984).** The legal foundation for the National Drug Enforcement Board, the act serves two primary purposes: (1) to maintain a national and international coordinated effort against drugs, and (2) to provide a high-level federal organizational focus to coordinate, and be responsible for, the accomplishment of drug suppression efforts.

**National Organization of Black Law Enforcement Executives (NOBLE).** Founded in 1976 with support and assistance from the Police Foundation, the Law Enforcement Assistance Administration (LEAA), and the Joint Center for Political Studies, NOBLE is the professional organization for black police and law enforcement administrators and managers nationwide.

**National Reporter System.** The various reports (the *Supreme Court Reporter, Federal Reporter, Federal Supplement,* and appellate cases from all the states) are grouped into a series including the *Atlantic Reporter, North Eastern Reporter, North Western Reporter, Pacific Reporter, South Eastern Reporter, South Western Reporter,* and *Southern Reporter.* For two states, separate reporters are also published (*New York Supplement* and *California Reporter*).

**National Rural Crime Prevention Center** A creation of the Ohio State University (1979), its express purpose is to aid rural communities and police agencies in dealing with the expanding rural crime problem.

**National Security Agency (NSA).** The federal agency charged with the protection of the nation through the interception of electronic signals and messages, and providing the appropriate intelligence, police, and law enforcement agencies with the relevant intelligence.

**National Sheriffs' Association (NSA).** Located in Alexandria, Virginia, the NSA serves as the professional society and legislative action committee for American sheriffs' agencies and their respective functionaries.

**National Youth Survey (NYS).** A survey conducted annually, concerning activities from the previous year, to determine the types and breadth of conventional and deviant behaviors of American youth, sponsored by the National Institute of Mental Health and housed within the National Archive of Criminal Justice Data in Ann Arbor, Michigan.

M
N

**nativism.** *n.* A proclivity toward favoring native-born peoples, often out of fear, ignorance, and/or prejudice. See *ethnocentrism; xenophobia.*

**natural law.** The unwritten law and principles, not having been written by human authority, but discoverable through human reason, which existed before the creation of the sovereign nation states and their concomitant positive law codes. Natural law provides the underpinnings for much of the positive law generated by common-law countries, and it has provided the moral compass from which to evaluate positive law and governmental rectitude.

**natural rights.** The unwritten law involving the intrinsic rights of individuals that existed before the creation of the sovereign nation state. The philosophers of the Enlightenment—Milton, Locke, and Rousseau—articulated the fundamental elements of natural rights. Early American patriarchs later modified and expanded on the concept of natural rights as a justification and defense for the American Revolution.

**natus.** *(Lat.)* Born.

**Naval Criminal Investigative Service (NCIS).** That branch of the U.S. Navy charged with the responsibility of conducting felony criminal investigations. Its responsibilities parallel those of the Army Criminal Investigation Division (CID).

**ne exeat.** *(Lat.)* A writ ordering one's detention and forbidding him or her to leave the jurisdiction of the court.

**negligence.** *n.* Conduct falling short of what would be expected of a prudent, reasonable person under similar conditions or circumstances, and one of the four elements comprising the *mens rea,* necessary to define an act as a crime.

**negligent.** *adj.* Something remiss, irresponsible, ill-considered, injudicious, or derelict.

**negligent homicide** A homicide committed by one whose negligence amounts to the proximate cause of another's death. In vehicle traffic law, the death of another via the instrumentality of a motor vehicle operated in a negligent way. See also *manslaughter.*

**Neiderhoffer, Arthur (1917–1981).** The noted criminal justician whose pioneering research on police attitudes, subculture, personality, public perceptions, cynicism, and authoritarianism is legendary. One of his many notable works is *Behind the Shield.* Neiderhoffer characterized the police officer as "a 'Rorscharch' in uniform . . . ." To people in trouble, the officer is a "savior," but to others he is "a fierce ogre."

**neighborhood-oriented policing (NOP).** See *community-oriented policing.*

**neighborhood watch.** A voluntary program of community self-empowerment involving people who serve as the eyes and ears of the police in a partnership with the police involving coproduction. Neighbors watch one another's children, possessions, and property, as well as crime-promoting activities of others.

**neoclassicism.** *n.* A criminological perspective (theory) that emerged in Europe in the early nineteenth century, via an alteration of the classical school of criminology's precepts, through the inclusion of such concepts as diminished capacity and a reduction in sentencing severity for those under a certain age or those not of sound mind.

**nepotism.** *n.* The granting of privileges, favoritism, or appointments to one's relatives by blood or marriage, as the term derives from the favoritism toward "nephews" exercised by many medieval prelates.

**Ness, Eliot (1903–1957).** A Chicago-based FBI special agent who, along with his group of "untouchables," fought corruption and bootlegging throughout the Chicago metropolitan area during the prohibition era. In 1936, Ness left the Bureau and accepted the position of Director of Public Safety for the City of Cleveland, Ohio, where he created a dedicated group of officers, made in the image of the untouchables, dubbed the "secret six." Ness and his secret six became inveterate crime and corruption fighters; their efforts led to the indictment of at least a dozen high-ranking Cleveland police officials and the termination of many others. His inability to identify and arrest the "Mad Butcher/Torso Killer" who had murdered at least twenty-three people from Cleveland to Pennsylvania (most of whom were decapitated) dogged his career as Cleveland's top cop. Ironically, it was an unknown drinking problem that led to his resignation from the world of policing and law enforcement. While intoxicated, he was involved in an automobile collision and fled the scene. After his apprehension, he summarily resigned his post as director of public safety. In an attempt to regain a public career, he ran for mayor of Cleveland but lost in a humiliating 2–1 vote. After his death, he was cremated and his ashes were placed in a pond in Cleveland's most prestigious cemetery.

**netwidening.** *n.* The inclusion of a wider array or selection.

**neutron activation analysis (NAA).** Discovered in 1936, NAA is a method used by forensic scientists as a method of analysis, employing radioactivity, in the detection of the presence of trace elements found in gunshot residues, e.g., lead.

**newark foot patrol experiment (1978–1979).** An experiment, similar to the Kansas City experiment, but testing specifically the effect of foot patrol on both the crime rate and public perceptions. The study found that, for the most part, crime levels were not significantly affected by foot patrol, in either residential or commercial areas.

**New Mexico State Penitentiary riot (1980).** Ranking among one of the most violent prison riots in U.S. history, this riot spanned February 2 and 3 of 1980. The thirty-six-hour insurrection resulted in thirty-three deaths and over 50 million dollars in property damage. It was not until the state called in the National Guard that the rebellion was quelled.

**night court.** A criminal court sitting during the early evening hours for the immediate disposition of petty offenses and various pretrial procedural motions.

**nightstick.** *n.* See *truncheon.*

**nihil.** *(Lat.)* Nothing.

**nihilism.** *n.* (1) The denial of any basis for truth or knowledge. (2) A doctrine espousing the total destruction of the existing social, political, and economic order to be replaced by entirely new institutions; a political doctrine advocating the use of violence against established authority and entrenched power.

**ninhydrin.** *n.* A chemical used as a processing reagent in the development of latent prints. It is often used on porous surfaces, such as paper or cardboard, where raising a print can be troublesome. It is also used in blood enhancement procedures.

**Ninth Amendment (1791).** "The enumeration in the Constitution of certain rights shall not be construed to deny or disparage others retained by the people."

**no bill.** A ruling issued by a grand jury finding that available evidence is insufficient to sustain a "true bill" (an indictment or presentment). Unlike a verdict in a petit trial, a "no bill" does not create double jeopardy or an *estoppel*; as a result, the prosecutor may present the evidence anew to another grand jury.

**no knock law.** A law allowing officers, with a lawful search warrant, to enter a dwelling without the customary knocking or announcing of their presence, identity, and purpose, when it can be reasonably assumed that such announcement would place the officers in peril or provide an opportunity for the destruction or secretion of evidence. It has been suggested that no knock warrants should require the signature of two judges, to prevent state abuse of this invasive writ and practice.

***nolle prosequi.*** *(nol-pros, Lat.)* A formal motion by the prosecutor that he or she will not prosecute the case any further. No cause need be given for this cessation of prosecution.

***nolo contendere.*** *(Lat.)* "No contest or I will not contest it." A formal plea in a criminal adjudication, wherein the defendant neither admits nor denies the charges made by the state. Nonetheless, the effect of the plea is nearly identical to a guilty plea, as the defendant is sentenced afterward by the judge. It is necessary for the judge to approve such a plea. The plea is sometimes used to avoid the use of a guilty plea at the criminal trial that might be used against the defendant in a subsequent civil trial arising out of the same circumstances.

***non comos mentis.*** *(Lat.)* Not of sound mind.

**nonfeasance.** *n.* The nonperformance of a mandatory act; the neglect of duty; dereliction, failure to execute, and avoidance of responsibility.

**noninterventionist.** *n.* One who holds to the perspective (a justice philosophy) emphasizing the least intrusive intervention (treatment) possible. Found among its central tenets are decarceration, diversion, and decriminalization.

***non prosequitor.*** *(Lat.)* A judgment by the court against the plaintiff for failure to appear.

**nonsecretor.** *n.* One with bodily fluids that do not contain identifying group antigens.

***non vult.*** *(Lat.)* The defendant does not wish to contest. See *nolo contendere.*

**not guilty by reason of insanity.** An affirmative defense of diminished capacity, claiming that at the time of the commission of the act, the defendant suffered from a mental defect or lacked the mental ability to know right from wrong, thus making the element of *mens rea* unprovable. While the defense may disallow a criminal conviction and sentence, a civil commitment will likely result from the defendant's actions, which in all reality will extend well beyond the sanction from a criminal conviction.

**notice to appear.** See *summons*; show cause order. A type of summons for low-level offenses issued by police officers, somewhat like a traffic ticket..

**notorious cohabitation.** The statutory offense committed when two persons of the opposite gender live openly together outside of wedlock. These laws are seldom enforced.

***null.*** *(Lat.)* Of no legal or binding authority.

**nulla poena sine crimine.** *(Lat.)* No punishment without a crime (a written criminal statute); more liberally, "no law (crime), no offense."

**nullification.** *n.* The act of making a law null and void (nullifying). For example, during prohibition, many juries found defendants innocent, even when the state had proven its case, because they did not think the law should exist. State legislatures also have nullified federal laws within their borders, creating a nullification crisis for the federal government, a largely unsettled area of law in the United States.

**Nuremberg trials.** The popular name for the International Military Tribunal's war trials held at Nuremberg, Germany, by the allied forces, following the close of World War II (1945). Both Nazi Party officials and military commanders were tried for war crimes, i.e., crimes against humanity, as well as other international crimes. Twenty-two defendants were found guilty and sentenced; among them, eleven were sentenced to be hanged.

# O

**oath.** *n.* A declaration or affirmation of the truth of a statement, deriving from an appeal to God or another authority, required of a witness at trial or a fact finding hearing. An affirmation may be taken independent of a swearing (to God) for those who are not theists.

**obit.** *(Lat.)* He or she died.

**obiter.** *(Lat.)* Incidentally; by the way.

**obiter dictum.** *(Lat.)* A concise opinion embedded in a decision by a judge, not necessary for the ruling.

**objection.** *n.* A formal opposition, made in court and noted in the official record, to a statement or evidence presented. Something presented in opposition, as a rebuttal, or refutation.

**oblique angle.** An angle of any degree, other than a right angle.

**obscenity.** *n.* A debauchery tending to injure public morals, as a function of its indecency.

**obstruction of justice.** Any act that tends to hinder or prevent, or attempts to hinder or prevent, the execution of legal process, e.g., obstructing or hindering the testimony of a witness.

**odium.** *(Lat.)* Hatred or antipathy.

**odontologist, forensic.** That specialized area of dentistry used by the justice system to identify victims and aid in the apprehension and prosecution of criminal offenders, which centers on the structure, maturation, and diseases of the mouth and teeth.

**offender.** *n.* A term frequently found in the criminal law for one implicated in a criminal act, including quasi-criminal acts like traffic offenses.

**offense.** *n.* Any breach of the criminal law, including felony and misdemeanor violations as well as quasi-criminal violations, e.g., traffic offenses and municipal ordinance violations.

**Office of Justice Programs (OJP).** Located in Washington, DC, the OJP is a program office housed within the U.S. Department of Justice, offering grant funding, specialized training, technical assistance, and statistical research to criminal justicians and state and local criminal justice agencies.

**Office of Juvenile Justice and Delinquency Prevention (OJJDP).** Authorized under the Juvenile Justice and Delinquency Prevention (JJDP) Act of 1974 (Public

Law 93–415, 42 USC 5601), the agency provides resources, through grants and other programs, to address nationwide the problems associated with juvenile delinquency and victimization.

**Office of Law Enforcement Assistance (OLEA).** Created by an act of Congress in 1965 (Public Law 89–197), the OLEA focused on improving police and law enforcement agencies throughout the nation through the administration of federal grants for training and equipment. The OLEA's functions were terminated and transferred to the newly created Law Enforcement Assistance Administration under the authority of the Federal Omnibus Crime Control and Safe Streets Act of 1968.

**Office of Special Investigations (OSI).** The criminal investigative agency within the U.S. Air Force, charged with the investigation of crimes against the Air Force, any of its interests, and/or its personnel. A separate agency from the Air Force Security Police. The parallel agency to the Army Criminal Investigative Division (CID) or the Naval Criminal Investigative Service (NCIS).

**official crime statistics.** Statistics collected by an official agency of criminal justice at the national, state, county, or local level. The FBI's *Uniform Crime Reports* (UCR) stands as a well-known example of official statistics, gathered by the Bureau from approximately 96 percent of all police and law enforcement agencies nationwide. Official statistics, as a general rule, are better at gathering data on serious offenses than unofficial statistics (e.g., the *National Crime Victimization Survey*), which are better at gathering data on less serious offenses.

**official immunity doctrine.** The doctrine posits that governmental officials can claim absolute privilege from civil liability, if the action in question falls within their lawful authority and if the questioned action requires the application of discretion. Seealso *sovereign immunity.*

**officially arrested.** One is officially arrested only after the police or law enforcement officer makes out an official arrest report, with the intent of proceeding with adversarial proceedings.

**Ohlin, Lloyd, E. (1928– ).** Widely known for his collaborative work with colleague Richard Cloward in the development of Differential Opportunity Theory, see, e.g., *Delinquency and Opportunity: A Theory of Delinquent Gangs* (1960). This theory is an integration of a number of different theoretical orientations. Most notably, Differential Opportunity brings together two divergent criminological theories: Edwin Sutherland's Differential Association and Robert K. Merton's Anomie.

**oligarchy.** *n.* A form of government under which only a few privileged people rule.

**ombudsman/ombudsperson.** *n.* A government official to whom people having grievances associated with the government may apply for relief, redress, or remedy. The ombudsman/ombudsperson serves as the citizen's representative before the government.

**Omnibus Crime Control and Safe Streets Act of 1968.** A Title I congressional act providing financial assistance to police and law enforcement agencies nationwide to improve services. Block grants were given to the various states, which in turn directed federal dollars to agencies in order to improve infrastructure, hardware, training, and crime fighting programs.

O
P

**open fields doctrine.** Police and other law enforcement agents are legally allowed to enter upon outdoor property to seek evidence, without a warrant or other justification. Paradoxically, the doctrine applies even when the property is posted "no trespassing." Anything observed in the "open fields" and in course of their activity is admissible in court under the "plain view rule."

**opening statement.** A statement made by both the prosecution and defense at the beginning of the trial, outlining in summary terms an overview of the case and evidence or proof that will be presented to the jury. Its purpose is to orient the jury and to give advanced notice as to the types of evidence that will be presented in order to provide a general picture of the facts and situations involved in the case.

**operant conditioning.** Pioneered by psychologist B. F. Skinner, this explanation for human learning posits that when a behavior is followed by positive consequences, it is more likely to be repeated; however, when a behavior is followed by negative consequences, it is less likely to be repeated.

**Operation Greylord.** A four-year long, mid-1980s FBI undercover operation targeting judges in the nation's largest unified court system, i.e., Cook County, Illinois. The investigation resulted in the indictment of twenty-eight people, six of whom were judges, thirteen of whom were Cook County-based lawyers. During the course of the operation, the FBI lawfully bugged the chambers of a judge, perhaps for the first time in American history.

**opiate.** *n.* Any controlled substance containing opium or any derivative thereof, acting as a narcotic sedative.

**opiate narcotic.** A drug having both sedative and analgesic properties.

**opinion.** *n.* (1) A document generated by an attorney for his client, laying out his understanding of the law and its applicability to the case at hand. (2) The official statement by a judge about a decision or judgment in a particular case. (3) The opinion of an attorney general concerning an issue over which there is no precedent, or the interpretation of existing case law. Opinions may be oral or written. Formal written opinions include the following: majority opinions, minority opinions, separate opinions, plurality opinions, *per curiam* opinions, slip opinions, and advisory opinions.

**opinion evidence.** Evidence regarding what a witness thinks, believes, or may infer from the facts and behaviors of those in dispute, as opposed to his or her mere perception of acts and behaviors. The rules of evidence disallow the use of opinion evidence by lay witnesses; however, opinions of expert (opinion) witnesses who are certified by the courts as experts are allowed. See, e.g., *Federal Evidentiary Rule 702.*

**opium.** *n.* The narcotic drug deriving from the juice of the seeds of the opium poppy; it contains alkaloids including morphine, codeine, and papaverine, with the ability to mask pain and induce sleep.

**Opportunity-Structure Theory.** Any of the criminological perspectives (theories) holding that crime derives from the situation in which it occurs; three separate explanatory approaches exist: environmental criminology, rational choice theory, and routine-activity theory.

**oral evidence.** Any evidence uttered by word of mouth, e.g., testimonial evidence. See *parol evidence.*

**order.** *n.* (1) An authoritative mandate, command, direction, rule, or regulation. A direct command of a court or judge, issued in writing and separate from any judgment. Numerous types of orders exist, e.g., restraining orders, day orders, final orders, general orders, and interlocutory orders. (2) The formal order of a chief executive, i.e., an executive order, having the force of law. (3) A command given by a military officer or noncommissioned officer to troops. (4) A command given to police officers by their superiors.

**order maintenance.** One of the primary nonlaw enforcement or noncriminal responsibilities of the police, involving the handling of interpersonal conflicts and public nuisances.

**order *nisi*.** *(Lat.)* A conditional order, providing a specified time within which to comply. Failure to satisfy the provisions of the order triggers the making of the order absolute and subjects the violator to a show cause order and/or contempt proceedings.

**order to show cause.** An order to appear and present to the court such reasons as why the original order should not be executed.

**ordinance.** *n.* Historically and generically an ordinance was a "public law or act" or statute; however, in modern usage it denotes a law created by the legislative body of a municipal corporation, i.e., local-level government. Such local government laws regulate traffic and zoning, e.g., and, as such, are civil laws and not criminal laws.

**ordinary care.** The level of care an ordinary, reasonable, competent, and prudent person involved in the same endeavor would exercise under similar circumstances; i.e., due care. Such degree of care is not absolute, but, rather, relative, as the totality of the circumstances dictate.

**ordnance.** *n.* In military usage, weapons, ammunition, and explosives.

**organic law.** The constitution of a sovereign state or nation; the fundamental law; the general principles from which all statutory law are given viability.

**organizational culture.** The culture, i.e., value system, attitudes, folkways, informally approved methods of operation, and rituals that exist within the social context of a formal organization. For example, in a police agency there is frequently a formal mode of operation, codified in a standard operating procedures manual (SOP), whereas an informal code (supported by the organizational culture) often determines actual operational modalities, often in contravention of the official SOP.

**organized crime.** An illegal pattern of activity conducted by a consortium of people and/or organizations, acting in concert, to carry out fraud, theft, extortion, intimidation, and a host of other offenses in a syndicated fashion. While historically not in and of itself a criminal offense in terms of being proscribed by statute, such activity has been addressed by federal authorities. See e.g., The Kefauver Committee of 1951, The Federal Omnibus Crime Control Act of 1970, and The President's Commission on Organized Crime (PCOC) of 1984.

**Organized Crime and Racketeering Section (OCRS).** Established in 1954 as a subdivision within the Criminal Division of the United States Department of Justice (USDOJ), located in Washington, DC. The OCRS coordinates enforcement programs nationwide to address the illicit activities of organized crime.

**Organized Crime Control Act (1970).** A bill signed by President Richard M. Nixon in order to broaden the fight against organized crime. The bill authorizes the FBI to investigate bombings and attempted bombings of all federal properties and institutions receiving financial assistance from the federal government.

**Originating Agency Identification (ORI).** Codes developed by the FBI for data storage, retrieval, and analysis on policing and law enforcement agencies in the United States.

**overcriminalization.** *n.* See *hyperlexis.*

**overrule.** *v.* To supersede, abrogate, nullify, invalidate, supplant, or overturn a former decision; to deprive the use of an earlier appellate decision; to reject, as a result of subsequent legal action or decision. To disallow, disaffirm, reject, or override.

**overt act.** The physical act done in the furtherance of a crime, essential to the establishment of a crime. This act must be more than a simple act of preparation to commit a crime (except in inchoate offenses); it must be directly involved in the accomplishment of the crime, which if not for extraneous causes, will lead to the actual commission of the crime. See *actus reus* "the guilty act," which in combination with *mens rea* constitutes a criminal offense.

**own recognizance (OR).** A release from bail on one's own recognizance, i.e., his or her signature that he or she will appear at the appropriate date and time before the court. This type of bond is generally extended only to stable members of a given community.

**oyez.** *interj.* "Hear ye." A phrase often used by the bailiff or other public crier to direct public attention to the reading and promulgation of a judicial paper or proclamation.

# P

PA, prosecuting attorney
PCR, police–community relations; also polymerase chain reaction
PERF, Police Executive Research Forum
PMG, Provost Marshal General
PMO, Provost Marshal's Office
PMSS, Prosecution Management Support System
POP, problem-oriented policing
PPU, Police Paramilitary Unit

**paddy rollers.** A term deriving from the antebellum American South for those involved in slave patrols. Paddy rollers established an unofficial policing institution in the American South that maintained the plantation economy by suppressing slave insurrections, tracking down runaway slaves, and by rendering punishments within the "plantation social control system."

**paddy wagon.** It is a term common among large urban police departments in the United States during the early- to mid-twentieth century, for a police van used in the transportation of prisoners. The van was usually a black-panel truck, with no windows in the cargo area, two wooden benches along both sides, and two windowless doors at the rear. While the origins of the term are somewhat obscure, it is believed to have derived from the derogatory term for Irishmen (paddies), who at the time dominated many large urban police departments. See also *black mariah.*

**pander.** *v.* To cater to the base-level illicit sexual gratification of another. The enticement of a woman into a place of prostitution. See *pimping.*

**panderer.** *n.* A pimp; one who procures sexual and/or lustful favors for others. See *procurer, madam, hustler, supplier, and purveyor.*

**panel.** *n.* (1) A group of people selected for service in some cause by the court. (2) A roll having the names of jurors summoned for duty.

**panhandle.** *v.* To beg or petition as a pauper.

**panopticon plan.** A 1791 architectural model for prisons, developed by Jeremy Bentham. The plan calls for a circular design having the guards in a central tower (for purposes of observation) with cells for prisoners lining the circular outer wall. Few jurisdictions followed the plan, although Stateville Penitentiary, in Joliet, Illinois, stands as one of the largest and best known prisons in the world.

**paraffin test.** A test wherein one's hand is coated with melted paraffin, which is later removed and tested for gunpowder residue, using a chemical solution (diphenylamine). When nitrates are found to be present, a distinctive color is produced, indicating gunpowder residue.

O
P

**paralegal.** *n.* One not licensed as an attorney, but having a course of study for legal technicians, who works for a law firm conducting interviews, legal research, and the filing of various motions in court.

**paramedic.** *n.* A type of emergency medical technician (EMT) holding advanced training allowing him or her to perform difficult pre-hospital medical procedures. See *EMT.*

**pardon.** *n.* Considered an "act of grace" on the part of the chief executive of the sovereignty, it is a remission for criminal acts and one of the numerous types of executive clemency recognized by the law. The authority for pardoning federal offenders is found in Article II § 2 of the U.S. Constitution; pardon authority for state offenders is found in the constitutions of the various states. Two types of pardons exist: (1) the absolute (full) pardon that restores all rights and privileges of citizenship taken at the time of conviction (see *civil death*), and (2) the conditional pardon, requiring that a specified condition be met, without which the pardon will not proceed. Most state governors have full pardoning powers, whereas some must share that power with a pardoning board or the state senate.

**pardon attorney.** An office within the U.S. Department of Justice that processes all petitions for federal executive clemency. The pardon attorney prepares the recommendation of the U.S. attorney general for the president of the United States.

**parens patriae.** *(Lat.)* "Parent of the country." The term derives from English common law, where the King had the prerogative to intercede as guardian for infants and idiots in their behalf. It refers to a concept of standing used by the state to protect those under legal disability of some form or another, generally juveniles. State attorneys general also hold the power of *parens patriae* to bring actions on the behalf of state residents in cases of antitrust offenses and to recover losses on their behalf.

**parish.** *n.* A political and administrative subdivision of the state of Louisiana, equivalent to a county elsewhere in the United States.

**park police.** Park police operate at the federal, county, and municipal level. At the federal level, they are part of the U.S. Department of Interior and operate within the Washington, DC, area. At the municipal level, park police are generally sworn officers of the municipal government and operate within the park system. (Many cities have consolidated their park police departments with the municipal police department). A parallel policing organization often operates at the county or township level of government, protecting parks and forest preserves, e.g., the Cook County, Illinois Park Rangers.

**park rangers.** Many park rangers are sworn police officers operating within a park at the state or county level. However, some park rangers have expanded responsibilities and function as conservation police protecting plant and animal life and ecosystems. The rangers of the National Park Service function in this capacity, while rendering other services to park visitors.

**Park, Robert Ezra (1864–1944).** An influential personage in sociology and criminology, Park emerged as a central figure in the "Chicago school" of sociology. See *Chicago school.*

**parole.** *n.* The discretionary and conditional release from prison, under the authority of a parole board. Parolees are placed under the supervision of a parole agent for the duration of the sentence of incarceration. During the parole period, parolees may suffer reduced civil liberty protections, as they are wards of the state serving the remainder of their sentences outside the walls of the penitentiary.

**parole board.** Envisioned by Alexander Maconochie, under his ticket-of-leave system, it is an administrative board charged with the responsibility of hearing parole applications and, when appropriate, granting parole to prisoners.

**parole contract.** A legal document setting forth the conditions under which a parolee is to conduct his or her life outside the prison walls. A violation of the provisions of the contract (a technical violation), or any criminal offense, may lead to a revocation hearing and reconfinement in a penal facility.

**parolee.** *n.* One conditionally released from a sentence of incarceration by the paroling authority, prior to the expiration of his or her judicially imposed sentence. The parolee is placed under the supervision of a parole agent and required to observe all conditions stipulated in the parole contract as well as other conditions of parole.

**parole officer.** An official of a parole agency (state or federal) charged with the responsibilities of supervising parolees and the conducting of preparole investigations.

**parole revocation.** An administrative action taken by the paroling agency (after a negative ruling emanating from a revocation hearing) removing the parolee from the status of parole, as a result of a technical violation of the parole contract or a violation of the criminal law. A revocation proceeding generally results in reincarceration.

**parol evidence.** Any oral evidence, e.g., words or speech, as opposed to written evidence.

**parole violation.** Any act or failure to act by a parolee under a conditional release from prison, not conforming to the conditions of parole stipulated in the parole contract, or any violation of a criminal statute.

**particeps criminis.** *(Lat.)* One who is a participant in a crime; an accomplice or confederate.

**Part I offenses.** That category within the FBI's *Uniform Crime Reports* (UCR) containing the major offenses; they are criminal homicide, forcible rape, robbery, aggravated assault, burglary, larceny,theft, motor vehicle theft, and arson.

**Part II offenses.** That category within the FBI's *Uniform Crime Reports* (UCR) including the following offenses: simple assault, forgery or counterfeiting, fraud, embezzlement, stolen property, vandalism, weapons offenses, prostitution and other commercial vice offenses, sex offenses, drug-use offenses, gambling, offenses against the family or children, driving under the influence, liquor law violations, drunkenness, disorderly conduct, vagrancy, curfew and loitering offenses, and juvenile runaway.

**particularity.** *n.* Specificity in delineation; providing exacting details.

**party.** *n.* (1) One whose name appears on the record as bringing a legal action or who is the one litigated against. (2) One holding an interest in or who takes part in the performance of an act or action. (3) A group empaneled for a shared purpose.

**patent print.** Often referred to as a plastic print, usually a fingerprint, it is an impression readily visible to the naked eye. This type of print is easily left in wet paint or clay; it is the reverse of a latent print.

**pathogenic.** *adj.* Of or causing disease.

**pathological.** *adj.* Diseased.

**pathology.** *n.* The science dealing with the causes, development, and effects of diseases; a diseased or abnormal condition.

*patria postestas. (Lat.)* Paternal power; the lawful authority a parent exercises over his or her children.

**patricide.** *n.* The act of intentionally killing one's father.

**Patriot Act.** See *USA Patriot Act.*

**patrol district.** (1) In municipal-level policing, the geographical area of responsibility for a large subdivision of the municipality, sometimes including more than one patrol beat and having its own station house. (2) In state-level policing organizations, it is a geographical division of the state (usually including one or more counties, depending on the population), more often than not commanded by a captain. Some highway patrol agencies refer to a district and its headquarters as a post.

**patrol officer.** The lowest ranking sworn officer of a municipal police department, the equivalent of a deputy sheriff or a state trooper.

**pauperism.** *n.* The state of being a pauper; one without financial means and who often lives on public welfare or charitable gifts.

**Pavlov, Ivan Petrovich (1849–1936).** The Russian physiologist who received the Nobel Prize in 1904 and who pioneered the concept of classical conditioning.

**peace officer.** A conservator of the peace; one vested with the police authority of the state. See *police officer.*

**peculation.** *n.* The act of stealing or the misuse of money or property entrusted to one's care, custody, or control; embezzlement.

**pecuniary value.** The money value of an object, negotiable instrument, concept, or other thing of value.

**pederasty (paederasty).** *n.* A form of sodomy practiced by adult men with young boys.

**pedophile.** *n.* An adult who uses a minor child for sexual gratification. Generally a male, this type of offender constitutes approximately one-third of all incarcerated sex offenders.

**Peel, Sir Robert (1788–1850).** The home secretary of England and "father" of modern policing during the time of the Industrial Revolution, who was mandated by Parliament with the task of constituting the first public, full-time, paid municipal police force. In 1829, he and his assistant Charles Rowan instituted London's "Bobbies," largely copying the organizational structure of the British Army, under the authority of the Metropolitan Police Act.

**Peeping Tom.** The common name for one who seeks sexual gratification by secretly spying on or invading the privacy of another; oftentimes a man viewing a woman in her bedroom. See *voyeur.*

*peine forte et dure. (Fr.)* An apparatus that used heavy weights for torturing criminal suspects. The procedure stretched the suspect's back until death or until the suspect spoke to the king's prosecutor.

**penal.** *adj.* Concerning a penalty, as in a penal statute; punitive, disciplinary, punishing.

**penal code.** The formal statutory codification of crimes of a state or nation. See *revised statutes, compiled statutes, and titles.*

**penal laws.** See *penal code.*

**penal servitude.** A form of punishment involving a confinement and labor for the purpose of working off debt. Such servitude is disallowed by the Constitution's Thirteenth Amendment and federal statute. See 18 USCA § 1581, 42 USCA § 1994.

**penalty.** *n.* The judgment or verdict of a court following a criminal conviction or a civil or administrative ruling; a sanction. In criminal trials, the penalty may involve a fine, incarceration, community service, and/or restitution, or any combination of the preceding; in capital cases it may involve the death penalty. For civil trials, the penalty may include a fine, restitution, and loss of privilege or license, or any combination of the preceding.

**pendens.** *(Lat.)* Pending; hanging.

**Pendleton Act (1833).** The federal act bringing civil service protection, through the establishment of a Civil Service Commission, applicable to most federal employees; *United States Statutes at Large* 22 (1883): 403.

**penetration.** *n.* A necessary element of the criminal law in order to prove rape, wherein the male sex organ is inserted into a female's vagina. The degree of insertion is not an issue and can be established without proof of emission.

**penitentiary.** *n.* A prison, correctional facility, or place of confinement where those convicted of a state or federal felony violation serve out their judicially prescribed sentences. The word derives from penitence—to be penitent or repentant for one's transgressions.

**Penn, William (1644–1718).** Governor of Pennsylvania from 1682 to 1692 and author of the *Great Laws,* authorizing the substitution of prison for hard labor for serious crimes in early Pennsylvania.

**Pennsylvania system.** A penal modality holding that prisoners should be separated to avoid the harmful influences that may be caused by communication between inmates, i.e., solitary confinement. This penal philosophy influenced the construction of the Eastern State Penitentiary (Pennsylvania) in 1829 at Cherry Hill.

**penology.** *n.* The formalized study of prison management and administration, as well as the reform, rehabilitation, and custody of inmates.

**pen register.** A device for tracing the source of phone calls dialed from a specific number, recording the time and date of all calls but not the conversation. As a pen register does not invade the privacy of the conversation, such practice is not disallowed under the Fourth Amendment. See *Smith v. Maryland,* 442 U.S. 735, 99 S.Ct. 2577, 61 L.Ed.2d 220 (1979).

**penumbra.** *n.* The peripheral or grey area; boundary area; shadow area; areas of uncertainty.

**penumbra doctrine.** A doctrine regarding the implied powers of the federal government deriving from the Necessary and Proper Clause of the Constitution, Article I § 8(18), permitting one implied power to be appended to another implied power.

**peonage.** *n.* The state or condition of penal servitude (where one is compelled to perform labor in order to work off indebtedness). Such penal servitude is disallowed by the Constitution's Thirteenth Amendment and statute 18 USCA § 1581, 42 USCA § 1994.

**per annum.** *(Lat.)* "By the year."

**per capita.** *(Lat.)* Per person; "by heads."

**per curiam.** *(Lat.)* "By the court."

**per diem.** *(Lat.)* "By the day."

**peremptory challenge.** The limited right to challenge a potential juror without citing a specific reason for doing so. In most jurisdictions, only a small number of peremptory challenges are allowed, after which all subsequent challenges must be for cause. See *Fed.R.Crim.P. 24.*

**perfidious.** *adj.* Characterized by treachery; faithlessness.

**perjury.** *n.* The intentional false statement made by one under oath in a judicial proceeding or during a matter of material inquiry. See *Model Penal Code*, § 241.1 or 18 USCA § 1621.

**permit.** *n.* Any legal document granting the right to something; license; legal right or privilege; empowerment. The permit, like a license, is an abstraction; thus, the paper document is little more than physical evidence of such permit or license.

**perpetrator.** *n.* One who directly or by his or her immediate agency commits a crime.

**perquisites.** *n.* Fringe benefits, emoluments, or profits attached to one's employment, office, title, or position.

**per se.** *(Lat.)* By itself alone; or one's self alone.

**person.** *n.* In legal usage, a human being, or, e.g., any municipality, firm, partnership, association, or corporation trustee.

**personal recognizance.** The pretrial release of a defendant based on his or her promise to show up for trial. It constitutes a type of bail when the judge is satisfied that the defendant will appear without posting a surety bond. Commonly referred to as release on recognizance (ROR). Judges often allow this type of bail if the person arrested is a real estate owner or has other significant assets or attachments within the jurisdiction of the court.

**Peters.** *n.* The appellate case law reporter for U.S. Supreme Court rulings, spanning 1828–1842. Before the introduction of the *United States Reports (U.S.)* and the *United States Supreme Court Reports Lawyer's Edition/Second Edition (L.Ed., or L.Ed.2d),* a series of lesser-known reports covered the decisions of the High Court; they include *Dallas* (1790–1800), *Cranch* (1801–1815), *Wheaton* (1816–1827), *Peters* (1828–1842), *Howard* (1843–1860), *Black* (1861–1862), and *Wallace* (1863–1874). Today, these early reports have been catalogued in the *United States Reports* and other reporters for the convenience of legal researchers.

**petition.** *n.* (1) A formal written document delivered to the court, requesting judicial action on a particular matter. (2) In the juvenile justice system, the formal charge; the equivalent to an information or indictment in the adult criminal process.

**petit jury.** A jury as trier of fact in an adjudication, either civil or criminal. In criminal cases, a jury panel comprised of as few as six or as many as twelve persons, depending on the jurisdiction and the severity of the alleged offense(s); see, e.g., *Duncan v. Louisiana,* 391 U.S. 145 (1968). As distinguished from a grand jury, composed of as few as eighteen to as many as twenty-three people for the purpose of determining whether an accused shall be formally accused of a criminal act and subjected to a criminal trial.

**petty offense.** An infraction or lower-level misdemeanor. Any offense for which the sanction does not extend beyond six months confinement or a fine of not more than $500 or both. See, e.g., 18 USCA § 1.

**peyote.** *n.* An hallucinatory drug deriving from the peyote plant, i.e., a spineless cactus found in the American Southwest. This drug has been traditionally used by Native Americans for centuries as a sacrament, generally in responsible quantities. The U.S. Supreme Court ruled in 1990 that state drug laws may prohibit the use of peyote for religious reasons, overturning an earlier ruling on the issue.

**pharmacology.** *n.* The organized study (science) of the preparation and use of drugs and their effect on living organisms.

**phenolphthalein test.** A field test used to determine the presence of blood.

**phenotype.** *n.* (1) A distinctive type identifiable via microscopically visible characteristics as opposed to genetic traits. (2) In forensic science usage, a person's genetic composition, e.g., one's blood type resulting from a specific gene.

**phonoscopy.** *n.* The organized scientific study of voice patterns (prints), their analysis, and their identification.

**photogrammetry.** *n.* A procedure used to obtain measurements from photographs by using two cameras located at different known points of reference, from which accurate measurements may be made.

**photo lineup.** The procedure whereby several photographs of uninvolved persons are mixed with that of a suspect, from which a witness must select the correct photographic image.

**photomacrograph.** *n.* A procedure used to magnify microscopic images sufficiently to be seen by the naked eye with some detail.

**phrenology.** *n.* A nineteenth-century criminological perspective (theory) holding that criminal types could be identified by their personality traits through a detailed measurement of the head. The first book on the subject, *The Outlines of Phrenology* (1832), was authored by J. K. Spurzheim, M.D., of the University of Vienna.

**phylasist.** *n.* A jailer.

**physiognomy.** *n.* A criminological perspective (theory), developed in the nineteenth century, holding that physical appearance can be used in the identification of criminal types. Italian criminologist Cesare Lombroso (1836–1909) held that it was possible to identify such criminal types by their atavistic anomalies.

**pickpocket.** *n.* A thief who specializes in the taking of valuables from the pockets of victims' garments.

**pied poudre.** *(Fr.)* Translated as "dusty feet," it was an early court in England, located near Winchester, and established to deal with minor affairs authorized by the Bishop of Winton, under a grant from Edward IV. The term derives from the French term for vagabond, a *pied poudreux*.

**piggybacking.** *n.* Jargon for a type of cyberspace trespassing.

**pilfer.** *v.* To steal, especially small sums of money or property.

**pillory.** *n.* A device used to sanction, upon conviction, those who violate social conventions and lower-level criminal offenses. A wooden restraining device that clamped around the wrists and neck of the offender, used in colonial America as a form of public ridicule.

**pinch.** *n.* Police jargon (in many midwestern cities) for an arrest by an officer.

**Pinkerton, Allan (1819–1884).** A celebrated American private detective, who was born in Scotland, but rose to fame in the United States. His skill as a detective was largely the result of his work for the Chicago and Northwestern Railroad, on the Galena Division. Later, he worked in both the Kane and Cook County Sheriffs' Offices. Eventually he left to open a private detective agency, and during the Civil War his service to the Union Army as an intelligence agent is well documented. Today the legacy of his work is the Pinkerton Detective Agency, one of the world's largest and most respected private detective and security guard agencies.

**PINS/CHINS/JINS/MINS.** Acronyms classifying juveniles, often consisting of status offenders, but named differently by the various jurisdictions. (INS means "in need of supervision"; P stands for person; C stands for child; J stands for juvenile; and M stands for minor.)

**piracy.** *n.* (1) Robbery on the high seas; air piracy; (2) a specialized form of larceny like music piracy, where high-tech methods are employed.

**pistol.** *n.* A handgun capable of being fired with the use of only one hand; two types exist: revolvers (wheel guns) and magazine-loaded automatics (semiautomatics).

**plagiarism.** *n.* The unlawful appropriation of the written composition, ideas, or intellectual property of another.

**plaintiff.** *n.* One who brings an action, i.e., complains. Complainant; petitioner; accuser.

**plain-view rule.** Things readily observable by an officer, who is in a place he or she has a legal right to be, that are not the object or product of a search but that are illegal and subject to seizure.

**plastic print.** See *patent print.*

**plastic white phosphorus.** Melted white phosphorus that is combined with a solution of synthetic rubber, used in many incendiary devices.

**platoon system.** A system used by many police departments to deploy their line officers across a twenty-four-hour period, with each eight-hour shift receiving an equal number of officers. One of the many problems associated with this scheduling method is that crime and calls for police services are not equally distributed across a twenty-four-hour period.

**plea.** *n.* The answer of a defendant to a formal charge in open court. In criminal procedure, it is a response to a criminal complaint, information, or indictment accusing a person of violating a specified statute. Pleas include not guilty, guilty, not guilty by reason of insanity, or *nolo contendere.*

**plea bargaining.** The process of negotiation between the state and the defendant, generally involving a guilty plea on the part of the defendant for a more favorable sentence, a reduction in charges, or both.

**pleadings.** *n.* The formal arguments posited by the various parties involved in an adjudication, regarding their claims and defenses.

**plebiscite.** *n.* See *referendum.*

**plenary.** *adj.* Full and complete without qualifications; unequivocal.

**plenipotentiary.** *n.* One given complete and unequivocal authority to act as an official representative of a given government or organization, and whose signature is binding.

**poaching.** *n.* The unlawful taking of another's fish or game.

**poena.** *(Lat.)* Punishment; penalty.

**pogrom.** *n.* A slaughter, massacre, killing, or homicide, often against an unpopular group.

**police.** *n.* The governmental department, bureau, or agency of a city, township, county, or state or nation charged with the responsibilities of maintaining public order, preserving the peace, providing emergency services, preventing crime, the detection of criminal activity, and the enforcement of the criminal law.

**police academy.** A training institute for police officers, usually mandated by state law, where recruits are taught basic skills and where veteran officers are given advanced instruction in various police skills and practices. Training academies are most often found at the state level, although they may also be found at the county and municipal level.

**police aids.** A generic name given to nonsworn (civilian) personnel who are employed to handle low-level calls for service, specific nonenforcement-type services, and technical services freeing sworn officers for more critical tasks.

**police authority.** The legal authority of the state to direct, command, and regulate. In the United States, it is conferred by the Tenth Amendment of the Constitution to the various states, which in turn have delegated such authority to counties, townships, and local-level governments. The term is often mistaken to mean police power, which is the force by which the state's police authority is enforced.

**police brutality.** The excessive, unnecessary, or extralegal use of force on citizens by police officers. The use of force beyond that which is necessary to accomplish lawful police objectives.

**police chief.** The top administrative officer of a police department; he or she may be a sworn officer, or in some jurisdictions, merely an appointed administrator without police arrest authority (i.e., nonsworn). Often, the position of chief of police is not a permanent rank; it is an appointed administrative position. If the person holding the position is an up-through-the-ranks officer, his or her permanent rank is that rank he or she held immediately before appointment to chief of police. The chief of police is accountable to the municipal board and/or the city manager or mayor, as a member of the executive branch of government.

**police civilian (complaint) review boards.** A board designed to provide independent citizen oversight of police practices through the creation of a complaint process and the investigation and formal disciplinary review of specific charges against individual officers. Most boards do not have punishment powers; their findings are advisory and may recommend to the chief of police discipline or termination of errant officers.

**police commander.** See *commander.*

**police commission.** A board composed of civilians appointed by the city, township, or county administrator, the mayor, or city council to act in an oversight capacity in matters related to the hiring, testing, promotion, and disciplining of officers. Members of the commission frequently hold the title of police commissioner, but hold no direct supervisory authority. See *commission* and *commissioner.*

**police community relations (PCR).** A formal program intended to enhance the relationship of police with their community constituents, especially minorities. According to many minority groups, during the 1960s, most police community relations programs were little more than public relations con games. Today, many departments are attempting to make inroads into police community relations through the establishment of Citizen Police Academies, which attempt to inform concerned citizens, by providing a comprehensive understanding of the role of the police in civil democratic society. Critics argue that such programs merely "preach to the choir."

**police corruption.** Any act by a police officer involving the misuse of his or her official authority in a way intended to produce personal gain for the officer or another.

**police counselor.** A commissioned police officer who is assigned to work at a local high school to form a bridge between the police department and the students and staff. There are a number of employment arrangements; e.g., the officer may be a sworn police department employee or a school employee who holds a commission with the local department or sheriff's office. He or she also deals with crime related problems at the school. The program was begun in the 1960s under a grant from the Mott Foundation.

**police court.** An inferior court in some states, having jurisdiction over minor offenses and infractions, including municipal ordinances, parallel with the jurisdiction of justice of the peace courts. These courts hold the power of committing magistrates with limited jurisdiction.

**police decoys.** Nonuniformed officers who pose as victims, e.g., drunks, disabled individuals, and tourists, with the intention of apprehending street muggers who prey on the weak.

**police department.** (1) A duly constituted police agency of a municipality, i.e., village, town, city, or township. (2) The duly constituted police agency of any special district, e.g., New York City's Port Authority Police. (3) The duly authorized police department of a state, e.g., the Illinois State Police.

*police des mouers.* *(Fr.)* "Police of the pouters." A specialized policing entity, developed about the time of the Statute of Winchester (1285), assigned to patrol the "red-light district" and control prostitution in the City of London.

**Police Executive Research Forum (PERF).** The national-level professional police administrator's association sponsoring research into police issues for jurisdictions with populations of 100,000 or greater.

**Police Foundation.** A private research-sponsoring institution dedicated to the improvement of policing in the United States, established with funding from the Ford Foundation. In 1970, a separate fund was established to become a catalyst for innovation in policing across the nation. The Police Foundation is located in Washington, DC.

**police jurisdiction.** In some southern states, the extension of the police authority of municipal police, by state law, into the unincorporated areas of the county, usually two or three miles beyond the corporate limits of the municipality.

**police jury.** In the state of Louisiana, the board of supervisors for a parish (the functional equivalent of a county board in other states).

**police officer.** A peace officer; a sworn member of a public organization (e.g., a police department) usually within a city, township, county, or state, charged with the responsibilities of protecting public safety, preserving the peace, providing emergency services, the detection of crime, and the enforcement of the law. The term should not be confused with a law enforcement officer, although popular culture often does so, as a law enforcement officer is charged with a much narrower band of responsibilities. Generally, a law enforcement officer is limited to reactive enforcement of the criminal code, as distinguished from the broad range of proactive responsibilities with which the police are charged.

**Police Officers' Bill of Rights.** Originally envisioned as a protection for police officers who were investigated by the internal affairs division of their respective departments, it has expanded to become a collective bargaining instrument that has been enacted into public law in some states.

**Police Paramilitary Unit (PPU).** PPU is the international community's acronym for the American SWAT team (Special Weapons and Tactics). See *SWAT.*

**police power.** The force by which the state's inherent police authority is enforced.

**police pursuit.** See *hot pursuit, vehicular* and *police vehicle pursuit.*

**police service style.** Any mode of operation to which a police agency subscribes, e.g., zero-tolerance policing or community-oriented policing.

**police state.** A totalitarian government, kept in power by an oppressive centralized secret police organization, accountable only to the dictator.

**police-to-population ratio.** The number of sworn police officers to the population of a given venue per thousand, expressed as a ratio, e.g., 2.3 police officers per 1,000 population. The distribution of police per one thousand population in the United States, when placed on a graph, forms a U-shaped configuration. That is, the highest ratios are found among the smallest and largest departments and municipalities, whereas the lowest ratios are found among the mid-sized departments and municipalities, i.e., suburban police departments.

**police unions.** Collective bargaining units representing the rank-and-file police officer, generally up through the rank of sergeant. Affiliation may be with a nationally recognized union or a locally based association. Police unions have been a viable reality since the 1960s. Critics argue that police unionization has militated against the police professionalization movement.

**police vehicle pursuit.** See *hot pursuit, vehicular.*

**policy, departmental.** Technically, policy involves major organizational principles; however, it has come to encompass procedures, rules, and regulations. It is the formal written document for guiding officer behavior. Often referred to as departmental standard operating procedures (SOPs), they are intended ideally to create a conceptual road map for officers in the field. The trend, however, has been to create extensive SOPs, as police organizations become larger, more complex, and bureaucratized. The result, only too often, is that officers cannot remember much of the policy, and, as such, policies frequently fail to serve their intended purposes.

***polis.*** *(Gr.)* Deriving from the Greek word *politer* (state citizenship), it evolved to become *politia* (Fr.), meaning "administration of the commonwealth." The word is associated with the early Greek "city states," and evolved to mean "city" (a municipal form of local government) in a more contemporary context. It is the progenitor of the modern word "police."

**political crimes.** Those crimes or prohibited acts directed at the established political order, its laws, and institutions.

**political patronage.** The process of giving favor to those of the same political persuasion for services rendered. Political favors distributed through a political system under a *quid pro quo* arrangement.

**polity.** *n.* A society within an organized government, i.e., the body politic. The people as the government within an organized political entity, e.g., the state.

**polling the jury.** The process of formally requesting that each juror, having heard the evidence and rendered a verdict in a specific case, state his or her individual verdict in open court.

**polyandry.** *n.* A form of polygamy allowing women to have multiple husbands at the same time; plural marriage for women.

**polygamy.** *n.* The state of having two or more wives at the same time; plural marriage for men.

**polygraph.** *n.* Commonly known as a lie detector, it is an electro-mechanical instrument that measures and records numerous involuntary physiological responses to an act of deception. The majority of courts disallow the admissibility of polygraph results, although some courts allow polygraph results under stipulation.

**polymerase chain reaction (PCR).** A method used in a forensic laboratory to amplify the amount of DNA in a biological strain sample.

**pornography.** *n.* Obscene, debauched, or indecent writing, pictures, art, or public behavior that arouses the prurient base-level sexual interest. See *Miller v. California*, 413 U.S. 15, 93 S.Ct. 2607, 37 L.Ed.2d 419 (1973).

**poroscopy.** *n.* The study of the patterns and arrangement of sweat pores in fingerprint impressions, for the purpose of identification.

**port warden.** The official responsible for the protection and safety of a given navigable port.

**positive evidence.** Evidence directly proving a fact or point in issue, without the need for a presumption.

**positive law.** That law that is formally written and adopted by the duly authorized governmental authority, i.e., the legislature, e.g., state statutory law.

**positivist.** *n.* One holding fast to the principles of positivism, i.e., scientific empiricism.

**posse.** *(Lat.)* A body of men and/or women summoned by the sheriff with full legal authority to assist him or her in keeping the peace or enforcing the law of the state.

**posse comitatus.** *(Lat.)* (1) "The power of the county (state)." (2) Under common law, the entire population of able-bodied males over the age of fifteen who could serve the sheriff if summoned to do so in a law enforcement capacity. Modern law provides for the *posse comitatus* to include all able-bodied persons over the age of eighteen.

**Posse Comitatus Act (1878).** A federal law passed shortly after the Civil War, prohibiting the military from functioning in a civil law enforcement capacity, except when martial law had been lawfully declared. This act was largely eclipsed during the tenure of President Reagan in an attempt to more efficiently police the drug problem and to suppress unlawful immigration. It was further eroded after September 11, 2001, when military police patrolled civilian airport terminals. Critics argue that this trend is a step toward police-state operations.

**possession.** *n.* The state of possessing; the custody, detention, control, or occupancy of anything that is the subject of property. As a general rule, the law recognizes two types of possession: actual and constructive possession; that is, the knowing and direct physical control over something, and possession without the actual custody or control by a person who has both the power and intention to exercise some form of possession or control over something.

**postconviction remedies.** The procedure or procedures under which one convicted of a crime may challenge such a conviction, either through the judicial system or through the chief executive via clemency.

**post facto.** *(Lat.)* "After the fact." See *ex post facto.*

**post hoc, ergo propter hoc.** *(Lat.)* The faulty presumption that an occurrence following one prior must be the result of the first occurrence. In social science methodology, it is the error of assuming causation from mere correlation.

**postmortem.** *adj.* "After death." Some activity occurring after death, e.g., a postmortem examination (an autopsy).

**postmortem lividity.** See *lividity, postmortem.*

**post obit.** *(Lat.)* "After death." Something pledged or to be done after death.

**posttrial motions.** Any of the motions used by either party in an litigation to prepare for appeal.

**posthumous.** *adj.* Something occurring, arising, granted, or continuing after death.

**Pound, Roscoe (1870–1964).** Legal scholar, educator, and administrator who postulated the well-known jural postulates. He taught at numerous law schools, beginning with the University of Nebraska Law School, in his home state, Northwestern University Law School, the University of Chicago Law School, and Harvard University Law School, where he was appointed dean from 1916 to 1936. Pound was universally acclaimed to be one of the nation's leading jurists.

**powder burn.** A burn caused by the ignition of gunpowder, generally from a firearm.

**power of attorney.** A legal document authorizing another to act in one's behalf, as his or her agent or attorney. Power of attorney ceases after the death of the one authorizing it; however, if a durable power of attorney is executed, the power continues in effect should the issuing party become disabled or have diminished mental faculties.

**praecipe.** *(Lat.)* A writ commanding a subject to do a required act, or to show cause for failure to carry out the required act. It is often a formal order to the clerk of the court to take a particular action.

**Praetorian Guard.** *(Lat.)* Under the reign of Augustus, the first Roman emperor (27BC), 500–600 soldiers (about a tenth of a legion) were used as palace guards and in a nascent policing (peace-keeping) function throughout the city.

**prearraignment lockup.** A custodial facility for those awaiting arraignment or pretrial release. Generally one may remain in this facility for no more than two days, or the next session of the court, barring exigent circumstances.

**precedent.** *n.* A decision by an appellate court serving as the ruling authority on the issue in question; court-generated law. See *stare decisis doctrine.*

**precept.** *n.* (1) An admonishment, rule, or directive regarding moral conduct. (2) In law, a judicial writ, warrant, order, or command, in both civil and criminal law, sent to the proper public official, commanding him or her to carry out some duty within the scope of his or her authority.

**precinct.** *n.* A small geographical unit of local-level government carrying out administrative responsibilities, although it does not constitute a subdivision of local government, and, as such, has no governmental powers in and of itself. A geographical district within a municipal government constituting a patrol bailiwick for the police department.

**precipe.** *(Lat.)* A document containing written instructions to the court clerk.

**precipitan reaction test.** A laboratory test determining whether blood is of human origin.

**predisposition investigation.** An investigation ordered by the juvenile court, generally conducted by the department of juvenile probation, after an adjudication leading to a finding of involvement, for the purpose of assisting the court in determining the appropriate disposition in a pending adjudication.

**preempt.** *v.* To seize by preemption; to establish ownership, control, or custody before others, thereby excluding all others.

**prefect.** *n.* (1) In the Roman Empire, a high-ranking official overseeing a civil government office, a high magistrate, or a military department head. (2) In modern usage, a civil administrative official in France, e.g., the head of the Paris Police Department.

**preliminary hearing.** The first appearance and screening by the court to determine whether one charged with a crime should be held for trial. In felony cases, a hearing wherein the state must establish probable cause that the suspect has committed the crime in question, usually conducted when no grand jury hearing is utilized, although some jurisdictions employ both. See *habeas corpus.*

**preliminary injunction.** A temporary court order intended to preserve the current state of affairs *(status quo)* pending a subsequent ruling.

**premeditation.** *n.* In law, the planning and forethought sufficient to establish the requisite intent to commit a crime. See *mens rea.*

**preponderance of evidence.** Evidence outweighing that which is offered in opposition.

**presentence investigation (PSI).** An investigation conducted in order to assist the court in drafting the appropriate sentence for a convicted offender, taking into account the broad social history of the offender. This report is conducted at the request of the court and is generally carried out by the department of probation and parole.

**presentence report** The final report prepared by the probation department at the court's request, for the purpose of assisting the court in determining the appropriate sentence that is in the best interest of the state and the defendant.

**presentment.** *n.* (1) An official report of a grand jury investigation, which usually contains a recommendation or an indictment. For example, a grand jury may be charged with the annual investigation of the condition and management of the county jail. In its report, the grand jury may recommend various changes or additional funding by the county board. The grand jury may also find certain individuals criminally responsible for poor conditions at the jail and hand up an indictment calling for an arrest and a criminal prosecution. (2) A written observation noted by a grand jury regarding an offense, in and of its own volition, knowledge, or observation, independent of the prosecutor's request or a bill of indictment issued before it. That is, a presentment constitutes an accusation, initiated by the grand jury independently of the prosecutor, requesting that an indictment be drafted or a public censure of an un-indictable coconspirator.

**President's Crime Commission (1965).** The short title for the President's Commission on Law4 Enforcement and Administration of Justice, requested by then President L. B. Johnson after declaring "war on crime." The commission provided task force reports on the police, courts, corrections, juvenile delinquency, organized crime, science and technology, drunkenness, narcotics, and drugs. The commission's final report was entitled *The Challenge of Crime in a Free Society.*

**presumption.** *n.* In legal usage, the inferring that a fact exists, based on the already proven existence of other facts.

**presumption of innocence.** The prosecution has the entire burden of proving all elements of the alleged criminal offense at trial beyond a reasonable doubt. That is, the defense has no obligation to prove the defendant's innocence. See *burden of proof.*

**presumptive evidence.** Evidence adequate to establish a fact, which if not rebutted, remains. See *prima facie.*

**presumptive sentencing.** A graduated sentencing model that incorporates sentencing guidelines with mandatory sentencing requirements while also providing some discretion to the sentencing judge.

**pretermit.** *v.* To pass over; to omit; to take no action. Grand juries sometimes take "pretermit" on issues, leaving them unaddressed until another grand jury may consider them.

**pretrial conference.** A conference between the prosecutor and the defense (oftentimes in the presence of a judicial officer) with the intention of stipulating those things that will expedite the trial.

**pretrial detention.** The detention of a defendant or a material witness prior to trial. Upon conviction, pretrial detention time may be subtracted from the time the defendant is sentenced to serve.

**pretrial discovery.** The disclosure by either the prosecution and/or the defense of evidence in their possession, prior to trial, generally in compliance with a discovery order. The direction today is toward full discovery in state courts; federal procedure lags behind state procedure in this matter.

**pretrial publicity.** Information provided by the media concerning a specific crime or offender.

**preventive detention.** The pretrial custody of a material witness or a defendant held without bail.

**Prévôts de maréchaux.** *(Fr.)* A military organization created under the authority of Francis I (1494–1547), consisting of mounted archers who protect the highways of France against robbers and thieves.

O
P

**prima facie.** *(Lat.)*  On the face of it; at face value; a fact assumed to be correct unless contrary evidence can show otherwise.

**primogeniture.** *n.*  The exclusive right of the eldest son to inherit his father's estate.

**principal.** *n.*  In criminal law, the chief actor in a criminal act or conspiracy. The lead perpetrator or aider and abettor, whether actively or constructively present at the crime scene, distinguished from a mere accessory.

**principle of proportionality.**  The principle that acts causing lesser harms should receive lesser sanctions than more serious acts producing greater harms.

**prison.** *n.*  A state or federal penal institution housing those convicted of felony violations and sentenced to a period of incarceration for no less than one year.

**prisoner.** *n.*  (1) One held in police custody. (2) One detained in jail awaiting trial, awaiting transportation to the state or federal prison after conviction, or serving time in jail for a misdemeanor conviction. (3) One sentenced to a state or federal penal facility for which the sentence was a period of incarceration of one year or greater, and who is under the physical custody of prison officials. (4) One held by military authorities for violations of the UCMJ or as an enemy of war or an unlawful combatant.

**prison farm.**  (1) A custodial facility operated by a county where misdemeanants are held for relatively short periods. (2) A penal facility operated as an adjunct to the state prison system to segregate special offenders. (3) Privately operated custodial facilities in the American South, where prisoners are leased in return for their labor. (4) A penal facility operated by a state (a southern state) where prisoners are sent for evaluation, diagnostic, and classification purposes.

**prisonization.** *n.*  The negative socialization process through which a prisoner learns to incorporate the values, lifestyle, and attitudes of the prison subculture; a painful process of institutional resocialization.

**prison labor.**  The labor of inmates at penal institutions, which is sometimes used as an institutional management tool, having its roots in both retributive and rehabilitative penal philosophies.

**prison psychosis.**  The term is not a clinical one, as it refers to the mentality of many inmates that results from the unpleasant strictures of prison life. Because of the seemingly endless boredom, monotony, and lack of initiative, the repressive nature of prison life causes many inmates to lapse into an inner fantasy world that sometimes takes the form of destructive behavior. The accompanying stupor is referred to as prison psychosis. See *prisonization.*

**private detective.**  One whose occupation involves the investigation of civil or criminal issues or other areas unrelated to the law. Generally, one who is licensed to conduct investigations for hire by state law; some states, however, do not license private detectives. Private investigators often work for private security companies or law firms, although some are independent contractors. Their work most often concerns civil cases, as criminal investigations are conducted by the police and law enforcement agencies free of charge. Occasionally, however, private detectives investigate criminal cases for defendants or their defense counsel. They are not granted the police power of the state and cannot make arrests other than as private citizens; nor may they lawfully carry concealed weapons. Private security agencies, in states licensing private investigators, are required to have at least one licensed private investigator on staff.

**private investigator.** See *private detective.*

**private security agency.** Generally an incorporated private detective, contract-guard, and/or armored car agency, operating for profit under a state license. As a general rule, private security agencies must have at least one licensed private detective on staff in order to conduct business, and if firearms are involved, some form of mandatory state training and certification are generally required. It is worth noting that private detectives may not legally carry a concealed weapon. Only uniformed security guards may carry a firearm that is not concealed and then only while in uniform.

**privilege.** *n.* A right, favor, advantage, or immunity granted to persons of a protected class or status, not extended to others.

**privileged communications.** Private communications between persons in a confidential relationship. Historically, the privilege was extended to three classes of people: (1) the clergy, (2) lawyers, and (3) medical doctors. The trend in recent years has extended the privilege; however, only the preceding categories enjoy the privilege in its fullest form. Other categories exist, such as the husband–wife communications privilege.

**proactive.** *adj.* A term used widely in contemporary criminal justice literature, involving activities that anticipate contingencies through thoughtful planning and community input via open institutions, with the intent of producing a relatively crime-free community. Proactive measures are the reverse of reactive measures, associated with governmental agencies of the past. A term for what in earlier times simply would have been "active."

**probable cause.** While no court has rendered an exact definition of probable cause, it can be said that it is the reasonable grounds to support a belief in a reasonable person of average intelligence that the accused was responsible for the crime in question. Perhaps, the most frequently cited definition, while falling short of a "bright-line" definition, was issued by the High Court in *Draper v. United States*, 358 U.S. 307, 79 S.Ct. 329, 3L.Ed.2d. 327 (1959). Probable cause exists where known facts and circumstances that are reasonably trustworthy are sufficient to justify a person of reasonable prudence in his or her belief that a crime is either in process or has already occurred, i.e., the "reasonable person standard;" or "probable cause is the sum total of layers of information and synthesis of what police have heard, know, or observe as trained officers" (*Smith v. United States*, 1949), i.e., the "reasonable officer standard."

**probation.** *n.* The conditional release of one convicted of a crime into the community during a period of supervision under an assigned probation officer. Probation is a court-ordered sanction, in lieu of incarceration.

**probative value.** That which tends to support or prove an issue in controversy.

**problem-oriented policing (POP).** A philosophy of policing envisioned by political scientist Herman Goldstein of the University of Wisconsin. This mode of policing holds that the police should work in unison with the community, seeking low-level quality-of-life problems, not necessarily in crime terms, which if adequately addressed at their root-level will translate into lowered crime rates. This places the service-level police officer in the position of a proactive community advocate and problem solver, as opposed to a reactive after-the-fact law enforcer.

**procedural law.** In criminal law, that body of law prescribing how the law is to be executed and the manner in which police officers and law enforcement officers carry out their law enforcement duties, i.e., the rules of criminal evidence and procedure. More generally, a body of law prescribing the methods for enforcing certain rights or of garnering redress for the invasion on those rights by government agents. Sometimes codified, procedural law is continually altered by case law, redefining the legal parameters of governmental behavior.

**proceeding.** *n.* Any action in the furtherance of conducting judicial business.

**profanity.** *n.* The state of being profane; profane language; irreverence toward the sacred; cursing and vulgarity. In some jurisdictions, it is an offense to use profanity in public.

**profession.** *n.* An occupational category requiring advanced educational and training components, often requiring a state-granted license, and generally involving greater conceptual input than manual labor, i.e., the learned professions: law, medicine, theology, and higher learning.

**professional degree.** A degree required for employment in a particular occupation (profession), narrower in focus than a liberal arts degree, e.g., a bachelor of science in architecture, as opposed to a bachelor of arts in history. A professional degree must be accredited by the appropriate professional association, e.g., the American Institute of Architects. Professional degrees may be earned at either public or private colleges and/or universities, or at freestanding professional schools (those not associated with a college or university). The entry-level law degree, e.g., may be earned at either a university (with a professional school of law) or at a freestanding institution. In either case, the degree was originally intended to be a bachelor's degree, an LLB, or bachelor of laws degree, as originally entry to professional schools occurred immediately after graduation from high school. In the United States, by the 1950s many institutions offering law degrees began requiring two or three years of college for admission and changed the title of the degree form an LLB to a juris doctor (JD), although the course content remained virtually unchanged. (Actually, graduate education in law begins at the master's level—an LLM or master of laws degree, beyond which stands the SJD, the doctor of juridical science). With only a few exceptions, the entry-level professional degree is all that is required to practice a given profession. A professional degree is intended for those wishing to practice within a specific profession and not for those who intend to conduct research in that field, unlike those pursuing graduate academic (research) degrees. As a result, there is little incentive for lawyers, e.g., to pursue graduate education. In medicine or dentistry, however, this is often not the case. Many of the specialties in medicine and dentistry require a master's degree; thus, there is incentive for many physicians and dentists to seek graduate education (but again, for the purpose of garnering specialized skills in order to better practice—not in order to conduct research).

**professional-model policing.** Also known as traditional-model policing, it is the model of policing that emerged as a result of the Progressive Era, narrowing the police mission to one of law enforcement (for the purpose of increasing organizational efficiency), the separation of police officers from the contaminating influences of society (for the purpose of eliminating corruption), and the imposition of a paramilitary organizational structure on urban police organizations. The separation of the department from the corruptive influence of the mayor's office was the final step in the development of a "professional" police force, under the Progressive agenda. The model further called for the professionalization of the upper echelons of the organization, similar to that of the U.S. Army of the early 1900s. This model, although arguably outdated, persists to this day, and has largely frustrated the implementation of more innovative modes of policing, like community-oriented policing.

**profiler.** *n.* In law enforcement, one who develops a profile for a criminal suspect whose identity is unknown, often in celebrated and violent criminal cases. Profiling is an art and not a science, although social science data are used by the profiler to construct an image of the suspect and his or her likely lifestyle, habits, and desires. Only a handful of law enforcement agencies have profilers, most notably the Federal Bureau of Investigation.

*pro forma.* *(Lat.) adj.* Done for appearances and in a superficial and perfunctory way as a matter of form; merely for the purposes of ritual and ceremonial formality.

**Progressive Era (1880-1920).** The American reform era spanning 1880–1920, comprising state and local progressivism (1880–1900) and federal progressivism (1900–1920). While some sources place the dates rigidly between 1900 and 1917, the movement actually began shortly after the end of the Civil War and held influence until the early 1930s. The perfectibility of government, in all its forms, was the primary objective of the movement, although it addressed numerous other issues and concerns. Its companion movement, known as the "Social Gospel" (also known as Christian socialism), provided legitimacy for progressivism as well as spiritual uplift. Numerous notable personages enlisted in the cause but none were more influential than the Baptist minister Walter Rauschenbusch, the "Prophet" of the Social Gospel. The movement was focused on the perfectibility of government in all its forms, and its effects are notable to this day; it included such things as the city manager form of government, the referendum, the eight-hour workday and laborer protections, and many others. No era in U.S. history has had more impact on the entire criminal justice system than the Progressive Era.

*pro hac vice.* *(Lat.)* "For this occasion only." For example, permission may be granted by the court allowing a lawyer the right to practice law within its jurisdiction where he or she is not licensed, for the purpose of a particular case only, or a sheriff may deputize for a specific time, place, or event.

**Prohibition Era (1920-1933).** Taking effect in January of 1920, the Eighteenth Amendment prohibited the manufacture, possession, sale, production, or transportation of alcoholic beverages in the United States. Numerous laws and organizations emerged to accommodate the drying-up of America under the Thirteenth Amendment, including the Anti-Saloon League and the Women's Christian Temperance Union. Despite the high hopes of many rural Christian fundamentalists in the South and Midwest, the movement proved to be disappointing. Critics argue that the movement actually led to the expansion of organized crime and did more damage than good.

**promulgate.** *v.* To officially proclaim or announce; to formally and officially disseminate.

**proof.** *n.* The substantiation of a proffered fact through evidence; a logically established assertion of a proposition.

**proof beyond a reasonable doubt.** Proof that a reasonable person would require to render a decision regarding a given controversy.

**property.** *n.* (1) Something capable of possession or subject to ownership, whether tangible or intangible, as in a right or interest. (2) The right to ownership. (3) A trait or attribute.

**property clerk.** The title given to the police or law enforcement official charged with the safekeeping of all property in police care, custody, and control.

**property rights.** Under common law, the right of ownership of private property, protecting the owner against unreasonable public restraint. Individual property rights may be put aside when public safety or welfare are involved, but are subject to due process procedures and just compensation. See the *doctrine of eminent domain.*

**pro se.** *(Lat.)* For one's self; on one's own behalf; generally referring to one who acts as his or her own attorney.

**prosecute.** *v.* To institute legal proceedings against a defendant, whether criminal or civil.

**prosecuting attorney (PA).** (1) In some states, e.g., Missouri and Michigan, he or she is a licensed attorney, who is an elected public official, representing the interests of the state in criminal and quasi-criminal prosecutions of state law and/or county ordinance violations. A PA is the equal of a state's attorney (SA) or district attorney (DA) in other states, at the county or parish level of government. It is important to note that a prosecutor prosecutes cases within a state trial court circuit or district, only within the county in which he or she was elected, even though the trial court's circuit or district may span a number of counties. (2) A generic title for a public prosecutor at any level of government.

**prosecution.** *n.* The party who initiates and carries out a criminal or civil proceeding against a defendant.

**Prosecution Management Support System (PMSS).** A system that provides data to prosecutors, allowing them to make informed decisions regarding the realignment of case loads relative to the seriousness of charges, within the parameters of established prosecutorial policies. The system is the result of years of research by the Bureau of Justice Assistance (BJA). The program is sponsored by the PMSS Program of the Bureau of Justice Assistance, Washington, DC.

**prosecutor.** *n.* In a criminal law context, the official who represents the government and conducts the prosecution in a criminal trial. Prosecutors represent the level of government they are employed by and go by a number of official titles, e.g., corporate counsel and city attorney (for municipal governments in local courts); county prosecutor, district attorney, prosecuting attorney, or state's attorney (for county governments in state trial courts); U.S. attorney (for the federal government in federal courts); and attorney general (for state governments and the federal government in state and federal courts).

**prosequi** *(Lat.)* To pursue or follow up through adjudication. See *nolle prosequi.*

**prostitution.** *n.* The act of prostituting; the state of being a prostitute.

**protective custody.** Custody provided for the purpose of ensuring the safety of a person, often a material witness.

**protective search.** A search conducted for the purpose of ensuring the safety of an officer, the subject, or another; one not initiated for the purpose of discovering evidence, e.g., a Terry frisk. See *Terry v. Ohio*, 392 U.S. 1, 88 S.Ct. 1868, 20 L.Ed.2d 889 (1968).

**provisional exit.** A conditionally authorized temporary release from confinement for a specified reason, with the full expectation of a timely return, e.g., for the sake of an appearance in court or other proceedings, an appeal, or medical treatment.

**proviso.** *n.* A condition; agreement; stipulation; or clause.

**provocation.** *n.* The provoking, inducement, instigation, stimulus, or motivation to behave in some way or to do a particular act.

**provost.** *n.* (1) The commissioned officer in charge of a military police command (MPC) at a military reservation, post, camp, or tactical unit in a theater of combat; superintendent of a military prison or prisoners of war (see *provost* [pronounced "provo"] *marshal*). (2) In American higher education, the chief operational officer, immediately below the president or chancellor. (3) In ecclesiastical usage, the administrative head of a cathedral or church.

**provost guard.** (1) A somewhat dated title for a contingent of military police, overseen by a provost (pronounced "provo") marshal. (2) During the American Revolutionary War and continuing until post–Civil War times, the official title for soldiers detailed for what today would be known as military police duty; troops similar to the French "troops of *Marechaussee."*

**provost marshal (PM).** In military usage, the word *provost* is pronounced "provo." Under military law, the commissioned officer in charge of a military police command, at any military reservation or other place subject to military law, occupation, or martial law. The provost marshal has the authority to carry out all military related policing and law enforcement functions, and as the officer of the court for military tribunals, carries out the execution of punishments adjudicated by courts-martial or other military tribunals. He or she is responsible for the custody and transportation of military prisoners or those under the jurisdiction of the military. The multiple functions and responsibilities of the provost marshal make his or her office most like that of the county sheriff in the civilian criminal justice system. Major criminal investigations, however, are delegated to the Army Criminal Investigation Division (CID) or other such agency in the U.S. Air Force or Marine Corps. Separate from the criminal justice functions of the provost marshal, he or she is responsible in the theater of combat for the custody of prisoners of war and numerous other combat responsibilities carried out by the military police in the furtherance of military objectives.

**provost marshal general (PMG).** The general officer (usually a two-star major general or three-starlieutenant general) overseeing all army provost (pronounced "provo") marshal, military police, and Criminal Investigation Division (CID) operations worldwide.

**Provost Marshal's Office (PMO).** (1) The office held by the army provost (pronounced "provo") marshal; the chief police or law enforcement executive (commissioned officer) at a given military reservation or within a tactical military command. (2) The physical structure similar in function to a civilian police station, including a communications center, sergeant's desk, roll-call room, lockup, and administrative offices on a military reservation or within a tactical military command. Note that the U.S. Air Force and Marine Corps have similar arrangements.

**proximate cause.** The primary moving cause or causal element, without which an effect would not have been produced resulting in injury, if the injury was one that could have been reasonably anticipated or foreseen as a result of such act or actions. See also *causality; concurrent cause;* and *efficient cause.*

**proxy.** *n.* The authority to act on another's behalf; a substitute or envoy.

**prurient.** *adj.* Lustful, lascivious, or lewd desire for the lecherous; a predilection for base-level sexuality.

**psychedelic drugs.** Drugs having the properties requisite to alter sensory perceptions and cause sensory crossovers, e.g., seeing sounds.

**psychiatrist.** *n.* A licensed physician holding a speciality in psychiatry; one holding a graduate degree beyond the entry-level MD degree, i.e., a medical master's degree.

**psychoactive drug.** A controlled substance capable of altering one's mood or behavior because of induced alterations in brain function.

**psychological drug dependence.** A dependency that is psychologically based, as opposed to one that is physiologically based.

**psychologist.** *n.* A professional holding an advanced academic degree (a graduate degree) in psychology, i.e., MA, Ph.D,. or Psy.D. The term *psychologist* must not be confused with *psychiatrist*, as psychiatrists are medical doctors.

**psychopath (sociopath).** *n.* One with a severe personality disorder; one lacking the ability to feel guilt or empathize with others.

**psychosis.** *n.* An abnormal or pathological mental state, constituting a clearly diseased entity.

**public defender.** A licensed attorney employed by a governmental entity, or one appointed by the court, to defend indigent defendants in criminal adjudications. Public defenders may be found, depending on the jurisdiction, working at the local, county, state, or federal level.

**public enemy.** A term used by police and law enforcement officers to describe a criminal who poses a clear danger to the public.

**public-interest disputes.** Labor conflicts leading to a strike jeopardizing national or state security, safety, health, and welfare. Strikes by police or air traffic controllers, e.g., fall under this category. Such strikes may invoke the emergency striking provisions found in either federal or state laws, e.g., the Taft–Hartley Act.

**public investigator.** One employed by a public agency in an investigative capacity, for purposes other than criminal law enforcement. That is, an agency other than a police or law enforcement agency, e.g., the health department, which enforces administrative or civil code regulations.

**public law.** A law or statute passed by a sovereign entity, regulating the organization of the state or nation, the relationship between its people, and the duties and responsibilities of public officials between citizens or other sovereigns. Public laws may be found in constitutional provisions, criminal law, and civil and administrative codes.

**public nuisance.** Anything creating an unreasonable interference with a commonly held right of the general population. Behavior may fall within the category of a public nuisance if such behavior in some way injures or interferes with public health, safety, morals, peace, or the general convenience of the people collectively.

**public place.** A place where the general public has a right to use, although not necessarily a place dedicated entirely to public use, but rather a place that is public rather than private. Such places are readily accessible to local neighborhoods and are in fact for public use, e.g., a public beach and public ways.

**public safety department.** A public agency organized to provide policing and/or other emergency services, e.g., fire, ambulance, and rescue services under one organizational administration.

**punishment.** *n.* In law, a sanction consisting of a fine, restitution, confinement, public service, or any combination thereof, imposed by law for the commission of an act or the failure to perform a required duty. In extreme cases, a penalty of death may be imposed in jurisdictions providing for it.

**punitive damages.** Damage awards that have been increased for the plaintiff beyond what is necessary to compensate him or her for the actual property loss, in instances where the wrong imposed was amplified by circumstances involving malice, fraud, or wanton conduct by the defendant.

**pyromania.** *n.* A chronic compulsion to set unwanted, illegal, and destructive fires.

O
P

# Q

**quarstionarius.** *(Lat.)* Dating to circa 300 BC, they were those mandated under Roman law to investigate the origins of fires—the equivalent of a contemporary fire marshal's arson investigator.

**quash.** *v.* To suppress, invalidate, rescind, terminate, abrogate, annul, put down, or vacate.

**quasi.** *(Lat.)* As if; like, just as; seemingly, similar, almost, pseudo.

**quasi-judicial powers.** Those powers granted to an administrative agency by the Congress or a state legislature to hold inquiries and to make decisions having the force of law, despite the doctrine of the separation of powers, holding that only courts of law (judges) have such powers. The universal rule against the delegation of powers (as it applies to the creation of criminal laws) has been argued as construing that because an administrative law may hold a criminal sanction, it is, therefore, a criminal law, and, thus, an improper delegation of the legislature's exclusive power to generate criminal law. This is a relatively unsettled area of law.

**questors.** *(Lat.)* Nascent investigative agents instituted in fifth-century Rome.

**Quetelet, Lambert Adolphe Jacques (1796–1874).** One of the earliest pioneers in criminological thought, he argued that no two persons could have identical physical measurements. This supported the Bertillon method of classification; however, in 1903 the warden of the prison at Leavenworth, Kansas, found two inmates with identical measurements but different fingerprints. This led to the abandonment of Quetelet's hypothesis.

**queuing system.** In police usage, a system by which police dispatchers assign responses to a list of waiting calls for service.

**quid pro quo.** *(Lat.)* "Something for something." In legal usage, a term for the rendering or exchange of one thing of value for another.

**Quinney, Earl Richard (1934– ).** One of the most celebrated critical criminologists of the twentieth century, his theoretical orientation has evolved to include phenomenological philosophy, the spiritualization of Marxism, and peace studies. His first book on Marxist criminology was *The Social Reality of Crime* (1970), whereas his publication of *Providence* (1980) echoed his return to religious interests.

**quorum.** *n.* (1) The minimal number of authorized members of a committee or panel necessary to conduct business. (2) A select committee, group, or panel.

**quo warranto.** *(Lat.)* A legal remedy challenging the continued exercise of alleged unlawful authority, generally brought about on the behalf of the people of a state, challenging the usurpation of a public office.

# R

RFLP, restriction fragment length polymorphism
RICO, Racketeer Influenced and Corrupt Organizations Act
ROR, release on recognizance

**race.** *n.* A primary biological subdivision of humans, as distinguished by such characteristics as body structure, color and texture of hair, eyes, and other features. Any population differing from others in some way that is genetically determined. Ethnologists generally agree that three major races exist: Caucasian, Negroid, and Mongoloid. Much confusion surrounds the term *race* as a result of cultural and unscientific connotations; scientists prefer the use of the term *ethnic* when referring to those who comprise a subgroup not entirely distinguished by genetic differences.

**racial profiling.** The selective enforcement of the criminal law by police and law enforcement officers, based on a profile regarding a specific criminal activity, heavily influenced by racial or ethnic characteristics. Some police agencies, for example, have had a policy of stopping automobiles with license plates from certain states, when the vehicle bearing those plates is being driven on a specified highway by a person of a particular racial origin.

**racism.** *n.* A belief system based on perceived differences in racial groups, leading to prejudice, bias, segregation, and injustice, underpinned by a doctrine of racial supremacy.

**Racketeer Influenced and Corrupt Organizations Act (RICO).** A federal statute originating in 1970 and amended in 1986; the statute (Title 18, USC § 1961–1968) was intended to target the continuing operations of organized crime. RICO expressly disallows the use of racketeering activities and/or profits to conduct the transactions of another business. The primary enforcement tool in the RICO law is the forfeiture provision against illegally gained interests in other business enterprises. Many states have legislated statutes similar to the federal RICO law. Many civil libertarians argue that the statute and similar state statutes represent numerous threats to constitutionally based civil liberty protections.

**racketeering.** *n.* (1) The ongoing organized conspiracy or activities of a group of criminals to extort money, services, or goods from legitimate businesses through threats of violence or the overt use of violence. (2) A criminally organized involvement in prostitution, gambling, or narcotics.

**radar.** *n.* An acronym for radio detecting and ranging; a scientific method of measurement based on the Doppler principle, discovered by Christian Doppler (1803–1853). Through the use of radio waves, a transmitter sends out a high-frequency radio signal that is returned, whereupon the distance between the transmitter and the object is measured. Doppler's theory postulates that as the source and observer move closer to one another, the frequency increases. Although originally developed in World War II for military purposes, the use of radar has been heavily employed in civilian policing, e.g., radar used to detect speeders.

**radical criminology.** A criminological perspective (theory) focusing on the political aspects of crime and criminal law, emphasizing the inherently repressive nature of the criminal justice process, especially in a capitalist state.

**railroad police.** Often referred to as special agents, they are the private police officers and investigators for the various railroads throughout the United States and Canada, holding public police or law enforcement commissions and authority.

**rampart scandal.** The LAPD scandal of the late 1990s, located within the Rampart Division of the City of Los Angeles, where Rampart officers were found to be involved in drug thefts, bank robberies, false imprisonment of defendants, the planting of evidence, and the horrific beating of defendants.

**Rand Corporation.** A nonprofit "think tank" serving the public interest through independent research and analysis on important public safety issues.

**ransom.** *n.* The money, consideration, or demand paid for the return of a kidnapped person.

**rape.** *n.* Sexual intercourse with another without lawful consent.

**rape shield laws.** Laws enacted by numerous state legislatures within the past three decades to protect victims of rape, when serving as witnesses, from having many of their personal relationships being brought into the criminal trial. Intended to shield the victim from impeachment by the defense counsel, critics argue that these laws provide only minimal protection against this painful defense tactic.

**Rational Choice Theory.** A criminological perspective (theory) pioneered by Ronald Clarke and Derek Cornish, grounded in two primary theoretical assumptions, i.e., utilitarianism and free will.

**rationalization.** *n.* A psychological process for explaining away behaviors by providing reasons for why they occurred, which places the transgressor in a more favorable light.

**Ray, Isaac (1807–1881).** One of the most influential authors on forensic psychiatry in nineteenth-century America. Among his most notable works is *The Medical Jurisprudence of Insanity* (1838).

**Ray, James Earl (1929–1998).** The person arrested for the 1968 assassination of civil rights leader Martin Luther King, Jr. Although his confession helped convict him, he later recanted it, and many believe that he was wrongly convicted. Nonetheless, he died in prison of liver failure on April 23, 1998.

**re.** *(Lat.)* In the case of; concerning the matter of. Commonly used to designate a judicial proceeding wherein only one party is represented in an issue; this frequently occurs in juvenile proceedings, e.g., *In re Gault*, 254, 303, 473, 486, 387 U.S. 1, 875 S.Ct. 1428, 18 L.Ed2d 527 (1967).

**reaction subculture.** A concept pioneered by Albert Cohen regarding delinquent subcultures whose negative and antisocial behaviors are the result of a reaction to socially induced stressors that mainstream society places on lower-class juveniles where delinquency is concentrated.

**reactionary subculture.** A group seeking to counteract or undo the progressive trends of a given period, favoring a return to a bygone era, e.g., the American "Know Nothings" or the "Luddites" of early industrial England.

**reactive crime strategies.** Crime control strategies that target the symptoms as opposed to the root causes of criminality, through reactive measures.

**reagent.** *n.* A chemical substance used in the detection or measurement of another substance. A reagent may also be used to transform one substance into another via the reaction it initiates.

**real evidence.** Evidence obtained through the inspection and analysis of material objects, artifacts, or physical characteristics.

**reality therapy.** The therapy envisaged by William Glasser. It focuses on forcing offenders to accept personal responsibility for their actions and to face the consequences stemming from them. Unlike psychotherapy, which permits offenders to make excuses for their behaviors, reality therapy makes offenders come face-to-face with their social transgressions.

**reasonable doubt.** Doubt that a reasonable and prudent person may have that would lead to an acquittal, based on reason and springing from the evidence or lack thereof.

**reasonable man (person) standard.** A standard required by the law concerning one's actions, whereupon one is deemed either in or out of compliance, if he or she acted in a manner that an ordinary prudent person would have under like circumstances.

**rebellion.** *n.* A resistance to the laws and authority of government, involving the use of force by arms.

**rebuttable presumption.** Sometimes called a disputable presumption, it is a term found in legal usage, especially the law of evidence or procedural law, asserting a presumption that may be refuted by evidence contrary to the presumption, e.g., the presumption that the driver of a vehicle involved in a high-speed pursuit with the police was driven by the owner, creating grounds for the immediate seizure of the automobile.

**rebuttal.** *n.* A refutation of something asserted.

**rebuttal evidence.** That evidence submitted to counteract, disprove, or erode and debilitate evidence provided by the opposing party.

**recall.** *n.* A lawful method for the removal from office of an elected public official after that person has been installed in office, before the expiration of his or her term.

**recant.** *v.* To repudiate, withdraw, or nullify prior testimony formally and publicly.

**recidivism.** *n.* The repeated commission of criminal behavior after one has been adjudged a criminal or a delinquent.

**recidivism statutes.** State and federal laws providing for increased sanctions against those who have been previously convicted of a crime(s).

**recidivist.** *n.* In penology, one who is an habitual offender and has reoffended after a criminal conviction.

**reciprocity.** *n.* (1) In law, especially international law, a *quid pro quo* arrangement between two or more states providing mutually specified privileges for citizens of any of the participating states. (2) Any reciprocal agreement between two parties, i.e., a mutual exchange.

**reckless driving.** The operation of a motor vehicle with reckless, willful, and wanton disregard for the rights and safety of others. That is, the operation of a vehicle in such a way as to knowingly, and with willful and wanton indifference to other's rights and safety, continue such operation, with the full knowledge that continuing such driving will likely injure another, but disregarding the consequences. It should be noted that reckless driving in most jurisdictions may be charged on private property, and the vehicle does not have to be motorized. However, the difficult part for the prosecution is the wanton element. That is why many jurisdictions have a lesser included offense known as careless or heedless driving that may be charged without the wanton element. According to the *Uniform Vehicle Code*, § 11–901, "Any person who drives any vehicle in a willful or wanton disregard for the safety of persons or property is guilty of reckless driving."

**reckless homicide.** A category of criminal homicide in some jurisdictions characterized by a reckless and/or willful disregard of such activities and consequences that result in the death of another. See *vehicular homicide* and *manslaughter*, *Uniform Vehicle Code*, § 11–903.

**Reckless, Walter Cade (1899–1988).** Reckless received his Ph.D. in sociology from the University of Chicago in 1931 and went on to author a number of influential articles and books on criminology and juvenile delinquency. One of his foci was the self-concept as an insulator against delinquency. Many of his theoretical propositions involved a combination of various aspects of symbolic interactionism, social disorganization, and social integration. He stands as one of the major contributors to control and containment theories.

**recognizance.** *n.* In law, an obligation, usually in place of a money bond, to comply with a court order, binding the person to do or not to do a specific act(s).

**record.** *n.* A written account of an act, action, or event, i.e., the court record or governmental criminal record.

**recuse.** *v.* In legal usage, to challenge a judge, juror, court, or tribunal for reasons of bias, prejudice, or incompetency.

**redirect examination.** *n.* The examination of a witness by the original (direct) examiner after the cross-examination of a witness by opposing counsel.

**redress.** *n.* The compensation, adjustment, satisfaction, or corrective action for abuses, damages, injuries, or afflictions suffered.

**reeve.** *n.* The high police official over a political subdivision (shire) in early England. Thus, this individual became the reeve of the shire; spoken together, the shire-reeve later evolved into the word "sheriff."

**referee.** *n.* One to whom a judge refers a case—for the purpose of serving as the court's go-between, facilitator, arbiter, and mediator—to take testimony and eventually write a report for the court's edification.

**referendum.** *n.* A device for seeking the direct approval of the electorate to change a statutory law, by superseding, overriding, or bypassing the legislature.

**reformatory.** *n.* An institution to which youthful offenders are sent following an adjudicatory hearing, where correction and reform are expected, as opposed to punishment, as juveniles, unlike adult offenders, have a right to treatment.

**refoulemant.** *v.* In international law, the prohibited surrender or purposeful transfer of a person against his or her will (often a refugee or alleged criminal and/or terrorist) to a third sovereign state, where that person faces a grave risk of abuse and/or torture.

**refreshing memory.** The practice of allowing a witness at trial to review documents and other memoranda for the purpose of aiding his or her memory.

**regiment.** *n.* In traditional military usage, a unit consisting of several battalions, generally commanded by a general-grade officer, often a major general (two stars). The basic organizational unit directly beneath a full division.

**regulatory justice system.** The system of justice that stems from the regulatory authority delegated by the legislature of the sovereign state to various administrative agencies, e.g., OSHA. See *administrative law, justice, law,* and *procedural law.*

**rehabilitation.** *n.* One of the goals of the criminal justice system and penal institutions, seldom found today, as it conflicts with the dominant goal of retribution (a conflicting goal of the criminal justice system and penal institutions). The intent of rehabilitation is to reform the offender into a productive member of society, as opposed to the mere warehousing of inmates.

**Rehnquist, William H. (1924–2005).** Sixteenth Chief Justice of the U.S. Supreme Court, he was appointed by President Ronald Reagan in 1986. In 1971, he was appointed as associate justice of the High Court by President Richard M. Nixon. A graduate of Stanford University Law School (1952), he clerked for Supreme Court Justice Robert H. Jackson (1052–1953). As a conservative member of the Court, he was instrumental in reversing the more liberal civil liberties–oriented trend of the Warren Court in criminal cases. Rehnquist died of cancer in office and was replaced by Chief Justice John G. Roberts, Jr., who was nominated by President George W. Bush in 2005.

**reintegration.** *n.* A correctional philosophy advocating positive methods for the reentry of offenders into open society.

**rejoinder.** *n.* Also known as a surrebutter, it is a pleading or answer to the plaintiff's or prosecution's reply.

**Relative Deprivation Theory.** A criminological perspective (theory) that did not come to fruition in criminological circles until the 1980s under theorists S. Stack and John Braithwaite and various left realists, who see it as an elemental concept. It occurs when people or groups subjectively view themselves as unfairly disadvantaged in relationship to others having similar qualities.

**release on recognizance (ROR).** The pretrial release of an accused without the posting of a money bond, with the defendant's promise to appear for trial. Often, ROR is provided when the defendant has real property that the state can seize (in an *ex parte* procedure) should the defendant not appear as commanded.

**relevance.** *n.* The state or quality of being pertinent to the issue at hand.

**remand.** *v.* (1) To return by court order for review or further consideration. Appellate courts sometimes remand a case back to the lower court for reconsideration. (2) To send a defendant back to custody.

**remedial.** *adj.* Providing or tending to provide a remedy; the correction of a wrong or abuse, i.e., a remedial action.

**remission.** *n.* (1) A release from indebtedness. (2) The partial or full arrest of a isease.

**removal proceeding.** A preconviction federal judicial procedure for transferring a defendant from one federal court district to another. The removal order authorizes the U.S. marshal to move the defendant to another federal court district.

**rendition.** *n.* The formal term for the extradition of a fugitive between the various states comprising the United States of America. The surrender of an alleged criminal offender by an asylum state to the state where the criminal offense was committed. This is accomplished via an order (often called a governor's warrant) by the governor of the prosecuting state.

**reparation.** *n.* The restitution for an injury, made directly to the injured party. Under international law, nations may be required to present reparations to injured sovereign states at the end of armed hostilities.

**repeal.** *n.* The abrogation or annulment of a preexisting law by the legislative enactment of a later law, overriding the first law and making it a nullity.

**repeat offender.** One who is a recidivist; one who repeatedly becomes involved in criminal activity after a criminal conviction.

**replevin.** *n.* A civil court order intended to recover property from another that has been wrongfully detained. In cases where a civil seizure of property, allegedly involved in a crime (especially as an instrumentality of the crime), was made, the defendant's property may be recovered via a replevin order.

**reports or reporters.** The published volumes of appellate case law of a state, court, or group of courts, e.g., the *Illinois Reports*, the *Northeastern Reporter* of the *National Reporter Series*, or the *Supreme Court Reporter.*

**reprieve.** *n.* A form of executive clemency; a stay of judgment; a temporary relief from a court-ordered sanction.

**res adjudicata.** *(Lat.)* "Things judged." Sometimes spelled *res judicata*, it is a thing judicially decided; a settled case. A rule in law that a decision by a court of competent jurisdiction is conclusive and, thus, cannot be relitigated. See also the *doctrine of collateral estoppel; double jeopardy.*

**rescind.** *v.* To cancel, invalidate, or annul a legal document, order, or mandate.

**res gestae.** *(Lat.)* "Things done." See *res gestae declaration.*

**res gestae declaration.** An excited utterance made by perpetrators, victims, or witnesses of a criminal act immediately before, during, or after its commission; such utterances must be induced by the intensity of the occasion and where there is no time for the declarant to purposely fabricate his or her utterance.

**resident.** *n.* (1) One who lawfully resides in a state, nation, or other political subdivision; (2) one who domiciles in a place; (3) one who physically occupies a dwelling.

**residential facility.** A correctional facility where offenders are permitted unaccompanied leave to use community-based resources and programs, e.g., schools or treatment programs.

**resisting an officer.** In criminal law, the offense of obstructing or preventing a peace officer or law enforcement agent who is attempting to execute a lawful writ or effect an apprehension.

**resocialization.** *n.* The process of reforming an individual through a sociopsychological conditioning process by a resocialization agent, regiment, or institutional environment. The resocialization process is most apparent in total institutions, where the process is virtually unconstrained. The process is often a painful one with notable effects, where one is virtually made over in the image of the organization.

**respondeat superior.** "Let the master answer." A legal doctrine holding that the master is liable for the wrongful acts of his or her servant (employee). The doctrine holds that the master is responsible for the lack of care on the part of the servant toward others to whom the master has a duty to extend proper care.

**respondent.** *n.* One who must answer a claim or allegation of another; the party against whom an appeal is lodged.

**response time.** The time between the reporting of a crime and the arrival of the police.

**restorative justice.** A deterrence model using restitution programs, community service, victim mediation, and other strategies both to rehabilitate the offender and to deal with the harm done to the victim and community.

**restriction fragment length polymorphism.** (RFLP). A time-consuming DNA typing technique, wherein organisms are differentiated through an analysis of discernable patterns derived from cleavages in their respective DNA.

**retreatism.** *n.* An adaptation in Merton's Anomie Theory whereby a person rejects the goal of economic advancement and any legitimate means of attaining it.

**retreatist subculture.** A subculture into which one retreats in response to perceived problems in the dominant culture. Some argue that the drug culture serves as a retreatist subculture, for example.

**retribution.** *n.* Punishment for wrongs committed. A concept in justice that a debt must be paid to society for wrongful acts by the defendant; an eye for an eye.

**return (search warrant).** The written portion of a search warrant citing the actions of the police or law enforcement agents during its execution, including a description of the places searched and an inventory of items seized.

**reversal.** *n.* In law, the overturning or setting aside of a lower court's decision by an appellate court.

**reverse discrimination.** A claim by one holding a majority status that antidiscrimination laws and policies are in fact discriminatory to majority persons. For example, when a person holding a majority status is refused entry into an educational institution, even though he or she has higher entrance examination scores than a minority person who is admitted into the institution because of a racial quota system, reverse discrimination is said to have occurred.

**review.** *n.* A judicial or administrative reexamination. In a judicial context, the examination of a decision rendered by a trial court on an issue of law by an appellate court or by a supreme court on an issue reviewed by an intermediate court of appeal; this does not constitute a rehearing of the case.

**revocation hearing.** A hearing concerning the withdrawal of either privilege of probation or parole, as a result of the offender's behavior that has allegedly violated the conditions of the parole or probation contract or the criminal law, which may result in reincarceration.

**RICO laws.** Laws at both the federal and state level constructed to prosecute organized crime activities. See *Racketeer Influenced and Corrupt Organizations Act (1970)* 18 USC § 1961–1968.

**ridge.** *n.* A line (friction ridge) found on the dactyls, a number of which create a fingerprint or footprint pattern.

**ridge count.** The number of ridges on a dactyl intervening or crossing an imaginary line drawn from the delta to the core.

**ridge line.** A line formed by a ridge in a fingerprint or footprint pattern.

**right of allocution.** The right of a defendant to speak in his or her own behalf before judgment is rendered.

**rights of defendants.** Those constitutionally provided protections (civil liberties) that a criminal defendant may claim, e.g., the right to counsel.

**right of sanctuary.** Laws that date from antiquity, allowing certain offenders to evade punishment by secular authorities once they have reached specified areas or structures designated as places under the protection of God.

**right to bear arms.** A civil liberty found in the Constitution's Second Amendment, which many civil libertarians argue applies exclusively to the right of the states to maintain a well-organized militia. The National Rifle Association argues otherwise, maintaining that it applies directly to the people individually. The courts have ruled, however, that the Second Amendment's safeguard is not infringed upon by state or federal laws making unauthorized possession of a firearm a crime. In mid-2008, the Supreme Court held in the *District of Columbia v. Heller* 554 US__(2008), that the right to bear arms does not pertain exclusively to the militia or armed forces, as previously alluded to in the earlier ruling in *US v. Miller* 307 US 174 (1939).

**right to counsel.** A constitutionally based protection (Sixth Amendment) of criminal defendants to be represented by counsel, even when he or she is indigent. *Federal Rules of Criminal Procedure* 44 and 18 USCA § 3006A provide for competent counsel. A triad of appellate cases have guaranteed the right to counsel, even in misdemeanor cases if a jail term is possible, see *Gideon v. Wainright,* 372 U.S. 335, 83 S.Ct. 792 (felony cases); *Argersinger v. Hemlin,* 407 U.S. 25, 92 S.Ct. 2006 (misdemeanor cases); and *In re Gault,* 387 U.S. 1, 87 S.Ct. 1428 (juvenile cases).

**Rikers Island Penitentiary.** The nation's largest penal institution, constructed in 1933 and located in New York City, housing nearly 8,000 prisoners on a daily average.

**riot.** *n.* In legal usage, a public disturbance by three or more persons assembled unlawfully causing a tumult and thereby creating a risk of injury to persons, property, or the public peace.

**Riot Act.** A 1775 English law making it a felony, in cases where twelve people or more are gathered unlawfully in a manner that is disruptive of the public peace, if they do not disband within one hour after a reading of the Riot Act.

**riot-control agent.** Any chemical agent used in riot control by military or police personnel, having the ability to temporarily irritate the eyes or respiratory system upon contact, generally CN and CS agents.

**riot grenade.** A nonlethal hand grenade, containing either an eye or respiratory irritant (CN or CS agents) or a combination of both, having a short fuse that detonates quickly after release.

**riot gun.** Sometimes called a scatter gun or a sawed-off shotgun, it is a generic name for a shotgun with a short barrel and open chock, intended to allow for the widest spread of shot (lead or steel projectiles, often double 00 buckshot). These types of shoulder weapons are generally 12 gauge and of the slide-action (pump) variety. They are frequently used by police or the National Guard during riot control, although many police agencies provide them to all marked patrol units as one of the most powerful weapons in the police arsenal.

**rites of passage.** The ceremonies, trials, and requisite accomplishments (often phys-ically, emotionally, and/or socially demanding) associated with the transition from one status to another, whether that transition be from puberty to adulthood, from one occupational category to another, or from one social status to another. The hazing ceremony associated with the admission into a college fraternity provides a graphic example.

**robber baron.** Originally a nobleman during the feudal period, who virtually or literally robbed people who made passage through his lands and ways (including waterways). During America's "Gilded Age" the term became a metaphor for the "captains of industry," who made enormous profits in amoral business ventures, at the cost of great suffering for those of the working classes. Progressive reformers sought to remedy the unbridled authority of the robber barons through governmental controls on their business practices.

**robbery.** *n.* (1) The unlawful taking of money or other items of value, while in the possession of another (whether actual or constructive) against his or her wishes, by means of arms, force, intimidation, or fear. (2) The taking or attempting to take anything of value under confrontational circumstances from the control, custody, or care of another person by force or threat of force or violence and/or by putting the victim in fear of immediate harm (FBI Uniform Crime Reporting Definition).

**Roberts, John G., Jr. (1955– ).** Appointed as the seventeenth Chief Justice of the U.S. Supreme Court, by President George W. Bush (2005), Mr. Roberts experienced a relatively noncontentious nomination process. Graduating from Harvard *summa cum laude* with a bachelor's degree in 1976, he went on to earn a Harvard law degree *magna cum laude* (1979). From 1980–1981, he served as law clerk to then Associate Justice William Rehnquist of the U.S. Supreme Court. From 1982 to 1986, he was the Associate Counsel to the President under the Chief White House Counsel. He was appointed principal United States Deputy Solicitor General from 1989 to 1993, and in 2003, he was appointed as a Justice of the U.S. Court of Appeals for the Washington DC circuit. Judge Roberts was initially nominated to fill retiring Associate Justice Sandra Day O'Connor's position, but with the death of Chief Justice Rehnquist, the president renominated him to fill the Chief Justice's vacancy. He was approved overwhelmingly by the full senate in September of 2005.

**role-playing.** A tool or procedure used in clinical psychology as a therapeutic tool. The client is required to act out a social role in order to experience another's world, with the intention of providing the role player new insights.

**Roman legal system.** The legal system and code used in early Rome, i.e., the Twelve Tablets of approximately 450 B.C., where the Romans first attempted to formally codify legal procedures. Following the fall of the Roman Empire, the Byzantine Empire built on the earlier Roman Code and developed the Justinian Code of 530 B.C.

**roping.** *n.* A method of surveillance where the investigator intends to let the subject know he or she is being observed.

**Ross, Edward A. (1866–1951).** Considered the originator of the term *social control*, Ross introduced the term in a series of articles published between 1896 and 1898 in the *American Journal of Sociology.* He later published a criminology text, *Social Control,* in 1901.

**Rotten-Apple Theory.** A simplistic theory and metaphor for police corruption, emphasizing the moral failings of a few rotten apples in the organizational barrel. This is appealing for administrators because it suggests that the problem is not widespread and not an institutional issue, with a simple remedy. In all reality, the theory describes only a small amount of corruption, which is generally an embedded department wide organizational cultural problem that is extremely difficult to remedy.

**Rousseau, Jean-Jacques (1712–1778).** A French philosopher, author, and social theorist. In 1754, he wrote *Discourse on the Origin and Foundations of Inequality,* emphasizing the inherent goodness of man. In 1762, he wrote *The Social Contract,* stating that "Man is born free, and everywhere he is in chains."

**Rowan, Sir Charles (1782–1852).** A former colonel in the British Army, he later became a police magistrate in Ireland. It was in this capacity that he became acquainted with Sir Robert Peel, who in 1829 appointed him as one of two commissioners (along with Richard Mayne) of the newly formed London Metropolitan Police Force.

**Royal Canadian Mounted Police (RCMP).** The national police department of Canada. While the United States has no such force, its individual state police departments serve many of the same functions and were originally modeled after similar federal police forces found across the globe.

**rule of four.** A rule governing whether a case is selected for appellate review by the Supreme Court; four justices must be in favor in order for it to proceed to review and a granting of *certiorari.*

**rule of law.** Also known as "the supremacy of law," it is a generally applicable legal principle, establishing a standard of conduct. A rule of law is not absolute, but rather a guide that is generally followed.

**rules.** *n.* Established standards and regulations created by legitimate institutions, e.g., a court, the legislature, a public regulatory agency, or a public office.

**rules of court.** The published and promulgated rules governing the practice and procedure before a given court system, usually generated by the supreme court of the sovereign.

**rules of evidence.** Either the case law or the codified law governing the admissibility of evidence. Some jurisdictions, similar to the federal government, have codified rules of evidence and procedure, as opposed to a reliance on case law alone.

**ruling.** *n.* (1) A judicial or administrative verdict, order, or mandate; (2) a determination concerning the admissibility of evidence; (3) the granting or refusal of a motion; or (4) an interpretation of law or constitutional provision.

**runaway.** *n.* The adjudicated status of a minor child who, without the permission of his or her parents or guardians, has left their custody and domicile and has failed to return home within a reasonable time frame.

**Rush, Benjamin (1745–1813).** An American physician and professor of chemistry, who devoted a great deal of his life to reforming the treatment of the mentally ill. He was one of the original leaders in the Philadelphia Society for Alleviating the Miseries of the Public Prisons, founded in 1787. He was opposed to capital punishment, calling it an offspring of the monarchical divine right and a practice contrary to a republican form of government. He condemned the practice in his book *On Punishing Murder By Death* (1792), advocating the replacement of capital and corporal punishment through a reformed prison system.

# S

SARA, scanning, analysis, response, and assessment
SART, sexual assault response team
SDS, Students for a Democratic Society
SEC, Securities and Exchange Commission
SEM, scanning electron microscope
SES, socioeconomic status
SIDS, sudden infant death syndrome
SJD, Doctor of juridical science (see *doctorate*)
SMA, Standard Metropolitan Area
SMART, Specialized Multi-Agency Response Team
SMSA, Standard Metropolitan Statistical Area
SOP, standard operating procedures
SPR, small particle reagent
SRO, school resource officer
STG, security threat group
SWAT, Special Weapons and Tactics

---

**sabotage.** *n.* Deriving from the French word for wooden shoe (*sabot*), it is the act of intentionally obstructing or destroying something; the organized activity, process, or effort to debilitate by destruction.

**Sacco–Vanzetti case.** This case stands as one of the most celebrated American criminal cases of the twentieth century, which eventually became a "cause *célèbre*," virtually around the globe. The arrest of Nicola Sacco and Bartolomeo Vanzetti occurred during one of the most politically repressive eras in American history, the "Red Scare." As committed anarchists, they were treated harshly and without proper regard for due process, resulting in their eventual execution on August 23, 1927. Despite compelling exculpatory evidence and efforts by many to gain an appeal or new trial, all failed. Their ordeal became a watershed in American history, as it dashed any remaining hopes that American democracy and its criminal justice system was the "bright line" against governmental tyranny. Intellectuals around the world raged against the flawed process that had sent two men to their deaths, in what many called judicial murder. Having been arrested and convicted largely as a result of their political persuasions, it was the underbelly of American cultural values and the intense nativism that fueled the serious due process violations, ignored by the judge, prosecutor, and jury. Whether guilty or not, legal and academic scholars agree that the system failed Sacco and Vanzetti utterly.

**sadomasochism.** *n.* A psychological disorder wherein sexual arousal is gained through the infliction of pain by one sexual partner, the sadist, on a cooperative sexual partner, the masochist.

**Saint Valentine's Day massacre (1929).** The mob assassination of several members of a bootlegging gang operated by "Bugs" Moran in Chicago on Saint Valentine's Day. The gangland slaying allowed Al Capone to consolidate his control over mob activities across the Chicago metropolitan area.

**Sam Browne belt and holster assembly.** A belt and holster (generally made of leather) consisting of a wide waist belt, supported by a strap originating at the officer's waist, then going diagonally across the officer's chest and connecting once again on the waist belt near the small of the officer's back. Part of the traditional police officer's uniform until the 1960s, it fell into disuse because of concerns regarding officer safety.

**sanction.** *n.* (1) The penalty part of a criminal statute; (2) a punishment imposed in order to gain compliance; (3) to confirm, authorize, or grant imprimatur.

**sanity hearing.** A hearing conducted under court or administrative order to determine whether or not one is legally sane.

**sans.** *(Fr.)* Without.

**sapphist.** *n.* Lesbian.

**SARA model.** The four activities involved in police/community problem-solving under either a problem- or community-oriented policing strategy, i.e., scanning, analysis, response, and assessment.

**satanic cult.** (1) A group of individuals holding that Satan was originally an archangel who had transgressed against God, and was summarily cast out of heaven, along with his heavenly followers (fallen angels). (2) A subculture following a charismatic leader whom the group believes is a deity.

**scanning, analysis, response, and assessment (SARA).** See *SARA model.*

**scanning electron microscope (SEM).** A microscope using electrons rather than light waves to examine very small objects, which appear in color and are three-dimensional. The process is especially useful in examining gunshot residue, when energy dispersive x-ray analysis is added to the process.

**school resource officer (SRO).** A program to fund the placement of police officers in schools under the Community-Oriented Policing Services (COPS) Office, during the late 1990s and early 2000s. Nearly $420 million was appropriated to hire over 3,800 school resource officers (SROs). This program in many ways paralleled the police counselor program of the 1960s and the 1970s.

**Schur, Edwin M. (1930– ).** A celebrated criminologist of the interactionist perspective, whose definition of deviance is basic to understanding his approach to explaining crime. He states, "Human behavior is deviant to the extent that it comes to be viewed as involving a personally discreditable departure from a group's normative expectation, and it elicits interpersonal and collective reactions that serve to 'isolate,' 'treat,' 'correct,' or 'punish' individuals engaged in such behavior." A proponent of radical noninterventionism, his position as an ardent supporter of symbolic interactionism was evident in his notable service to criminology and his publications such as *Radical Non-Intervention* (1973) and *Labeling Women Deviant* (1984), to cite only two.

**scienter.** *(Lat.)* Knowingly. Commonly used during a pleading to convey a defendant's guilty knowledge.

**scintilla of evidence.** A figurative phrase meaning the smallest spark of evidence.

**scopolamine.** *n.* A drug producing drowsiness, sometimes used in polygraph examinations. During the drug-induced semisleep, it is believed that the subject's inhibitions are lowered and truthful responses are attained. Polygraph examinations employing this process are of dubious utility.

**Scotland Yard.** The name commonly associated with the headquarters of the London Metropolitan Police Office (MPO), since its inception in 1829. Originally, the MPO was located at Whitehall Place, where the courtyard behind the building was called Scotland Yard—the venue through which the public had to pass in order to gain entrance into the MPO building. Today, the MPO is on Victoria Street.

**Scottsboro Boys incident (1931).** A celebrated criminal case where nine black men (some yet boys), ranging in age from thirteen to twenty-one, were arrested for having raped two white women; they were vagrants illegally riding in an open railroad freight car, near Paint Rock, Alabama. All were convicted; only one escaped the court-ordered death sanction. The Supreme Court ruled that the defendants had been denied their constitutionally protected right to the affirmative assistance of counsel and reversed the decision. See *Powell v. Alabama*, 287 U.S. 45 (1932).

**search.** *n.* The probing for something concealed or secreted, in places where the items/persons sought may be reasonably concealed.

**search and seizure.** A phrase encompassing that body of procedural and evidentiary law dealing with the Fourth Amendment's protections (and/or those embodied in state constitutions) against unreasonable searches and seizures, executed by governmental authorities (at either the state or federal level) on private persons and public and private agencies and institutions. Search and seizure law has historically relied on an elaborate body of case law handed down by the state and federal appellate courts, defining the legal parameters for police and law enforcement agents at both the state and federal level. Some search and seizure law derives from statutory law, in other situations by court rules, and in still other situations under codified rules of evidence and procedure. In some instances, these codified rules largely override the need for agencies and the courts to rely on appellate law, i.e., the *Federal Rules of Evidence*, established in 1945 by an act of Congress.

**search incident to arrest.** The right of officers to search, without a warrant, a person and the area around him or her to which he or she might reach, "arms-reach doctrine," or lunge, the "lunge doctrine." Under *Chimel v. California,* 395 U.S. 752 (1969), the High Court ruled that the police and law enforcement agents may search the area to which a subject may reasonably reach, and most appellate courts have liberally construed the ruling to variants of the area to which the subject may lunge.

**search of containers.** The fact that the High Court has upheld the warrantless search of automobiles (based on probable cause, i.e., *Carroll v. U.S.*, 267 U.S. 132 [1925]). The Court expanded the right to the warrantless search of containers in the passenger compartment in *N.Y. v. Belton*, 453 U.S. 454 (1981), but in *United States v. Ross*, 456 U.S. 798 (1982) limited the search authority of the police to exclude closed movable containers found in the trunk.

**search warrant.** A written court order, i.e., a writ issued by a judge in the name of
the state, directing authorized peace officers and law enforcement agents to
search a specific place and seize specified items as evidence in a criminal investigation. The warrant is limited in terms of the place or places to be searched, the
specificity of the item or items to be seized, and the time period within which the
warrant is enforceable (warrants become stale within ninety-six hours in many
jurisdictions).

**Second Amendment (1791).** "A well regulated Militia being necessary to the security
of a free State, the right of the people to keep and bear arms shall not be infringed."

**secondary deviance.** Deviant acts that follow after one has been labeled deviant
and has accepted the negative label.

**secondary evidence.** That evidence that is inferior to the "best evidence" or primary evidence available, i.e., a photocopy of an original document. The rules of
evidence have established the best-evidence rule, generally disallowing secondary
evidence when original evidence is available.

**second-hand evidence.** A phrase referring to hearsay evidence.

**Secret Service.** Charged with the protection of the president and members of his or her
immediate family, the vice president, any president elect, and numerous others, the
U.S. Secret Service is composed of nearly 3,500 employees under the panoply of the
Secretary of the Treasury. Divided into five major divisions, i.e., administrative,
inspection, investigations, the Office of Protective Services, and the Office of
Protective Intelligence, the agency first appeared in its present iteration under the
Treasury Department in June of 1860, for the purpose of suppressing counterfeiting.
After the death of President Lincoln, the protection of the president and his or her
family was included. Arguably, the agency can claim its lineage from the colonial
Secret Service under Aaron Burr (1778), an intelligence agency for the U.S. Army.

**Security and Exchange Commission (SEC).** The federal regulatory watchdog
agency charged with policing virtually all aspects of the securities industry, e.g.,
brokerage firms, stock exchanges, and investment companies. The commission
was established under the Securities Exchange Act of 1934 and consists of five
presidentially appointed members who serve five-year terms of office.

**security classifications.** A security classification scheme employed under the
Department of Defense Industrial Security Program, including a four-tiered system:
confidential, restricted, secret, and top-secret levels.

**security threat group.** A group that poses a threat to officers working within a penal
institution, as defined by the Federal Bureau of Prisons. The bureau has termed
any identifiable group (gang) of individuals who pose a threat or hazard to the
necessary order inside a penal institution as a security threat group.

**sedition.** *n.* The agitation and stirring up of resistance against the sovereign government but falling short of overt treason. Advocating for the overthrow of the government by means of violence.

***sed quis custodiet ipsos custodes?*** *(Lat.)* "But who is to guard the guardians
themselves?"A question posed by the Roman satirist Juvenal (circa AD60).

**seduction.** *n.* The overt act of seducing, baiting, or inducing another to do wrong,
often in a sexual context.

**segregation.** *n.* The separation of things, often social, ethnic, or racial groups. Racial and ethnic segregation in the United States was made illegal under *Brown v. Board of Education*, 347 U.S. 483 (1954), reversing the "separate but equal doctrine" established under *Plessy v. Ferguson*, 163 U.S. 527 (1896).

**seizure.** *n.* In law, the taking of something into one's possession, as in a court-ordered search and seizure process. See *confiscation, expropriation, forfeiture,* and *impoundment.*

**selective enforcement.** A phrase used in policing to indicate the enforcement of a particular law to the exclusion of others, or the enforcement of the law in selected geographical areas, or at selected times, or against a particular group, or any combination of the preceding.

**selectmen or women.** *n.* Elected municipal government officials in a town (usually a town in the northeastern region of the United States) who conduct business for the municipality. The equivalent of municipal aldermen or alderwomen elsewhere in the United States.

**self-defense.** An affirmative criminal defense, claiming that one used force in the defense of himself, herself, or another, to repel a perceived imminent danger or injury, likely to result in grave bodily harm or death. Some jurisdictions require that before self-defense can be claimed, the subject must establish an attempt to retreat, unless the attack is attempted within the home.

**self-incrimination.** An act, statement, or utterance incriminating oneself in criminal activity, i.e., rendering incriminating evidence against oneself. See also *admissions* and *confessions.*

**self-report studies.** A survey methodology intended to measure criminal activity by asking respondents about their criminal activities over a stipulated time period. Criminologist James Short is well known for this type of data collection strategy.

**self-report survey.** The actual structured data collection instrument (questionnaire) used in self-report studies.

**Sellin Center for Studies in Criminology and Criminal Law.** Named after a noted criminologist, this institution, founded in 1960 and housed at the University of Pennsylvania, conducts research on crime, delinquency, and the various components of the criminal justice system.

**semiautomatic.** *n.* A category of firearm that fires a projectile automatically each time the trigger is depressed. Unlike a fully automatic firearm, where bullets are fired repeatedly while the trigger is depressed, semiautomatics require that the trigger be depressed each time a bullet is to be fired. The loading mechanism operates either from the recoil produced by the bullet being fired or by the expanding gasses resulting from ignition. It should be noted that long guns or shoulder weapons (rifles and shotguns) use this designation. Handguns that fire semiautomatically are referred to as automatics, erroneously implying that they are fully automatic firearms.

**sentencing.** *n.* That stage of a trial where the judge imposes the sanction or sentence; in misdemeanor cases it is imposed immediately upon the rendering of a guilty verdict. In felony cases, the trial is bifurcated, and sentencing occurs at a separate date and time, after the judge receives a presentence investigation report (PSI) from the department of probation and parole.

**sentencing council.** A judicial panel consisting of three or more judges in place of a single judge, charged with the responsibility of determining the appropriate sanction for defendants after a criminal conviction.

**sentencing dispositions.** The various sanctions that may be imposed by the sentencing judge after a criminal conviction. The dispositions may vary among fines, incarceration, community service, probation, or any combination thereof. The death penalty may be imposed in some jurisdictions for some capital offenses.

**sentinel.** *n.* One who stands guard and gives notice when danger is imminent.

**sentry.** *n.* One who stands guard, usually at a specified location, admitting only those who are authorized to pass.

**separation of powers doctrine.** A political and legal doctrine holding that federal governmental powers are distributed among the three branches of the government, i.e., the executive, legislative, and judicial branches. The purpose of the doctrine is to ensure that no single branch has the authority to create law, interpret law, and enforce law.

**sequester.** *v.* To hold in isolation, as in the sequestration of a jury.

**sergeant.** *n.* In military usage, an enlisted rank for a noncommissioned officer; a rank immediately above corporal but below a warrant officer. Several ranks exist within the general category of sergeant, e.g., sergeant, staff sergeant, first sergeant, master sergeant, and sergeant major. In police usage, a supervisory rank above corporal, but below lieutenant (an administrative rank).

**serial murder.** A term for a number of similar killings by one offender or a group of offenders. According to the FBI, serial murder is the killing of several victims in three or more separate acts.

**serial number.** An identifying number (or alphanumerical digits) placed on an item by the originating manufacturer. In the case of automobiles, the term "serial number" has been supplanted by "vehicle identification number" (VIN). See *vehicle identification number (VIN).*

**Serpico, Frank.** A 1960 graduate of the New York Police Department's Police Academy who refused to participate in the graft and corruption schemes of his fellow officers. His reports of corruption to the appropriate NYPD officials fell on deaf ears, and he eventually went outside the department to the Knapp Commission on police corruption. By 1971, he was reviled by his peers and was shot in the face by a drug dealer while his partners failed to intervene. He now lives outside the United States.

**service of process.** The delivery of writs, summonses, and so forth; the delivery of formal notice to a defendant ordering him or her to appear in court for the purpose of answering to an allegation.

**session.** *n.* The time during which an official body sits and conducts its business, e.g., a court, grand jury, commission, or legislature.

**session laws.** A body of laws, published chronologically (according to the order they were enacted), as opposed to subject matter, during any given session of the legislature.

**Seventh Amendment (1791).** "In suits at common law, where the value in controversy shall exceed twenty dollars, the right of trial by jury shall be preserved, and no fact tried by a jury shall be otherwise reexamined in any Court of the United States, than according to the rules of the common law."

**severance.** *n.* In law, the state of being severed, or the act of severing, separating, or partitioning. It is a tactic used to deal with interwoven legal issues separately, by dividing the suit into two or more independent parcels, leading to separate judgments.

**sexism.** *n.* Chauvinism, bias, or discrimination according to assumed sexual superiority.

**sexual assault response team (SART).** A team of specially trained technicians who investigate sexual assault or sexual battery cases. Such teams are composed of a medical doctor or nurse, a rape crisis advocate, a police detective, and the first responder to the scene, e.g., a patrol officer or emergency medical technician (EMT).

**sexual harassment.** The unsolicited and unwelcome sexual advances or requests of another for sexual favors or other conduct of a sexual nature. See, e.g., *Illinois Annotated Statutes*, chapter 68 § 2–102(E) (Smith-Hurd).

**shakedown.** *n.* A type of extortion where police officers and other public enforcement officials solicit money in return for underenforcement or nonenforcement.

**Shaw, Clifford R. (1895–1957).** Along with his colleague Henry McKay, these Chicago-based criminological researchers modeled their longitudinal study of juvenile delinquency in Chicago, following the Zone Theory promulgated earlier by Park and Burgess (a spatial distribution of crime). Their thirty-three-year study demonstrated that despite the change of ethnicity in certain neighborhoods, the crime patterns remained largely unchanged—supporting their hypothesis that juvenile delinquency (crime) is learned and passed on from one generation to the next, through a process they termed cultural transmission. See *McKay, Henry D.* and *Cultural Transmission Theory.*

**Sheldon, William Herbert (1898–1977).** A criminological theorist and a disciple of biological determinism; he believed in the assumption that the primary determinants of human behavior were constitutional and inherited. His somatotyping led to the classification of physique typologies including endomorphy, mesomorphy, and ectomorphy.

**sheriff.** *n.* In most American states, a constitutional officer elected to the highest policing post within a county or parish. The sheriff is a multitasked policing official or administrator responsible for countywide policing and law enforcement duties; he or she is also an officer of the court, responsible for its security and the enforcement and service of its various writs, both civil and criminal. (In some anomalous situations, an independent city has a sheriff who is generally responsible for the transportation and detention/custody of defendants, as an officer of the court, absent any law enforcement duties.) Sheriffs have the power of *posse comitatus* and can legally command any able-bodied citizen, over age eighteen, to come to his or her aid—failure to comply is a criminal offense. Generally responsible for countywide warrant service, the sheriff has the broadest range of policing tasks and responsibilities of any police agency in the United States. As a county-based police official, he or she is constitutionally required in thirty-five of the fifty states, and provides essentially the same services at the county level as the U.S. marshal provides for a federal court district. As a result of the sheriff's constitutional basis, he or she is not directly accountable to the county board (commissioners, supervisors, or judges). The removal of the sheriff during his or her term of office is nearly impossible and must be done, if at all, through an extraordinary process using a writ of *quo warranto*, holding that the sheriff holds his or her office illegally. It is common for state law or the state constitution to protect the sheriff from arrest on state charges within his or her home county, providing for his or her arrest through the county coroner only. Sheriffs date back well over a thousand years in England and are among the oldest extant policing officials in the occidental world.

**sheriffdom.** *n.* (1) The venue within which a sheriff lawfully exercises his or her authority; the jurisdiction of a sheriff (in the United States, a county or parish). (2) The public office of the sheriff.

**sheriff's department.** A county-based policing agency that is not mandated by state constitution. Although the sheriff, under this arrangement, may be elected, he or she does not hold an office per se and generally comes under the oversight of the county board (commissioners, supervisors, or judges). The sheriff, under this arrangement, may be terminated without a writ of *quo warranto* as he or she cannot claim constitutional immunity from direct county board oversight.

**sheriff's office.** The official office held by a sheriff, which is most often required by the state's constitution (thirty-five out of fifty). As such, it is improper to refer to a sheriff's office as a department, as a department is a part of the executive branch of government, whereas a sheriff holds a constitutionally mandated office at the county level for the administration of the state's legal affairs, both criminal and civil, under the authority of the organic law of the state.

**sheriff's police.** Some populous states, having home rule provisions, allow for counties of certain sizes, usually over one million population, to appoint a chief of police who oversees a county police department, separate and apart from the sheriff's office (which is separately responsible for the service of court writs, court security, the transportation of prisoners, and the administration of the county jail). In other jurisdictions, other arrangements exist, e.g., an appointed county chief of police with the attendant county police department supplanting the sheriff's office; a sheriff's police department, with an appointed chief of police, under the umbrella authority of the sheriff's office. Under any of the preceding arrangements, officers working for these anomalous agencies (fewer than 1 percent of all countywide policing agencies nationwide) more fully replicate the duties of municipal police officers, only at the county level.

**sheriff's sale.** The sale of items seized or unclaimed, including real estate, usually via an auction by the sheriff (the officer of the court) or the court's designee.

**Sherman Report.** The short title for the three-part, two-year report entitled "The Quality of Police Education," authored by Lawrence Sherman and commissioned by the National Advisory Commission on Higher Education for Police Officers, looking into the problems of police education in the United States. The report recommends a detailed strategy for improving police higher education under the following categories: the purpose of police education, curriculum, institutions (community colleges, colleges, and universities), faculty, students, and changing the police. The report suggests that criminal justice undergraduate education should provide a broadly based educational experience, generally required by many existing professions; college-level credit should not be awarded for the completion of training academy courses; community college criminal justice programs should be eliminated; prior criminal justice employment should not be a requirement for instructors; and police agencies should focus on hiring college-educated personnel as opposed to attempting to educate in-service officers.

**shield law.** Any law enacted for the purpose of protecting certain classes of professionals (e.g., physicians, psychiatrists, or lawyers) from making disclosures concerning communications and facts learned during the privileged communications involved in professional consultation. See *privileged communications.*

**shire reeve.** The progenitor of the modern-day sheriff, the term derives from "shire" (the English equivalent of an American county) and "reeve" (the chief enforcement officer appointed by the king over a shire). As the language evolved, the word "shire" (pronounced in England as "sure") combined with the word "reeve" and became shortened to "sheriff."

**shock probation.** A form of split sentencing, employed in some states, allowing offenders sentenced to probation to be briefly incarcerated, before they are placed on supervised probation in the community for the duration of their respective sentences.

**shoofly.** *n.* A colloquialism for a police officer or other criminal investigator (sometimes in an undercover capacity) who investigates the wrongdoings of other police or law enforcement officials, e.g., an internal affairs investigator.

**shoplifting.** *n.* The act of stealing items from a commercial establishment; usually this form of amateur theft is of clothing from a retail distributor by would-be shoppers. "Professional" shoplifters use far more sophisticated methods, like booster boxes, and their larceny constitutes a far more serious threat to the profitability of retail establishments.

**shotgun.** *n.* A firearm of the shoulder-weapon category, usually having a smooth bore (no rifling), designed to shoot primarily any form of "shot," ranging from very small sizes (e.g., number 8 to very large double 00 buck). The purpose of a shotgun is to deliver a pattern of shot, making it easier to hit a moving target, e.g., in upland game hunting. A shotgun can facilitate a "rifled slug" where the slug has rifling, making it more or less a rifle, although the range of a rifled slug is considerably less than that of a conventional rifle. Shotguns may be purchased in a number of gauges (410, 28, 20, 16, 12, and 10) with virtually any action style—slide action (pump), semiautomatic, bolt, or breach load, and may be double-barreled. For police and military use, shotguns are generally of the 12-gauge slide-action (pump) variety and use double 00 buckshot, although rifled slug is occasionally used.

**show cause** A court order mandating one's appearance for the purpose of providing the reason(s) or rationale for particular conditions or circumstances to be continued or for them to be disallowed.

**showup.** *n.* See *police lineup.*

**shrapnel.** *n.* Shell fragments scattered by an explosive device, named after General Shrapnel (1761–1842) of the British Army, who designed the shrapnel artillery shell.

**silencer.** *n.* An illegal device used to muffle the sound of a firearm.

**Silver Platter Doctrine.** A legal procedure whereby evidence gathered by state officers was admissible in federal prosecutions if federal officers were not involved in the violation of the defendant's constitutional protections resulting from the illegal evidence seizure. This circumvention of the intended rules promulgated in *Weeks v. United States*, 232 U.S. 383, 34 S.Ct. 341 (1914) was made possible because of the wording found in *Weeks:* "Evidence illegally seized by federal officers is inadmissible . . . ." The doctrine was struck down during the Warren Court's due process revolution of the 1960s in *Elkins v. United States*, 364 U.S. 206, 216 (1960).

**sin.** *n.* A wrongful act; the breaking of a religious moral principle or rule; an offense, wrong, or encroachment.

**sine.** *(Lat.)* Without.

**sine qua non.** *(Lat.)* "Without exception." An absolutely requisite condition, without which something cannot be accomplished.

**single action.** A term associated with the activating mechanism of a firearm, meaning that before a revolver can be fired, the hammer must first be cocked manually each time the weapon is to be fired. With semiautomatic handguns, the hammer must be cocked the first time the weapon is to be fired; thereafter, the hammer is automatically cocked by the recoil of the preceding round.

**Sing Sing.** The common name for the New York State Penitentiary located at Ossining, New York, formally referred to as the Ossining Correctional Facility.

**Sirhan, Sirhan.** The convicted assassin of presidential aspirant Senator Robert F. Kennedy (former U.S. attorney general under President John F. Kennedy— his brother).

**Sixth Amendment (1791).** That amendment to the Constitution providing for the right to a speedy trial, an impartial jury, the right to confront witnesses against one's self, the provision for compulsory process to obtain witnesses, and the assistance of counsel.

**SJD.** The terminal law degree; see *doctorate*.

**skyjacking.** *n.* The crime of hijacking an airplane, also known as air-piracy.

**sky marshal.** One employed by the federal law enforcement unit organized in 1970 to protect against skyjackers; the unit was later disbanded and replaced by the State Department's hijacking task force (1985).

**slavery.** *n.* The status of involuntary servitude; being subordinate and entirely under the control of another. See *disenfranchisement, duress,* and *enslavement*.

**small arms.** A category of firearms including both hand and shoulder weapons of all types up to 60 caliber.

**small particle reagent (SPR).** A solution, composed of a mechanical suspension of molybdenum sulfide granules in a detergent-based solution, often used in the detection and photographing or lifting of latent fingerprints on wet surfaces.

**smoke grenade.** A grenade of either the hand or rifle type, used to produce smoke for a variety of purposes, including signaling.

**smuggling.** *v.* The act of taking out or bringing in items from one jurisdiction to another secretly and illegally, as a result of the item's legal status or because a duty is avoided by such practice.

**social anthropology.** See *anthropology, cultural*.

**Social Bond Theory.** A criminological perspective (theory) developed originally by Travis Hirschi (1969), later integrated with Social Control Theory, with his colleague Michael Gottfredson. Social Bond Theory posits that four social bonds induce positive socialization and conformity, i.e., attachment, commitment, involvement, and belief. As a result, his theory is more an explanation of why people choose to conform than one that seeks to explain why individuals act out. Delinquents are at odds with conventional moral codes only when their bonds (attachments to society) are weak.

**social class.** The position one holds within the social hierarchy, based on numerous socioeconomic indicators including level of and type of educational attainment, ethnicity, religious affiliation, place of residence, occupation, income, and numerous other variables.

**social constraint.** A negative form of social control exercised by legitimate authorities, subjecting offenders to detention with the intent of preventing repetition of offensive behavior.

**social contagion.** A process of social interaction whereby impulses are telegraphed between individuals resulting in a uniformity of response. The phenomenon is made manifest in fads, mass panic, and rioting.

**Social Containment Theory.** A criminological perspective (theory) pioneered by Walter C. Reckless, holding that there exists a containing external structure (external pulls) and a protective internal structure (internal pushes), providing both a defense and protection against crime and delinquency. Reckless suggests seven outer containment influences and six inner containment influences.

**Social Control Theory.** A criminological perspective (theory) pioneered as early as 1900 by E. A. Ross, focusing on the control mechanisms and techniques generally used in controlling human behavior and conformity to accepted societal rules. The perspective holds that people are not motivated to conform when social control mechanisms break down. More contemporary studies in Social Control Theory have been promulgated by Travis Hirschi and David Matza.

**Social Disorganization Theory.** A criminological perspective (theory) holding that the breakdown of effective social bonds, social controls at the neighborhood and community levels, and primary-group associations result in high–crime rate areas.

**social engineering.** A sociopolitical agenda involving governmental intervention in the plight of the disenfranchised, through the implementation of various social programs. Such programs require heavy taxation, and as such, are eschewed by conservative elements within American culture. The intent of social engineering is to level the social playing field by eliminating obstacles to social advancement.

**socialization.** *n.* The process of becoming socialized; a sociopsychological conditioning process whereby the personality is created under the influence of the socializing agent or institution.

**social justice.** A philosophical and sociopolitical perspective seeking cooperation within a community in order to provide equal opportunity for all citizens. Adherents of this perspective frequently champion the plight of the disenfranchised through initiatives intended to level the social and economic playing field, and it is often carried out by religious organizations.

**Social Learning Theory.**  A criminological perspective (theory) holding that delinquent behavior is learned behavior, occurring through the same learning processes as nondelinquent behavior. This perspective is closely linked with two other perspectives: Social Control Theory and Social Reaction Theory.

**social mobility.**  The movement from one social status to another.

**Social Process Theory.**  A criminological perspective (theory) holding that one's interactions with key social institutions, e.g., family, schools, or peer groups, largely shape one's behavior.

**social psychology.**  A transdisciplinary area involving the application of psychology and sociology. Social psychology courses are frequently cross-listed in both the sociology and psychology departments at collegiate institutions.

**social sanction.**  A penalty applied for the violation of social folkways, mores, or conventions, often informal in character.

**social scientist.**  One who studies, researches, and develops theory attempting to explain human behavior. Social scientists are found in a number of academic disciplines including sociology, psychology, anthropology, and criminology and generally hold terminal research degrees in their respective field, i.e., the Ph.D. Many social scientists cross disciplinary lines in order to conduct research and develop appropriate theory; this is especially true in criminology and criminal justice.

**social security number.**  First issued in 1936 by the Social Security Administration for the purpose of administering the national system of old-age worker benefits, the number has increasingly been used as a means of identification—something for which it was not intended. The first three digits indicate the state in which the number was assigned, e.g., 318–361 indicate Illinois-issued numbers.

**social status.**  One's location, relative position, rank, or standing in the social order of a given social group or society. The status one holds in the stratification of a given society, e.g., the upper, middle, or lower stratum. Social status results from a number of variables, including one's education, occupation, religious affiliation, income, place of residence, and so forth.

**social stratification.**  The arrangement, division, or layering of the social order into groupings that are unequal in terms of property, prestige, and power.

**Social Structure Theory.**  A criminological perspective (theory) holding that the causes of crime can be largely explained as a result of social relationships. Four resultant explanations emerge: choice, power, opportunity, and inequality.

**sociobiology.** *n.*  A criminological perspective (theory) developed during the 1980s that attempts to explain criminal behavior as a result of the connection between sociological factors and biological determinates that predispose some people to commit crime. Some well-known contemporary theoreticians include C. Ray Jeffery, Lee Ellis, Diana H. Fishbein, and Adrian Raine. Raine's book *The Psycholpathology of Crime: Criminal Behavior as a Clinical Disorder* stands as a stellar example of this perspective.

**socioeconomic status (SES).**  One's social rank, predicated on income, education, occupational category, religious affiliation, and numerous other variables.

**sociology.** *n.*  A social science that attempts to empirically explain human behavior resulting from group interaction.

**sociometry.** *n.* The measurement of social phenomena through the application of quantitative measures, i.e., sociological positivism.

**sodium amytal.** The technical name for one of the drugs commonly referred to as "truth serum."

**sodium pentothal.** The technical name for one of the drugs commonly referred to as "truth drug."

**sodomy.** *n.* (1) The act of engaging in oral or anal copulation between humans; (2) sexual acts between humans and animals.

**solicitation.** *n.* The overt act of urging or soliciting someone to commit a crime.

**solicitor.** *n.* In England, a lawyer other than a barrister. Solicitors are not members of the bar, and, as such, cannot plead cases before superior courts.

**solicitor general.** The U.S. solicitor general is charged with representing the federal government in cases before the Supreme Court and makes the decision as to what cases should be argued for final review before the High Court. Further, he/she formally presents the government's position, writes the government's appellate briefs, and often makes the oral arguments before the High Court.

**somatotypes.** *n.* A criminological perspective (theory) based on the assumption that various body types (endomorphy, mesomorphy, and ectomorphy) are correlated with certain proclivities that can predispose one to various types of criminality. This theory has a direct linkage with Cesare Lombroso's early theory of phrenology and the prediction of various types of criminality. See *Sheldon, William Herbert.*

**Southern Police Institute.** Located within the University of Louisville's School of Justice Administration, the Institute was established in 1951, with the intent of advancing professional police administration across the nation. The Institute publishes quarterly the *Southern Police Institute Alumni News.*

**sovereign immunity.** A centuries-old legal doctrine, deriving from the "divine right of kings," holding that the sovereign (the king, state, or nation state) cannot be sued in its own courts without first gaining its permission. Some sovereignties have essentially eschewed this doctrine by replacing it with another immunity hurdle, i.e., the "public duty doctrine," and requiring that the case, if it is permitted, be tried in the court of claims (a special court with summary jurisdiction and without a jury). The sovereign immunity of the various states within the federal union is addressed in the Eleventh Amendment to the U.S. Constitution (1798).

**sovereignty.** *n.* The absolute and supreme right, authority, and power under which an independent state or nation state is governed, without the consent or approval of others. Sovereignty is generally denoted by a standing military capability, e.g., an army or a national guard. The term infers unabridged police power within its borders.

**span of control.** A principle of management positing that a supervisor should oversee a limited number of subordinates, generally no more than six.

**special damages.** See *punitive damages.*

**special grand jury.** A grand jury empaneled to investigate a specific case or a grouping of cases, where similar crimes have been perpetrated.

**special judge.** A judge appointed to oversee a specific case only, in addition to the regularly appointed or elected judges of that particular trial court.

**Special Weapons and Tactics (SWAT).** A creation of Chief Darryl Gates of the LAPD, where officers are assigned to a heavily militarized and armed assault team to be used in cases of barricaded subjects, for example. These units have become increasingly popular across the nation and are now used in tactics like street sweeps. Critics argue that the overemphasis on militarism creates problems for newer modes of policing, where a close relationship between the police and the public is necessary, i.e., community-oriented policing. See *PPUs*.

**Specialized Multi-Agency Response Team (SMART).** A team comprised of various units of local government to address a specific community problem. For example, municipal housing inspectors may be teamed up with police to fight a growing drug problem, where a suspected drug house may have building code violations that will allow the team to condemn the building, essentially putting the drug dealers out of business in that locale.

**specific deterrence.** Deterrence focused exclusively on offenders, suggesting that punishment should be sufficiently severe to convince convicted offenders not to repeat their criminal conduct.

**specific intent.** Some crimes require the element of specific intent, i.e., that intent necessary in order to prosecute the offense, beyond the intent that can be inferred by the carrying out of the overt criminal act itself.

**Speck, Richard.** The twenty-five-year-old murderer of eight student nurses in Chicago in July of 1966, who had the XYY chromosome pattern. As a result of this horrific mass murder, a good deal of interest in the role that genetics play in violent crime was sparked.

**spectrograph.** *n.* A scientific instrument found in a forensic laboratory, used to photograph elements of the light spectrum in order to identify inorganic compounds and substances found in the composition of various items of evidence.

**spectrophotometer.** *n.* A forensic laboratory instrument used to both measure and record the absorption pattern of ultraviolet light and/or infrared light/radiation from an unknown chemical substance, from which an identification may be made.

**speedy trial.** The right of a criminal defendant to a timely trial for his or her alleged transgressions. This fundamental right is embodied in the Sixth Amendment to the U.S. Constitution. Most jurisdictions have enacted legislation specifically stating the maximum time that may elapse before the case is dismissed. The general rule is that the state must proceed with trial within 100 days, following a person's arrest or detention. Jurisdictions, however, are divided as to whether the violation by the state of the 100-day rule establishes a double jeopardy defense, if tried on related charges.

**spiral search.** A search method wherein the investigator begins the search at the core of the crime scene and continues outward in an ever-widening spiral. This method is especially useful in large crime scenes.

**split sentence.** Often referred to as "shock probation," this sentencing option requires the defendant to serve a specified period of incarceration, after which he or she is placed on probation. Critics argue that the purpose of probation is defeated by the mandatory incarceration, allowing the negative effects of labeling to attach.

**spoils system.** A patronage system awarding government appointments to party loyalists.

**spontaneous utterance.** See *res gestae declaration (excited utterance).*

**spur.** *n.* Sometimes referred to as a hook, it is a detail of a friction ridge found in some fingerprint ridge patterns, i.e., a ridge shaped like a hook or a small branch off a single ridge line.

**Spurheim, John Gasper (1776–1832).** An adherent of Franz Gall's notion of phrenology, who brought the concept to America.

**spurious.** *adj.* (1) False or counterfeit; something like in appearance but not in function or structure; an artifact but not the actual thing. (2) In quantitative measurement, the covariance of a variable that is only coincidental.

**staff.** *n.* That body of personnel of supervisory or administrative rank and/or responsibility, providing support for the actual service providers in an organization, i.e., the line personnel.

**staff functions.** Those functions within an organization concerned with the supervision or administration of the organization, as opposed to the actual provision of services or production capacity. In police usage, e.g., those functions associated with officers above the rank of sergeant, who manage the organization.

**stakeout.** *n.* An investigative technique for observing persons, places, or things, where the investigator, well secreted, makes note of the object of his or her observation.

**Standard Metropolitan Area (SMA).** The replacement term for the former Standard Metropolitan Statistical Area (SMSA). See *SMSA.*

**Standard Metropolitan Statistical Area (SMSA).** An urban zone where several municipalities expand until they form one continuous and contiguous urban area, although they have separate governments. For statistical reasons, the U.S. Census Bureau counts them as one metropolitan region, usually one large central city immediately adjacent to a number of smaller municipalities, i.e., the Chicago Metropolitan Statistical Area.

**standard of proof.** That level of proof necessary to legally effectuate a particular action, e.g., for an arrest, probable cause is necessary; yet for a conviction at trial, proof beyond a reasonable doubt is required. A continuum beginning with a mere hunch (the weakest of all levels of proof) and proceeding to the strongest level of proof, beyond a reasonable doubt.

**standard operating procedures (SOP).** The comprehensive written and codified manual of an organization, generally containing the organization's mission statement, organizational policy, procedures, rules, and regulations. In police organizations, an SOP manual serves ideally as a conceptual road map, assisting officers in the field as an intuitive guide.

**standing.** *n.* The legal right to initiate legal and or judicial action, i.e., the requirement that one must have sufficient interest in a case to proceed with it.

**standing order.** An order that is permanently in place as part of an organization's formal written standard operating procedures.

**star chamber proceeding.** In law or criminal justice usage, a metaphor for secret, invasive, and forceful inquisitorial-like proceedings by the prosecution, usually referring to the oppressive techniques used under the heavy authority of the grand jury, where those under subpoena are given inadequate opportunity to be represented by counsel and without the observation of customary judicial formalities and a number of constitutional protections. The term derives from the Court of the Star Chamber established under King Charles I of England, where the king's inquisitor would have subjects placed on the rack, inside a building having stars on the domed ceiling.

**stare decisis.** *(Lat.)* A legal principle in the doctrine of precedent, meaning "let the former decision stand." Appellate courts will not overturn an earlier ruling and apply it to future cases, unless there is compelling reason to do so.

**state.** *n.* (1) An independent and sovereign nation among the community of nations. (2) The body politic, politically organized under one government with established boundaries. (3) One of the sovereignties constituting a federated federal republic, as in the United States, where the states (as lesser sovereignties) are held to be sovereign in specified spheres but have ceded specified powers to an overarching national government through a constitution.

**state constitution.** The organic law of a state (in the United States), largely functioning in the same capacity and somewhat parallel to the federal Constitution. It is important to note, however, that state constitutions are considerably longer and are used to explicitly grant certain powers. Critics argue that many state constitutions are considerably dissimilar to the federal Constitution in that they are not as focused on civil liberties as is the latter and are used in place of statutory law. Nonetheless, proponents of state constitutions argue that, as a result of the chipping away at federal civil liberty protections by the High Court in recent decades, state constitutions actually afford greater protections than the federal Constitution and serve an important role in that capacity for criminal defendants charged in state action.

**state courts.** Those courts organized under state constitutional authority and imprimatur and consisting of trial courts and appellate courts. Many states have a three-tiered system of trial courts (courts of general jurisdiction), intermediate appellate courts, and a court of last resort (supreme court), while other states have only a two-tiered system, absent an intermediate court of appeals. Local government (inferior) courts are not part of a state court system.

**state-mandated training.** Training required by state law for various public agencies. Police and correctional training, e.g., are mandated as to the areas of instruction and the number of hours devoted to each topic.

**state police.** A state-level police agency having wide-ranging police and law enforcement authority, as opposed to state highway patrol agencies with limited enforcement authority. Some argue that state police organizations date back to the Texas Rangers, although that organization resembled more closely an irregular militia and border patrol than a true state police agency. Modern state police agencies, as we know them today, derive from the establishment of the Pennsylvania State Constabulary of 1905, now the Pennsylvania State Police, organized as a strike-breaking force in the coal and iron fields during the formative years of the organized labor movement. The four archetypal state police departments are Pennsylvania (1905), New York (1917), Michigan (1917), and West Virginia (1919). As a general rule, states with heavy concentrations of industry and/or mining tend to have state police departments, whereas those states with more agrarian economies tend to use the highway patrol model, with limited enforcement authority.

**state police power** The absolute power of the state to direct and command as a sovereign entity. The power to enact laws (especially criminal laws) for the protection of the citizenry's safety, health, morals, and welfare. The various states within the Union derive this power from the Tenth Amendment of the Constitution.

**state reports.** The decisions rendered by the state's highest appellate court (often referred to as the state supreme court) are reported and bound in volumes known as the state reports. States using intermediate appellate courts, placed between the trial courts and the Supreme Court, sometimes publish a separate series. Volumes include a subject index as well as a digest of cases reported therein; cases are also indexed alphabetically.

**state secrets.** Those secrets that a sovereign government may claim are not discoverable in court as a matter of state security. The claim of a state secret may provide a judicially recognized immunity from the customary discovery process, e.g., information concerning various classified intelligence information and materials, military strategies, or weaponry. See *government secrets.*

**state's attorney.** The chief prosecutor for the state, elected in a particular county, to represent the state's interests, generally in criminal matters. See also *county attorney, district attorney,* or *prosecuting attorney.*

**state's evidence.** That testimony given by a participant in a crime, incriminating others and given as a *quid pro quo* for a blanket of immunity from prosecution.

**state's rights.** Those "powers not delegated to the United States by the Constitution, nor prohibited by it to the States, are reserved to the States respectively, or to the people" (Tenth Amendment). States rights have been a source of enduring tension in the federated republic that defines the American union and was the underlying source for the Civil War. States have on occasion resorted to nullifying federal law within their borders, leading to nullification crises, many of which have never been fully settled. When state's rights have been infringed upon by the national government, the action has been justified under the "due process" clause of the Fourteenth Amendment.

**status offender.** A juvenile who violates a status offense (one declared an offense by virtue of the offender's age and that is legal for those of adult status). Status offenses include truancy, underage drinking, smoking, and incorrigibility.

**status quo.** *(Lat.)* "The state in which." The existing state of affairs or the customary state of affairs.

**statute.** *n.* An enactment of the legislative body of a sovereign state or nation, declaring, commanding, or prohibiting things, as distinguished from an ordinance enacted by a non sovereign governmental legislative body, e.g., a municipal board or council.

**statute of limitations.** The specified time period under which a crime may be charged. Capital crimes are not subject to statutes of limitations.

**Statute of Winchester.** A law instituted under King Edward I (1285) to establish a systematic policing program, involving a watch (nighttime shift) and a ward (daytime shift), both in and outside London.

**Statutes at Large.** The official codified compilation of the acts and resolutions of the various sessions of the Congress of the United States.

**statutory.** *adj.* Of or having the characteristics of a statute; conforming to a statute.

**statutory law.** Law enacted by the legislative branch of a sovereign state or nation, i.e., a state general assembly or the Congress.

**statutory rape.** The act of an adult male having unlawful sexual intercourse with a female under the legally defined age of consent (usually age seventeen). Whether the perpetrator engages in this illicit sexual activity knowing or not knowing the age of the female is irrelevant.

**stay.** *n.* The lawful suspension of a judicially sanctioned proceeding by either court or executive order.

**steal.** *v.* The misappropriation of another's property, money, ideas, or emoluments, generally with stealth; a form of larceny.

**stereotypes.** *n.* Fixed ideas, notions, or patterns, commonly associated with individuals or groups.

*stet. (Lat.)* "Let it stand."

**stigmata.** *n.* (1) Marks or wounds similar to those of the crucified Christ, said to appear supernaturally. (2) In criminological usage, the criminal label that one must endure after conviction or processing by the criminal justice system, which may lead to secondary deviance.

**stimulant.** *n.* A substance that stimulates any bodily function, process, or organ, i.e., a drug.

**sting operation.** A form of police or law enforcement negative proactivity, involving undercover operatives, where the objective is to entrap the suspect for the purpose of making an arrest by deception.

**stipend.** *n.* A payment for services rendered; often associated with academic services.

**stipulation.** *n.* The admittance of proof via agreement between opposing counsel.

**Stockholm syndrome.** A term used for the bond that is sometimes created between the victims of terrorist activities (who are held unlawfully) and their captors. The term derives from a group that was held captive in a bank vault in Stockholm, Sweden.

**Stone, Harlan Fiske (1872–1946).** The successor to Chief Justice Charles Evans Hughes, appointed by President Franklin D. Roosevelt in 1941. Stone started his law career in New York City in 1899, and by 1925 had risen to the post of U.S. attorney general, having been appointed by President Calvin Coolidge.

**stop and frisk.** The phrase "stop and frisk" derives from the case of *Terry v. Ohio,* 392 U.S. 1, 88 S.Ct. 1868, 20 L.Ed.2d 889 (1968): the stopping (a temporary detention falling short of an arrest) and frisking (a superficial pat-down search) of suspects by police officers, for the purpose of officer safety or the safety of others. Stop and frisk actually consists of two separate acts, predicated on two separate sets of causation. That is, officers must have reasonable suspicion that a crime was committed or was about to be committed (a reasonable suspicion that crime is afoot), before officers may legally detain the suspect(s). Second, there must be grounds beyond that which justified the stop to conduct a frisk. In its ruling in *Terry,* the High Court held that officers have the right to stop citizens when they have reasons to believe that crime is afoot, and to conduct a pat-down type search if there is a sound reason that they can articulate leading a reasonable person to believe that the life or safety of the officer(s) or others might have been in jeopardy at the time of the frisk.

**street crime.** A category of aggressively assaultive street-level offenses that place the safety of the public in serious jeopardy, e.g., robbery, car jacking, and assault, which are targeted by police departments for preventive or suppression efforts. Some preventive efforts involve aggressive police practices like street sweeps and other types of negative proactivity including undercover sting operations.

**striated impressions.** Impressions left by the combined forces of pressure exerted on a given surface, plus the movement by another object across that surface, which leaves scratches on the first object's surface.

**strict liability offenses.** (1) A category of criminal and quasi-criminal offenses for which the proof of *mens rea* is not required. See *absolute liability*. (2) In civil law, the responsibility for injury or damages whether or not caused innocently or by negligent behavior.

**struck jury.** A jury of twelve derived by allowing opposing counsel to eliminate (strike) twelve names from the original venire of forty-eight potential jurors, and from that list to strike twelve more by using the right to challenge.

**strychnine.** *n.* An extremely poisonous crystalline alkaloid, made from *nux vomica* (a plant); in small dosages it can act as a stimulant to the central nervous system.

**Students for a Democratic Society (SDS).** A politically radicalized student organization, influential during the 1960s. During that decade, the SDS became the most powerful national-level, white, left-wing organization in America, with membership reaching an estimated 100,000. The SDS was largely eclipsed by the more overtly revolutionary Weathermen, who were involved in bombings and other terrorist acts against the establishment.

**stun gun.** A handheld weapon producing approximately 45,000 volts of electricity, capable of immobilizing victims for well over a full minute. Such weapons have been made unlawful in a number of states, with other states severely limiting the weapon's use.

***sua sponte.*** *(Lat.)* By one's own volition; without encouragement or prompting.

**subculture.** *n.* A social group whose members have shared values and ideas differing from those of the dominant culture.

**subject.** *n.* In law, a neutral term for a person of some interest to the criminal justice system or the police or law enforcement specifically. Should evidence later point toward the culpability of the subject, he or she becomes reclassified as a suspect. At this juncture, *Miranda* warnings become necessary if questioning follows.

**suborn.** *v.* To cause another to commit perjury, through persuasion, bribery, or other inducements.

**subornation of perjury.** See *suborn*.

**subpoena.** *n.* "Under penalty." A formal written writ, issued by a judicial officer, demanding a person to appear in court at a specified date and time, to testify concerning a matter in controversy or to bring specified materials with him or her. Failure to comply with a subpoena is chargeable with a contempt of court citation, and depending on the type of failure, it may be either civil or criminal contempt. Three types of subpoenas exist. Those who have been uncooperative or recalcitrant may be served an "instanter," a subpoena requiring their immediate appearance before the court. The common subpoena calling one to testify is known as a subpoena *ad testificandum.* A subpoena requiring one to "bring with" him or her specified documents and or materials is known as a subpoena *duces tecum.*

**subpoena ad testificandum.** *(Lat.)* The proper name for the ordinary subpoena calling one to testify. See *subpoena.*

**subpoena duces tecum.** "Bring with." A court-ordered process compelling the production of various materials, documents, or chattels under one's control for inspection by the court. This particular subpoena is often used by a grand jury panel to compel the production of documents, materials, chattels, or oral testimony.

*sub rosa.* *(Lat.)* Privately; secretly; confidentially, and not for publication.

**substantial capacity test.** A test for legal insanity proposed under the *Model Penal Code,* § 4.01, in order to determine whether one is chargeable criminally for an alleged offense, as a result of mental disease or defect. A test to determine whether he or she substantially lacks the capacity to appreciate the wrongfulness of his or her conduct or to conform his or her conduct to legal requirements.

**substantive evidence.** That category of evidence presented in order to prove a fact in issue, as contrasted against evidence introduced for the purpose of corroborating the testimony of a witness or the discrediting of a witness.

**substantive law.** That category of law creating, defining, and regulating rights, as contrasted against procedural law providing allowable methods for enforcing rights.

**substantive rights.** Basic rights providing for the equal protection of fundamental rights, privileges, and immunities, and distinguished from procedural rights.

**subterfuge.** *n.* The evasion of anything unpleasant or with painful consequences through plan or action.

**subversion.** *n.* Anything that subverts or overthrows an established government.

**sudden infant death syndrome (SIDS).** The death of an infant, often in its crib, for no apparently discernable reason.

*sui generis.* *(Lat.)* Of its particular class or kind, i.e., one of a kind. In law, something acting outside the usual parameters. For example, a military tribunal for unlawful combatants, which is nearly independent of the existing legal system, its rules of evidence, due process, procedures, and oversight.

*sui juris.* *(Lat.)* "Of one's own right." The ability to manage one's own affairs.

**summary.** *adj.* In law, something done swiftly and without formality; something carried out without a jury or appellate review and from which no recourse is available.

**summary judgment.** (1) In criminal law, a sanction imposed immediately by the proper authority without ceremony or the possibility of appellate review. (2) In civil law, a stage at which the judge must decide whether a suit will proceed.

**summary jurisdiction.** The authority (jurisdiction) of a given court to render a judgment in and of itself, e.g., in cases where one is tried by a justice of the peace where the conviction and sanction is rendered without committing the defendant to trial by jury or review by a higher court.

**summons.** *n.* A formal order issued by a judicial officer directing someone to appear in court at a specified time and date to answer alleged charges. When police officers issue a summons, without going through a judicial officer, as in the case of a traffic ticket or a notice to appear for a minor infraction, it is called a citation.

**sumptuary legislation.** Laws enacted to limit excesses in food, alcoholic beverages, or clothing on religious or moral grounds.

**sunset laws.** Originating in 1976, they are laws designed to decommission agencies and other governmental organizations no longer serving the public interest.

**superior court.** (1) In states utilizing a nonunified court system, the state trial-level court of general jurisdiction, superior only to the justice of the peace or magistrate's court at the local level of government. (2) A title generically given to any court above another.

**super-maximum-security prison.** A penal facility housing dangerous felons and maintaining a strict security protocol including high walls, gun turrets, and very limited prisoner contact with the outside world. A twenty-three-hour a day lockdown is common, with prisoner court appearance frequently held within the physical confines of the penal facility.

***supersedeas.*** *(Lat.)* A formal writ commanding a stay of legal proceedings.

**suppression hearing.** A pretrial criminal proceeding, wherein the defendant seeks to make inadmissible evidence against him or her that was allegedly obtained illegally by police or law enforcement officials.

***supra.*** *(Lat.)* "Above." When used by itself, it refers the reader to something mentioned earlier in the text or document.

**supremacy clause.** That clause found in Article VI of the Constitution declaring that all laws made in the furtherance of the Constitution and all treaties made under the authority of the federal government shall be superior to and will preempt any conflicting enactment of a state constitution, act, or statute.

**Supreme Court.** (1) The highest appellate court in the federal judiciary; this court may function as a trial court in cases of treason, without a jury and with no available appeal. (2) The highest appellate court in a state judiciary. (3) In the state of New York, the trial court of general jurisdiction.

**surety.** *n.* Something that guarantees or gives assurance against loss or default, i.e., bail or a bond; a person who takes on the responsibility for another; one who makes himself/herself liable for another's liabilities, e.g., a bail bondsman/bondswoman.

**surrebuttal.** *n.* See *rejoinder.*

**surreptitious.** *adj.* Conducted in a clandestine, secret, or stealthy way.

**surrogate.** *n.* A substitute acting in place of another; in law, known as a subrogate.

**surveillance.** *n.* The covert observation of a person, place, or thing, especially for one suspected of criminal behavior or under some form of correctional supervision.

**suspect.** *n.* One who is of particular interest to a criminal justice agency (especially the police or law enforcement) as a material witness or possible defendant, but who has not yet been charged with the violation of a specific offense.

**suspended sentence.** A court-ordered sanction imposed after conviction for a criminal offense, specifying the penalty to be imposed, but holding the execution of the sanction in abeyance, and discharging the defendant, pending good behavior for a specified period of time or the successful completion of a treatment program.

**Sutherland, Edward H. (1883–1950).** Perhaps the most prominent American criminologist of the twentieth century, and well known for his collaborative work with fellow criminologist Donald Cressey in the development of the theory of Differential Association in his seminal text *Principles of Criminology* (1939).

**swindler.** *n.* One who knowingly and criminally defrauds another.

**sworn officer.** A police or law enforcement officer who receives a commission as a state or federal officer upon swearing an oath to protect and defend the Constitution and laws of the United States (and in the case of state, county, and local officers, the state constitution and laws in addition to the federal Constitution and laws). These officers constitute the ranks from patrol officer (agent) to administrators of police and law enforcement agencies and are separated from civilian and other technical support personnel.

**Sykes, Gresham M'Cready (1922– ).** Living one of the most notable careers in the field of criminology, his academic affiliations range widely, and his contributions are many. Some of his more influential earlier writings include *Crime and Society* (1956) and *The Society of Captives* (1958). Sykes's primary contributions to criminology involve the prison system and Neutralization Theory, along with colleague David Matza. Neutralization Theory posits that individuals will comply or avoid social rules depending on their ability to rationalize their infractions, thereby distorting reality and concomitantly protecting their self-image, which would otherwise be liable to assault from self-blame.

**symbolic interactionism.** A school of sociological and criminological thought, founded by George Herbert Mead (1863–1931), focusing on the primacy of communication, especially oral communications, and the social construction of reality. Mead's follower Martin Blumer coined the term "symbolic interactionism," arguing that one's self-image is largely the product of social perceptions turned inward. See *Labeling Theory*.

**synnomie.** *n.* The opposite condition to that of anomie; a social state marked by social cohesion maintained by shared values.

**synthesis.** *n.* The bringing together of individual parts in an effort to form a cohesive whole; the opposite of analysis.

# T

Taser, Thomas A. Swift's Electric Rifle
TQM, total quality management

**talesman/woman.** *n.* One summoned from the bystanders in court to act as a juror, to act as the tail added to the jury.

**Tammany Hall.** The corrupt political machine in New York City under the leadership of William Marcy Tweed, "Boss Tweed," spanning 1869–1871. A New York Democratic political machine controlling patronage that swindled the city out of so much money that when *Harper's Weekly* ran articles exposing Tweed's graft, bankers feared that the bond debt caused by the corruption might affect the city's bond rating. Tweed was tried, convicted, and died in jail in 1876. Tammany Hall stands as a metaphor for corrupt municipal government. See *Tweed, William Marcy (Boss Tweed.)*

**Taney, Roger Brooke (1777–1864).** Chief justice of the U.S. Supreme Court from 1836 to 1864; under his leadership the High Court's ruling in *the Dred Scott v. Sanford* (1857) case gave the death knell to settling the differences that separated North from South. He spent two hours arguing that because blacks had been considered inferior beings when the Constitution was drafted, the framers could not have included them within the meaning of the word "citizen." And, as such, the right of citizens from different states to sue in federal court could not apply to former slaves or their descendants.

**Tannenbaum, Frank (1893–1969).** A noted criminologist and one of the pioneers of the school of symbolic interactionism in criminology, his work included what he termed the "tagging" process in his 1938 book *Crime and the Community.*

**Tarde, Gabriel (1843–1904).** A noted early French sociologist and criminologist, who had been a magistrate earlier in his life, was attracted to the study of crime, especially the psycho-social basis of crime. He authored a number of treatises, including *Penal Philosophy* in 1890 (the translation was republished in 1912), wherein he was critical of Cesare Lombroso's concept of atavism.

**target hardening.** A crime-prevention technique attempting to make it difficult to successfully commit a criminal offense by intentionally increasing the protection of the property, object, or person.

**task force.** In police and law enforcement usage, a specially organized, specially trained, and self-contained unit assigned to a specific case. The task force is usually composed of specialized detectives and evidence technicians from several law enforcement or policing agencies, sometimes even crossing state lines.

**Taser.** The acronym for "Thomas A. Swift's Electric Rifle." The Taser was originally introduced in 1975 as a nonlethal weapon for police and security personnel. Depressing the trigger dispatches two barbed contacts that are connected to the gun by wire. Because of the extremely high voltage of the weapon, the barbed contacts need not penetrate the skin in order for the weapon to be effective.

**team policing.** A mode of policing that began in Scotland in the 1950s and was experimented with in the United States beginning in the mid-1960s, lasting until the very early 1980s. Police officers were to work in teams of approximately twenty or thirty officers, as generalists, assigned on a permanent basis to a given locale or neighborhood. Although it was not largely successful, it planted the seeds for the next police modality, i.e., problem-oriented policing.

**tear gas.** The common name for a chemical agent causing temporary but intense irritation of the eyes and respiratory difficulty; used by the police and military to quell riots and to force subjects out of buildings. Two types of chemical agents are used in tear gas: CN and CS.

**technical parole violation.** A violation of one of the stipulated technical rules in the parole contract, as opposed to a criminal violation.

**ten signals.** The police brevity code, used on the radio; each of the nearly 100 "signals" begin with 10 followed by a dash and another number, e.g., 10–50 (a traffic collision). The most commonly used ten signals are those published by the APCO, although others exist. The Army Military Police, e.g., uses a different code. Critics of the ten-signal code argue that it does not save time on the radio.

**Tenth Amendment (1791).** "The powers not delegated to the United States by the Constitution nor prohibited by it to the States, are reserved to the States respectively, or to the people."

**tenure.** *n.* An employment status granted to those who meritoriously survive a probationary period, whereupon they cannot be summarily dismissed. College professors, e.g., hold tenure, and, as a result, cannot be dismissed for lecturing on unpopular subjects. Police and law enforcement officials hold similar tenure, and federal judges hold lifetime tenure.

**territorial jurisdiction.** The jurisdiction of a court, policing authority, or other governmental agency, limited to cases and issues arising within a specified territory, e.g., a county or a judicial circuit. The geographical area over which a government or any subdivision thereof has jurisdiction.

**terrorism.** *n.* Intimidation through violence used as a political weapon, usually by the weak, to subjugate various groups or to break the will of a culture. By definition, terrorism nearly always involves some sort of violent criminal acts.

**Terrorism Research and Communication Center.** A center created in 1978 and located in New York City, providing operational and educational materials on terrorism to police and law enforcement organizations.

**testimony.** *n.* Verbal evidence uttered by a competent witness, under oath or affirmation.

**Texas Rangers.** An investigative unit within the Texas Department of Public Safety, functioning as a statewide agency. Originally organized in 1836, during the time of the Texas Republic, Sam Houston increased the agency's numbers to over 1,600 men to serve as an irregular militia with some civil policing and law enforcement functions, including border patrol, Indian control, and a force applied against rustlers, bandits, and highwaymen. During the Civil War, the Rangers served the Confederate army. Some argue that the Texas Rangers represent the first attempt at state policing in the United States, although most scholars consider the Pennsylvania State Constabulary (the forerunner to the Pennsylvania State Police) as the first modern state police agency.

**thanatology.** *n.* The organized study of death and dying.

**theft.** *n.* The unlawful taking of another's property or services; a larceny.

**theocracy.** *n.* (1) A government ruled by God or a god. (2) A government by priests, ministers, or churchmen/women claiming divine authority to rule. (3) A government by and of religious rule and or teachings to the exclusion of all others.

**theory.** *n.* An empirically based explanation and system of concepts and knowledge explaining facts and phenomena.

**Theory X and Theory Y Management Styles.** A perspective on management styles, as envisioned by Douglas McGregor by contrasting two polar extremes. Theory X managers view their employees as people who inherently dislike work and who must be forced to be productive. This perspective assumes that the typical person wants to be directed, as opposed to self-directed, with little ambition, seeking little more than security in his or her employment. Theory Y managers, however, assume that those they supervise are self-motivated and consider work to be as natural as play. The most significant motivators for the typical worker are self-fulfillment, self-actualization, and ego gratification. As a result, this type of manager allows his or her workers greater latitude in conducting their work in a more harmonious and supportive environment.

**thief-takers.** The forerunners to bounty hunters and modern private detectives, emerging as a result of the lawlessness on the public ways of England during the seventeenth century. The Parliamentary Act of 1693 established a reward of forty pounds for the capture and conviction of any highwayman. Only too frequently, the thief-takers would become thieves and "thief-takers" themselves by perverting the intent of the 1693 Act. That is, they would entrap young men to commit crimes only to arrest them for the bounty.

**Third Amendment (1791).** "No soldier shall, in time of peace be quartered in any house, without the consent of the owner, nor in time of war, but in a manner to be prescribed by law."

**third degree.** The unlawful infliction of pain, whether physical or psychological, for the purpose of eliciting an admission or confession.

**Thomas, William Isaak (1863–1947).** An influential member of the "Chicago School" of sociology and an inveterate symbolic interactionist; he pioneered the concept that "If men define situations as real, they are real in their consequences." He and his colleague Florian Znaniecki attributed the rise in urban crime in Chicago to "social disorganization," the breakdown of effective social bonds in neighborhoods and the greater community. Among his classic works is the *Polish Peasant in Europe and America.*

**Thrasher, Frederick M. (1892–1962).** A graduate student in the Sociology Department at the University of Chicago. Along with cohorts Reckless and Hayner, he was heavily influenced by Park, Burgess, and Faris. In 1927, he published *The Gang,* a well-known field study of delinquents in the Chicago area, emphasizing the impact of social process.

**threat.** *n.* A communication of some sort of one's intent to inflict injury to another's person, property, or rights in order to restrain his or her freedom of action. The mailing of threatening letters is a federal offense (18 USCA § 876).

**ticket-of-leave.** A system of conditional release from prison envisioned by Alexander Maconochie of England and Sir Walter Crofton of Ireland during the 1840s.

**time-in-rank system.** An employment system where seniority helps determine rank, not simply by the overall time one has vested in the system, but rather by time in the system overall plus the time vested in a particular rank. That is, should two persons hold the identical rank, e.g., captain, in a military organization, and they both have approximately the same number of years in the organization, but one has been a captain for even one day longer than the other, he or she outranks the other captain.

**tithing.** *n.* In early English society, a unit of civil government comprised of ten families. Ten families made a hundred, the administrative division of an English shire, perhaps equivalent to a township, while an English shire is the functional equivalent of an American county.

**tokenism.** *n.* The practice of admitting only the minimal number of minority applicants into an organization for the purpose of satisfying the minimal requirements of civil rights legislation or of placating public opinion.

**tool marks.** Impressions made when tools come in contact with material surfaces, leaving chips or striations that may be matched with a specific tool under microscopic examination at crime laboratory.

**Top Ten Most Wanted Criminals.** A program that publishes a list of the FBI's most wanted criminals. The list is highly publicized, including photographs and descriptions.

**tort.** *n.* A personal wrong; a civil as opposed to a criminal wrong or injury.

**total institution.** A term coined by Erving Goffman to describe institutions whose express purpose is to resocialize its members in order to reform them and change their values in accord with its value system; examples include prisons, military boot camps, and mental hospitals.

**total quality management (TQM).** An organizational management perspective holding that employees should care about their work and become involved in a participatory management style of organizational accountability, where they are expected to take the initiative in improving the quality of their work and work environment.

**township.** *n.* In some states, the name for a political subdivision of a county. In some states, e.g., the northeastern states, it is an active unit of government, whereas in others, e.g., the midwestern states, it is relatively dormant, save its tax collection and rural fire protection responsibilities.

**toxicology.** *n.* The organized study (science) of poisons and their impact on living organisms.

**trace elements.** Microscopic amounts of chemical elements or minerals found in or on objects of interest to the police, law enforcement, and the crime laboratory.

**trace evidence.** Evidence of microscopic proportions, such as small particles or residues of hair, fibers, elements, minerals, glass fragments etc., requiring detailed laboratory examination or other instrumentation.

**tracer bullet.** In the military, a bullet or projectile having a substance that, once ignited, illuminates the trajectory of the projectile, even during full daylight, for the purpose of target acquisition.

**tracking.** *v.* The following and recording of an offender through the criminal justice system and its various stages and processes.

**Traditional-Model Policing.** See *Professional-Model Policing.*

**traffic offenses.** (1) The quasi-criminal statutes regulating the operation of motor vehicles upon the public highways of a given state, often in accord with the *Uniform Vehicle Code;* (2) the civil ordinances of a municipal corporation regulating the operation of vehicles upon the ways within the corporate limits of the municipality; (3) the civil ordinances of a county regulating the operation of vehicles upon the public ways throughout a given county.

**transfer evidence.** Physical evidence that is transferred between victim and assailant or between subjects (e.g., victims, offenders, or other relevant actors) and the crime scene. This type of evidence is also known as associative evidence.

**transfer hearing.** A hearing where the state requests that a case exclusively under the jurisdiction of the juvenile court be transferred to adult court, based on the violence involved and/or the potential threat the minor child may pose to general society, should he or she be released at age twenty-one, when the juvenile court's authority terminates. These hearings are called, variously, certification and bind over hearings and have become increasingly more common within the past twenty years.

**transactional immunity.** The absolute blanket of immunity granted a witness against future prosecution for any evidence, event, or transaction about which he or she is compelled to give testimony (usually before a grand jury).

**transit police.** A special district police agency, established by state authority, for the express purpose of protecting public safety on an established public transit system, e.g., the policing agency for the Chicago Transit Authority (CTA).

**transnational crime.** A criminal act occurring in more than one sovereign nation, in the furtherance of the criminal act or conspiracy. Examples include money laundering, international terrorism, and drug trafficking.

**transponder warrant.** A special-purpose search warrant permitting the covert placement of a transponder on or within one's property (generally an automobile) in order to track its movement.

**treason.** *n.* The only crime mentioned in the Constitution of the United States (Article III § 3): "Treason against the United States shall consist only in levying war against them, or in adhering to their enemies, giving them aid and comfort." See *sedition.* In general terms, the violation of one's allegiance to his or her sovereign state by an overt act, e.g., bearing arms against the sovereign; in the United States this applies equally to the U.S. government and the various state governments, although treason against a state is largely nonexistent.

**treaty.** *n.* A formal legal document or compact recognizing a binding agreement between two or more sovereign nation states regarding issues of public welfare. Treaties must be signed by duly authorized commissioners and ratified by the proper authority (in the United States, senatorial approval is required, see Article II § 2,

Constitution). As such, a treaty constitutes an international law and contract between two or more nation states.

**trespass.** *v.* In its broadest legal sense, the unlawful infringement, transgression, or interference with another's person, property, and/or property rights. In a more narrow criminal law sense, trespass is the knowing and unlawful entering or remaining upon the land, building, or other structure, or vehicle (to include airplanes, watercraft, or other specialized vehicles) by a person without the legal authority to do so. Trespass includes the remaining on the land or within a structure or vehicle in defiance of a court order.

**trial.** *n.* The formal legal adjudication and examination of the facts in a case, cause, or controversy, whether civil, criminal, or administrative, before a court of competent jurisdiction.

**trial by ordeal.** In feudal times, a primitive draconian type of trial wherein the defendant was subjected to impossible odds in order to prove his or her innocence. For example, defendants were placed in a burlap bag filled with rocks and thrown into ice-cold water; if the bag came to the surface he or she was deemed innocent; if the bag sank, he or she was guilty, as God would not allow an innocent person to perish.

**trial court.** At the state or federal level, a court of general jurisdiction litigating cases and rendering judgments, verdicts, and rulings on both civil and criminal matters. The lowest court in a unified court system.

**trial de novo.** *(Lat.)* The trying of a case as new, as though it had never before been litigated and no judgment rendered. A trial *de novo* occurs in nonunified court systems, where the inferior court judge is often not a licensed attorney and a record of the trial is not made, e.g., a trial at the municipal level of government in some states. As the state appellate court would require a transcript of the trial, no appeal is available. As such, the case must be heard anew within the state's three-tiered judicial system, in the trial court of general jurisdiction. This is not to be considered an appeal; it is truly a trial anew at the trial-court level, from where an appeal may be made, should it be necessary.

**trial judge.** In both civil and criminal law, the judicial officer who presides over the trial, whether bench or jury, of a defendant or defendants, making necessary evidentiary and procedural rulings during the course of the trial. In a jury trial, the judge acts as the trier of law, whereas in a bench trial, he or she acts as both the trier of law and fact.

**triangulation.** *n.* (1) In the social sciences, it is a methodology for increasing either the validity and/or reliability of data, from separate sources, upon which inferences may be drawn.(2) In crime-scene investigations, a method of measurement wherein measurements are made from crime-scene items to two permanent fixtures or locations, e.g., a street crub, utility pole, or fire hydrant.

**tribunal.** *n.* (1) A seat where a judge sits in a court. (2) The entire body of judges and justices composing a given judicial jurisdiction. (3) A court of justice, whether civil or military. (4) The entire jurisdiction over which the court and/or judge presides.

**trifurcation.** *v.* The dividing up of a trial into three separate and distinguishable parts, each serving a separate purpose and function.

**trooper.** *n.* Deriving originally from the fact that troopers were mounted police employed by the commonwealth, the title in a modern context denotes a rank within a state-level police organization, i.e., a state police department or highway patrol department. A trooper is the lowest rank within a state-level policing agency, the functional equivalent of a deputy sheriff in a sheriff's office, or patrol officer within a municipal police department. The term can also be generically applied to all state-level police officers regardless of rank, to imply a distinction between state officers and officers of the county, township, or municipal level.

**truant.** *n.* A juvenile who is absent from school without permission. Truants fall under the jurisdiction of the school as well as the juvenile justice system.

**truant officer.** A school-based official charged with the responsibility of dealing with truant pupils.

**true bill.** An indictment or bill of indictment. An endorsement by an empaneled grand jury, finding the evidence before it to be sustained. The true bill may lead to the issuance of a warrant for the arrest of the defendant to be tried on criminal charges. Should the defendant be in custody, pending a grand jury ruling, he or she is then brought before a judge for arraignment.

**truncheon.** *n.* A wooden or plastic cudgel or club used primarily as a police officer baton.

**trusty.** *n.* A prison convict granted special privileges, as a result of his or her good behavior during incarceration.

**truth in sentencing.** A series of laws at both the state and federal levels, requiring that offenders serve most of their judicially imposed sentences; many states and the District of Columbia require 85 percent of the sentence be served. These laws began appearing as early as the 1980s and became very politically popular during the 1990s and beyond.

**Tweed, William Marcy (Boss Tweed, 1823–1878).** During his rule of "Tammany Hall" in the 1860s, he was one of a group of New York City aldermen known as the "Forty Thieves." He became the epitome of political corruption during the era. As a New York senator, Tweed along with his protégé Governor John Hoffman spread his corruption scheme statewide, collecting a percentage of all public contracts. Largely through the efforts of reformers and political cartoonist Thomas Nast, Tweed's corruption was brought under public scrutiny. Eventually, Samuel Tilden and his "Committee of Seventy" brought the ring to the bar of justice. Tweed was jailed for a brief period but managed to flee to Spain to avoid an ensuing trial necessary to recover much of his graft money; he was extradited and later died in jail.

**typographic printing.** A style of printing used to frustrate counterfeiting, where overprinting, through a process known as *intaglio*, is used to provide changeable images including serial numbers, seals, signature, and the like.

**typology.** *n.* A classification scheme used to organize data, where items are placed into discrete categories, based on common characteristics.

S
T

# U

UCMJ, Uniform Code of Military Justice (1951)
UCR, *Uniform Crime Reports*
USBP, United States Border Patrol
USC, United States Code
USCA, United States Code Annotated
USCBP, United States Customs and Border Protection
UCMJ, United States Code of Military Justice
USCS, United States Customs Service
USMS, United States Marshals Service
USNCB, United States National Central Bureau (INTERPOL)
USR, *United States Reports*

---

**ulnar loop.** A friction-ridge pattern found in fingerprints deriving from the ulna bone of the forearm.

**ultra vires.** *(Lat.)* Any action conducted outside the legal authority or power of a governmental official or agency.

**ultraviolet light.** Short-wavelength light (electromagnetic waves), ranging from 100 to 400 nanometers. It is divided into three classes: UC-A, UV-B, and UV-C. For forensic purposes, it is the UV-A (often called black light) that is of greatest utility, as it is relatively harmless; it may cause fluorescent material to glow.

**ultraviolet light imaging.** The use of ultraviolet lighting to enhance various details in photography.

**under color of law.** Any action taken abusing or misusing the power otherwise vested in an official by virtue of state law; the appearance of authority or actual invocation of power, without the actual legal right to act; any unlawful act done under circumstances where it would not have occurred but for the fact that the offender committing it was a lawful official exercising his or her powers beyond the limits of lawful authority. See 42 USCA § 1983.

**undercover work.** (1) Activities conducted by a police or law enforcement official or an agent (whether sworn or otherwise) covertly for the purpose of collecting strategic or tactical intelligence; (2) any covert activity done for the purpose of conducting a criminal investigation with the intent of making an arrest or arrests; (3) any negative proactivity conducted covertly in the furtherance of a sting operation.

**undersheriff.** *n.* (1) A deputy sheriff serving as a peace officer within a sheriff's office; (2) sometimes used as a title for the second in command in a sheriff's office, i.e., the undersheriff/chief deputy.

**unfounding.** *n.* The process of asserting that certain crimes (unsolved) never were crimes in the first place.

**Uniform Code of Military Justice (UCMJ).** The criminal code and procedure applicable to all of the armed services, including the Coast Guard. It provided for a military trial and appellate court system during the 1960s. See 10 USCA § 801.

***Uniform Crime Reports* (UCR).** The UCR is the product of a reporting program begun in 1927 by the International Association of Chiefs of Police (IACP). Under the program, participation is voluntary, and since the program's first reporting year (1930) the responsibility for sustaining the national clearing house for crime statistics was transferred to the FBI by congressional action. The program's annual report, *Crime in the United States,* is published by the FBI, showing data about crimes reported to the police only. It is divided into Part I and Part II offenses and organized according to geographical locale.

**Uniform Juvenile Court Act (1968).** A suggested model act, initiated by Congress, recommending standards for the formal processing of juvenile offenders in the various juvenile justice systems found across the nation.

**uniform state laws.** A compilation of model codes created by the Conference of Commissioners on Uniform State Laws for ready enactment by the various states on a series of areas, with the intent of bringing about a standardization among and between the various states.

**United States Attorney.** The lead federal prosecutor for a federal court district. U.S. attorneys have a staff of assistant U. S. attorneys who work under their supervision. U.S. attorneys and their assistants report to the U.S. attorney general, in Washington, DC. The function of U.S. attorneys parallels that of state prosecutors working at the county level, within a particular trial court of the state trial court system.

**United States Border Patrol (USBP).** Tracing its origins from 1904 under the aegis of the Commissioner General of Immigration, the USBP is the uniformed federal policing agency, mandated to secure the nation's borders against illegal immigration. The USBP has over 8,000 border patrol agents, patrolling nearly 8,000 miles of international boundaries. Recruit officers are required to successfully complete a nineteen-week academy in Glynco, Georgia, or Charleston, South Carolina. Reorganized in 2003 as a part of the United States Customs and Border Protection (USCBP). See *USCBP.*

**United States circuit courts.** The intermediate-level appellate courts within the federal judicial system. These courts hear appeals from the federal trial (district) courts within their given circuits. Appeals from the U.S. circuit courts of appeals go directly to the U.S. Supreme Court.

**United States Code (USC).** The official compilation of all federal statutes organized by subject area, including the U.S. Constitution.

**United States Code Annotated (USCA).** The annotated compilation of federal statutes published by the West Publishing Company, organized by subject area, including the U.S. Constitution.

**United States Code of Military Justice (USCMJ).** The federal statutory code applicable to the armed forces of the United States (see Title 10 [Armed Forces], Chapter 47 USCMJ).

**United States commissioner.** A low-level federal magistrate having nearly the identical functions of those of a justice of the peace at the state/local level. He or she is

U
V

not considered a judge within the federal judiciary and does not preside over a court. A commissioner is, however, empowered to issue certain warrants, to act as an officer for commitment, to set bail, and to bind over defendants for trial.

**United States Court of Appeals for the Federal Circuit.** The sole federal appellate court reviewing cases from the U.S. Claims Court and the Court of International Trade.

**United States Court of Claims.** See *United States Court of Federal Claims.*

**United States Court of Federal Claims.** The federal court with original jurisdiction in all cases of suit by individuals against the U.S. government or its appendages for alleged damages. Since October of 1982, the court was reorganized under Article I of the U.S. Constitution, via the Federal Courts Improvement Act, and was renamed the United States Court of Federal Claims. The court consists of sixteen judges who are nominated by the president for a fifteen-year term, after Senate confirmation. See *Federal Court Administration Act* of 1992, Public Law No. 102–572, 106 Stat. 4506 (1992).

**United States Customs Court.** Known officially as the United States Court of Customs and Patent Appeals, it is a specialized appellate tribunal founded in 1909, as the United States Court of Customs Appeals. In 1929, the court's jurisdiction expanded to include patent appeals and was given the full name cited above. The court consists of five justices who review (1) U.S. Customs Court decisions, (2) issues of law in findings of the lower court and the U.S. Tariff Commission regarding unfair practices in the area of import trade, and (3) decisions of the Patent Office regarding trademarks and patent applications.

**United States Customs and Border Protection (USCBP).** The police/federal law enforcement agency charged with the inspection of goods and materials entering or leaving the United States or any of its protectorates and the protection of the borders of the United States against smuggling and illegal immigration. This newly formed agency came into existence on March 1, 2003, under the aegis of the newly created Department of Homeland Security, and combined the former U.S. Customs Service with the U.S. Border Patrol. The new agency, the USCBP, has approximately 18,000 inspectors.

**United States Customs Service (USCS).** See *United States Customs and Border Protection (USCBP).*

**United States district courts.** The trial courts of general jurisdiction within the federal judiciary; appeals from these courts are heard by the U.S. circuit courts of appeals.

**United States Fish and Wildlife Service (USF&WS).** Dating back to its inception in 1871, this federal policing agency is housed within the U.S. Department of the Interior, with its research function being transferred to the U.S. Geological Survey in 1996. It functions as the federal equivalent to the Department of Natural Resources found throughout the various states.

**United States Immigration and Naturalization Service.** Originally organized within the Department of the Treasury, it was transferred to the Department of Justice in 1940. It has been recently relocated within the Department of Homeland Security, as a result of the September 11, 2001, tragedy. The agency has the responsibility of administering the immigration and naturalization laws of the nation, related to the admission or exclusion, deportation, and naturalization of aliens.

**United States Internal Revenue Service.** See *Internal Revenue Service.*

**United States Marshals Service (USMS).** Originally the Office of the U.S. Marshal, this federal police/law enforcement agency was begun under the Judiciary Act of 1789 and holds the distinction of being the oldest federal police/law enforcement agency. The duties and responsibilities of this federal agency replicate nearly identically those of the sheriff's office at the state/county level, e.g., the transportation of prisoners, acting as the officers of the court, and so forth.

**United States National Central Bureau (USNCB).** The national headquarters (located in Washington, DC) for the U.S. sector of the International Criminal Police Organization (INTERPOL).

**United States Parole Commission (USPC).** The independent federal agency, within the U.S. Department of Justice, reporting to the U.S. attorney general, charged with the responsibility of reviewing parole applications from those incarcerated in any facility under the Federal Bureau of Prisons. As of 2002, Congress has extended the life of this agency until November of 2005.

***United States Reports (USR).*** Cited simply as "U.S." it is one of three main sets of reports chronicling the decisions of the U.S. Supreme Court. The two other reports are West Publishing Company's *Supreme Court Reporter* and the Lawyers' Co-operative Publishing Company's *United States Supreme Court Reports,* cited as (L.Ed.) or (L.Ed.2d).

**United States Secret Service.** See *Secret Service.*

**United States Sentencing Commission.** Mandated by the Comprehensive Crime Control Act of 1984, this commission functions independently within the judicial branch of the federal government. After consultation with representatives including judges, prosecutors, defense attorneys, law enforcement officials, and numerous others, and with the approval of the U.S. Senate, the president appoints the voting members of the commission. No fewer than three voting members must be federal judges, and no more than four members may be from the same political party. The commission's purpose is to develop the means by which sentencing and penal or correctional practices affect the intended purposes of sentencing and to generate sentencing policies and practices for the federal system of criminal justice.

**United States Statutes at Large.** The official compilation of all the known congressional acts and resolutions for each Congress; the document is published by the Office of the Federal Register at the National Archives and Records Service. It consists of two parts; the first includes public acts and joint resolutions, whereas the second holds private acts and joint resolutions, concurrent resolutions, presidential proclamations, and treaties.

**United States Supreme Court.** The highest court in the land, functioning almost exclusively as the highest appellate court, although in a limited number of cases it functions as a trial court from which there is no appeal available, e.g., in cases of treason; the chief justice presides over impeachment cases. The Court consists of nine justices: eight associate justices, and a chief justice. Justices are nominated by the president contingent on the approval of the Senate for lifetime terms of office.

U
V

**United States Supreme Court Reports.** The official reports of the decisions of the U.S. Supreme Court, published by the Lawyers' Co-operative Publishing Company, abbreviated in legal citations as L.Ed. (lawyers' edition) or L.Ed.2d. (lawyers' edition, second edition).

**unlawful assembly.** The gathering of three or more persons under an agreed upon plan that if allowed to come to fruition, will likely cause a riot.

**unlawful combatant.** A legal category or status for a person who is not a member of the armed forces of a sovereign foreign state, or its militia, who engages in armed conflict against the United States; it was resurrected under the administration of President George W. Bush during the Iraqi War (2003). Many of the detainees held at the American detention center at Guantanamo Bay, Cuba, were/are held under this newly created and unsettled legal status, wherein the detainees' legal rights to counsel and protection under the rules of warfare are withheld. According to the U.S. Department of Justice, this legal status applies even to citizens of the United States who carry arms against the United States. This is a legal status and area of law that is clearly unsettled, and likely to be visited by the Supreme Court in the near future. See *Ex Parte Quirin,* 317 U.S. 1, 63 S.Ct. 1 (1942).

**unlawful entry.** A form of trespassing; the unlawful entering upon the lands or property of another without force and in a peaceable manner but without the legal right to do so.

**unlawful flight to avoid prosecution.** The intentional flight from one state or nation to another to avoid a felony criminal prosecution. A federal statute, commonly referred to as the Fugitive Felon Act, makes such unlawful flight a federal felony violation.

**unlawful flight to avoid testifying.** The intentional flight from one sovereign state or nation to another in order to avoid giving testimony as a material witness in a criminal prosecution, whether state or federal. A federal law, known as the Fugitive Witness Act, makes it a felony to avoid testifying via such flight.

**urban ecology.** The demographic study of spatial distributions of people and institutions in urbanized areas, especially incorporated cities, in an attempt to explain urban growth patterns as well as urban decline and dispersion.

**USA Patriot Act.** A federal act passed only forty-five days following the September 11, 2001, terrorist attack on the World Trade Center in New York City. This legislation (HR 3162 RDS, 107th Congress, 1st Session, October 24–25, 2001) gave sweeping authority to federal law enforcement and intelligence agencies for the purpose of enhancing national security. Among the act's many provisions are enhanced surveillance procedures, antiterrorism financing investigative authority, and law enforcement and intelligence information sharing. Critics argue that this piece of legislation has opened the door for federal law enforcement abuses of constitutionally based protections that have been the hallmark of American civil liberties for centuries. Proponents argue that the legislation provides law enforcement with the tools necessary to deal with contemporary intelligence and law enforcement problems of a global nature impinging on the security of the nation.

**use immunity.** A phrase used to denote a type of immunity under which the witness is compelled to render testimony of a self-incriminating nature, providing, in turn, that such testimony may not be used against the witness in a subsequent prosecution. If, however, the prosecution independently discovers the same evidence that was related to the court (generally the grand jury), a prosecution of the compelled witness using that evidence may proceed. Failure to testify after being granted use immunity may lead to a contempt of court ruling.

**usury.** *n.* The intentional lending of money at an unlawfully or immorally high interest rate. Usury laws exist in most jurisdictions setting limits on the maximum amount of lawful interest that may be assigned.

**utilitarianism.** *n.* A doctrine holding that the best purpose for all action is to bring about the greatest good for the greatest number. See *Jeremy Bentham (1748–1832).*

**utter.** *v.* To put forth, to offer, to dispatch or purvey, to publish, to place in circulation (as with a forged document or counterfeit note), to declare or assert, directly or indirectly by either words or actions, that something is genuine.

**uxoricide.** *n.* The intentional murder of a woman by her husband.

# V

**vacate.** *v.* To abandon, withdraw, retire, annul, rescind, quash, or set aside.

**vagabond.** *n.* One who wanders from one locale to another with no permanent abode, demonstrating a shiftless and irresponsible lifestyle.

**vagrancy.** *n.* The condition of wandering from one place to another in an irresponsible manner and without visible means of legitimate support.

**vandalism.** *n.* The willful damaging of property. It may be prosecuted as either a misdemeanor or felony depending on the value of the object(s) damaged or destroyed; it is similar to the charge of criminal damage to property.

**varieties of police behavior.** A typology of police service styles and organizational behavior developed by James Q. Wilson, including watchman, legalistic, and service styles. Wilson argues that the organizational culture of a police agency is not necessarily a result of formal policy; moreover, it is the result of informally transmitted values and traditions.

**vector.** *n.* (1) A line segment drawn from a known point of origin to a specified location. (2) The movement of an object (often a projectile) in relation to a given surface or plane.

**vehicle identification number (VIN).** A combination of numbers and letters, used to identify a specific vehicle by manufacturer, year, category, style, color, and so forth. The VIN is imprinted on a metal strip that is affixed to the vehicle with special rivets available only to the manufacturer in order to frustrate attempts by auto thieves to transfer the VIN from one vehicle to another. The VIN was known in earlier decades as an automobile's serial number.

**vehicular homicide.** An unlawful homicide caused by the negligent operation of a motor vehicle. See *reckless homicide.*

**venire.** *(Lat.)* "To appear in court." (1) Frequently, the name of a writ for gathering a jury pool. (2) The list of jurors summoned for jury service during a particular term of the court.

**venire facias.** *(Lat.)* The technical name for a writ issued to the sheriff of the county in which a cause is to be litigated, ordering him or her to summon a panel of prospective jurors.

**venireman.** *n.* (1) The title for a member of a jury panel. (2) The entire empaneled jury summoned via a writ of *venire facias.*

**venue.** *n.* In law, the specific geographical area over which the court has the authority to litigate and determine a case. Venue must not be confused with jurisdiction, which implies the inherent right of the court to legally decide a particular type of case.

**Vera Institute of Justice (1966).** Founded by Louis Schweitzer as the Vera Foundation, the Vera Institute of Justice is a research organization seeking to achieve a fundamentally fair justice system in America. It has sponsored such well-known research projects as the Manhattan Bail Project and the Bronx Sentencing Project; the institute is located in New York City.

**verbal act.** An action by words; statement showing motive, character, and the object of a given act.

**verdict.** *n.* In the original Latin form *"veredictum,"* it means a true declaration. The final judgment or ruling in an adjudication, made by the judge in a bench trial or the jury in a jury trial.

**vicarious liability.** The liability associated with the acts or actions of another. Examples include negligent hiring, improper or inadequate training, and negligent retention. See *respondeat superior doctrine ("let the master answer").*

**vice offenses.** Those offenses associated with victimless crimes, e.g., pornography, prostitution, drugs, and obscenity.

**vice squad.** That division of a police department charged with the investigation, abatement, and suppression of vice and vice-related incidents, e.g., drugs, prostitution, and gambling.

**victim.** *n.* In criminal justice usage, any person having suffered death, physical or mental injury, and/or loss of property or property rights as a result of the criminal activity or attempted criminal activity of another.

**Victim Assistance Program.** A formal program offering services to victims of crime through counseling, crisis intervention, and information concerning their legal rights as victims.

**victim compensation.** The creation of the 1984 Victims of Crime Act provided federal moneys to assist state victim compensation funds. State-operated funds exist in forty-four states, the District of Columbia, and the U.S. Virgin Islands, providing compensation for medical bills and wage losses resulting from a crime. The act does not generally provide for property loss.

**victim impact statement.** A statement allowed in court during the sentencing phase of the trial, allowing the victim or another to inform the court of the personal impact of the offender's behavior.

**victimization.** *n.* The harming of a person, i.e., the criminal harming of another as a result of a criminal incident.

**victimization rates.** The rates at which people are victimized by crime, generally presented as a ratio of victims to the population in thousands.

**victimless crime.** Crime where no traditional or official victim (outside of the perpetrator or society at large) exists, e.g.., gambling, prostitution, and drug usage.

**victimology.** *n.* That part of criminology examining the role the victim plays in precipitating a criminal incident.

**vigilante.** *n.* A member of a vigilance committee or organization committed to enforcing certain laws and maintaining moral standards and codes without legal authority. Between the mid-1700s and the early-twentieth century, vigilante groups were an ever-present element in American culture. Such groups as the

South Carolina Moderators, the East-Texas Regulators, the Ku Klux Klan, and the Southwestern Missouri Bald Knobbers are well-known examples of this social phenomenon.

**vigils.** *(Lat.)* During the reign of Augustus, the first emperor of Rome (27BC), a *Praetorian Guard* was established and augmented by *vigils* and *lectores*, i.e., those who were responsible for patrolling the streets, forerunners to modern-day police officers.

**Vinson, Frederick Moore (1890–1953).** The twelfth chief justice of the U.S. Supreme Court, appointed by President Harry S. Truman in 1946.

**visual average speed computer and recorder (VASCAR).** A manually actuated electronic speed detection device widely used by police, measuring and computing the time–distance relationship.

**voiceprint.** *n.* A metaphor for the spectrographic recording of the patterns made by the energy used to produce words and sounds.

**void for vagueness.** A legal doctrine that provides for making unenforceable any law that is either so obscure in its promulgation or unclear in its reading that a reasonable person could not determine its requirements. This doctrine rests on due process principles. See *Connally v. General Construction Co.,* 269 U.S. 385 (1926) and *City of Mesquite v. Alladen's Castle, Inc.,* 455 U.S. 283 (1982).

**voir dire.** *(Fr.)* "To speak the truth." The preliminary examination of prospective jurors.

**Vollmer, August (1876–1955).** Considered the "father" of police professionalism, he began his career in policing in 1905, as town marshal for the city of Berkeley, California. He was a supporter of police higher education and promoted the curriculum at San Jose State College in the early 1900s. In 1929, he was appointed professor of police administration at the University of Chicago and later became a professor at the University of California (1931).

**Volstead Act (1919).** The National Prohibition Act was a product of the Eighteenth Amendment, prohibiting the manufacture, transportation, and sale of alcoholic beverages consisting of more than 0.5 percent alcohol. The act was repealed with the adoption of the Twenty-First Amendment in 1933. Among the unintended consequences of the act's passage were political and police corruption, the expansion of organized crime, and the violence associated with the enforcement of the act.

**Voltaire, Francois Marie Arouet (1694–1778).** A French philosopher positing that the number of offenses for which the death sentence can be applied should be reduced, in an effort to make punishment for criminal offenses more socially useful. He further argued that punishment should be proportional to the crime, holding that only those acts contrary to society's existence should be made criminal.

**voluntariness.** *n.* In legal usage, the state of self-induced willingness to comply, unconstrained, and unimpelled by the influence of another. Statutorily, the term implies knowledge of facts essential to the issue at hand and a knowing surrender of one's right to remain silent.

**voluntary statement.** A statement given knowingly, intelligently, and without coercion; one not impelled by the influence of another; one given intentionally.

**voyeurism.** *n.* The act of secretly observing sexual objects, scenes, or the private parts of the human body unlawfully, for the purpose of sexual gratification. Persons so disposed are commonly known as Peeping Toms.

# W

**Waite, Morrison Remick (1816–1888).** The sixth chief justice of the U.S. Supreme Court from 1874 to 1888. Appointed by President Ulysses S. Grant, Waite died in office.

**waiver.** *n.* The intentional and voluntary relinquishment of a right, claim, or privilege.

***Wallace.****n.* The appellate case law reporter for U.S. Supreme Court rulings, spanning 1863–1874. Before the introduction of the *United States Reports (U.S.)* and the *United States Supreme Court Reports Lawyer's Edition/Second Edition (L.Ed., or L.Ed.2d),* a series of lesser-known reports covered the decisions of the High Court; they include *Dallas* (1790–1800), *Cranch* (1801–1815), *Wheaton* (1816–1827), *Peters* (1828–1842), *Howard* (1843–1860), *Black* (1861–1862), and *Wallace* (1863–1874). Today, these reports have been catalogued in the *United States Reports* and other reporters for the convenience of legal researchers.

**Walnut Street Jail.** Conceived of as an alternative to corporal punishment, this 1773 jail, later known as a penitentiary, was to serve as an American model of humane penal reform, earlier adopted by European penologists. It was assumed that convicted felons incarcerated therein would reflect on their injuries to society and become penitent. Notable characteristics included the separation of men and women, the forbidding of corporal punishment, and mandatory religious instruction.

**wanton.** *adj.* Actions are said to be wanton when they are deliberate, unnecessary, reckless, indifferent, and knowingly carried out with no regard for their consequences. Wantonness connotes a willful, knowing, intentional, and malicious reckless disregard for the rights and safety of others.

**war crimes.** Crimes committed by nations and their agents in open violation of the established international norms and laws governing war. For example, the Nuremberg trials following World War II were conducted to try Nazi war criminals for crimes against humanity.

**war power.** The legal authority and power of the U.S. government to prosecute a war. This power includes the right to protect the national defense apparatus, including its materials, instruments, and personnel, from injury or danger. The abridgement of constitutional protections may be legally justified under the nation's "war powers" only when the danger to the government is imminent.

**warden.** *n.* A prison superintendent; the highest prison administrative official; the administrator responsible for overall prison operations.

**warrant.** *n.* A writ or judicial order authorizing police and other law enforcement officers to arrest or seize specified persons or articles or to search places specified therein. The Constitution requires that warrants issue on probable cause only and be supported by oath or affirmation.

**warrantless arrest.** The arrest of a person or group of persons without a warrant. Officers in most jurisdictions may arrest without a warrant if they have probable cause to believe that a crime has been committed. Other jurisdictions require that officers have first-hand knowledge of the crime, i.e., the crime must be committed in their presence if the offense is a misdemeanor; in felony cases, an arrest may be made without a warrant in all jurisdictions.

**warrantless search.** Searches conducted without the authority of a search warrant may be made under a number of exceptions to the Constitution's warrant requirement, found in the Fourth Amendment. One such exception is the consensual search of the dwelling place of another, his person, articles, containers, baggage, or vehicle. Warrantless searches may be made under exigent circumstances, where obtaining a warrant is not practicable. Another exception is the probable-cause-based search of a motor vehicle because of its high degree of mobility, rendering a search warrant unworkable in certain circumstances; however, in all cases, probable cause must be established. See *Carrol v. United States,* 267 U.S. 132, 45 S.Ct. 280, 69 L.Ed. 543 (1925).

**Warren Commission.** The commission established by executive order 11130 in 1963 to independently investigate the assassination of President John F. Kennedy. The commission's report followed in 1964, focusing on Lee Harvey Oswald as the lone assassin, rejecting any conspiracy theories. The commission was headed by Chief Justice Earl Warren.

**Warren, Earl (1891–1974).** The fourteenth chief justice of the U.S. Supreme Court from 1953 to 1969; he was appointed by President Dwight D. Eisenhower as a conservative replacement for the exiting chief justice. To Eisenhower's surprise, Warren departed from his former conservative ideological posture and the long-standing doctrine of "judicial restraint" by creating a social agenda for the High Court involving "judicial activism." In a litany of landmark rulings, the High Court expanded the civil liberty protections found in the Constitution and permanently changed police investigative procedures across the nation to the liking of civil libertarians but to the chagrin of conservatives.

**watch and ward.** The watch involved the compulsory policing of a city during the nighttime hours by adult males, whereas the ward involved the policing of the city during the daytime hours. The watch was overseen by the constable in the larger walled cities of England; Boston established a night watch in 1636, and it served as the first iteration in the evolution of municipal-level American policing.

**watch system.** An historical system of policing wherein all adult males within a city were required to serve during the night watch. Eventually the watch was expanded to cover the daytime hours, known as the ward (Boston, 1634). The watch system eventually evolved into a full-time paid occupation, i.e., full-time, paid, public police.

**W**
**X**

**Watergate affair.** During the 1972 presidential campaign, the Democratic Party headquarters, located in the Watergate Hotel, Washington, DC, was broken into by members of an organization working for the Nixon reelection committee. Implicated in the conspiracy were such high-ranking administration officials as John Ehrlichman, H. R. Haldeman, and John Mitchell (former attorney general). Despite White House denials of complicity, the ongoing investigation led to the impeachment and later resignation of President Richard M. Nixon. Nixon was later pardoned (before trial) by his successor, Gerald R. Ford.

**watermark.** *n.* A design or mark on paper produced during the manufacturing process, which can be clearly observed when the paper is held up to a light source.

**weapon.** *n.* An instrument or substance of any kind used for offensive or defensive combat; anything used or designed to be used in destroying, injuring, or defeating another.

**Weathermen.** *n.* The radical and militant faction of the Students for a Democratic Society (SDS), which fomented unrest on American college campuses nationwide during the 1960s. This faction broke off from the main body of the SDS in 1969 and formed a splinter group, calling itself the Weathermen. The Weathermen resorted to terrorist tactics in order to further their political agenda.

**Weber, Max (1864–1920).** Before the "shaking out" of the academic disciplines, Weber was an academic interested in, what we call today, the social sciences. As a result, several disciplines claim him, e.g., sociology, economics, and political science. Nonetheless, his impact on the social sciences collectively has been long lasting, especially his interest in bureaucracies. Weber envisioned bureaucracies as rational organisms designed to most efficiently conduct their work. His impact on the sociology of formal organizations is monumental and has influenced generations of scholars of organizational sociology, including criminal justice scholars.

**weight of evidence.** The balance or inclination of evidence. See the *preponderance of evidence.*

**Wells, Alice Stebbins.** A leader in the early policewomen's movement in the United States, she was instrumental in the establishment of the International Association of Policewomen (1915).

**weregild (wergild).** *n.* The pecuniary amount for the commission of a homicide or other egregious personal felony paid by the offender to the king, lord, and next of kin, during the feudal period. According to Anglo-Saxon law, the amount depended on the social rank of the party slain. If the responsible party failed to pay the weregild, private vengeance could be extracted against the offender and his kin by the kin of the injured party or his or her family.

**West's National Reporter System (Regional Reporters).** The published rulings and opinions of the state-level appellate courts within the United States of America. A federal reporter system also exists including, for example, the *United States Reports (U.S.)* and the *United States Supreme Court Reports Lawyer's Edition (L.Ed.).* West's National Reporter organizes state appellate court decisions by grouping them according to a system of seven geographical regions across the nation, although some anomalies to the pattern exist. For example, some states are clearly not contiguous nor even found within the region to which they have been assigned, e.g., Oklahoma is found in the *Pacific Reporter.* See *law reports/reporters* for a fuller explanation.

**Wharton rule.** A rule disallowing the charge of conspiracy when the full participation of the involved parties is required, e.g., adultery.

**Wheaton.** *n.* The appellate case law reporter for U.S. Supreme Court rulings, spanning 1816–1827. Before the introduction of the *United States Reports (U.S.)* and the *United States Supreme Court Reports Lawyer's Edition/Second Edition* (L.Ed., or L.Ed.2d), a series of lesser-known reports covered the decisions of the

High Court; they include *Dallas* (1790–1800), *Cranch* (1801–1815), *Wheaton* (1816–1827), *Peters* (1828–1842), *Howard* (1843–1860), *Black* (1861–1862), and *Wallace* (1863–1874). Today, these early reports have been catalogued in the *United States Reports* and other reporters for the convenience of legal researchers.

**white-collar crime.** A term coined by noted criminologist Edwin H. Sutherland to categorize and label business crimes such as embezzlement and other business-related offenses. This offense category includes nonviolent crime for financial gain, conducted as a deception by persons whose employment status is essentially entrepreneurial or professional and who exploit their occupational skills and opportunities for financial gain.

**White, Edward Douglass (1845–1921).** Appointed to the U.S. Supreme Court by President Grover S. Cleveland, he is remembered for his conservative opinions and support of American nationalism. He also served on the Louisiana Supreme Court from 1879 to 1880, before his election to the Senate in 1890. He began his tenure with the High Court in 1894 as an associate justice before being elevated to chief justice by President William H. Taft.

**white slave traffic (Mann Act).** This federal act provides for a $5,000 fine and/or five years in prison of any person who knowingly transports or causes another to transport any female for the purpose of prostitution or other immoral purposes across state lines or to a foreign nation. The act was supported by eighteen nations at the Paris conference of 1904. The act also proscribes the importation of females into the United States for such purposes.

**Whitman, Charles.** Born in 1941, he later joined the U.S. Marine Corps, where he learned a good deal about firearms and marksmanship. After leaving the corps, he attended college. During the predawn hours of August 1, 1966, he murdered his mother and went to the clock tower on the University of Texas, Austin campus. From this vantage point high above the campus, he proceeded to shoot and kill seventeen students and to wound thirty-one others. He was shot and killed by a police officer; later an autopsy revealed that he had a brain tumor. Whether this was the cause of his murderous rampage is unknown. This incident, coupled with the Kent State University incident, fueled the impetus for creation of campus police departments with sworn officers for postsecondary educational institutions in the United States.

**Wickersham Commission (1931).** Created in 1929 by President Herbert Hoover, and formally known as the National Commission on Law Observance and Enforcement, its members conducted a nationwide study of the American criminal justice system. The fourteen separate reports were published in 1931, including the *Report on Lawlessness in Law Enforcement.* The report found that police across the nation routinely beat suspects to gain confessions, and used the third degree, including the infliction of pain.

**wildlife forensic laboratory.** The Clark Bavin Fish and Wildlife Laboratory, located in Ashland, Oregon, was established in 1988 as the only such forensic laboratory in the nation and much of the world. It serves the United States Fish & Wildlife Service (USF&WS) as well as conservation police agencies from the fifty states and 120 signatory nations.

W
X

**Wilson, Orlando W. (1900–1972).** An ardent police reformer and disciple of August Vollmer, Wilson served as chief of police of Wichita, Kansas, in 1928. Critical of the political influence on Wichita police, he left the department to accept a professorship at the University of California, Berkeley, establishing the first professional school of criminology just after World War II. Appointed superintendent of the Chicago Police Department in 1960, he served until 1967, when he left feeling unable to extract the mob influence from the department.

**Wines, Enoch (1806–1879).** Originally a clergyman and schoolmaster, he became a well-known prison reformer in 1861, along with his associate Zebulon Brockway. As secretary of the Prison Association of New York, he authored the *Report on the Prisons and Reformatories of the United States and Canada* (1867).

**wiretapping.** *v.* (1) The act of conducting a surreptitious electronic eavesdropping on private conversations and/or communications via court order or warrant (intercept order). Various state and federal statutes govern the procedures and circumstances under which a legal wiretap may be authorized. See *Federal Crime Control and Safe Streets Act*, 18 USCA § 2510 et seq. (2) The unlawful act of conducting a surreptitious electronic eavesdropping on private conversations and/or communications.

**witness.** *n.* In criminal law, a sworn layperson who testifies to accounts from his or her personal perceptions and experiences concerning the issue at hand. Expert (opinion) witnesses testify as to their opinions regarding the issue in controversy.

**witness list.** The complete list of witnesses to be called during a trial by both the prosecution and defense. This list is generally required by both prosecution and the defense in preparation for trial.

**Witness Relocation Program.** A program established for the protection of witnesses in mob-related cases, where the witness is given a new identity and relocated to a secret location, at government expense. At the federal level, the program is run by the U.S. Marshals Service.

**work product rule.** A rule holding that the "work product" of an attorney may be protected against discover. Work product includes material prepared by an attorney in anticipation of future litigation, involving legal theories, or legal strategies, private memoranda, and so forth. See *Hickman v. Taylor*, 329 U.S. 495, 67 S.Ct. 385, 91 L.Ed 451 (1947).

**work release.** A prison-based program under which inmates are temporarily released into the community to perform employment tasks, usually during the daytime, but requiring their return to a secure facility during the nighttime hours and/or on weekends.

**World Court.** Known earlier as the International Court of Justice, this court was founded in 1945 under U.S. authority to settle issues concerning international law. The court has fifteen justices elected for nine-year terms. Located at the Hague, it holds court in the Peace Palace, erected in 1903 under a grant from industrialist Andrew Carnegie. Although without enforcement power over its rulings, the court has moral suasion throughout the world. Its orders are enforceable through a voluntary withdrawal of entitlements by various nations and various U.N. sanctions.

**writ.** *n.* A judicial order requiring that an act specified therein be performed or discontinued.

**writ of assistance.** In criminal law, a general warrant failing to specify the person(s) or place(s) to be searched or the person(s) or item(s) to be seized, leaving the time and manner of the search to the judgment of the officer. Writs of assistance and general warrants are forbidden by the Constitution, Article I § 9.3.10.

**writ of attachment.** A writ used to enforce a court's order or judgment; it often takes the form of ordering the sheriff (or in federal jurisdiction, the U.S. marshal) to attach the nonconforming party to stand before the court in order to answer his or her contempt.

**writ of audita querela.** An arrest of judgment; a writ setting aside the execution of the judgment of a court where an injustice was performed by the party obtaining such judgment.

**writ of *certiorari.* (*Lat.*)** "To be informed of." A writ seeking appellate review; the Supreme Court may grant or deny the writ.

**Writ of error.** See *coram nobis* and *coram vobis*.

W
X

# X

**xenophobia.** *n.* The fear, suspicion, and hatred of outsiders (foreigners). See *ethnocentrism; nativism.*

**x-ray diffractometer.** A scientific instrument used in a forensic laboratory (in x-ray diffractometry) to identify solid substances (often of powder form) by subjecting such substances to x-ray bombardment. The rays of light that are deflected by this process show characteristic colors and patterns associated with various minerals, substances, and compounds.

**XYY chromosomes.** A rare chromosomal pattern found among males where an extra Y chromosome is present. It is argued that the presence of the extra Y chromosome produces an overly aggressive male prone to violence, and as an inherited trait, the subject should not be held criminally culpable for his actions. This has become a defense for some murderers, although mass murderer Richard Speck was unsuccessful in vindicating himself using it as a defense in his 1966 trial for the murder of eight student nurses in Chicago.

# Y

**year and a day rule.** A common-law rule, still in effect in some jurisdictions, that death cannot be criminally attributed to a defendant's unlawful act or acts unless the death occurs within a year and a day of the act or acts. Justification for this ancient rule was the imprecision of medicine in determining the causality of death after an extended period. Many legal experts argue that, given today's medical and forensic advances, the year and a day rule is dated and should be done away with.

**Youth Correction Authority Act** The American Law Institute's 1940 model act that served as the catalyst for various state youth authority statutes that followed.

# Z

**zero-tolerance policing.** A policing model (crime-attack model) that emerged during the 1990s, emphasizing police negative proactivity, i.e., the aggressive enforcement of minor criminal violations, especially those that undermine quality-of-life issues. Many police administrators mistakenly think that zero-tolerance policing is in the furtherance of community-oriented policing, as it too places strong emphasis on low-level quality-of-life issues. However, community-oriented policing stresses positive proactivity, i.e., where enforcement of the criminal law is the last option—not the first, as with zero-tolerance policing.

**zone search.** A method used by crime-scene evidence technicians to methodically search for physical evidence, wherein the area to be searched is segmented into rectangular grids (zones). Evidence from each zone is catalogued and marked on the zone sketch. Each zone is completely searched before the next is examined.

**zone theory.** There are numerous approaches to crime causation or reduction; some are more theoretically based, whereas others are more applied. Nonetheless, all are based on an environmentally focused perspective (theory) of crime causation, resting on the premise that structural elements in society, e.g., location, environmental design, architectural design, landscaping, and others, play an influential role in human behavior and interaction, leading to crime or the lack thereof; they include, e.g.,(1) Concentric Zone Theory (Park's and Burgess's original Chicago study); (2) Defensible Space Theory (Oscar Newman); (3) Crime Prevention Through Environmental Design (CPTED by C. Ray Jeffery); Environmental Criminology (Brantigan and Brantigan); and Deviant Places Theory (Rodney Stark).

**zoning.** *n.* A system for the division of a municipality or county into separate zones or districts for the purpose of segregating commercial, industrial, residential, and other usages. Zoning requirements may include building codes, architectural design, environmental design, historic preservation, and others.

# Index of Major Appellate Cases

# Major Appellate Cases

## Abandoned Property

*Abel v. United States*, 362 U.S. 217, 80 S.Ct. 683, 4 L.Ed.2d 688 (1960). The leading case regarding the warrantless but lawful seizure of abandoned property by law enforcement officers, after a subject has deposited articles in the trash container in his hotel room and subsequently checked out of the hotel.

## Admissibility of Evidence

*Elkins v. United States*, 364 U.S. 206, 4 L.Ed.2d 1169, 80 S.Ct. 1437 (1960). The Supreme Court overturned an earlier decision found in *Wolf v. Colorado* (1949), allowing evidence garnered contrary to the federal exclusionary rule by state officers to be admissible in federal trials. Under *Wolf*, federal officers could have admitted at trial evidence which, if seized by them, would have been found inadmissible, but was admissible if seized for them by state officers. The *Wolf* decision created a process of serving up otherwise inadmissible evidence, known as the "silver platter" doctrine.

## Arrest and Detention

*Brower v. County of Inyo*, 489 U.S. 593, 103 L.Ed.2d 628, 109 S.Ct. 1378 (1989). In a narrow decision for the majority (5–4), the Court held that placing a police roadblock, without any avenue of escape, across the entire roadway for the purpose of stopping a fleeing suspect constitutes a seizure under the Fourth Amendment. The Court further ruled that such an unreasonable seizure would establish civil liability within Title 42 USC 1983.

*Delaware v. Prouse*, 440 U.S. 648, 663, 99 S.Ct. 1391, 1401, 59 L.Ed.2d 660, 673 (1979). The Court held that the arbitrary stopping of a motor vehicle for the purpose of inspecting the driver's license to be unreasonable under the Fourteenth Amendment, absent an articulable and reasonable suspicion that the driver is unlicensed. The Court also indicated that random vehicle checks are potentially a form of discriminatory law enforcement.

*Sibron v. New York* and *Peters v. New York*, 392 U.S. at 62, 88 S.Ct. at 1902, 20 L.Ed.2d at 934 (1968). The two companion cases to the *Terry v. Ohio* (1968) decision handed down by the Supreme Court regarding the authority of the police to stop and frisk individuals, without a warrant or probable cause to make a full-custody arrest. The Court made clear the underlying justifications for demanding a temporary detention of possible offenders based on the contextual circumstances, and the permissibility of a "protective" search based on officer safety and/or the safety of others. Lastly, the Court ruled on the inadvertent discovery and subsequent seizure of evidence of a crime, fruits of a crime, or instrumentalities of a crime. As in *Terry v. Ohio* (1968), officers may stop and temporarily detain suspicious individuals, when they have reason to believe (based on contextual variables and their occupational experience) that a crime has been committed or that crime is afoot—a *Terry* stop. Officers have authority to conduct a limited search of the subject's outer clothing when they reasonably believe that their lives are in danger or the life of another is in jeopardy—a *Terry* frisk. This limited search is only justified as a pat-down search for possible weapons, not for the discovery of evidence. Evidence of a crime or instrumentalities of a crime that may be found as a result may be used in a subsequent trial as evidence found incident to a limited search for weapons. See *Terry v. Ohio* (1968).

*State v. MacKenzie*, 161 ME 123, 137, 210 A.3d 24, 32–33 (1965). The Supreme Judicial Court of Maine ruled that despite the fact that the definition of an arrest, as contrasted against a mere detention, eludes exact definition, a criminal arrest ". . . signifies the apprehension or detention of the person of another in order that he may be forthcoming to answer for an alleged or supposed crime."

*Terry v. Ohio*, 392 U.S. 1, 88 S.Ct. 1868, 20 L.Ed.2d 889 (1968). The Supreme Court ruled in this case and its companion cases, i.e., *Sibron v. New York* (1968) and *Peters v. New York* (1968), that police officers have the lawful authority to stop (detain) persons when they have a "reasonable suspicion" that crime is afoot, but lacking sufficient probable cause to make a full-custody arrest. They may search those individuals only when they have a reasonable fear that their lives or the lives of others may be in jeopardy. The search, however, is not for the purpose of discovering secreted proof of a crime, but, moreover, is limited to a search of the outer clothing for the discovery of a weapon that may be used to assault the officer or others nearby.

*United States v. Mendenhall*, 446 U.S. 544, 100 S.Ct. 1870, 64 L.Ed.2d 497 (1980). The Court clarified what constitutes a seizure under the meaning of the Fourth Amendment; it held: "A person has been 'seized' within the meaning of the Fourth Amendment only if, in view of all of the circumstances surrounding the incident, a reasonable person would have believed that he was not free to leave." As a result, the Court found no seizure of the person when DEA agents in plain clothes and displaying no weapons approached a suspect in an airport, identified themselves as federal enforcement agents, and requested her identification and airline ticket. When she obediently accompanied the agents to their office, no seizure occurred, as there were no threats, nor was there any show of force.

*United States v. Santana*, 427 U.S. 38, 96 S.Ct. 2406, 49 L.Ed.2d 300 (1976).The Supreme Court ruled that the warrantless arrest of a person who is in a public place at the initiation of the arrest may not defeat the lawful process of arrest by the person's retreating into his or her home. The Court made clear that the doorway of one's home is a public place, under the meaning of the Fourteenth Amendment.

## Death Penalty and Deadly Force Issues

*Coker v. Georgia*, 433 U.S. 584, 97 S.Ct. 2861 (1977). The High Court ruled that the death penalty was disproportionate to the offense of rape and found it unconstitutional under the Eighth Amendment's cruel and unusual punishment provision.

*Furman v. Georgia*, 408 U.S. 238, 33 L.Ed.2d 346, 92 S.Ct. 2726 (1972). The Court struck down the death penalty laws in both Georgia and Texas, holding that "the imposition and carrying out of the death penalty in these cases constitutes cruel and unusual punishment in violation of the Eighth and Fourteenth Amendments."

*Gregg v. Georgia*, 428 U.S. 153, 49 L.Ed.2d 859, 96 S.Ct. 2909 (1976). The Court ruled that the new Georgia death penalty statute had basically remedied the discretionary imposition of the death penalty found earlier in *Furman v. Georgia* (1972), where the law violated the Eighth and the Fourteenth Amendments to the Constitution. Because the new statute required that the jury find at least one "aggravating circumstance" out of ten before imposing the death penalty, the discretionary and even "freakish" imposition of sentencing was reasonably controlled.

*Stanford v. Kentucky*, 492 U.S. 361, 106 L.Ed.2d 306, 109 S.Ct. 2969 (1989). The Supreme Court ruled that the fact that the Federal Anti-Drug Abuse Act of 1988 does not provide capital punishment for offenders under eighteen years of age does not establish a rule or precedent disallowing the sentence of death for youthful offenders.

*Tennessee v. Garner*, 471 U.S. 1, 85 L.Ed.2d 1, 105 S.Ct. 1694 (1985). The Court ruled that the use of deadly force to prevent the escape of a felon was in contravention to the Fourth Amendment. This decision was the death knell to the centuries old "fleeing felon" rule. According to the Court, deadly force may be used by officers to prevent the escape of a felon only when his or her escape is likely to lead to the death or serious bodily harm to officers or others, e.g., the flight after direction to stop by police for a forcible felony.

*Witherspoon v. Illinois*, 391 U.S. 510, 20 L.Ed.2d 776, 88 S.Ct. 1770 (1968). The Supreme Court held that excluding jurors for cause, based on their conscientious scruples, moral, religious, or ethical principles against the use of capital punishment, is a violation of the Sixth Amendment. Calling such a "death qualified" jury a "hanging jury," the Court argued that such a process would virtually stack the deck against the defendant. A ". . . sentence of death cannot be carried out if the jury that imposed or recommended it was chosen by excluding veniremen for cause simply because they voiced general objections to the death penalty or expressed conscientious or religious scruples against its infliction."

## Double Jeopardy

*Ashe v. Swenson*, 397 U.S. 436, 90 S.Ct. 1189 (1970). In reversing the conviction of a defendant for robbery, in a second trial arising out of the same set of circumstances, the High Court ruled that despite the fact that the defendant may have committed the robbery of six men who had been playing poker, his acquittal at the first trial for the robbery of only one of the men constituted a barrier (an *estoppel*/double jeopardy) against any future trials for the robbery of any of the other five poker players.

APP

*Bartkus v. Illinois*, 359 U.S. 121 (1959). The Supreme Court ruled that one may be lawfully subjected to a criminal trial for the same offense under the laws of two separate sovereignties, and that such second punishment does not constitute double jeopardy. That is, in the American federal system, both the federal government and the various state governments remain sovereign, within their respective spheres. As such, one may be punished for the same criminal act by both a state and federal government, if both sovereigns have a statute proscribing such conduct.

*Benton v. Maryland*, 395 U.S. 784, 23 L.Ed.2d 707, 89 S.Ct. 2056 (1969). The Supreme Court ruled that the federal Constitution's double jeopardy clause is so fundamental to the American scheme of justice that it be applied to the states regardless of whether it is addressed in their respective state constitutions. (At the time of the decision, forty-five of the fifty states had such a provision in their respective constitutions, while the remainder of states applied double jeopardy protections via common law). The *Benton* decision, therefore, did not forcefully apply an unfamiliar concept on the states; it simply formally applied a nearly universally accepted principle to all American criminal adjudications, whether state or federal.

*Breed v. Jones*, 421 U.S. 519, 44 L.Ed.2d 346, 95 S.Ct. 1779 (1975). The Supreme Court ruled unanimously that the prosecution of a juvenile in adult court, after receiving an adjudicatory hearing in juvenile court, constitutes double jeopardy and is, therefore, disallowed under the Fifth and Fourteenth Amendments of U.S. Constitution.

*Illinois v. Vitale*, 447 U.S. 410, 65 L.Ed.2d 228, 100 S.Ct. 2260 (1980). A divided Supreme Court (5–4) ruled that the double jeopardy provision of the Constitution does not disallow an involuntary manslaughter prosecution stemming from a vehicle code violation, where the defendant's one act is punishable under two types of law. That is, a trial for the violation of a state vehicle code provision (failure to reduce speed to avoid an accident) arising out of the same incident does not prevent a lawful (involuntary manslaughter—another Illinois statute) criminal prosecution based on the same act. In the instant case, the defendant was arrested, tried, and convicted for the violation of a state vehicle code statute (failure to reduce speed to avoid an accident), while he was also arrested, tried, and convicted of involuntary manslaughter. The U.S. Supreme Court ruled that this type of dual prosecution does not constitute double jeopardy under the Constitution because "Whether the offense of failing to reduce speed to avoid an accident is the 'same offense' for double jeopardy purposes as the manslaughter charges, depends on whether each statute in question requires proof of a fact which the other does not. *Blockburger v. United States*, 284 U.S. 229."

## Due Process Issues

*Bordenkircher v. Hayes*, 434 U.S. 357, 54 L.Ed.2d 604, 98 S.Ct.663 (1978). In a narrow 5–4 decision, the Court held that a prosecutor does not infringe on a defendant's due process rights when he or she carries out a threat made earlier to reindict the defendant on more serious charges if the defendant fails to plead guilty to the plea bargained charge.

*Gitlow v. New York*, 268 U.S. 652, 45 S.Ct. 625, 69 L.Ed. 1138 (1925). The Supreme Court defined the phrase "due process" of law to mean essentially "without abridgement of certain of the rights guaranteed by the Bill of Rights." The ruling implies that the concepts supporting the Bill of Rights, as opposed to the guarantees themselves, are so fundamental to the American scheme of federalism and of justice that, as one nation, they must be applied in state criminal action as well as federal.

*In re Gault*, 387 U.S. 1, 87 S.Ct. 1248 (1967). The Court ruled that despite the intent of the juvenile justice system, and its restorative foundation in civil law, juveniles hold basic constitutional protections previously thought applicable in adult criminal trials only. They include (1) the notice of timely and specific charges, (2) the right to counsel, (3) the right to confront witnesses against them and to cross-examine them, (4) the privilege against self-incrimination, and (5) the right to seek appellate review.

*In re Winship*, 397 U.S. 358, 25 L.Ed.2d 368, 90 S.Ct. 1068 (1970). Holding that the Constitution's "due-process clause" requires proof beyond a reasonable doubt, the Court extended the same level of proof required in adult criminal trials to juvenile delinquency adjudications.

*Kent v. United States*, 383 U.S. 541, 86 S.Ct. 1045, 16 L.Ed.2d 84 (1966). A divided Supreme Court (5–4) ruled that a juvenile has basic due process rights, including the right to counsel at waiver, transfer, or certification hearings.

## Entrapment

*Sherman v. United States*, 356 U.S. 78 S.Ct. 819 (1958). The Supreme Court reversed the conviction of a drug user, based on the entrapment defense promulgated in *Sorrells v. United States* (1932), looking at the defendant's predisposition to commit the crime, stating that "A different question is presented when the criminal design originates with the officials of the government, and they implant in the mind of an innocent person the disposition to commit the alleged offense and induce its commission in order that they may prosecute. . . ."

*Sorrels v. United States*, 287 U.S. 435, 53 S.Ct. 210 (1932). The Court ruled that undercover law enforcement operations often require some deception and trickery, but those tactics may not be used to ensnare innocent law-abiding citizens into criminal activity. When the design for the crime originates with the enforcement officer, and not the accused, for the purpose of ensnaring and arresting him or her, entrapment has occurred. Allowing such activity on the part of police or law enforcement officers would be tantamount to a court sanctioned method for the manufacturing of crime.

## Exclusionary Rule

*Mapp v. Ohio*, 367 U.S. 643, 655, 81 S.Ct. 1684, 1691, 6 L.Ed.2d 1081, 1090 (1961). The Court's ruling made inadmissible any evidence from a search in violation of one's Fourth Amendment protections. This rule had been in effect for federal prosecutions since *Weeks v. United States* (1914); however, the *Mapp* ruling made the provisions of the Bill of Rights binding on state officers in state criminal action through the due process provision of the Fourteenth Amendment (the selective incorporation doctrine). In fact, the larger impact of the ruling was to make inadmissible in a criminal trial against a suspect any evidence gathered against him or her that was obtained in violation of his or her constitutionally based civil liberty protections found in the Bill of Rights.

*United States v. Calandra*, 414 U.S. 338, 38 L.Ed.2d 561, 94 S.Ct.613 (1974). The Court made clear that the purpose of the Fourth Amendment-based but court-generated "exclusionary rule" was expressly to deter police and law enforcement misconduct.

*Weeks v. United States*, 232 U.S. 383, 34 S.Ct. 341, 58 L.Ed. 652 (1914). The High Court, for the first time in the nation's history, ruled that evidence obtained by police or law enforcement officers in violation of a defendant's constitutionally protected civil liberties would be excluded from subsequent criminal trials against him or her. This ruling applied only to federal police and law enforcement officers; it was not until *Wolf v. Colorado* (1949) that it applied in any way to state officers in state criminal prosecutions.

## Forcible Abduction of Defendant by Enforcement Officers

*Frisbie v. Collins*, 342 U.S. 519, 72 S.Ct. 509 (1952). The Supreme Court ruled, relying heavily on an earlier such case, i.e., *Ker v. Illinois* (1886), that the unlawful abduction of a defendant does not impair the authority of the court to try him or her. Known as the *Ker–Frisbie* rule, the two cases make clear that a court retains its jurisdiction over the crime and defendant even when the means by which the defendant is delivered to the court are clearly illegal.

*Ker v. Illinois*, 119 U.S. 436, 7 S.Ct. 225 (1886). The High Court ruled that the way in which a defendant is delivered into the jurisdiction of a court does not impact the legality of the court's jurisdiction over the defendant, the trial, or the verdict. Ker, who was indicted by an Illinois grand jury for felony violations, was living in South America. The governor of Illinois requested that the president of the United States have a warrant issued for Ker's arrest, authorizing a private Pinkerton agent to take Ker into custody and deliver him to the proper Illinois court for trial. The Pinkerton agent failed to serve the warrant and forcibly abducted Ker, placing him aboard an American ship for transport. Ker was later convicted but appealed, claiming that he had been unlawfully placed in the custody of the court and that, as such, the Illinois trial court's ruling was invalid. The Supreme Court ruled the trial was legal regardless of the illegalities of the Pinkerton agent in taking custody of the defendant. The *Ker* case along with the *Frisbie* case led to the development of the *Ker–Frisbie* rule.

*United States v. Rauscher*, 119 U.S. 407 (1886). Handing down its ruling on the same day in 1886 that it ruled on *Ker v. Illinois*, the High Court made clear in *Rauscher* that no American court holds jurisdiction over a defendant standing before it who has been produced in violation of a valid treaty. While the *Ker* decision evinces that where no treaty violation has occurred, due process does not disallow the trial of the defendant whose attendance before the court was produced via forceful abduction, trickery, luring, or other illegality.

## Free Speech

*Skokie, Village of v. National Socialist Party of America*, 69 Ill.2d 605, 14 Ill. Dec. 890, 373 N.E.2d 21 (1978). The Illinois Supreme Court held that the swastika as a symbol of Nazi storm trooper repression could not be disallowed under the "fighting-words" doctrine exception to free speech and that it be allowed to be displayed under the Constitution's free speech provision of the First Amendment, despite its offensiveness to the mostly Jewish community of Skokie.

*Tinker v. Des Moines Independent Community School District et al.*, 393 U.S. 503, 383 F.2d 988 (1969). The Court held that the Board of Education, which had sought an injunction against students wearing black armbands to protest the nation's policy in Southeast Asia, was a violation of the free-speech clause of the First Amendment and the due process clause of the Fourteenth. The Court stated that "A prohibition against expression of opinion, without any evidence that the rule is necessary to avoid substantial interference with school discipline or the rights of others, is not permissible under the First and Fourteenth Amendments."

## General Warrants and Writs of Assistance

*Boyd v. United States*, 116 U.S. 616, 625, 6 S.Ct. 524, 528–29 L.Ed. 746, 749 (1886). The Supreme Court ruled on whether the compulsory disclosure, under a subpoena *duces tecum* during a forfeiture procedure, is subject to the limitations imposed by the Fourth and Fifth Amendments. Holding that a nexus exists between the two amendments, the test for the reasonableness of a search is dependent on whether the purpose of a search is actually the discovery of incriminating evidence.

## Grand Juries

*Hurtado v. California*, 110 U.S. 516, 28 L.Ed. 232, 4 S.Ct. 292 (1884). The Supreme Court held that a grand jury indictment may be supplanted by a state prosecutor's information, even for serious felony offenses like murder, despite the U.S. Constitution's requirement found in the Fifth Amendment. The grand jury requirement holds for federal prosecutions only.

*United States v. Calandra*, 414 U.S. 338, 94 S.Ct. 613, 38 L.Ed.2d 561 (1974). In accordance with a discernable pattern of refusing to extend the exclusionary rule any further, the High Court ruled that illegally obtained evidence is not prevented from consideration by a grand jury.

## Informant Information

*Aguilar v. Texas*, 378 U.S. 108, 84 S.Ct. 1509, 12 L.Ed.2d 723 (1964). This case is one of two U.S. Supreme Court cases determining probable cause for informant-based complaints and affidavits (often using confidential informants); see also *Spinelli v. United States* (1969). Through these two cases, the Court articulated a specified requirement for the preparation of complaints and affidavits to ensure the veracity and reliability of the informant and his or her information, known as the "two-pronged test." First, the affidavit was required to provide sufficient circumstances from which a magistrate could determine whether the informant had an adequate basis for his or her proffered knowledge and that the information was not the product of simple suspicion. Second, the affidavit needed to explain the underlying circumstances leading to the use of a confidential informant to assist the magistrate in determining whether the informant was credible and the information reliable. That is, prong one determines whether the affidavit needed to establish that the informant personally (first-handedly) perceived the information provided or that the informant's information was provided by an independent source, but that there was compelling reason to believe it anyway. In prong two, officers needed to provide convincing proof of the informant's veracity and reliability. Subsequently, the *Illinois v. Gates* (1983) decision retreated from the rigid *Aguilar–Spinelli* two-pronged test, by creating the "totality of the circumstances" approach for determining hearsay probable cause; see *Illinois v. Gates*, a lesser standard.

*Illinois v. Gates*, 462 U.S. 213, 103 S.Ct. 2317, 76 L.Ed.2d 527 (1983). As a major ruling on determining probable cause based on informant information, commonly known as the "hearsay method," the High Court signaled a retreat from the rigid standards promulgated in two earlier rulings, i.e., *Aguilar v. Texas* (1964) and *Spinelli v. United States* (1969). In abandoning the *Aguilar–Spinelli* "two-pronged" test for determining the informant's veracity, although not disallowing it, the Court opted for allowing anonymous tips under the "totality of circumstances" test.

*McCray v. Illinois*, 386 U.S. 300, 306–07, 87 S.Ct. 1056, 1060, 18 L.Ed.2d 62, 68 (1967). The Supreme Court ruled that police officers need not reveal the identity of informants if their prior credibility has been satisfactorily established.

*Spinelli v. United States*, 393 U.S. 410, 89 S.Ct. 584, 21 L.Ed.2d 723 (1969). In this companion case to *Aguilar v. Texas* (1964), where informant hearsay is used to establish probable cause, the Court ruled that specific requirements for police and law enforcement officers needed to be met. These requirements established the "two-pronged" test for informant veracity and reliability; see *Aguilar v. Texas* (1964). The rigid adherence to the *Aguilar–Spinelli* "two-pronged test" was greatly relaxed in *Illinois v. Gates* (1983), under a more permissively conservative Court.

## Judicial Review

*Marbury v. Madison*, 1 Cranch 137 (1803). The original issue in this noteworthy case had to do with the Court ruling on the failure of President Thomas Jefferson to appoint William Marbury as a federal justice of the peace. The commission to the judgeship was made during the eleventh hour of President John Adams's tenure, and Marbury appealed to the Supreme Court to enforce his appointment; however, that is of little importance, as the larger issue in the case lies in the sagacious way Chief Justice John Marshal used the case to bolster the Court's role in American government. Through Marshal's decision, the Supreme Court was ensured its place as an equal member in the American system of government, i.e., along with the executive and legislative branches, by asserting its role as the exclusive interpreter of the laws and Constitution of the United States, via the right of "judicial review." This is the process that allows the Supreme Court to determine whether federal and state statutes comport with the Constitution.

## Juries (Petit) and Jury Trials

*Apodica v. Oregon*, 406 U.S. 404, 92 S.Ct. 1628, 32 L.Ed.2d 184 (1972). The Supreme Court held that convictions by less than unanimous jury verdicts in noncapital cases are not disallowed under the Constitution's Sixth and Fourteenth Amendments.

*Bloom v. Illinois*, 391 U.S. 194, 20 L.Ed.2d 522, 88 S.Ct. 1477 (1968). The High Court ruled that the right to a jury trial in grave criminal contempt cases originating in state courts is protected by the U.S. Constitution.

*Duncan v. Louisiana*, 391 U.S. 145, 20 L.Ed.2d 491, 88 S.Ct. 1444 (1968). The Court held that criminal defendants are entitled to a jury trial for all serious offenses, under the protections found in the Sixth Amendment. That is, defendants must be provided the option of a jury trial for all offenses that are punishable by a sanction of more than six months in jail and/or a fine of more than $500, as the Supreme Court held that petty offenses are those punishable by a jail term of less than six months and/or a fine of less than $500.

*In re Winship*, 397 U.S. 358, 25 L.Ed.2d 368, 90 S.Ct. 1068 (1970). The Court ruled that the level of proof for a finding of "delinquency" in a juvenile adjudication is proof beyond a reasonable doubt, i.e., the same level of proof as for a guilty verdict in an adult criminal trial.

*McKeiver v. Pennsylvania*, 403 U.S. 528, 91 S.Ct. 1776 (1971). The High Court held that the right to a trial by jury for juvenile offenders is not constitutionally protected under the Sixth Amendment.

*Williams v. Florida*, 399 U.S. 78, 26, L.Ed.2d 466, 90 S.Ct. 1893 (1970). Justice White, writing for the majority, held the traditional twelve-person jury to be an historical misconception; smaller juries are allowable under the Constitution's Sixth Amendment. In fact, six-person juries are permissible if state law allows.

*Witherspoon v. Illinois*, 391 U.S. 510, 20 L.Ed.2d 776, 88 S.Ct. 1770 (1968). The Supreme Court held that excluding jurors for cause, based on their conscientious scruples, moral, religious, or ethical principles against the use of capital punishment, is a violation of the Sixth Amendment. Calling such a "death qualified" jury a "hanging jury," the Court argued that such a process would virtually stack the deck against the defendant. A ". . . sentence of death cannot be carried out if the jury that imposed or recommended it was chosen by excluding veniremen for cause simply because they voiced general objections to the death penalty or expressed conscientious or religious scruples against its infliction."

## Juveniles

*Breed v. Jones*, 421 U.S. 519, 44 L.Ed.2d 346, 95 S.Ct. 1779 (1975). The Supreme Court ruled unanimously that the prosecution of a juvenile in adult court, after receiving an adjudicatory hearing in juvenile court, constitutes double jeopardy and is, therefore, disallowed under the Fifth Amendment to the Constitution of the United States.

*In re Gault*, 387 U.S. 1, 87 S.Ct. 1248 (1967). The Court ruled that despite the intent of the juvenile justice system, and its restorative foundation in civil law, juveniles hold basic constitutional protections previously thought applicable in adult criminal trials only. They include (1) the notice of timely and specific charges, (2) the right to counsel, (3) the right to confront witnesses against them and to cross-examine them, (4) the privilege against self-incrimination, and (5) the right to seek appellate review.

*In re Winship*, 397 U.S. 358, 25 L.Ed.2d 368, 90 S.Ct. 1068 (1970). Holding that the Constitution's due process clause requires proof beyond a reasonable doubt, the Court extended the same level of proof required in an adult criminal trial to juvenile delinquency adjudications.

*Kent v. United States*, 383 U.S. 541, 86 S.Ct. 1045, 16 L.Ed.2d 84 (1966). A divided Supreme Court (5–4) ruled that a juvenile has basic due process rights, including the right to counsel at waiver, transfer, or certification hearings.

*McKeiver v. Pennsylvania*, 403 U.S. 528, 91 S.Ct. 1776 (1971). The High Court held that the right to a trial by jury for juvenile offenders is not constitutionally protected under the Sixth Amendment.

*Stanford v. Kentucky*, 492 U.S. 361, 106 L.Ed.2d 306, 109 S.Ct. 2969 (1989). The Supreme Court ruled that the fact that the Federal Anti-Drug Abuse Act of 1988 does not provide capital punishment for offenders under eighteen years of age does not establish a rule or precedent disallowing the sentence of death for youthful offenders.

*Tinker v. Des Moines Independent Community School District et al.*, 393 U.S. 503, 383 F.2d 988 (1969). The Court held that the Board of Education, which had sought an injunction against students wearing black armbands to protest the nation's policy in Southeast Asia, had violated the free-speech clause of the First Amendment and the due process clause of the Fourteenth. The court stated that "A prohibition against expression of opinion, without any evidence that the rule is necessary to avoid substantial interference with school discipline or the rights of others, is not permissible under the First and Fourteenth Amendments."

*Vernonia School District v. Acton*, 515 U.S. 646, 115 S.Ct. 2386, 132 L.Ed.2d 564 (1995). The High Court ruled that the suspicionless drug testing of all students who have chosen voluntarily to participate in interscholastic sports does not constitute an unreasonable search under the Fourth Amendment.

## Lineups, Showups, and Confrontations

*Gilbert v. California*, 388 U.S. 263, 87 S.Ct. 1951, 18 L.Ed.2d 1178 (1967). The Court held in both the *Gilbert* and *Wade* cases that in a confrontation (any presentation of a suspect to witnesses or victims of a crime) the defendant has a right to the assistance of counsel, as it constitutes a "critical stage" in the legal process, thereby creating the *Wade–Gilbert* rule. See *Wade v. United States* (1967).

*Stovall v. Denno*, 388 U.S. 293, 87 S.Ct. 1967, 18 L.Ed.2d 1119 (1967). The Court held that the due process clause found in the Fifth and Fourteenth Amendments forbids any type of pretrial identification method that is suggestive or likely to lead to mistaken identifications.

*United States v. Wade*, 388 U.S. 218, 87 S.Ct. 1926, 18 L.Ed.2d 1149 (1967). See *Gilbert v. California* (1967), the *Wade–Gilbert* rule above.

## Miranda Warnings, Admissions, Confessions, and Interrogations

*Beckwith v. United States*, 425 U.S. 341, 96 S.Ct. 1612, 48 L.Ed.2d 1 (1976). The Court ruled that Miranda warnings need not be given in "non-custodial" interrogations, despite the fact that the "focus" of the investigation has centered on the suspect, if the person so interrogated is not in formal custody or deprived of freedom of action in a significant way. This was a departure from the High Court's ruling of only a few years earlier, in *Escobedo v. Illinois* (1964).

*Brown v. Illinois*, 422 U.S. 590, 603–04, 95 S.Ct. 2254, 2261–62, 45 L.Ed.2d 416, 427 (1975). The U.S. Supreme Court ruled that a confession gained through the exploitation of an illegal arrest is inadmissible at trial, even after Miranda warnings have been administered.

*Brown v. Mississippi*, 297 U.S. 278, 56 S.Ct. 461, 80 L.Ed. 682 (1936). The Supreme Court held that a coerced confession derived from police brutality violated the due process protection found in the Fourteenth Amendment to the U.S. Constitution. A series of cases followed extending this protection to cases employing other forms of police coercion, including subtle psychological pressures, e.g., *State v. Jennings* (1979), *United States v. Koch* (1977), and *Brady v. United States* (1970).

*Escobedo v. Illinois*, 378 U.S. 478, 84 S.Ct. 1758, 12 L.Ed.2d 977 (1964). The Supreme Court ruled that when a criminal investigation moves from a general inquiry concerning an unsolved crime to one that focuses on a particular individual or group of individuals, with the purpose of eliciting incriminating utterances, warnings regarding the defendant's right to counsel need to be administered, under the "assistance of counsel" obligation of the Sixth Amendment. This requirement is made applicable in state criminal action through the due process provision of the Fourteenth Amendment to the U.S. Constitution. The *Escobedo* decision created the "focus test."

*Hoffa v. United States*, 385 U.S. 293, 87 S.Ct. 408, 176 L.Ed.2d 374 (1966). The Court held that subjects who are unaware that they are speaking to police or law enforcement officers cannot possibly think they are in custody; thus, situations involving undercover officers and agents cannot be considered custodial. As a result, according to the High Court, Miranda warnings do not apply in these "non-custodial" settings.

*Jenkins v. Delaware*, 395 U.S. 213, 23 L.Ed.2d 253, 89 S.Ct. 1677 (1969). The Court ruled that the standards imposed under *Miranda v. Arizona* (1966) are not applicable to pre-Miranda trials that have been remanded back for retrial after the Miranda decision was promulgated.

*Mallory v. United States*, 354 U.S. 449, 1 L.Ed. 1479, 77 S.Ct. 1356 (1957). The Supreme Court held that the unreasonably long detention of a defendant by police, before bringing him before a magistrate for a *habeas corpus* (committing) hearing, made the confession police had elicited inadmissible in court.

*McNabb v. United States*, 318 U.S. 332, 63 S.Ct. 608, 87 L.Ed. 819 (1943). The Court ruled that obtaining a statement, admission, or confession during an unreasonable delay between a defendant's arrest and arraignment makes inadmissible any such statement, admission, or confession at a subsequent trial. Together with the *Mallory v. United States* (1957) ruling, these twin cases have produced the *McNabb–Mallory* rule.

*Miranda v. Arizona*, 384 U.S. 436, 86 S.Ct. 1602, 16 L.Ed.2d 694 (1966). The High Court shifted from the "focus test" articulated in *Escobedo v. Illinois*, under the "totality of the circumstances" approach based on the Sixth Amendment, to the Fifth Amendment based on the prohibition against self-incrimination. In short, the Court held that the prosecution may not introduce statements, admissions, or confessions garnered from a "custodial" interrogation of the defendant unless the necessary procedural safeguards were in place to prevent self-incriminating statements made without the defendant's consent. The formal warnings include (1) the defendant's right to remain silent, (2) statements made by the defendant can and will be used against him or her in a court of law, (3) the defendant has the right to be represented by counsel, during the interrogation, and (4) should the defendant not be able to afford a lawyer, one will be appointed to represent him or her. However, should the defendant waive his or her Miranda rights, all statements, admissions, or confessions are admissible at trial.

*New York v. Quarles*, 467 U.S. 649, 81 L.Ed.2d 550, 104 S.Ct. 2626 (1984). The Court's decision in this case created what has come to be known as the "public safety" exception to the Miranda warnings. The Court ruled that if officers have an articulable reason to believe that a weapon has been discarded, abandoned, or secreted immediately prior to the arrest, in the interest of public safety, they may ask where the weapon is without first administering the Miranda warnings.

*Nix v. Williams*, 467 U.S. 431, 81 L.Ed.2d 377, 104 S.Ct. 2501 (1984). This case led to the establishment of the "inevitable discovery" doctrine, where the body of a homicide victim was disclosed during an illegal interrogation and where afterward the defendant led the police to the location of the corpse. The Court reasoned that the Fourth Amendment did not demand suppression of the evidence, given that the state would have inevitably found the body anyway, providing the state with no advantage at trial as a result of the illegal interrogation, as search parties were nearing the location at the time of discovery.

*Rhode Island v. Innis*, 336 U.S. 291, 64 L.Ed.2d 297, 100 S.Ct. 1682 (1980). A divided Court (5–4) held that Miranda warnings are required when a suspect is in custody and is subjected to "express" questioning that the police or law enforcement officers know will likely lead to the elicitation of incriminating statements.

*Zucconi v. State*, 50 N.J. 361, 235 A.2d 193 (1967). The New Jersey Supreme Court held that the questioning of a hospitalized suspect, who is not under arrest, is not generally considered a custodial interrogation. The questioning of heavily drugged or intensely ill suspects, however, may constitute a custodial interrogation, given the diminished capacity of the defendant; see *State v. Ross*, 183 Neb, 1, 157 N.W.2d 860 (Supreme Court of Nebraska, 1968).

## Probable Cause

*Beck v. Ohio*, 379 U.S. 89, 85 S.Ct. 223, 13 L.Ed.2d 142 (1964). The High Court ruled that the Court's warrant requirement is so strongly preferred over a warrantless search that the probable cause supporting a court-order search warrant could be somewhat less than that for a warrantless search. The Court's rationale hinged on the fact that the intervention of a neutral and detached judicial officer served the constitutionally based right of citizens from the potentially harried and overzealous police or law enforcement officer's independent judgment.

*Draper v. United States*, 358 U.S. 307, 79 S.Ct. 329, 3 L.Ed.2d 327 (1959). The Court, in attempting to define the elusive meaning of probable cause, posited that probable cause exists where facts and circumstances that are reasonably trustworthy are sufficient to justify a person of reasonable prudence in his or her belief that a crime has been committed. For police officers, "probable cause is the sum total of layers of information and synthesis of what police have heard, know, or observe as trained officers." When police are attempting to build sufficient probable cause based on information coming from an informant, the problem lies in "probable cause hearsay" built on hearsay, thus, the Court's ruling in *Aguilar v. Texas* (1964).

APP

## Religious Freedom

*Reynolds v. United States*, 98 U.S. 145, 25 L.Ed. 244 (1879). The Court ruled that the practice of polygamy may lawfully be proscribed and punishable by law, despite the fact that a church may endorse the practice. The Court reasoned that to place the doctrines of a church above the laws of the secular state would allow every person to become a law unto himself or herself, providing government in name only.

## Revocation Hearings

*Gagnon v. Scarpelli*, 411 U.S. 778, 36 L.Ed.2d 656, 93 S.Ct. 1756 (1973). The Court held that probationers and parolees are entitled to revocation hearings identical to those outlined in *Morrissey v. Brewer*. Where an indigent probationer or parolee is incapable of relaying his or her version of the incident, the state is generally required to provide counsel at state expense.

## Right to Counsel

*Argersinger v. Hamlin*, 407 U.S. 25, 32 L.Ed.2d 530, 92 S.Ct. 2006 (1972). The Court held that defendants facing the possibility of jail time (this includes petty misdemeanor offenses) are entitled to representation by counsel if they so desire and that a lawyer will be appointed at no cost if defendants are indigent.

*Betts v. Brady*, 316 U.S. 455, 86 L.Ed. 1595, 62 S.Ct. 1252 (1942). The U.S. Supreme Court ruled that an indigent defendant had no right to counsel in a noncapital state case, under the Fourteenth Amendment's due process provision. This decision was later overturned in *Gideon v. Wainwright* (1963).

*Brady v. United States*, 397 U.S. 742, 25 L.Ed.2d 747, 90 S.Ct. 1463 (1970). The Court emphasized the importance of counsel during the pleading process, citing two other significant companion cases on the issue: *McMann v. Richardson* (1970) and *Parker v. North Carolina* (1970), during the same session.

*Brewer v. Williams*, 430 U.S. 387, 51 L.Ed.2d 424, 97 S.Ct. 1232 (1977). In a narrow decision for the majority (5–4), the Supreme Court held that any indirect questioning of the defendant after the arraignment stage, without his or her counsel in attendance, constituted an incursion into his constitutionally protected right to the affirmative assistance of counsel. Known as the "Christian burial" speech, the ploy used by the police was to attempt to get the defendant to reveal more information about the whereabouts of the victim's body. They appealed to his deep religious beliefs while transporting him, without his attorney in attendance, asking him questions during the trip about where they could find the young girl's body, in order to give her a proper Christian burial. The Court ruled that the Christian burial speech was tantamount to an interrogation and disallowed the admissibility of the statements at trial.

*Gideon v. Wainwright*, 372 U.S. 335, 83 S.Ct. 792, 9 L.Ed.2d 799 (1963). As one of a series of cases enforcing the Sixth Amendment's right to counsel, the Supreme Court expanded that right to all felony violations as well as "petty offenses" if a jail term is a possibility upon conviction. According to the ruling, counsel must be provided at state expense to indigent defendants.

*Johnson v. Eisentrager*, 399 U.S. 763, 790–791, 949–950 (1950). The second court of appeals ruling for the District of Columbia held that aliens captured abroad during military operations and held in U.S. military custody on foreign soil are not entitled to Constitutional protections (including the right to counsel and *habeas corpus*) because they are "aliens outside the sovereign territory of the United States."

*Johnson v. Zerbst*, 304 U.S. 458, 82 L.Ed. 1461, 58 S.Ct. 1019 (1938). The Supreme Court held that the Sixth Amendment's right to counsel applies to indigent federal defendants, and, as such, they are entitled to counsel at government expense.

*Kirby v. Illinois*, 406 U.S. 682, 32 L.Ed.2d 411, 92 S.Ct. 1877 (1972). The Court held that a suspect has the right to counsel at a police lineup if the lineup follows a formal charge, i.e., a preliminary hearing, indictment, information, or arraignment.

*Massiah v. United States*, 377 U.S. 201, 12 L.Ed.2d 246, 84 S.Ct. 1199 (1964). The Court held that a federal criminal defendant under indictment may not be lawfully interrogated without his or her attorney being present; such an interrogation constitutes a violation of the defendant's Sixth Amendment right to counsel. Later in *McLeod v. Ohio* (1965) the Court extended the *Massiah* ruling to the states under the due process provision of the Fourteenth Amendment, i.e., through the selective incorporation doctrine.

*Powell v. Alabama*, 287 U.S. 45, 77 L.Ed 158, 53 S.Ct. 55 (1932). The Court's decision in the "Scottsboro Boys" case held that the Sixth Amendment's right to counsel was violated, as the state trial court did not provide "effective appointment of counsel," which created a denial of due process within the meaning of the Fourteenth Amendment. The Court stated in conclusion, "The judgments must be reversed and the causes remanded for further proceedings not inconsistent with this opinion."

## Search, Seizure, and the Exclusionary Rule

### *Arms-length (lunge) doctrine*

*Chimel v. California*, 395 U.S. 752, 89 S.Ct. 2034, 23 L.Ed.2d 685 (1969). The Supreme Court ruled that the warrantless search of an offender and the area "within his immediate control" incident to a lawful arrest is permissible. This ruling led to the "arms-length" doctrine, which later was expanded by other appellate courts to include any area where the subject might reasonably be able to leap; this later became known as the "lunge" doctrine. In creating the rule, the Court noted that ". . . it is entirely reasonable for the arresting officer to search for and seize any evidence on the arrestee's person in order to prevent its concealment or destruction. And the area into which an arrestee might reach in order to grab a weapon or evidentiary items must, of course, be governed by a like rule."

## Consent searches

*Florida v. Royer*, 460 U.S. 491, 103 S.Ct. 1319, 75 L.Ed.2d 229 (1983). The Supreme Court held that the illegality of the subject's detention invalidated his consent to allow the police to search his luggage. The Court ruled that the defendant's consent was, therefore, tainted and the seizure of items in the luggage became "fruit of the poisonous tree."

*Schneckloth v. Bustamonte*, 412 U.S. 218, 229, 93 S.Ct. 2041, 2048–49, 36 L.Ed.2d 854, 864 (1973). The Court ruled that when ". . . properly conducted, [a consent search] is a constitutionally permissible and wholly legitimate aspect of effective police activity." However, the Court requires, in cases of consent searches, "clear and convincing evidence" that the proffered consent was in fact voluntarily given and was not the product of duress or coercion, whether express or implied.

## Electronic surveillance

*Berger v. New York*, 388 U.S. 41, 18 L.Ed.2d 1040, 87 S.Ct. 1873 (1967). The Supreme Court held that New York's wiretap statute was too permissive, allowing for a trespassing into the Fourth Amendment's protections from unreasonable search and seizures. In its ruling, the High Court found the New York statute permitting electronic surveillance to be issued without adequate justification and to have been nearly automatically renewed upon request by police and law enforcement officials for extended periods.

*Katz v. United States*, 389 U.S. 347, 19 L.Ed.2d 576, 88 S.Ct. 507 (1967). The Supreme Court ruled that the Fourth Amendment "protects people, not places"; as such, eavesdropping conducted electronically constitutes both a search and a seizure, making it subject to the Fourth Amendment's warrant requirement. This decision overturned the earlier *Olmstead v. United States* (1928) decision.

*Olmstead v. United States*, 277 U.S. 438, 48 S.Ct. 564, 72 L.Ed. 944 (1928). In its holding that a wiretapping was not subject to the Fourth Amendment's warrant requirement, the Court reasoned that there had been no physical intrusion into the premises of the defendant. The Court stated, "The evidence was secured by the use of the sense of hearing and that only. There was no entry of the houses or offices of the defendants. . . . The intervening wires are not part of his house or office. . . ." The venerable Justice Louis Brandies forcefully dissented, stating, "Our government is the potent, the omnipresent teacher. For good or for ill, it teaches the whole of the people by its example. . . . If the government becomes a law breaker, it breeds contempt for the law; it invites every man to become a law unto himself; it invites anarchy."

*Smith v. Maryland*, 442 U.S. 735, 61 L.Ed.2d 220, 99 S.Ct. 2577 (1979). The High Court held that the use of a pen register (a device for recording the telephone numbers dialed from a particular telephone) is not a violation of a suspect's "reasonable expectation of privacy" and, as such, does not require a court-ordered warrant (intercept order). The Court reasoned that because the device does not record any of the conversation, no Fourth Amendment violation can possibly occur.

## Exclusionary rule and search and seizure generally

*Mapp v. Ohio*, 367 U.S. 643, 655, 81 S.Ct. 1684, 1691, 6 L.Ed.2d 1081, 1090 (1961). The Court's ruling made inadmissible any evidence from a search in violation of one's Fourth Amendment protections. This rule had been in effect for federal prosecutions since *Weeks v. United States* (1914); however, the *Mapp* ruling made many of the provisions of the Bill of Rights binding on state officers in state criminal action, through the due process provision of the Fourteenth Amendment (the selective incorporation doctrine). In fact, the larger impact of the ruling was to make inadmissible in a criminal trial against a suspect any evidence gathered against him or her that was obtained in violation of his or her constitutionally based civil liberty protections found in the Bill of Rights.

*United States v. Calandra*, 414 U.S. 338, 38 L.Ed.2d 561, 94 S.Ct. 613 (1974). The Court made clear that the purpose of the Fourth Amendment-based but court-generated "exclusionary rule" was expressly to deter police and law enforcement misconduct.

*Warden v. Hayden*, 387 U.S. 294, 18 L.Ed.2d 782, 87 S.Ct. 1642 (1967). In its over-turning of the "mere evidence" rule, the Court held that police and law enforcement officers may seize various items, including clothing, during a lawful search of a suspect's domicile or other locations.

*Ybarra v. Illinois*, 444 U.S. 85, 100 S.Ct. 338, 62 L.Ed.2d 238 (1979). The Court held that when police officers have a warrant for the search of a suspect and/or the premises, he or she and the premises may naturally be searched; however, simply because another person happens to be on the premises does not give officers the authority to search him or her, as a general rule.

## Good-faith exception

*United States v. Leon*, 468 U.S. 897, 82 L.Ed.2d 677, 104 S.Ct. 3405 (1984). In creating what has come to be known as the "good-faith" exception, the Court held that the seizure of evidence produced as a result of a defective warrant, issued by a detached and neutral judge, will not be excluded from trial if the officers acted in objective good faith.

## Open-fields doctrine

*Hester v. United States*, 265 U.S. 57, 44 S.Ct. 445, 68 L.Ed. 898 (1924). The Court held that "The special protection accorded by the Fourth Amendment to the people in their 'persons, houses, papers and effects' is not extended to the open fields."

## Plain-view doctrine and mere evidence

*Coolidge v. New Hampshire*, 430 U.S. 443, 91 S.Ct. 2022, 29 L.Ed.2d 564 (1971). The Supreme Court made clear that evidence seized by police or law enforcement agents under the "plain-view" doctrine must clearly be inadvertently discovered. The Court

APP

reasoned that ". . . where the discovery is anticipated, where the police know in advance the location of the evidence and intend to seize it, the situation is altogether different. The requirement of a warrant to seize imposes no inconvenience whatever, or at least none which is constitutionally cognizable in a legal system that regards warrantless searches as '*per se* unreasonable' in the absence of 'exigent circumstances.' "

*Warden v. Hayden*, 387 U.S. 294, 18 L.Ed.2d 782, 87 S.Ct. 1642 (1967). In its overturning of the "mere evidence" rule, the Court held that police and law enforcement officers may seize various items, including clothing, during a lawful search of a suspect's domicile or other locations.

## Vehicles

*Carroll v. United States*, 267 U.S. 132, 45 S.Ct. 280, 69 L.Ed. 543 (1925). In creating the "*Carroll* doctrine," the High Court ruled that the warrantless search of a motor vehicle on a public way by police officers or law enforcement agents, having probable cause to believe that the vehicle holds items that offend against the law, is constitutionally permissible. That is, the stopping and search of a vehicle, where officers have probable cause, is not unreasonable under the Fourth Amendment's protection against unreasonable search and seizure. This "automobile exception" to the warrant requirement is based on the near impossibility of procuring a warrant, given the mobility of the vehicle, which can quickly find its way into another jurisdiction.

*Chambers v. Maroney*, 399 U.S. 42, 90 S.Ct. 1975, 26 L.Ed.2d 419 (1970). The High Court expanded the warrantless search authority of automobiles by police and law enforcement officers under the *Carroll* doctrine to include impounded vehicles, that is, those vehicles already seized and removed from the public highway. The Court argued that "For constitutional purposes, we see no difference between on the one hand seizing and holding a car before presenting the probable cause issue to a magistrate and on the other hand carrying out an immediate search without a warrant. Given the probable cause to search either course is reasonable under the Fourth Amendment."

*Maryland v. Wilson*, 519 U.S. 408 (1997). The Supreme Court held that police officers may, without a warrant, order both the driver and passenger(s) out of a vehicle that has been legally detained. Further, evidence seized as a result of the subjects' exiting of the vehicle is legally admissible at a subsequent criminal trial.

*New York v. Belton*, 453 U.S. 454, 69 L.Ed.2d 768, 101 S.Ct. 2869 (1981). The Supreme Court ruled that the search of an automobile is permitted if conducted incident to a lawful full-custody arrest of an occupant of that vehicle. Officers may search the passenger compartment of the vehicle, including the glove box, console, and articles of clothing.

*Robbins v. California*, 453 U.S. 420, 69 L.Ed.2d 744, 101 S.Ct. 2841 (1981). The Supreme Court ruled that police and law enforcement officers may not open closed opaque containers during the warrantless search of an automobile. This decision was reversed only a year later in *United States v. Ross* (1982).

*South Dakota v. Opperman*, 428 U.S. 364, 96 S.Ct. 3092, 49 L.Ed.2d 1000 (1976). After the U.S. Supreme Court ruled that police conduct in searching and seizing evidence during an automobile inventory search was reasonable, and, therefore, admissible at trial, the South Dakota Supreme Court in *State v. Opperman*, 247 N.W.2d 673 (S.D. 1976) found the search to have violated not the Fourth Amendment of the U.S. Constitution, but rather the search and seizure protections of the South Dakota constitution. Here, a state supreme court had actually extended greater protections under the state constitution than those found under the federal Constitution.

## Warrantless searches

*Cupp v. Murphy*, 412 U.S. 291, 93 S.Ct. 2000, 36 L.Ed.2d 900 (1973). The Supreme Court ruled that police and law enforcement officers may conduct a limited search of detained persons absent a search warrant. In its ruling, the Court held that a person detained by authorities for investigative purposes only may nevertheless be searched, relying heavily on its earlier *Chimel v. California* (1969) decision, noting that while officers did have probable cause for an arrest, the officers had merely detained the subject; however, the detention was against the subject's will and constituted a seizure under the Fourth Amendment, thereby providing grounds for the warrantless search.

*Kyllo v. United States*, 533 U.S. 27 (2001). The Supreme Court ruled, in a split 5–4 decision, that police and law enforcement agents may not legally use thermal imaging devices on a subject's home without a court-ordered search warrant.

*Payton v. New York*, 445 U.S. 573, 100 S.Ct. 1371, 63 L.Ed.2d 639 (1980). The Supreme Court ruled that without exigent circumstances or lawful consent, police officers and law enforcement agents may not, as a general rule, enter a suspect's home to make a routine warrantless felony arrest. However, despite the lower protections afforded by an arrest warrant, if officers have a valid arrest warrant, it extends the limited authority to enter the premises to make the apprehension if officers have a reasonable belief that the suspect is inside.

*Robbins v. California*, 453 U.S. 420, 69 L.Ed.2d 744, 101 S.Ct. 2841 (1981). The Supreme Court ruled that police and law enforcement officers may not open closed opaque containers during the warrantless search of an automobile. This decision was reversed only a year later in *United States v. Ross* (1982).

*South Dakota v. Opperman*, 428 U.S. 364, 96 S.Ct. 3092, 49 L.Ed.2d 1000 (1976). After the U.S. Supreme Court ruled that police conduct in searching and seizing evidence during an automobile inventory search was reasonable, and, therefore, admissible at trial, the South Dakota Supreme Court in *State v. Opperman*, 247 N.W.2d 673 (S.D. 1976), found the search to have violated not the Fourth Amendment of the

U.S. Constitution, but rather the search and seizure protections of the South Dakota constitution. Here, a state supreme court had actually extended greater protections under the state constitution than those found under the federal Constitution.

*United States v. Chadwick*, 433 U.S. 1, 97 S.Ct. 2476, 53 L.Ed 538 (1977). The Supreme Court's decision in the *Chadwick* case severely limited the warrantless search of containers, luggage, and other personal items that have been seized incident to an arrest. The Court ruled that ". . . warrantless searches of luggage or other property seized at the time of an arrest cannot be justified as incident to that arrest either if the 'search is remote in time or place from the arrest' . . . or no exigency exists."

*United States v. Leon*, 468 U.S. 897, 82 L.Ed.2d 677, 104 S.Ct. 3405 (1984). In creating what has come to be known as the "good-faith" exception, the Court held that the seizure of evidence produced as a result of a defective warrant, issued by a detached and neutral judge, will not be excluded from trial if the officers acted in objective good faith in gaining and/or executing the warrant.

*United States v. Mendenhall*, 446 U.S. 544, 100 S.Ct. 1870, 64 L.Ed.2d 497 (1980). The Court clarified what constitutes the seizure of a person under the meaning of the Fourth Amendment; it held: "A person has been 'seized' within the meaning of the Fourth Amendment only if, in view of all of the circumstances surrounding the incident, a reasonable person would have believed that he was not free to leave." As a result, the Court found no seizure of the person when DEA agents, in plain clothes and displaying no weapons, approached a suspect in an airport, identified themselves as federal enforcement agents, and requested her identification and airline ticket. When she obediently accompanied the agents to their office, no seizure occurred, as there were no threats, nor was there any show of force.

*United States v. Ross*, 456 U.S. 798, 102 S.Ct. 2157, 72 L.Ed.2d 572 (1982). The Court ruled that "The scope of the warrantless search authorized by [the *Carroll*] exception is no broader and no narrower than a magistrate could legitimately author- ize by warrant. If probable cause justifies the search of a lawfully stopped vehicle, it justifies the search of every part of the vehicle and its contents that may conceal the object of the search."

*United States v. Santana*, 427 U.S. 38, 96 S.Ct. 2406, 49 L.Ed.2d 300 (1976). The Supreme Court ruled that the warrantless arrest of a person who is in a public place at the initiation of the arrest may not defeat the lawful process of arrest by the person's retreating into his or her home. The Court made clear that the doorway of one's home is a public place under the meaning of the Fourteenth Amendment.

*Vernonia School District v. Acton*, 515 U.S. 646, 115 S.Ct. 2386, 132 L.Ed.2d 564 (1995). The High Court ruled that the suspicionless drug testing of all students who have chosen voluntarily to participate in interscholastic sports does not constitute an unreasonable search under the Fourth Amendment.

## Status or Condition Made Criminal

*Robinson v. California*, 370 U.S. 660, 82 S.Ct. 1417 (1962). The Court held that the status or condition of an individual may not be defined as a crime. The Court opined that the state may not punish an individual for being "mentally ill, or a leper, or . . . afflicted with a venereal disease," or, for that matter, being a drug addict. "Even one day in prison would be a cruel and unusual punishment for the 'crime' of having a common cold."

## Suppression of Evidence

*Franks v. Delaware*, 438 U.S. 154, 98 S.Ct. 2674, 57 L.Ed.2d 667 (1978). The Supreme Court ruled that a defendant may lawfully challenge the veracity of the affidavit supporting a search warrant if the defendant can make a substantial preliminary showing that false statements were made knowingly and intentionally in order to provide sufficient probable cause to convince a judicial officer to issue the warrant.

## Unlawful Combatants

*Ex Parte Quirin*, 317 U.S. 1, 63 S.Ct. 1 (1942). The Supreme Court ruled during World War II that "unlawful combatants" were subject to capture and detention as prisoners of war and subject to trial and sanctioning by military tribunals. The case arises out of a group of Nazi spies who, after receiving sabotage training in Germany, came ashore from German submarines on the beaches of New York and Florida. The ruling from this case is that civilian "unlawful combatants" may not be tried by military courts *within* the United States unless they are spies.

*Johnson v. Eisentrager*, 399 U.S. 763, 790–91, 949–50 (1950). The second court of appeals, ruling for the District of Columbia, held that aliens captured abroad during military operations and held in U.S. military custody on foreign soil are not entitled to Constitutional protections (including the right to counsel and habeas corpus) because they are "aliens outside the sovereign territory of the United States."

## Void for Vagueness Doctrine

*Connally v. General Construction Co.*, 269 U.S. 385 (1926). The Court held that "The dividing line between what is lawful and unlawful cannot be left to conjecture. The citizen cannot be held to answer charges based upon penal statutes whose mandates are so uncertain that they will reasonably admit of different constructions. A criminal statute cannot rest upon an uncertain foundation. The crime, and the elements constituting it, must be so clearly expressed that the ordinary person can intelligently choose, in advance, what course it is lawful for him to pursue."

# Federal Investigative Agencies

| Agency | Areas of Responsibility | *Approximate Number of Investigators/Inspectors* |
|---|---|---|
| Federal Bureau of Investigation | Counterterrorism<br>Drugs<br>Organized crime<br>Foreign counterintelligence<br>Violent crime<br>White-collar crime | 11,000 |
| Immigration and Naturalization Service | Unauthorized entry into the United States | 8,000 |
| Drug Enforcement Administration | Narcotics and controlled substances | 3,500 |
| United States Marshals Service | Prisoner transportation and custody<br>Witness protection Program<br>Service of federal court writs<br>Prisoner escape<br>Probation and parole violations<br>Court security services | 2,500 |
| Internal Revenue Service (Criminal Investigation) | Federal income tax violations | 2,900 |
| United States Secret Service | Counterfeiting offenses<br>Presidential protection | 3,225 |
| United States Customs Service | Customs law violations<br>Export law violations<br>Money laundering | 2,900 |
| Bureau of Alcohol, Tobacco, and Firearms | Firearms and explosive law violations<br>Alcohol and tobacco law violations | 2,000 |

| Agency | Areas of Responsibility | Approximate Number of Investigators/Inspectors |
|--------|------------------------|------------------------------------------------|
| United States Postal Inspection Service | Mail fraud violations Postal security | 2,225 |
| National Park Service | Criminal offenses with the national park system | 650 |
| United States Capitol Police | District of Columbia Criminal Code violations Security of Capitol complex | 1,100 |
| Bureau of Diplomatic Security | Personnel background investigations Passport and visa fraud | 700 |
| United Forest Service (Law Enforcement and Investigations) | Offenses within the national forests | 500 |
| United States Department of Agriculture (Office of Inspector General) | Food safety issues Crimes involving food stamps | 250 |
| Bureau of Indian Affairs | Criminal and quasi-criminal offenses in Indian country | 335 |
| United States Fish and Wildlife Service (Division of Law Enforcement) | U.S. wildlife statutes | 240 |
| Bureau of Land Management (Law Enforcement Division) | Violation of federal statutes regarding federal lands, archaeological sites, various wild animals, and other federal resources | 200 |
| Department of the Interior (Office of the Inspector General) | Federal land fraud violations | 40 |

APP

| Agency | Areas of Responsibility | Approximate Number of Investigators/Inspectors |
|--------|-------------------------|-----------------------------------------------|
| United States Department of Labor (Office of the Inspector General) | Violations of federal statutes concerning labor employees | 160 |
| United States Office of Labor Management Standards | Labor-Management Reporting and Disclosure Act Violations | 130 |
| United States Department of Health and Human Services (Office of the Inspector General) | Medicare and Medicaid fraud | 180 |
| United States Food and Drug Administration | Federal Food and Drug Acts, Cosmetic Act, Public Health Service Act, and the Federal Anti-Tampering Act | 110 |
| United States Environmental Protection Agency (Office of Criminal Enforcement, Forensics, and Training) | Violations of environmental and regulatory statutes | 160 |
| United States Environmental Protection Agency (Office of the Inspector General) | Environmental Protection Program fraud | 55 |
| National Oceanic and Atmospheric Administration, National Marine Fisheries Service (Staff Office for Law Enforcement) | Violations of the Larceny Act, Marine Mammal Protection Act, and the Endangered Species Act | 115 |
| United States Bureau Export Administration (Office of Export Enforcement) | Dual-use export violations | 70 |

| Agency | Areas of Responsibility | Approximate Number of Investigators/Inspectors |
|---|---|---|
| United States Social Security Administration (Office of the Inspector General) | Social Security Program fraud | 85 |
| United States Public Buildings Service (Federal Protective Service) | Offenses against the General Services Administration's controlled buildings | 65 |
| United States General Services Administration (Office of the Inspector General) | Corruption and financial crime against GSA programs | 60 |
| United States Department of Justice (Office of the Inspector General) | Misconduct and fraud within the Department of Justice | 120 |
| United States Department of Housing and Urban Development (Office of the Inspector General) | Fraud Concerning Housing and Urban Development Programs | 110 |
| United States Department of Education (Office of the Inspector General) | Federal Student Aid Program fraud | 80 |
| United States Department of Transportation (Office of the Inspector General) | Fraud against the Department of Transportation | 65 |
| United States Department of Veterans Affairs (Office of the Inspector General) | Fraud against Veteran Healthcare, Procurement, and Entitlement Programs | 65 |
| Federal Deposit Insurance Corporation (Office of the Inspector General) | Violations against the interests of the Federal Deposit Insurance Corporation | 30 |

| Agency | Areas of Responsibility | Approximate Number of Investigators/Inspectors |
|---|---|---|
| United States National Aeronautics and Space Administration (Office of the Inspector General) | Violations against National Aeronautics and Space Administration programs | 50 |
| United States Department of Energy (Office of the Inspector General) | Violations against Energy Department programs | 55 |
| Small Business Administration (Office of the Inspector General) | Fraud of SBA programs | 40 |
| United States Department of the Treasury (Office of the Inspector General) | Fraud and misconduct of Treasury Department Employees | 40 |
| United States Department of State (Office of the Inspector General) | State Department Fraud, including the Arms Control and Disarmament Agency, the U.S. Information Agency, and the Broadcasting Board of Governors | 30 |
| Amtrack Police Department | Offenses against Amtrack property | 310 |
| United States Tennessee Valley Authority Police | Criminal violations on or against Tennessee Valley Authority Properties | 180 |
| United States Tennessee Valley Authority (Office of the Inspector General) | Fraud perpetrated against Tennessee Valley Authority Programs | 30 |
| Library of Congress Police | District of Columbia code violations | 105 |
| United States Supreme Court Police | Violations of federal statutes concerning the protection of the high court and its justices | 75 |

# Abbreviations and Acronyms for Federal Organizations

**AEF,** Army Expeditionary Force
**AFOSI,** Air Force Office of Special Investigations
**AG,** Attorney General
**ATAC,** Antiterrorist Alert Center
**BLM,** Bureau of Land Management
**CGIS,** Coast Guard Investigative Service
**CID,** Criminal Investigation Command (Formerly, Criminal Investigation Division)
**CITF,** Criminal Investigation Task Force
**CIOD,** Computer Investigations and Operations Department
**CTD,** Counterterrorism Division
**DCIO,** Defense Criminal Investigation Organization
**DCIS,** Defense Criminal Investigative Service
**DEA,** Drug Enforcement Administration
**DODIG,** Department of Defense Inspector General
**DONCAF,** Department of the Navy Central Adjudication Facility
**DIS,** Defense Investigative Service
**DS,** Bureau of Diplomatic Security
**DSS,** Defense Security Service
**EPA,** Environmental Protection Agency
**FBI,** Federal Bureau of Investigation
**FDA,** Food and Drug Administration
**FLETC,** Federal Law Enforcement Training Center
**GAO,** Government Accountability Office (Formerly, Government Accounting Office)
**IG,** Inspector General
**IRS,** Internal Revenue Service
**LEPS,** Law Enforcement and Physical Security Department
**MA,** Master-at-Arms (Navy)
**MCIO,** Military Criminal Investigative Organization
**MP,** Military Police (Army and Marine Corps)
**MPC,** Military Police Command
**MPC,** Military Police Corps (Army)
**MPFU,** Major Procurement Fraud Unit
**MTAC,** Multi-Threat Alert Center
**NCIS,** Naval Criminal Investigative Service
**NIS,** Naval Investigative Service
**NISCOM,** Naval Investigative Service Command
**NSIC,** Naval Security and Investigation Command
**ODI,** Office of Defense Intelligence
**OIC,** Office of Criminal Investigations
**ONI,** Office of Naval Intelligence
**PMO,** Provost Marshal's Office
**PSI,** Postal Inspection Service
**PSO,** Protective Services Operations
**USACIDC,** United States Army Criminal Investigation Command

# Justices of the U.S. Supreme Court

## Chief Justices

### John Jay (1745–1829)

| | |
|---|---|
| Nominated by: | George Washington |
| Sworn in: | October 19, 1789 |
| Tenure: | 5 years, 8 months[*] |
| Party: | Federalist |
| Religion: | Episcopalian |
| State: | New York |
| Prior public service: | President of the Congress, U.S. Commissioner to Spain and France, negotiator of the "Jay Treaty" (1793–1794), Secretary of Foreign Affairs, and two-term governor of New York |

### John Rutledge (1732–1810)

| | |
|---|---|
| Nominated by: | George Washington |
| Sworn in: | August 12, 1795 |
| Tenure: | 5 years, 10 months[*] |
| Party: | Federalist |
| Religion: | Church of England |
| State: | South Carolina |
| Prior public service: | Associate Justice of the U.S. Supreme Court, later Chief Justice |

### Oliver Ellsworth (1745–1807)

| | |
|---|---|
| Nominated by: | George Washington |
| Sworn in: | March 8, 1796 |
| Tenure: | 4 years, 9 months[*] |
| Party: | Federalist |
| Religion: | Congregationalist |
| State: | Connecticut |
| Prior public service: | U.S. Senate, and Connecticut Supreme Court |

### John Marshall (1755–1835)

| | |
|---|---|
| Nominated by: | John Adams |
| Sworn in: | February 4, 1801 |
| Tenure: | 34 years, 5 months[*] |
| Party: | Federalist |
| Religion: | Episcopalian |
| State: | Virginia |
| Prior public service: | Virginia House of Delegates, U.S. Secretary of War, U.S. House of Representative, and U.S. Secretary of State |

## Roger B. Taney (1777–1864)

| | |
|---|---|
| Nominated by: | Andrew Jackson |
| Sworn in: | March 28, 1836 |
| Tenure: | 28 years, 6 months* |
| Party: | Democrat |
| Religion: | Catholic |
| State: | Maryland |
| Prior public service: | U.S. Attorney General |

## Salmon P. Chase (1801–1873)

| | |
|---|---|
| Nominated by: | Abraham Lincoln |
| Sworn in: | December 15, 1864 |
| Tenure: | 8 years, 4 months* |
| Party: | Republican |
| Religion: | Episcopalian |
| State: | Ohio |
| Prior public service: | U.S. Senator (Ohio), Governor of Ohio, and U.S. Secretary of the Treasury |

## Morrison R. Waite (1816–1888)

| | |
|---|---|
| Nominated by: | Ulysses S. Grant |
| Sworn in: | March 4, 1874 |
| Tenure: | 14 years* |
| Party: | Republican |
| Religion: | Episcopal |
| State: | Ohio |
| Prior public service: | None |

## Melville W. Fuller (1833–1910)

| | |
|---|---|
| Nominated by: | Grover Cleveland |
| Sworn in: | October 8, 1888 |
| Tenure: | 21 years, 8 months* |
| Party: | Democrat |
| Religion: | Episcopalian |
| State: | Illinois |
| Prior public service: | None |

## Edward D. White (1845–1921)

| | |
|---|---|
| Nominated by: | William Howard Taft |
| Sworn in: | December 19, 1910 |
| Tenure: | 27 years, 2 months* |
| Party: | Democrat |
| Religion: | Catholic |
| State: | Louisiana |
| Prior public service: | Associate Justice of the U.S. Supreme Court and the Louisiana Supreme Court, and the U.S. Senate |

APP

## William Howard Taft (1857–1930)

| | |
|---|---|
| Nominated by: | Warren G. Harding |
| Sworn in: | July 11, 1921 |
| Tenure: | 8 years, 6 months[*] |
| Party: | Republican |
| Religion: | Unitarian |
| State: | Connecticut |
| Prior public service: | President of the United States, Secretary of War, U.S. Court of Appeals for the 6th Circuit, and Governor General of the Philippines |

## Charles Evans Hughes (1862–1948)

| | |
|---|---|
| Nominated by: | Herbert Hoover |
| Sworn in: | February 13, 1930 |
| Tenure: | 30 years, 8 months[*] |
| Party: | Republican |
| Religion: | Baptist |
| State: | New York |
| Prior public service: | Associate Justice of the U.S. Supreme Court, U.S. Secretary of State, and U.S. Court of Appeals for the 11th Circuit |

## Harlan Fiske Stone (1872–1946)

| | |
|---|---|
| Nominated by: | Franklin Delano Roosevelt |
| Sworn in: | July 3, 1941 |
| Tenure: | 21 years, 2 months[*] |
| Party: | Democrat |
| Religion: | Episcopalian |
| State: | New York |
| Prior public service: | Associate Justice of the U.S. Supreme Court and U.S. Attorney General |

## Fred M. Vinson (1890–1953)

| | |
|---|---|
| Nominated by: | Harry S. Truman |
| Sworn in: | June 24, 1946 |
| Tenure: | 7 years, 2 months[*] |
| Party: | Democrat |
| Religion: | Methodist |
| State: | Kentucky |
| Prior public service: | U.S. Court of Appeals for the D.C. Circuit |

## Earl Warren (1891–1974)

| | |
|---|---|
| Nominated by: | Dwight David Eisenhower |
| Sworn in: | October 5, 1953 |
| Tenure: | 15 years, 8 months[*] |
| Party: | Republican |
| Religion: | Presbyterian |
| State: | California |
| Prior public service: | Governor of California and California Attorney General |

## Warren E. Burger (1907–1995)

| | |
|---|---|
| Nominated by: | Richard Milhous Nixon |
| Sworn in: | June 23, 1969 |
| Tenure: | 17 years, 3 months* |
| Party: | Republican |
| Religion: | Presbyterian |
| State: | Virginia |
| Prior public service: | U.S. Court of Appeals for the D.C. Circuit and Assistant U.S. Attorney General |

## William H. Rehnquist (1924–2005)

| | |
|---|---|
| Nominated by: | Ronald Wilson Reagan |
| Sworn in: | September 26, 1986 |
| Tenure: | 33 years, 7 months* |
| Party: | Republican |
| Religion: | Lutheran |
| State: | Arizona |
| Prior public service: | Associate Justice of the U.S. Supreme Court and Assistant U.S. Attorney General |

## John Roberts, Jr. (1955–)

| | |
|---|---|
| Nominated by: | George W. Bush |
| Sworn in: | September 29, 2005 |
| Tenure: | Incomplete |
| Party: | Republican |
| Religion: | Catholic |
| State: | New York |
| Prior public service: | U.S. Court of Appeals for the D.C. Circuit |

## *Associate Justices*

## Sammuel Alito (1950– )

| | |
|---|---|
| Nominated by: | George W. Bush |
| Sworn in: | January 31, 2006 |
| Tenure: | Incomplete |
| Party: | Republican |
| Religion: | Catholic |
| State: | New Jersey |
| Prior public service: | U.S. Court of Appeals for the 3rd Circuit |

## Henry Baldwin (1780–1844)

| | |
|---|---|
| Nominated by: | Andrew Jackson |
| Sworn in: | January 18, 1830 |
| Tenure: | 14 years, 3 months* |
| Party: | Democrat |
| Religion: | Trinity Church |
| State: | Pennsylvania |
| Prior public service: | U.S. House of Representatives |

APP

## Philip P. Barbour (1783–1841)

| | |
|---|---|
| Nominated by: | Andrew Jackson |
| Sworn in: | May 12, 1836 |
| Tenure: | 4 years, 9 months* |
| Party: | Democrat |
| Religion: | Episcopalian |
| State: | Virginia |
| Prior public service: | U.S. District Court (Eastern District of Virginia) and U.S. House of Representatives |

## Hugo L. Black (1886–1971)

| | |
|---|---|
| Nominated by: | Franklin Delano Roosevelt |
| Sworn in: | August 19, 1937 |
| Tenure: | 34 years, 1 month* |
| Party: | Democrat |
| Religion: | Baptist |
| State: | Alabama |
| Prior public service: | Alabama police court judge, and U.S. Senate |

## Harry A. Blackmun (1908–1999)

| | |
|---|---|
| Nominated by: | Richard Milhous Nixon |
| Sworn in: | June 9, 1970 |
| Tenure: | 24 years, 2 months* |
| Party: | Republican |
| Religion: | Methodist |
| State: | Minnesota |
| Prior public service: | U.S. Court of Appeals for the 8th Circuit |

## John Blair (1732–1800)

| | |
|---|---|
| Nominated by: | George Washington |
| Sworn in: | February 2, 1790 |
| Tenure: | 5 years, 9 months* |
| Party: | Federalist |
| Religion: | Presbyterian |
| State: | Virginia |
| Prior public service: | Virginia Supreme Court of Appeals and the Virginia Constitutional Convention |

## Samuel Blatchford (1820–1893)

| | |
|---|---|
| Nominated by: | Chester Arthur |
| Sworn in: | April 3, 1882 |
| Tenure: | 11 years, 3 months* |
| Party: | Republican |
| Religion: | Presbyterian |
| State: | New York |
| Prior public service: | U.S. District Court and U.S. Court of Appeals for the 2nd Circuit |

## Joseph P. Bradley (1813–1892)

| | |
|---|---|
| Nominated by: | Ulysses S. Grant |
| Sworn in: | March 23, 1870 |
| Tenure: | 21 years, 10 months* |
| Party: | Republican |
| Religion: | Presbyterian |
| State: | New Jersey |
| Prior public service: | None |

## Louis D. Brandeis (1856–1941)

| | |
|---|---|
| Nominated by: | Woodrow Wilson |
| Sworn in: | June 5, 1916 |
| Tenure: | 22 years, 8 months* |
| Party: | Democrat |
| Religion: | Jewish |
| State: | Massachusetts |
| Prior public service: | None |

## William J. Brennan, Jr. (1906–1997)

| | |
|---|---|
| Nominated by: | Dwight David Eisenhower |
| Sworn in: | October 16, 1956 |
| Tenure: | 33 years, 9 months* |
| Party: | Democrat |
| Religion: | Catholic |
| State: | New Jersey |
| Prior public service: | New Jersey Supreme Court Justice, New Jersey Superior Court, Appellate Division, and Judge, Superior Court, New Jersey |

## David J. Brewer (1837–1910)

| | |
|---|---|
| Nominated by: | Benjamin Harrison |
| Sworn in: | January 6, 1890 |
| Tenure: | 20 years, 3 months* |
| Party: | Republican |
| Religion: | Protestant |
| State: | Kansas |
| Prior public service: | Kansas Supreme Court and U.S. Court of Appeals for the 8th Circuit |

## Stephen G. Breyer (1938– )

| | |
|---|---|
| Nominated by: | William Jefferson Clinton |
| Sworn in: | August 3, 1994 |
| Tenure: | Incomplete |
| Party: | Democrat |
| Religion: | Jewish |
| State: | California |
| Prior public service: | U.S. Court of Appeals for the 1st Circuit |

APP

## Henry B. Brown (1836–1913)

| | |
|---|---|
| Nominated by: | Benjamin Harrison |
| Sworn in: | January 5, 1891 |
| Tenure: | 15 years, 5 months[*] |
| Party: | Republican |
| Religion: | Protestant |
| State: | Michigan |
| Prior public service: | U.S. District Court (Michigan) |

## Harold Burton (1888–1964)

| | |
|---|---|
| Nominated by: | Harry S. Truman |
| Sworn in: | October 1, 1945 |
| Tenure: | 13 years[*] |
| Party: | Republican |
| Religion: | Unitarian |
| State: | Ohio |
| Prior public service: | U.S. Senate (Ohio) and Mayor of Cleveland |

## Pierce Butler (1866–1939)

| | |
|---|---|
| Nominated by: | Warren G. Harding |
| Sworn in: | January 2, 1923 |
| Tenure: | 16 years, 10 months[*] |
| Party: | Democrat |
| Religion: | Catholic |
| State: | Minnesota |
| Prior public service: | None |

## James F. Byrnes (1879–1972)

| | |
|---|---|
| Nominated by: | Franklin Delano Roosevelt |
| Sworn in: | July 8, 1941 |
| Tenure: | 1 year, 3 months[*] |
| Party: | Democrat |
| Religion: | Episcopalian |
| State: | South Carolina |
| Prior public service: | U.S. Senate (South Carolina) |

## John A. Campbell (1811–1889)

| | |
|---|---|
| Nominated by: | Franklin Pierce |
| Sworn in: | April 11, 1853 |
| Tenure: | 8 years[*] |
| Party: | Democrat |
| Religion: | Episcopalian |
| State: | Alabama |
| Prior public service: | None |

## Benjamin N. Cardozo (1870–1938)

| | |
|---|---|
| Nominated by: | Herbert Hoover |
| Sworn in: | March 14, 1932 |
| Tenure: | 6 years, 4 months* |
| Party: | Democrat |
| Religion: | Jewish |
| State: | New York |
| Prior public service: | New York Court of Appeals |

## John Catron (1786–1865)

| | |
|---|---|
| Nominated by: | Andrew Jackson |
| Sworn in: | May 1, 1837 |
| Tenure: | 28 years, 1 month* |
| Party: | Democrat |
| Religion: | Presbyterian |
| State: | Tennessee |
| Prior public service: | Chief Justice, Tennessee Supreme Court |

## Samuel Chase (1741–1811)

| | |
|---|---|
| Nominated by: | George Washington |
| Sworn in: | February 4, 1796 |
| Tenure: | 15 years, 4 months* |
| Party: | Federalist |
| Religion: | Episcopalian |
| State: | Maryland |
| Prior public service: | Chief Judge, General Court of Maryland |

## Tom C. Clark (1899–1977)

| | |
|---|---|
| Nominated by: | Harry S. Truman |
| Sworn in: | August 24, 1949 |
| Tenure: | 17 years, 9 months* |
| Party: | Democrat |
| Religion: | Presbyterian |
| State: | Texas |
| Prior public service: | U.S. Attorney General, Assistant Attorney General, and Special Assistant, Department of Justice |

## John H. Clarke (1857–1945)

| | |
|---|---|
| Nominated by: | Woodrow Wilson |
| Sworn in: | October 9, 1916 |
| Tenure: | 5 years, 11 months* |
| Party: | Democrat |
| Religion: | Protestant |
| State: | Ohio |
| Prior public service: | U.S. District Court (Ohio) |

## Nathan Clifford (1803–1881)

| | |
|---|---|
| Nominated by: | James Buchanan |
| Sworn in: | January 21, 1858 |
| Tenure: | 23 years, 6 months[*] |
| Party: | Democrat |
| Religion: | Congregational and later Unitarian |
| State: | Maine |
| Prior public service: | None |

## Benjamin R. Curtis (1809–1874)

| | |
|---|---|
| Nominated by: | Millard Fillmore |
| Sworn in: | October 10, 1851 |
| Tenure: | 6 years[*] |
| Party: | Whig |
| Religion: | Unitarian and later Episcopalian |
| State: | Massachusetts |
| Prior public service: | Massachusetts House of Representatives |

## William Cushing (1732–1810)

| | |
|---|---|
| Nominated by: | George Washington |
| Sworn in: | February 15, 1790 |
| Tenure: | 5 years, 10 months[*] |
| Party: | Federalist |
| Religion: | Unitarian |
| State: | Massachusetts |
| Prior public service: | Vice President of the Massachusetts ratifying convention of 1788 and justice of the peace and judge of probates |

## Peter V. Daniel (1784–1860)

| | |
|---|---|
| Nominated by: | Martin Van Buren |
| Sworn in: | January 10, 1842 |
| Tenure: | 18 years, 5 months[*] |
| Party: | Democrat |
| Religion: | Episcopalian |
| State: | Virginia |
| Prior public service: | U.S. District Court (Virginia) |

## David Davis (1815–1886)

| | |
|---|---|
| Nominated by: | Abraham Lincoln |
| Sworn in: | December 10, 1862 |
| Tenure: | 14 years, 3 months[*] |
| Party: | Democrat |
| Religion: | Not a member of any church |
| State: | Illinois |
| Prior public service: | Illinois 8th Judicial Circuit |

## William R. Day (1849–1923)

| | |
|---|---|
| Nominated by: | Theodore Roosevelt |
| Sworn in: | March 2, 1903 |
| Tenure: | 19 years, 8 months[*] |
| Party: | Republican |
| Religion: | Protestant |
| State: | Ohio |
| Prior public service: | U.S. Court of Appeals for the 6th Circuit |

## William O. Douglas (1898–1980)

| | |
|---|---|
| Nominated by: | Franklin Delano Roosevelt |
| Sworn in: | April 17, 1939 |
| Tenure: | 36 years, 7 months[*] |
| Party: | Democrat |
| Religion: | Presbyterian |
| State: | Connecticut |
| Prior public service: | Advisor to President Franklin D. Roosevelt |

## Gabriel Duvall (1752–1844)

| | |
|---|---|
| Nominated by: | James Madison |
| Sworn in: | November 23, 1811 |
| Tenure: | 23 years, 2 months[*] |
| Party: | Democrat-[*]Republican |
| Religion: | French Protestant |
| State: | Maryland |
| Prior public service: | Chief Justice, General Court of Maryland |

## Stephen J. Field (1816–1899)

| | |
|---|---|
| Nominated by: | Abraham Lincoln |
| Sworn in: | May 20, 1863 |
| Tenure: | 34 years, 6 months[*] |
| Party: | Democrat |
| Religion: | Episcopalian |
| State: | California |
| Prior public service: | California Supreme Court |

## Abe Fortas (1910–1982)

| | |
|---|---|
| Nominated by: | Lyndon Baines Johnson |
| Sworn in: | October 4, 1965 |
| Tenure: | 3 years, 7 months[*] |
| Party: | Democrat |
| Religion: | Jewish |
| State: | Tennessee |
| Prior public service: | Assistant director, U.S. Securities and Exchange Commission and Under Secretary, Interior Department |

APP

## Felix Frankfurter (1882–1965)

| | |
|---|---|
| Nominated by: | Franklin Delano Roosevelt |
| Sworn in: | January 30, 1939 |
| Tenure: | 23 years, 7 months[*] |
| Party: | Democrat |
| Religion: | Jewish |
| State: | Massachusetts |
| Prior public service: | Advisor to President Franklin D. Roosevelt |

## Ruth Bader Ginsburg (1933– )

| | |
|---|---|
| Nominated by: | William Jefferson Clinton |
| Sworn in: | August 10, 1993 |
| Tenure: | Incomplete |
| Party: | Democrat |
| Religion: | Jewish |
| State: | Washington, D.C. |
| Prior public service: | U.S. Court of Appeals for the D.C. Circuit |

## Arthur J. Goldberg (1908–1990)

| | |
|---|---|
| Nominated by: | John Fitzgerald Kennedy |
| Sworn in: | October 1, 1962 |
| Tenure: | 2 years, 10 months[*] |
| Party: | Democrat |
| Religion: | Jewish |
| State: | Illinois |
| Prior public service: | U.S. Secretary of Labor |

## Horace Gray (1828–1902)

| | |
|---|---|
| Nominated by: | Chester Arthur |
| Sworn in: | January 9, 1882 |
| Tenure: | 20 years, 8 months[*] |
| Party: | Republican |
| Religion: | Unitarian or Congregational |
| State: | Massachusetts |
| Prior public service: | Chief Justice, Massachusetts Supreme Court |

## Robert C. Grier (1794–1870)

| | |
|---|---|
| Nominated by: | James K. Polk |
| Sworn in: | August 10, 1846 |
| Tenure: | 23 years, 6 months[*] |
| Party: | Republican |
| Religion: | Presbyterian |
| State: | Pennsylvania |
| Prior public service: | Pennsylvania (Allegheny County) District Court |

## John M. Harlan (1899–1971)

| | |
|---|---|
| Nominated by: | Dwight David Eisenhower |
| Sworn in: | March 28, 1955 |
| Tenure: | 16 years, 6 months* |
| Party: | Republican |
| Religion: | Presbyterian |
| State: | New York |
| Prior public service: | U.S. Court of Appeals for the 2nd Circuit |

## Oliver Wendell Holmes, Jr. (1841–1935)

| | |
|---|---|
| Nominated by: | Theodore Roosevelt |
| Sworn in: | December 8, 1902 |
| Tenure: | 29 years, 1 month* |
| Party: | Republican |
| Religion: | Unitarian |
| State: | Massachusetts |
| Prior public service: | Chief Justice, Massachusetts Supreme Court |

## Charles Evans Hughes (1862–1948)

| | |
|---|---|
| Nominated by: | William Howard Taft |
| Sworn in: | October 10, 1910 |
| Tenure: | 30 years, 9 months* |
| Party: | Republican |
| Religion: | Baptist |
| State: | New York |
| Prior public service: | None |

## Ward Hunt (1810–1886)

| | |
|---|---|
| Nominated by: | Ulysses S. Grant |
| Sworn in: | January 9, 1873 |
| Tenure: | 9 years* |
| Party: | Republican |
| Religion: | Episcopalian |
| State: | New York |
| Prior public service: | New York Court of Appeals |

## James Iredell (1751–1799)

| | |
|---|---|
| Nominated by: | George Washington |
| Sworn in: | May 12, 1790 |
| Tenure: | 9 years, 5 months* |
| Party: | Federalist |
| Religion: | Episcopalian |
| State: | North Carolina |
| Prior public service: | Superior Court of North Carolina |

APP

## Howell E. Jackson (1832–1895)

Nominated by:           Benjamin Harrison
Sworn in:               March 4, 1893
Tenure:                 2 years, 5 months*
Party:                  Democrat
Religion:               Baptist
State:                  Tennessee
Prior public service:   U.S. Court of Appeals for the 6th Circuit

## Robert H. Jackson (1892–1954)

Nominated by:           Franklin Delano Roosevelt
Sworn in:               July 11, 1941
Tenure:                 13 years, 3 months*
Party:                  Democrat
Religion:               Episcopalian
State:                  Pennsylvania
Prior pubic service:    U.S. Solicitor General and U.S. Attorney General

## Thomas Johnson (1732–1819)

Nominated by:           George Washington
Sworn in:               August 6, 1792
Tenure:                 5 months*
Party:                  Federalist
Religion:               Episcopalian
State:                  Maryland
Prior public service:   Chief Judge, General Court of Maryland, Continental Congress,
                        Maryland House of Delegates, and Governor of Maryland

## William Johnson (1771–1834)

Nominated by:           Thomas Jefferson
Sworn in:               May 7, 1804
Tenure:                 30 years, 3 months*
Party:                  Democrat–Republican
Religion:               Presbyterian
State:                  South Carolina
Prior public service:   Court of Common Pleas (South Carolina) and South Carolina
                        General Assembly

## Anthony Kennedy (1936– )

Nominated by:           Ronald Wilson Reagan
Sworn in:               February 18, 1988
Tenure:                 Incomplete
Party:                  Republican
Religion:               Catholic
State:                  California
Prior public service:   U.S. Court of Appeals for the 9th Circuit

## Joseph R. Lamar (1857–1916)

| | |
|---|---|
| Nominated by: | William Howard Taft |
| Sworn in: | January 3, 1911 |
| Tenure: | 5 years* |
| Party: | Democrat |
| Religion: | Church of Disciples |
| State: | Georgia |
| Prior public service: | Georgia Supreme Court |

## Lucius Q.C. Lamar (1825–1893)

| | |
|---|---|
| Nominated by: | Grover Cleveland |
| Sworn in: | January 18, 1888 |
| Tenure: | 5 years* |
| Party: | Democrat |
| Religion: | Methodist |
| State: | Mississippi |
| Prior public service: | U.S. Senate and U.S. Secretary of the Interior |

## Brockholst Livingston (1757–1823)

| | |
|---|---|
| Nominated by: | Thomas Jefferson |
| Sworn in: | January 20, 1807 |
| Tenure: | 16 years, 2 months* |
| Party: | Democrat–Republican |
| Religion: | Presbyterian |
| State: | New York |
| Prior public service: | New York Supreme Court and New York General Assembly |

## Horace H. Lurton (1844–1914)

| | |
|---|---|
| Nominated by: | William Howard Taft |
| Sworn in: | January 3, 1910 |
| Tenure: | 4 years, 6 months* |
| Party: | Democrat |
| Religion: | Episcopalian |
| State: | Tennessee |
| Prior public service: | Tennessee Supreme Court and U.S. Court of Appeals for the 6th Circuit |

## Thurgood Marshall (1908–1993)

| | |
|---|---|
| Nominated by: | Lyndon Baines Johnson |
| Sworn in: | October 2, 1967 |
| Tenure: | 24 years* |
| Party: | Democrat |
| Religion: | Episcopalian |
| State: | New York |
| Prior public service: | U.S. Court of Appeals for the 2nd Circuit and U.S. Solicitor General |

APP

## Stanley Matthews (1824–1889)

| | |
|---|---|
| Nominated by: | Grover Cleveland |
| Sworn in: | May 17, 1881 |
| Tenure: | 7 years, 10 months* |
| Party: | Republican |
| Religion: | Presbyterian |
| State: | Ohio |
| Prior public service: | Hamilton County Court of Common Pleas (Ohio) and Superior Court of Cincinnati, Ohio |

## Joseph McKenna (1843–1926)

| | |
|---|---|
| Nominated by: | William McKinley |
| Sworn in: | January 26, 1898 |
| Tenure: | 26 years, 11 months* |
| Party: | Republican |
| Religion: | Catholic |
| State: | California |
| Prior public service: | U.S. Court of Appeals for the D.C. Circuit and U.S. Attorney General |

## John McKinley (1780–1852)

| | |
|---|---|
| Nominated by: | Martin Van Buren |
| Sworn in: | January 9, 1838 |
| Tenure: | 14 years, 6 months* |
| Party: | Democrat |
| Religion: | Protestant |
| State: | Alabama |
| Prior public service: | U.S. Senate (two non-consecutive terms) |

## John McLean (1785–1861)

| | |
|---|---|
| Nominated by: | Andrew Jackson |
| Sworn in: | January 11, 1830 |
| Tenure: | 31 years, 3 months* |
| Party: | Democrat |
| Religion: | Methodist Episcopalian |
| State: | Ohio |
| Prior public service: | Ohio Supreme Court, U.S. House of Representatives, and U.S. Postmaster General |

## James C. McReynolds (1862–1946)

| | |
|---|---|
| Nominated by: | Woodrow Wilson |
| Sworn in: | October 12, 1914 |
| Tenure: | 26 years, 3 months* |
| Party: | Democrat |
| Religion: | Disciples of Christ |
| State: | Tennessee |
| Prior public service: | U.S. Attorney General |

## Samuel F. Miller (1816–1890)

| | |
|---|---|
| Nominated by: | Abraham Lincoln |
| Sworn in: | July 21, 1862 |
| Tenure: | 28 years, 3 months[*] |
| Party: | Republican |
| Religion: | Unitarian |
| State: | Iowa |
| Prior public service: | Justice of the Peace, Knox County, Kentucky |

## Sherman Minton (1890–1965)

| | |
|---|---|
| Nominated by: | Harry S. Truman |
| Sworn in: | October 12, 1949 |
| Tenure: | 7 years[*] |
| Party: | Democrat |
| Religion: | Catholic |
| State: | Indiana |
| Prior public service: | U.S. Court of Appeals for the 7th Circuit |

## William H. Moody (1853–1917)

| | |
|---|---|
| Nominated by: | Theodore Roosevelt |
| Sworn in: | December 17, 1906 |
| Tenure: | 3 years, 11 months[*] |
| Party: | Republican |
| Religion: | Episcopalian |
| State: | Massachusetts |
| Prior public service: | U.S. Attorney General |

## Alfred Moore (1755–1810)

| | |
|---|---|
| Nominated by: | John Adams |
| Sworn in: | April 21, 1800 |
| Tenure: | 3 years 9 months[*] |
| Party: | Federalist |
| Religion: | Episcopalian |
| State: | North Carolina |
| Prior public service: | Superior Court (North Carolina) and North Carolina General Assembly |

## Frank Murphy (1890–1949)

| | |
|---|---|
| Nominated by: | Franklin Delano Roosevelt |
| Sworn in: | February 5, 1940 |
| Tenure: | 9 years, 5 months[*] |
| Party: | Democrat |
| Religion: | Catholic |
| State: | Michigan |
| Prior public service: | Mayor of Detroit, Judge in the Detroit Recorder's Court, Governor of Michigan, and U.S. Attorney General |

APP

## Samuel Nelson (1792–1873)

Nominated by:          John Tyler
Sworn in:              February 27, 1845
Tenure:                27 years, 9 months*
Party:                 Democrat
Religion:              Protestant
State:                 New York
Prior public service:  Chief Justice, New York Supreme Court

## Sandra Day O'Connor (1930– )

Nominated by:          Ronald Wilson Reagan
Sworn in:              September 25, 1981
Tenure:                Incomplete
Party:                 Republican
Religion:              Episcopalian
State:                 Arizona
Prior public service:  Arizona Court of Appeals, Arizona State Senator,
                       and Arizona Assistant Attorney General

## William Paterson (1745–1806)

Nominated by:          George Washington
Sworn in:              March 11, 1793
Tenure:                13 years, 6 months*
Party:                 Federalist
Religion:              Protestant
State:                 New Jersey
Prior public service:  U.S. Senate and Governor of New Jersey

## Rufus Peckham (1838–1909)

Nominated by:          Grover Cleveland
Sworn in:              January 6, 1896
Tenure:                13 years, 9 months*
Party:                 Democrat
Religion:              Episcopalian
State:                 New York
Prior public service:  New York Court of Appeals

## Mahlon Pitney (1858–1924)

Nominated by:          William Howard Taft
Sworn in:              March 18, 1912
Tenure:                10 years, 9 months*
Party:                 Republican
Religion:              Presbyterian
State:                 New Jersey
Prior public service:  New Jersey Supreme Court

## Lewis F. Powell, Jr. (1907–1998)

Nominated by: Richard Milhous Nixon
Sworn in: January 9, 1970
Tenure: 15 years, 5 months[*]
Party: Democrat
Religion: Presbyterian
State: Virginia
Prior public service: None

## Stanley Reed (1884–1980)

Nominated by: Franklin Delano Roosevelt
Sworn in: January 31, 1938
Tenure: 19 years, 1 month[*]
Party: Democrat
Religion: Protestant
State: Kentucky
Prior public service: U.S. Solicitor General

## William H. Rehnquist (1924–2005)

Nominated by: Richard Milhous Nixon
Sworn in: January 7, 1972
Tenure: 33 years, 8 months[*]
Party: Republican
Religion: Lutheran
State: Arizona
Prior public service: Later became Chief Justice of the U.S. Supreme Court

## Owen J. Roberts (1875–1955)

Nominated by: Herbert Hoover
Sworn in: June 2, 1930
Tenure: 15 years, 2 months[*]
Party: Republican
Religion: Episcopalian
State: Pennsylvania
Prior public service: None

## John Rutledge (1739–1800)

Nominated by: George Washington
Sworn in: February 15, 1790
Tenure: 5 years, 10 months[*]
Party: Federalist
Religion: Church of England
State: South Carolina
Prior public service: Chief Justice, South Carolina Supreme Court, South Carolina
Chancery Court, and Chair of South Carolina's Delegation
to the U.S. Constitutional Convention

APP

## Wiley B. Rutledge (1894–1949)

Nominated by:        Franklin Delano Roosevelt
Sworn in:            February 15, 1943
Tenure:              6 years, 7 months*
Party:               Democrat
Religion:            Unitarian
State:               Iowa
Prior public service:  U.S. Court of Appeals for the D.C. Circuit

## Edward T. Sanford (1865–1930)

Nominated by:        Warren G. Harding
Sworn in:            February 19, 1923
Tenure:              7 years*
Party:               Republican
Religion:            Episcopalian
State:               Tennessee
Prior public service:  U.S. District Court (Tennessee)

## Antonin Scalia (1936– )

Nominated by:        Ronald Wilson Reagan
Sworn in:            September 26, 1986
Tenure:              Incomplete*
Party:               Republican
Religion:            Catholic
State:               Washington, D.C.
Prior public service:  U.S. Court of Appeals for the D.C. Circuit

## George Shiras, Jr. (1832–1924)

Nominated by:        Benjamin Harrison
Sworn in:            October 10, 1892
Tenure:              10 years, 4 months*
Party:               Republican
Religion:            Presbyterian
State:               Pennsylvania
Prior public service:  None

## David H. Souter (1939– )

Nominated by:        George Herbert Walker Bush
Sworn in:            October 9, 1990
Tenure:              Incomplete
Party:               Republican
Religion:            Episcopalian
State:               New Hampshire
Prior public service:  U.S. Court of Appeals for the 1st. Circuit and New Hampshire
                     Supreme Court

## John Paul Stevens (1920– )

| | |
|---|---|
| Nominated by: | Gerald R. Ford |
| Sworn in: | December 19, 1975 |
| Tenure: | Incomplete |
| Party: | Republican |
| Religion: | Protestant |
| State: | Illinois |
| Prior public service: | U.S. Court of Appeals for the 7th Circuit |

## Potter Stewart (1915–1985)

| | |
|---|---|
| Nominated by: | Dwight David Eisenhower |
| Sworn in: | October 14, 1958 |
| Tenure: | 22 years, 8 months[*] |
| Party: | Republican |
| Religion: | Episcopalian |
| State: | Ohio |
| Prior public service: | U.S. Court of Appeals for the 6th Circuit |

## Harlan Fiske Stone (1872–1946)

| | |
|---|---|
| Nominated by: | Calvin Coolidge |
| Sworn in: | February 5, 1925 |
| Tenure: | 21 years, 2 months |
| Party: | Republican |
| Religion: | Episcopalian |
| State: | New York |
| Prior public service: | U.S. Attorney General and later Chief Justice of U.S. Supreme Court |

## Joseph Story (1779–1845)

| | |
|---|---|
| Nominated by: | James Madison |
| Sworn in: | February 3, 1812 |
| Tenure: | 33 years, 7 months[*] |
| Party: | Democrat–Republican |
| Religion: | Unitarian |
| State: | Massachusetts |
| Prior public service: | Massachusetts General Assembly and U.S. House of Representatives |

## William Strong (1808–1895)

| | |
|---|---|
| Nominated by: | Ulysses S. Grant |
| Sworn in: | March 14, 1870 |
| Tenure: | 10 years, 9 months[*] |
| Party: | Republican |
| Religion: | Presbyterian |
| State: | Pennsylvania |
| Prior public service: | Pennsylvania Supreme Court |

APP

## George Sutherland (1862–1942)

| | |
|---|---|
| Nominated by: | Warren G. Harding |
| Sworn in: | October 2, 1922 |
| Tenure: | 15 years, 3 months* |
| Party: | Republican |
| Religion: | Episcopalian |
| State: | Utah |
| Prior public service: | None |

## Noah Swayne (1804–1884)

| | |
|---|---|
| Nominated by: | Abraham Lincoln |
| Sworn in: | January 27, 1862 |
| Tenure: | 19 years* |
| Party: | Republican |
| Religion: | Quaker |
| State: | Ohio |
| Prior public service: | U.S. Attorney (Ohio) and Ohio State Attorney General |

## Clarence Thomas (1948– )

| | |
|---|---|
| Nominated by: | George Herbert Walker Bush |
| Sworn in: | October 23, 1991 |
| Tenure: | Incomplete |
| Party: | Republican |
| Religion: | Catholic |
| State: | Washington, D.C. |
| Prior public service: | U.S. Court of Appeals for the D.C. Circuit |

## Smith Thompson (1768–1843)

| | |
|---|---|
| Nominated by: | James Monroe |
| Sworn in: | September 1, 1823 |
| Tenure: | 20 years, 3 months* |
| Party: | Democrat–Republican |
| Religion: | Presbyterian |
| State: | New York |
| Prior public service: | Chief Justice, New York Supreme Court and New York State General Assembly |

## Thomas Todd (1765–1826)

| | |
|---|---|
| Nominated by: | Thomas Jefferson |
| Sworn in: | May 4, 1807 |
| Tenure: | 18 years, 9 months* |
| Party: | Democrat–Republican |
| Religion: | Presbyterian |
| State: | Kentucky |
| Prior public service: | Governor of Kentucky and Chief Justice, Kentucky Court of Appeals |

### Robert Trimble (1776–1828)

| | |
|---|---|
| Nominated by: | John Quincy Adams |
| Sworn in: | June 16, 1826 |
| Tenure: | 2 years, 2 months* |
| Party: | Democrat–Republican |
| Religion: | Protestant |
| State: | Kentucky |
| Prior public service: | Kentucky Court of Appeals and U.S. District Court (Kentucky) |

### Willis Van Devanter (1859–1941)

| | |
|---|---|
| Nominated by: | William Howard Taft |
| Sworn in: | January 3, 1911 |
| Tenure: | 26 years, 5 months* |
| Party: | Republican |
| Religion: | Episcopalian |
| State: | Wyoming |
| Prior public service: | U.S. Court of Appeals for the 8th Circuit |

### Bushrod Washington (1762–1829)

| | |
|---|---|
| Nominated by: | John Adams |
| Sworn in: | February 4, 1799 |
| Tenure: | 30 years, 10 months* |
| Party: | Federalist |
| Religion: | Episcopalian |
| State: | Virginia |
| Prior public service: | Virginia House of Delegates (Virginia ratifying convention for the U.S. Constitution) |

### James M. Wayne (1770–1867)

| | |
|---|---|
| Nominated by: | Andrew Jackson |
| Sworn in: | January 14, 1835 |
| Tenure: | 32 years, 6 months* |
| Party: | Democrat |
| Religion: | Protestant |
| State: | Georgia |
| Prior public service: | Georgia Superior Court, Georgia General Assembly, and U.S. House of Representatives |

### Byron R. White (1917–2002)

| | |
|---|---|
| Nominated by: | John Fitzgerald Kennedy |
| Sworn in: | April 16, 1962 |
| Tenure: | 31 years, 2 months* |
| Party: | Democrat |
| Religion: | Episcopalian |
| State: | Colorado |
| Prior public service: | Deputy U.S. Attorney |

APP

## Edward D. White (1845–1921)

| | |
|---|---|
| Nominated by: | Grover Cleveland |
| Sworn in: | March 12, 1894 |
| Tenure: | 27 years, 2 months* |
| Party: | Democrat |
| Religion: | Catholic |
| State: | Louisiana |
| Prior public service: | Louisiana Supreme Court, later U.S. Senate, and Chief Justice U.S. Supreme Court |

## Charles E. Whittaker (1901–1973)

| | |
|---|---|
| Nominated by: | Dwight David Eisenhower |
| Sworn in: | March 25, 1957 |
| Tenure: | 5 years* |
| Party: | Republican |
| Religion: | Methodist |
| State: | Missouri |
| Prior public service: | U.S. Court of Appeals for the 8th Circuit and U.S. Judge for the Western District of Missouri District |

## James Wilson (1742–1798)

| | |
|---|---|
| Nominated by: | George Washington |
| Sworn in: | October 5, 1789 |
| Tenure: | 8 years, 10 months* |
| Party: | Federalist |
| Religion: | Episcopalian |
| State: | Pennsylvania |
| Prior public service: | Delegate to the first Constitutional Congress and member of the Constitutional Convention |

## Levi Woodbury (1789–1851)

| | |
|---|---|
| Nominated by: | James K. Polk |
| Sworn in: | September 23, 1845 |
| Tenure: | 5 years, 11 months* |
| Party: | Democrat |
| Religion: | Protestant |
| State: | New Hampshire |
| Prior public service: | New Hampshire Supreme Court, U.S. House of Representatives, U.S. Senate, and U.S. Secretary of the Treasury |

## William B. Woods (1824–1887)

| | |
|---|---|
| Nominated by: | Rutherford B. Hayes |
| Sworn in: | January 5, 1881 |
| Tenure: | 6 years, 4 months* |
| Party: | Republican |
| Religion: | Protestant |
| State: | Georgia |
| Prior public service: | U.S. 5th Circuit Court |

*Tenure has been rounded to the nearest whole month or year